The Census Book
Facts, Schedules & Worksheets for the U.S. Federal Censuses

by

William Dollarhide

Copyright © 2019
William W. Dollarhide and Leland K. Meitzler
All rights reserved.

No part of this book may be reproduced in any form without permission in writing from the author or publisher except in brief quotations in articles and reviews.

Published by Family Roots Publishing Co., LLC
PO Box 1682
Orting, WA 98360-1682
www.familyrootspublishing.com

Family Roots Publishing Co., LLC is an independent company and is not affiliated with FamilySearch.

Library of Congress Control Number: 2019939769.
ISBN: 978-1-62859-265-8. Softbound.
ISBN: 978-1-62859-266-5. Hardbound.

Cover Photo Credits: The montage of photos all came from the U.S. Census Bureau's History Page, 1790-2010 Image Gallery, see
www.census.gov/history/www/sights_sounds/photos.

Recommended Citation:
The Census Book: Facts, Schedules & Worksheets for the U.S. Federal Censuses, by William Dollarhide, publ. Family Roots Publishing Co., Orting, WA, 2019, 245 pages.

Printed in the United States of America

Contents

Preface 7

Introduction
   Growth of the U.S. Federal Census 9

Section 1 – Census Facts
   Historical U.S. Censuses 11
      Early Census Takers 13
      Censuses in U.S. Territories 13
      Compensation to the Census Takers 14
      The Census Day 15
      Table 1: Census Year/Day/Time Allowed 16
      Census Counting Machine 16
      Early Census Losses 17
      Table 2 – Statewide Census Losses 18
      Census Copies, 1790-1820 19
      Census Copies, 1830-1840 19
      Census Copies, 1850-1870 20
      Census Copies, 1880 22
      1880 Short Form 22
      Census Copies, 1890 22
      1890 Short Form 23
      1890 Veterans Schedule 23
      Copies/Microfilm/Digitizing, 1900-1940 23
      Soundex Indexes, 1880-1930 24
      Soundex Code 25
      Personal Census Search 25
      County Boundary Changes 25
      Table 3: Statistics, 1790-1940 Censuses 26
      References 27

Section 2 – Population Schedules
   Contents – Section 2 29
      Table 4: Availability of U.S. Federal
            Censuses, 1790-1950 30
      First Census of the U.S. – 1790 31
      Second Census of the U.S. – 1800 35
      Third Census of the U.S. – 1810 39
      Fourth Census of the U.S. – 1820 43
      Fifth Census of the U.S. – 1830 47
      Sixth Census of the U.S. – 1840 51
      Seventh Census of the U.S. – 1850 55
      Eighth Census of the U.S. – 1860 61
      Ninth Census of the U.S. – 1870 67
      Tenth Census of the U.S. – 1880 73
      State Censuses Taken in 1885 77
      Eleventh Census of the U.S. – 1890 79
      Table 5 – 1884-1896 State Censuses 82
      Twelfth Census of the U.S. – 1900 83
      Thirteenth Census of the U.S. – 1910 87
      Fourteenth Census of the U.S. – 1920 91

      Fifteenth Census of the U.S. – 1930 95
      Sixteenth Census of the U.S. – 1940 99
      Seventeenth Census of the U.S. – 1950 103

Section 3 – Non-Population Schedules
   Contents – Section 3 107
      Table 6: Availability of Non-Population
            Schedules 108
      Descriptions of the Non-Population
            Schedules, 1820-1935 109
   State Availability Tables:
      Alabama 113
      Alaska 114
      American Samoa 114
      Arizona 114
      Arkansas 115
      California 115
      Colorado 116
      Connecticut 117
      Dakota Territory (1861-1889) 117
      Delaware 118
      District of Columbia 118
      Florida 119
      Georgia 120
      Guam 121
      Hawaii 121
      Idaho 121
      Illinois 122
      Indiana 122
      Iowa 123
      Kansas 124
      Kentucky 124
      Louisiana 125
      Maine 126
      Maryland 126
      Massachusetts 127
      Michigan 128
      Minnesota 129
      Mississippi 129
      Missouri 130
      Montana 131
      Nebraska 131
      Nevada 132
      New Hampshire 132
      New Jersey 133
      New Mexico 133
      New York 134
      North Carolina 135
      North Dakota (1889-1935) 135
      Ohio 136
      Oklahoma 136

Contents, Cont'd

State Availability Tables, Cont'd

Oregon 136
Pennsylvania 137
Puerto Rico 138
Rhode Island 138
South Carolina 138
South Dakota (1889-1935) 139
Tennessee 139
Texas 140
Utah 141
Vermont 141
Virgin Islands of the U.S. 142
Virginia 142
Washington 143
West Virginia 144
Wisconsin 144
Wyoming 145

Section 4 – Census Samples & Worksheets

Contents – Section 4 147

Population Schedules:

1790 Federal Census 148
1800 Federal Census 150
1810 Federal Census 152
1820 Federal Census 154
1830 Federal Census 156
1840 Federal Census 158
1850 Federal Census 160
1860 Federal Census 162
1870 Federal Census 164
1880 Federal Census 166
1880 Short Form 168
1885 State Census – 5 states 170
1890 Short Form 172
1890 Veterans Schedule 174
1900 Federal Census 176
1910 Federal Census 178
1920 Federal Census 180
1930 Federal Census 182
1940 Federal Census 184
1950 Federal Census 186

Industry/Manufactures Schedules:

1820 Manufactures 188
1850 Products of Industry 190
1860 Products of Industry 192
1870 Products of Industry 194
1880 Manufactures-Products of Industry 196
1880 Manufactures-Boots, Shoes 198
1880 Manufactures-Flour & Grist Mills 199
1880 Manufactures-Lumber Mills 200
1880 Manufactures-Agri. Implements 201
1885 Manufactures Schedule 202

Agriculture Schedules:

1850 Agriculture 204
1860 Agriculture 206
1870 Agriculture 208
1880 Agriculture 210
1885 Agriculture 211

Mortality Schedules:

1850 Mortality Schedule 212
1860 Mortality Schedule 214
1870 Mortality Schedule 216
1880 Mortality Schedule 218
1885 Mortality Schedule 220

Slave Schedules:

1850 Slave Schedule 222
1860 Slave Schedule 224

Social Statistics Schedules:

1850, 1860, 1870 Social Statistics 226
1880 Defective, Dependent & Delinquent Classes:
1880 Insane Inhabitants & Idiots 227
1880 Deaf-Mutes & Blind Inhabitants 228
1880 Homeless Children & Prisoners 229
1880 Pauper & Indigent Inhabitants 230

Soundex Extraction Forms:

Soundex Indexes Description & Contents 231
1880 Soundex 232
1900 Soundex 234
1910 Soundex/Miracode 236
1920 Soundex 238
1930 Soundex 240

Census Comparison Sheets:

1790-1840 Census Worksheet 242
Census Comparisons Sheet 244

Preface

1999: The First *Census Book*

In 1999, the first *Census Book* was published. The full title was *The Census Book: A Genealogist's Guide to Federal Census Facts, Schedules and Indexes.* (Published by Heritage Quest, Bountiful, Utah, 182 pages). The original *Census Book* has been out of print for several years, but new and used copies of the book still appear for sale at various websites, such as eBay, Thriftbooks.com, and Amazon.com.

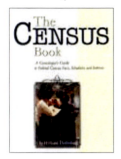

There were several good reviews of the *Census Book*, but my favorite was in 2007, when George C. Morgan, a nationally known author, lecturer, podcaster, and blogger, said this about the book, *"Bill Dollarhide's "The Census Book" is the best reference book on the subject among several that have been issued in the same time frame. While I respect Loretto Szucs'/Matthew Wright's excellent book and the detailed book by Kathleen Hinchley, this one is concise, has detailed dates and references, and is the one I return to again and again, Bravo, Bill! Great work."*

The organization of the first Census Book was as follows:
    Section 1 – Historical U.S. Censuses
    Section 2 – Published Statewide Censuses
    Section 3 – Countywide Census Indexes
    Section 4 – Non-Population Census Schedules
    Section 5 – Census Forms 1790-1930

Censuses Before the Internet

In the 1999 *Census Book*, the word "Internet" did not appear on any page. Although there was a World Wide Web in 1999, its use for genealogy was still in its infancy. My friend and former publisher John Sittner had just recently sold his Ancestry, Inc. publishing business, which soon after was the foundation for Ancestry.com. And, FamilySearch.org had just started online with an electronic card catalog Neither of these online genealogy giants of today had posted their first census database on the Internet.

There were a few genealogy-related websites on the Internet, but the main computer genealogy application in 1999 was not the Internet, it was the census indexes published on CD-ROM disks. The *Census Book* was the first book to identify the complete list of CD-ROM census indexes available, detailing the publications for every state, and then adding any printed indexes available as alternatives.

Computer Census Indexes

The progression from computer-generated printed census indexes to fully searchable Internet databases had actually begun much earlier. The first computer-generated printed census indexes began appearing in the late 1960s from Accelerated Indexing Systems (AIS), a company founded by Ronald V. Jackson of Bountiful, Utah. Jackson pioneered the use of main frame computers for indexing censuses several years before personal computers existed. Over a period of some twenty-five years, AIS head-of-household indexes were prepared for all states, 1790 through 1860.

Several years after AIS began indexing censuses, other companies began indexing projects as well. A small company called Index Publishing produced several statewide indexes in the mid 1980s using its Apple II computers. Soon after, Precision Indexing, a division of AGLL (dba Heritage Quest), began producing census indexes using IBM PCs, concentrating on the 1870 census. In addition, a few other individuals and groups prepared indexes to various statewide censuses. Eventually, most of the census indexes were licensed for use by CD-ROM publishers. By 1999, there were CD-ROM indexes of every state's U.S. Federal Census through 1900, and a smattering of states later than 1900.

Where are they Now?

If you were to visit the current Alabama Family History Research Page at the Ancestry.com website, you would find a database listed as *Alabama, Compiled Censuses & Substitutes, 1810-1890*, a database with 40,948 records. A similar database title can be found for each of the 50 states and DC. **Compiled Censuses & Substitutes** is the current name of the first census databases acquired by Ancestry.com from Ron Jackson's original AIS census indexes. They comprise the earliest census databases online and the reason for Ancestry's initial success online.

2019: A New *Census Book*

In 2019, a new *Census Book* was published. The full title: *The Census Book: Facts, Schedules & Worksheets for the U.S. Federal Censuses.* (Published by Family Roots Publishing Co., LLC, Orting, WA, 245 pages). What is different? Any references to CD-ROM publications were replaced with direct links to Internet databases. The printed countywide census indexes were removed, replaced by links to databases and alternative publications in the statewide section. The organization and description of the changes found in the new *Census Book* follows:

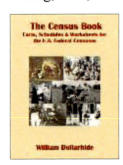

Section 1 – Census Facts. Historical U.S. Censuses. The original concept and layout is the same, but with considerable editing, rewriting, and added features.

Section 2 – Population Schedules. This section is where major changes took place. The 1999 edition had no references to the Internet for census population databases – this 2019 edition has links to over 630 URLs, providing instant access to over 600 million indexed census records online.

In the first *Census Book*, each census year had a table showing the CD-ROM indexes and any printed book indexes available. In the new *Census Book,* a table for each census year now includes the starting FHL film number for each state's population schedules at the FHL online catalog, providing links to over 580 FHL catalog title pages. It is the searchable roll number that gives a researcher quick access to the digital images of any census year, state, county, or town.

Census substitutes were added where available; better U.S. maps of each census year were included; and 1940 and 1950 census chapters were added. Also, a new census chapter was inserted for 1885, when 14 states took state censuses – they are good substitutes for the lost 1890 census.

Section 3 – Non-Population Schedules. This section identifies all non-population categories, adding those after 1900. All new statewide tables, Alabama to Wyoming, were expanded to 1935, and reorganized for appearance and adding URL links to 560 more online databases. The location of the original Non-Population schedules is repeated, and the locations of microfilm copies now features many direct links to a Family History Library online catalog page, in particular, those with digital images available.

Section 4 – Census Samples & Worksheets. The 1999 Census Book had no Samples and 34 Census Worksheets; the new 2019 Census Book has 57 Samples and 42 Worksheets. New worksheets were added for the 1890 Short Form; the 1940 Census; and the 1820, 1850, 1860, 1870, 1880, and 1885 Manufactures Schedules.

There are a total of 1,190 URLs giving access to over 1 billion census records/names. As a result, there is a very good chance genealogists can shorten the time to find their ancestors online using this new *Census Book.*

– bill$hide

Introduction

Growth of the U.S. Federal Census
Blame it on Thomas Jefferson and the American Statistical Association

The main users of the U.S. Federal Censuses are the millions of amateur genealogists in the U.S. They are the beneficiaries of a national census strategy that took on more than the Founding Fathers had asked for in 1787. The Constitution never used the word *census*, but asked for an *enumeration* of the population every ten years. The method of conducting the enumeration was left to the Congress *"in such manner as they shall by law direct."*

Beginning in 1790 there was more than just a counting of the population – the first census asked five questions: the name of a head of household, the number of males under 16, males over 16; females of any age, and the number of slaves. The number of questions increased in each census thereafter, and by 1840, a total of 66 questions were asked.

We should probably thank Thomas Jefferson, the first U.S. Secretary of State under President George Washington. Jefferson was in charge of the first census of 1790. He wrote copious instructions that were followed to the letter, and in fact, some of his rules for the 1790 census were used in every census thereafter, e.g., the age categories for males and females added to the name of the head of a household; and the use of a "census day" to enumerate households were first outlined by Thomas Jefferson.

We should also thank an organization formed in 1839 called the American Statistical Association. From its very beginning, members of this organization began lobbying Congress to add more vital statistical information in the decennial census schedules. There was no national standard for the collection of vital statistics in the U.S., yet the country was experiencing continual epidemics of various diseases that seemed to be localized in certain parts of the country. Gathering statistics about the number of deaths, causes of death, and so on, was a growing concern expressed eloquently by members of the American Statistical Association.

As a result, the law enacted for the preparation of the 1850, 1860 & 1870 censuses (9 Stat. 428, 23 May 1850) included a new concept in which much more information was gathered. An all new Census Office under the newly formed Department of the Interior was created just prior to each census year, and for the 1850-1870 censuses, the Population Schedules now listed the names of every member of a household, giving their name, age, and birthplace. In addition, in 1850, the new Census Office began a program of statistics gathering unheard of in the first six censuses, e.g., for all three census years, 1850-1870, special schedules were added for Products of Industry, Agriculture, Social Statistics, and in direct response to the American Statistical Association's lobbying, a *Mortality Schedule*, in which every person who had died during the previous 12 months was named, along with the cause of that person's death. Slave Schedules were also added for the 1850 and 1860 censuses.

By 1880, the Census Office had become nearly a full-time operation – the staff stayed for nearly eight years in compiling the 1880 reports. That is because the reports were extensive, complex, and numerous, e.g., for the Manufacturing schedules alone, ten (10) special schedules were added to collect statistics on such Products of Industry as Boots & Shoes; Flour & Grist Mils, Lumber & Sawmills, and Agricultural Implements.

Coinciding with these events, more vital statistical questions were added to each census from 1880 and on, and the Census Office had to keep up. A former employee of the Census Office saw the need and invented an electrical-mechanical calculating machine. It was used to tabulate the 1890 census statistics, cutting the time from nearly eight years for the 1880 tabulations to less then two years for the 1890.

Up to 1900, it was believed that the federal censuses could provide the means of collecting national vital statistics. The 1900 had more vital statistics questions than any previous census, e.g., it included an age, plus month and year of birth; number of children born to a mother, and number still living, etc. However, since the information came in ten year intervals, the statistics about births and deaths was not very meaningful for the period between census years.

In 1901, Congress passed a resolution asking each state to gather information about births and deaths on a statewide basis. But, because Congress gave no money to the states to do it, it took several more years before it happened in every state. By 1925, all 48 states had laws requiring statewide registration of all births and deaths.

The 1910 and 1920 census schedules asked less of these types of questions, mainly because the matter of vital statistics information had been handed over to the states. Still, the development of the census as a means of collecting diverse information continued to grow. There were other unique questions added for each subsequent census. For example, in the 1930 census, one of the questions was whether the household had a radio set.

The 1940 census was the first to employ statistical sampling. The 1940 population schedule featured a comprehensive format with space for 40 persons per sheet and 34 columns of questions. Lines 14 & 29 added 16 additional "Supplementary Questions." Also in 1940, there were some extra schedules that were not microfilmed, such as the Housing Schedules, which asked several questions about construction materials, running water, and whether the house was served by an indoor flush toilet or an outhouse. Another 1940 statistic was each person's address five years earlier: "In what place did this person live on April 1, 1935?, to which a full address was to be given if different from the 1940 address. Genealogists love that one!

The 1950 census had a comprehensive schedule format with space for 30 persons per sheet and 22 columns of questions. Lines 4, 9, 14, 19, 24 & 29 were sample lines, with an additional 20 columns of supplemental questions.

In 1951, the Census Bureau hired consultants to assist in tabulating the 1950 population schedules using a Universal Automatic Computer (UNIVAC), an updated version of the Electronic Numerical Integrator and Computer (ENIAC), the very first electronic computer, developed during World War II by the U.S. Army's Ballistic Research Laboratory.

Soon after their first computer experience, the Census Bureau purchased their own UNIVAC. They had a perfect application for their new computer: the upcoming 1960 U.S. Census, which became the first census to be tabulated and reported completely using an electronic computer.

UNIVAC was a thousand times faster than the Census Bureau's 1890 electrical-mechanical calculator. A typical home PC today is thirteen thousand times faster than UNIVAC.

To keep up and manage the growth of the U.S. census, the Census Bureau has always been quick to take on any new technology that could make their job easier. They are still on that leading edge and remain the world leader in statistics gathering. Genealogists are grateful.

Section 1 – Census Facts

Historical U.S. Censuses

Genealogists are avid users of the U.S. federal censuses available to the public. The numbers of users before the advent of personal computers and the World Wide Web were easier to count. By the mid-1990s, most libraries or archives in the U.S. with large collections of census records on microfilm could confirm the large numbers of amateur genealogists as daily visitors. In all of the regional branches of the National Archives, amateur genealogists represented 90 percent of the patrons using those facilities. Back then, most of the regional archives provided a complete set of microfilmed censuses, all in one room, an attraction most genealogists could not resist.

Today, there are millions of new census users due to the availability of all federal censuses on the Internet. Most census searching can now be done at home, although there are still a great number of libraries and archives worth visiting in person for census research or other genealogical resources. Wherever the research is conducted, the U.S. Federal Censuses remain the primary source for finding the names of American ancestors.

Though most genealogists are familiar with the use of U.S. census records to help identify their American ancestors, some facts about the censuses overall may not be obvious. Some hidden aspects to the various censuses may be missed by even experienced family historians.

Perhaps a review of some of these obscurities may help a researcher understand why certain census records exist while others do not, or why an ancestor does not appear when he should appear in a census. Hopefully, this information will encourage a genealogist to go back to the census records and look again for information that may have been missed the first time.

Why a Census?

Ask someone on the street why a census is taken in the United States every ten years. A common answer might be, "for taxes." Several people might answer, "for reapportioning the seats of the U.S. House of Representatives." Both answers would be correct. In Article I, Section 2, the Constitution of the United States says:

"Representatives and direct taxes shall be apportioned among the several states which may be included within this Union according to their respective numbers, which shall be determined by adding to the whole number of free persons, including those bound to service for a term of years, and excluding Indians not taxed, three-fifths of all other persons. The actual enumeration shall be made within three years after the first meeting of the Congress of the United States, and within every subsequent ten years, in such manner as they shall by law direct."

Beginning in 1790, the United States of America became the first country in the world to call for regularly held censuses. Note that the Constitution did not treat everyone as equal. "Free persons" excluded Indians living on treaty land and who were exempt from paying taxes (or voting).

"All other persons" meant slaves, who were counted as 3/5ths of a person for determining representation in Congress. This latter provision was to offset the large slave populations of states like Virginia and South Carolina, where, in 1790, slaves represented 39 and 43 percent of their population, respectively. In comparison, Connecticut and New Jersey had slave populations of 1.1 and 6.2 percent, respectively.

It may be overlooked by some that "direct taxes" were authorized in the Constitution of the United States. But, except for the national direct tax levied in 1797 to defray debts left over from the Revolutionary War, and the direct tax levied during the Civil War Era, Congress did not do it permanently until 1913, when personal income taxes were first levied directly on individuals.

The primary action of Article I, Section 2, was to authorize and carry out a national enumeration/census to be conducted every ten years. As in so many other areas of the U.S. Constitution, the wisdom of the document is revealed in how it simply states what must be done and leaves the details of carrying out a census to Congress *"in such manner as they shall by law direct."* For every ten years since 1790, Congress has enacted a law specific to and authorizing a census to be taken. None of the laws is the same, and each specifies more information to be gathered than in the preceding census.

After every census taken in the U.S., Congress first decides how many total seats there will be in the U.S. House of Representatives, then divides that number into the figure for the total U.S. population. This determines how many persons one congressman will represent. By dividing that number into each state's population, it can be determined how many U.S. representatives can come from each state. After each decennial census, it is the responsibility of the state legislatures to decide the new U.S. Congressional boundaries within their state, and to ensure that each area is equal to that portion of population for one U.S. representative. The exception to this rule applies to states whose entire population is less than one congressional allotment – all states must have at least one U.S. representative.

The phrase in the Constitution, *"the actual enumeration shall be made,"* was debated early in Congress, because one could say that it meant an "actual count" and nothing else. From the first census of 1790 forward, however, more information has been included than just the tally of persons; and each subsequent census has included more information than the previous one. For this, genealogists are very grateful. However, the language of the Constitution also stated that Congress should carry out the censuses *"in such manner as they shall by law direct."* That provision established that Congress could broadly determine the content and manner of taking censuses, and that provision has never been challenged judicially.

Ironically, in 1997 the Census Bureau proposed that the census for the year 2000 should be the first census ever taken that would not attempt an "actual enumeration" of every citizen. They wanted to collect an actual count of 90 percent of the population, based on the typical return of census forms; then use statistical sampling to count the remaining 10 percent rather than continually go back time and time again to find the persons who did not return the forms. But Congress denied permission for this statistical sampling proposal because of the constitutional provision for an *actual enumeration*.

Census accuracy and under-counting has always been a matter of contention. Over the years, several major cities have sued Uncle Sam because the cities thought they were unfairly deprived of numbers, therefore, a loss of federal block grants based on population. In most cases, the courts have held that under-counting is an inherent part of taking a census, and no compensation or recounts were due. Exceptions to this were in 1870, when the northern cities of Indianapolis, Philadelphia, and New York County were each granted a second enumeration. A few southern cities had also asked for a recount in 1870, without success. This may have been in keeping with the times; because after the Civil War, northern carpetbaggers were often used as census takers in the South. They were known to under-count their enumeration districts on purpose in an attempt to keep the political influence of the South less important in Congress. In 1880, the city of St. Louis was granted a second enumeration. All of these repeated enumerations in 1870 and 1880 are available as part of each state's microfilmed & digitized censuses. In 1890, the city of New York was convinced that the federal census was so bad, they undertook a census of their own, today called the 1890 New York Police Census. That NYC name list is extant, microfilmed & digitized online. (The 1890 NYC federal census, however, was later lost due to a fire).

The Early Census Takers

Since the first census of 1790, the states have not been involved in taking a national census except to review and act on the reports generated. The national census has always been a federal responsibility. The first few censuses were managed by a small staff as part of the U.S. Secretary of State's office. The initial set of rules and instructions were issued by Thomas Jefferson, the first Secretary of State under President George Washington. Congress did not get around to creating a Census Office until just before the 1850 census. If it were not a responsibility of a state, who was the agency responsible for taking the censuses?

The first nine censuses (1790-1870) were conducted by assistant federal marshals of the United States Federal Circuit Court system. One U.S. marshal was assigned to each federal court district, and it was his job to hire and manage assistant marshals to take the door-to-door censuses in his district.

The federal court districts did not always match up with state boundaries. For example, at the time of the 1790 census, there were 16 federal court districts, but only 14 states. Vermont entered the Union as the 14th state in early 1791. Soon after, Congress passed a special law to include Vermont in the first census, with a census day designated as the first Monday in April, 1791, and with five months allowed to take the census there.

In 1790, Virginia had two federal court districts, each with their own United States Courthouse. One Virginia district had the same boundaries as what was to become the state of Kentucky in 1792. Massachusetts also had two federal court districts, one of which had the same boundaries as the future state of Maine. The rest of the states had federal court district boundaries that were the same as their state boundaries in 1790. In subsequent censuses, several states had more than one federal court district. Today, some larger states have as many as four federal court districts.

Censuses in U.S. Territories

The 1790 census was taken for determining seats in the U.S. House of Representatives. Since people living in territories did not have voting representation in Congress, no perceived need existed for a census to be taken in the old Northwest Territory or the Southwest Territory, the first two territories of the U.S. Soon after the law providing for the 1790 census was enacted, Secretary of State Thomas Jefferson, perhaps as an afterthought, wrote a letter to the governor of the Southwest Territory (the territory that became the state of Tennessee in 1796). Jefferson asked Governor Blount if he wouldn't mind taking a census, even though it was not required under the law; and he had neither money allocated, nor a federal marshal to do it.

But, since he knew that Blount had "sheriffs who will be traversing their Districts for other purposes," Jefferson wondered if the Governor could ask them to take a census "arranged under the same classes prescribed . . . for the general census." Blount complied, in a way, by providing the Secretary with a count of the territory's inhabitants, but without listing their names. His report was dated 19 September 1791. Presumably, Jefferson would have asked the same of Governor St. Clair of the Northwest Territory in 1790, but St. Clair was up to his neck fighting off Indian attacks and not available for much else that year.

In the enabling law for the 1800 census, territories were officially included for the first time. Congress had determined that there was a good reason for including territories, if only to determine if a territory had met the minimum population required for statehood. Unfortunately, the 1800 censuses taken for Northwest Territory, Indiana Territory, and Mississippi Territory were all lost, with the exception of one county (Washington Co NW Territory, now Ohio).

Compensation to the Census Takers

Before the 1790 census, there was much debate in Congress about the various aspects of the first census, including the compensation for an assistant marshal. Several members of Congress were worried that the amount was not high enough to attract people to the job. One member of Congress reminded his colleagues of the Bible story about King David, who was blamed for a terrible plague in Israel immediately after a census was taken. The representative from New York remembered that back in the 1770s most of the residents of a New York town had fallen sick right after they had been visited by a British census taker. The representatives wondered if taking a census would ever be possible, given the prevailing superstitions about censuses overall.

Nevertheless, in the end, a sum of about $44,000 was spent in taking the 1790 census which was reported to the President in a pamphlet of fifty-six pages. (In comparison, the 2010 census was reported in over 1,500 volumes and cost 13 billion dollars).

In 1790, compensation paid to the assistant marshals was set by law to be $1.00 for every 300 persons in cities and towns containing more than 5,000 people, and $1.00 for every 150 persons in rural areas. The law allowed the U.S. marshal to pay $1.00 for every 50 persons in areas determined to be sparsely populated or difficult to reach, subject to a ruling by the federal judge in his district.

Each assistant marshal was given a sample copy of the 1790 census form; and he was expected to make all his own copies, ruling the lines of the forms himself. He was also required to pay for his pens, ink, paper, travel, shelter, meals, and all other expenses incurred in taking the census.

Samuel Bradford, the assistant marshal for the city of Boston, began his work door-to-door on 2 August 1790, and by 21 August had completed his enumeration. His notebook shows that the work required seventeen working days. He enumerated an average of more than one thousand persons per day. As his compensation was $1.00 for every 300 persons, his earnings amounted to about $3.30 per day, a figure much higher than his rural counterparts and not a bad wage for 1790.

Mr. Bradford could have learned how to increase his pay even more by the example of Clement Biddle, the U.S. Marshal for the district/state of Pennsylvania. Biddle was in charge of the 1790 census taken in that state. Coincidentally, in 1791, Biddle published a directory of the city of Philadelphia, which, apparently, was a profitable success. Comparing the names in the 1791 directory with the 1790 census returns for Philadelphia reveals that Mr. Biddle added very little to his directory. Publishing the city directory may have been a plan of Mr. Biddle's all along.

Biddle's Philadelphia census list included occupations for heads of household, not one of the 1790 columns on the sample form given to Mr. Biddle. And, of course, the occupation for each person was repeated in the Biddle directory, cover page below:

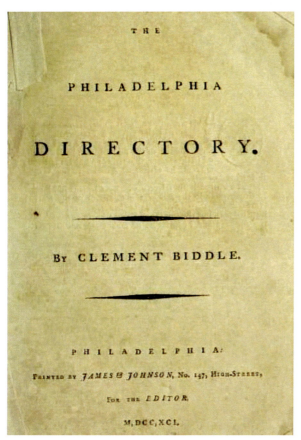

Still, most census takers were not having much job satisfaction. For example, after taking the Morgan County, North Carolina, census in 1790, the assistant marshal there wrote a few words of complaint at the end of his list of names:

"I have been Closely Employd Since the 25 of December Last. One Other man has been closely Employd Since the 6th of January; one other has been Employd Since the 12 of January; a third one Since the 1st of March and Two others A Week Each and all had Since to fall behind. After riding horses almost to Death. This is a True State of Facts. No one Man Can Number the People in the District of Morgan Going from House to House in 18 Months I Aver, and if there is no Provision to Collect the people in the Next Law, no man that understands will have anything to do with it."

At the end of the 1820 Hall County, Georgia schedules, the assistant marshal wrote the following:

"The difficulties were very considerable that attended taking the census, in the first place, the inhabitants are very dispersed, in the second place the country being but lately settled, there are but few roads, in the third place great part of the Country are very Mountainous, and in the fourth place it was, except in the oldest settled parts, difficult to get nourishment for either myself or horse, and often when got, had to pay very high, in the 5th place had often to travel a considerable distance through fields to get to the dwelling cabins, often, and generally, drenchd in dew, particularly in August and September; and often had to walk many miles where it was so steep that I could not ride, or even set on my horse."

The Census Day

In each enabling law authorizing a census to be taken, Congress specified a "census day" for gathering the census information from each household in America. From 1790 to 1820, the census day was the first Monday in August. The census day was not the day the enumerator arrived at a household; it was the day for which all the statistics of the census was collected. The original 1790 instructions given to all the U.S. marshals by Secretary of State Thomas Jefferson were repeated in every census law from 1790-1840:

. . . all the questions refer to the day when the enumeration is to commence; the first Monday in August next. Your assistants will thereby understand that they are to insert in their returns all the persons belonging to the family on the first Monday in August, even those who may be deceased at the time when they take the account; and, on the other hand, that they will not include in it, infants born after that day."

Similar instructions were given for every census, 1850-2010, but with different census days. Table 1 shows the census day for each census, 1790-1950, and the time allowed to take the census.

Table 1

Census Year	Census Day	Time Allowed
1790	2 August	9 Months
1800	4 August	9 Months
1810	6 August	10 Months
1820	7 August	13 Months
1830	1 June	12 Months
1840	1 June	18 Months
1850	1 June	5 Months
1860	1 June	5 Months
1870	1 June	5 Months
1880	1 June	1 Month
1890	1 June	1 Month
1900	1 June	1 Month
1910	15 April	1 Month
1920	1 January	1 Month
1930	1 April	1 Month
1940	1 April	1 Month
1950	1 April	1 Month

South Carolina could not complete its 1790 enumeration in nine months. The U.S. marshal complained that he was having great difficulty finding people to take the job because of the resistance to the census being taken. A Charleston jury met to decide the fate of six persons who had "refused to render an account of persons in their households as required by the census act." A South Carolina census taker was brought on trial for neglect of duty. He did not complete the census in his district. These and other problems led Congress to grant South Carolina an extension to complete the census there. South Carolina's 1790 census returns were dated 5 February 1792, nearly nineteen months after the original census day.

Genealogists should record two dates when copying information from the censuses, the census day and the enumeration date. No matter how many months it took for an enumerator to reach a house, he was supposed to gather the information as if time had stopped on the census day. However, we will never know for sure if the enumerator always followed his instructions. Every person whose regular abode was in a particular household on the census day was to be enumerated, even if a person were away at the time of the enumeration.

From Table 1 showing the census days, note that the census day changed from the first Monday in August in 1820 to the first day of June in 1830. If one is researching families appearing in the 1820 and 1830 censuses, looking at these censuses again may be important. Since the census days for 1820 and 1830 are not exactly ten years apart, the two-month difference may reveal some surprising results. For example, if a person were born between 1 June 1820 and 7 August 1820, that child would appear in the 1820 census in the "under 5" category. But in 1830, that same person would appear in the "under ten" rather than the "of 10 and under 16" category, since the person had not turned 10 yet. Comparing the other age categories for a person appearing ten years later and not in the correct age category may give a clue to a person's date of birth within a two-month period. NOTE: See the *1790-1840 Census Worksheet* on page 242 for a way to graphically visualize the age differences recorded from 1790 through 1840.

Census Counting Machines

Table 1 shows the time allowed in the legislative acts for taking each census. Note that in 1840, eighteen months were allowed to take the census; while in 1850, only five months were allowed. The reason for this change has an interesting history:

Soon after the first Census Office was created in early 1850, two young men from Poughkeepsie, New York, approached the director with a proposal. They had invented a "counting machine" they thought could help in tabulating the census returns. The two men demonstrated a prototype machine that used flat metal cards with slots and holes punched in them in a precise pattern so that a metal rod could be passed through the holes and slots and lift out certain cards with holes in the same location. By a process of elimination, cards with a particular pattern of holes could be removed; and in the process, they could be categorized, sorted, and counted.

The director of the newly established Census Office was impressed. The two men opened a business and with the Census Office's good recommendation, borrowed a small sum. The new company developed a working model of the machine; and within a few weeks, the machine proved so reliable that the Census Office decided to use it in the tabulation of the 1850 census. They estimated that it would cut the time to count the census figures from eighteen months to five months, and that is the time they recommended to Congress in their budget request.

Since the 1850 census, the Census Office has used a counting machine in every census taken. In fact, every year after that, the machine was improved in speed and accuracy. In 1890, an electrical-mechanical calculator was used; and in 1960, an electronic computer (UNIVAC) was employed.

That little two-man company that presented their invention to the Census Office back in 1850 goes by a different name today. It is called the IBM Corporation.

Early Census Losses

The 1790 law required the U.S. marshals to deposit the original returns from their assistants with the clerks of the U.S. District Courts. These name lists remained in the clerks' offices, while the marshals' summaries from the various districts were sent to the president of the United States. The law required that the president receive *"the aggregate amount of each description of persons within their respective district."* The marshals were to *"file the original returns of their assistants with the clerks of their respective district courts, who are hereby directed to receive and carefully preserve the same."* (1 Stat. 101, 1 March 1790).

This requirement was repeated in the enabling laws for the 1800, 1810, and 1820 censuses. The president was to receive not the name lists, but summaries of the census tallies. This fact contradicts what several well-known publications use as the reason for many early census losses. For example, several genealogical reference books say that when the British burned Washington in 1814, the earliest census returns were destroyed. This incorrect statement can be found in National Archives guides, State Archives guides, Family History Library guides, and repeated in many other publications.

The only census schedules that could have been in Washington, D.C., in 1814 were the 1810 schedules for the District of Columbia which had its own U.S. District Court (part of the U.S. Supreme Court). Since the 1810 D.C. schedules were lost, they may have been the only censuses destroyed when the British burned Washington in 1814.

In 1830, Congress passed a law calling for the return of the original censuses for the years 1790-1820. The original census returns were to be sent to Washington by the various clerks of the district courts – the same clerks who had been admonished in earlier laws to *"receive and carefully preserve"* the original census returns. Obviously, some clerks failed in their duties. According to the provisions of the 1830 law, the census schedules of 1790-1820 for the two districts of Massachusetts (Massachusetts and Maine) were transferred to Washington. Also transferred were the 1790-1820 original censuses for the states of New Hampshire, Vermont, Rhode Island, Connecticut, New York, Maryland, Pennsylvania, North Carolina, and South Carolina.

Certain original census returns were lost before enactment of the 1830 law, or the law was ignored by clerks of the district courts.

Georgia's 1790, 1800, and 1810 census returns never reached Washington; and what happened to them is not known. Even worse, the first four New Jersey censuses, 1790-1820, were never received at Washington. Also lost were the 1790 returns for Delaware and Virginia's two federal court districts (old Virginia, including present-day West Virginia and the district which later became the state of Kentucky) and the states of Virginia, Kentucky, and Tennessee for 1800. In addition, the census returns for Northwest Territory, Indiana Territory, and Mississippi Territory, all with complete censuses taken in 1800, never reached Washington. The 1810 census schedules for Tennessee and the territories of Michigan, Missouri, and Mississippi were also not received at Washington and are presumed lost. See Table 2 for a complete summary of census losses, 1790-1820.

All of the statewide census losses occurred in the first four censuses taken, 1790-1820, with the exception of the 1890 census. More than 99 percent of the original 1890 schedules were destroyed due to a fire in the Commerce Building in Washington in January 1921. The failure of some clerks of the district courts to comply with the 1830 law asking for the return of the original censuses may account for most of the losses. For example, the 1820 Michigan census returns were found where they had been all along – in the office of the clerk of the district court in Detroit, Michigan, but discovered many years after the 1830 law had demanded their transfer to Washington.

There is a slight possibility that some early 1790-1820 lost censuses still exist. If any of the old censuses have survived, they are probably buried in some subbasement or attic of a federal courthouse – because that is where they were first deposited.

Table 2 shows the status of censuses from 1790 to 1820. A dash in a column means a census was not taken for that state in that year. "Lost" means the census returns never reached Washington in 1830 and were probably lost. "Extant" means the manuscripts of the census returns survive, and microfilmed & digitized copies of them are available.

Table 2

Summary of Statewide Census Losses, 1790-1820

State/Territory	1790	1800	1810	1820
Alabama	—	—	—	lost
Arkansas	—	—	—	lost
Connecticut	extant	extant	extant	extant
District of Columbia	—	—	lost	extant
Delaware	lost	extant	extant	extant
Georgia (1)	lost	lost	lost	extant
Illinois	—	lost	(2)	extant
Indiana (3)	—	lost	lost	extant
Kentucky	lost	lost	extant	extant
Louisiana	—	—	extant	extant
Maine	extant	extant	extant	extant
Maryland (4)	extant	extant	extant	extant
Massachusetts	extant	extant	extant	extant
Michigan	—	—	lost	extant
Mississippi	—	lost	lost	extant
Missouri	—	—	lost	lost
New Hampshire (5)	extant	extant	extant	extant
New York	extant	extant	extant	extant
New Jersey	lost	lost	lost	lost
North Carolina (6)	extant	extant	extant	extant
Northwest Territory	—	(7)	—	—
Ohio	—	—	lost	extant
Pennsylvania	extant	extant	extant	extant
Rhode Island	extant	extant	extant	extant
South Carolina	extant	extant	extant	extant
Tennessee	—	lost	lost	(8)
Vermont	extant	extant	extant	extant
Virginia (9)	lost	lost	extant	extant

Table 2 Notes:
1. Three counties are missing from the 1820 Georgia schedules.
2. Of Illinois Territory's two counties in 1810, Randolph is extant and St. Clair is lost.
3. Missing from the Indiana 1820 schedules is Daviess County.
4. Three counties are missing from the Maryland 1790 schedules.
5. Missing from the 1790 New Hampshire schedules are thirteen towns in Rockingham County and eleven towns in Strafford County.

6. Missing from the North Carolina schedules are three counties in 1790, four counties in 1810, and six counties in 1820.
7. In 1800, about a fourth of the population of the Northwest Territory was in Washington County, whose original census was discovered among the papers of the Ohio Company in Marietta, Ohio. All other counties were lost.
8. In 1820, two federal court districts were in place in Tennessee, one with a U.S. Courthouse in Nashville, the other in Knoxville. The original censuses returned to Washington in 1830 were from the Nashville district only, representing the western two-thirds of the state. The twenty eastern counties enumerated with the 1820 Knoxville district were not received in Washington and are presumed lost.
9. The "Heads of Families" index to the 1790 census includes Virginia. However, these names were extracted and compiled from county tax lists of Virginia, 1785-1787.

Census Copies, 1790-1820

In the first four censuses, the assistant marshals were only required to make one set of the name lists they had collected. Sometimes, however, census takers made copies of their work. This can be seen in certain states of the 1790-1820 censuses where all the names are listed for a county in alphabetical order, obviously compiled from an earlier draft. With no requirement that a copy be made of the name lists, any such earlier drafts were probably discarded. The format of the schedules for the first six censuses (1790-1840) was a listing with only the names of the heads of household, but with age brackets for males and females included in each household.

A special consideration unique to the 1820 form asks for all males "16-18" years of age and in another column, all "males 16-26" years of age. The purpose of these two categories was to determine the number of young men in the U.S. of military age. If a male were shown in the 16-18 column, he would also be in the 16-26 column. To confirm this, add all the marks for males and females, then go to the far right-hand side of the form and find the "total number in the household" figure. If a male were in the 16-18 category, and at least one male was in the 16-26 category, the number in the "total number" column should confirm that a person was not counted twice. Further confirmation of this can be found in the 1820 instructions to the U.S. marshals which read as follows:

"It will be necessary to remember, that the numbers in the columns of free white males between 16 and 18 must not be added to the general aggregates, (they) will all be repeated in the column of those between 16 and 26."

Genealogists who have recorded the number of persons and age categories from the 1820 census need to understand the significance of the added male "16-18" category. One should go back to the same census sheets to confirm that the correct number of persons in the household were noted. It may be enlightening to learn about that "extra" young man in a family in 1820, but found no where else.

Census Copies, 1830-1840

In a change of policy, the laws authorizing the 1830 and 1840 censuses required that two copies of the census schedules be prepared. One would be retained by the clerk of the district court, the other sent to Washington. Congress had decided that one copy of the name lists was not enough; and after the experience of several earlier census returns disappearing, they asked that the clerks prepare a name-by-name copy. Most examples show that the copies, not the originals, were the census schedules usually sent to Washington.

Only the Washington copies of the censuses were transferred to the National Archives and microfilmed & digitized many years later. What happened to the various copies retained by the clerks for the 1830 and 1840 censuses is a mystery. Scanning through any microfilmed & digitized census schedules and looking at the handwriting is one way of learning if it is the clerk's copy or the original. If the handwriting changed from one assistant marshal's district to the next, then the records are probably the originals, not the copies. If page after page of the handwriting is by the same person, crossing over various town, district, or county boundaries, then it is probably the clerk's copy, not the original.

It is known that various clerks of the District Courts complained loudly about having to make extra copies of the census schedules – they did not think that Congress had provided enough funds for the extra work. As it turned out, the clerks' involvement with census taking ended with the 1840 census.

Census Copies, 1850-1870

The first Census Office began operations in 1850, and a new set of procedures for taking the census was put in place. Although the door-to-door census takers were still the assistant marshals of the Federal District Court system, the clerks of the District Courts were taken out of the census process. For the 1850 through 1870 censuses, they were replaced by the secretary of state in each state or territory.

The job of the new Census Office was to collect the census schedules and prepare the reports after the various U.S. marshals and secretaries of state had completed their work. The Census Office did not have complete control of the job, nor did it even hire its own census enumerators. After each enumeration and subsequent reporting period, from 1850 through 1900, the Census Office was disbanded, then recreated again ten years later. For the 1850-1870 censuses, the Census Office reported the constitutional population figures within a few weeks of receiving all of the census schedules, but remained in full operation until a comprehensive final report was issued to Congress. The final report included dozens of new tables, schedules, and special details, and would keep the Census Office is operation for a couple of years after the census was enumerated. The Census Office did not become a permanent federal agency until 1902, when it was named the Bureau of the Census. Since about the time of World War I, the agency has been often referred to as the "Census Bureau."

A single enabling law authorized the 1850, 1860, and 1870 censuses (9 Stat. 428, 23 May 1850). For all three census years, the law asked for an original and two additional copies of the census schedules to be prepared. This was a result of a new procedure for handling the census schedules that began in 1850. Upon completion of an enumeration, the original schedules for an entire county were placed in public view at a county courthouse. Copies of the census schedules were made using the following procedure:

• A complete set of the original census schedule for one county was displayed at each county courthouse after the censuses for 1850, 1860, and 1870.

• The supervising assistant federal marshal made a complete copy of the name lists for the county or counties under his jurisdiction. A "clean copy" of the countywide schedules was to be sent to the state or territorial secretary of state, and the original schedules were to remain in the courthouse for the applicable county. The new copy was to become the "state copy."

• The state or territorial secretary of state received all of the copies of county schedules for his state, then made a "federal copy." The state copy was to be retained at the secretary of state's office. The federal copy was to be sent to the Census Office in Washington.

The original copy of the census schedules made by a supervising assistant marshal in each county was supposed to remain in that county, but it is not known if the marshals always followed their instructions. It is disappointing that so few of the original censuses for 1850-1870 have ever been found in county courthouses. A few years ago, a genealogist looking through case files in a county probate court noticed that many packets of files were wrapped with strips of paper. Unwrapping these packets revealed that the strips of paper were torn off that county's original 1850 census pages. One county's officials obviously had little regard for their old censuses. They used them for scrap paper.

The same is true for the census schedules retained in the offices of the various secretaries of state. It is not known what happened to most of the state copies of the 1850-1870 censuses. One explanation is that they may have been given to various state representatives and senators as "mailing lists" for their counties and districts.

Genealogists should remember that when reading the microfilmed & digitized censuses for 1850-1870, they are handwritten copies of the original, or even copies of copies of the originals. If a genealogist is reading a copy (perhaps one that is twice removed from the original), does that explain why an ancestor's name is misspelled, or not there at all?

There is substantial evidence that the original county copies and state copies of the 1850-1870 censuses were better versions than the microfilmed & digitized federal copies. A few county originals and a few state copies, such as those that exist for New York, Michigan, Minnesota and Wisconsin, have been found. The Wisconsin State Historical Society has the complete original state copies of Wisconsin 1850-1870 federal censuses. By visiting the Society's library in Madison and comparing the original state copy with the microfilmed & digitized federal copy, one will see some dramatic differences. When Leland Meitzler was looking for his great grandparents in the 1860 census for New York, he compared the county copy and federal copy. He found the name was spelled "Mader" in the microfilmed federal copy, but correctly spelled "Meitzler" in the original county copy. There are many other examples of the federal copy being in error; and specifically, common human errors were made while transcribing handwritten names and information from one document to another.

Harry Hollingsworth reported some of these differences in his article, "Little Known Facts About the U.S. Census," *The American Genealogist* 53 (1977), page 11:

"I have personally found many discrepancies between the Federal and State copies themselves, and vast differences between them and the originals (i.e., the county copies)! Whole names have either been changed or omitted. Ages have been copied wrong. Whereas, in the originals, the surnames of each family are generally written over and over again, in the copies the word "ditto" or its abbreviation "do" appears instead. When written over and over, a surname has much less chance of being written incorrectly! In one Federal entry, I find Rebecca Gey but "Grey" in the original. In another Federal entry, Amanda Vandyke appears, but she is Amanda A. Vanslyke in the original. Esther Hollinsworth of the original – the correct name – appears as Esther Hollenback in the Federal copy!"

Unfortunately, the federal copies of the 1850-1870 censuses – the copies with the most errors – are the only ones available from the National Archives today, and the ones microfilmed & digitized for public use.

Census Copies, 1880

The last census conducted under the jurisdiction of the federal courts and the U.S. marshals was the 1870 census. In the enabling act for the 1880 census, the reconstituted Census Office was expanded and given a substantial boost in budget. However, the big change was that the Census Office was able to hire its own enumerators and take full control of the census nationwide. Five times the number of enumerators were used in conducting the 1880 census compared with the 1870. For the first time, the schedules listed relationships for every member of a household to the head.

The 1880 census tracts were organized into Enumeration Districts (E.D.s). Each E.D. had a supervisor who managed the enumerators under him and handled the work of making copies of the census schedules. Free-hand sketch maps or any local maps available were used, and the E.D. boundaries were sketched onto the maps. The E.D. maps were returned to Washington along with the original schedules, and both were microfilmed & digitized.

The 1880 Short Form

In 1880, an original and a "Short Form" copy of the census schedules were made. Unlike the 1850-1870 censuses, where the original schedules remained in the county courthouses, the 1880 original schedules were sent directly to the Census Office in Washington, while an abbreviated copy was made to remain in each county of the U.S. The 1880 Short Form, showing just the name, age, sex, and color of every person, was to be on public display at a county courthouse for 30 days after the enumeration.

The Short Form name list was arranged by the first letter of a surname. A family with each member having the same surname would appear as a family group, but there was no indication of relationships; and one would lose the connection to any other persons with a different surname shown as part of the household in the full schedules.

Still, the 1880 Short Form name lists were an instant success. Businessmen, politicians, government people, and others clamored to get their hands on the 1880 Short Form lists, because they were perhaps the only directory/index to the names of the inhabitants of a county at that time.

Before 1880, most commercial directories were primarily related to businesses, not individual households. There were very few countywide directories that named every head of household, let alone the names of spouses, children, boarders, etc. The popularity of the 1880 Short Form gave several directory publishers the incentive to produce their own versions, and some began producing a new publication every year thereafter. The initial popularity of the 1880 Short Form listing waned after a few years because the availability of updated every-name directories made them obsolete. For that reason, there are few of the original 1880 Short Form lists still around today.

There were 2,570 counties in the U.S. in 1880, all of which had a Short Form index to the county's inhabitants. A recent survey of all state libraries, state archives, and the Family History Library in Salt Lake City could identify fewer than 50 counties with surviving original 1880 Short Form name lists. See the GenealogyBlog article, *The 1880 Census Short Forms & Where to Find Them*, see www.genealogyblog.com/?p=41858.

Census Copies, 1890

The original 1890 census population schedules (the name lists) were involved in a 1921 fire that took place in the Commerce Building in Washington, DC. The fire was contained in the basement storage area that held the entire collection of the 1890 federal census originals (the only copy). Fragments of the schedules that survived the 1921 fire are together on one roll of microfilm, all indexed, listing 6,160 persons out of the entire 1890 population of 62.9 million people.

A recent publication has an annotated list of over 1,200 substitute name list databases from the period 1885-1895, see **Substitutes for the Lost 1890 Federal Census,** by William Dollarhide (publ. 2019, Family Roots Publishing Co., 103 pages). See www.familyrootspublishing.com/store/product_view.php?id=3577.

The tragedy of the lost 1890 Census was that it was the only copy. Why there was only one copy had to do with the form design of the census schedules. In 1890, the Census Office created a completely different method of recording the census enumeration, one that was unique to the 1890 census and never repeated. Up to 10 persons in one household were enumerated on both sides of one sheet of paper, making the 1890 census schedules at least ten times greater in volume than the 1880 schedules.

The 1890 Short Form

With the tenfold increase in paper volume, Congress decided to finance just one copy and make an 1890 Short Form copy an option to any county in the U.S. that wanted their own set. Unlike the 1880 Short Forms, which were free, the counties were required to pay for the cost of making a 1890 Short Form copy of the census schedules. The format of the 1890 Short Form was a simple listing of persons in the same order they appeared on the full census schedules, showing only a name, age, sex, and color; but there was no alphabetizing as was done in the 1880 Short Forms.

But by 1890, the demand for a Short Form census listing had been eliminated – there were now numerous every-name directories that did the same thing. Of the 2,813 counties in the U.S. in 1890, just two (2) counties were known to have a Short Form copy made:

1) **Washington County, Georgia,** originals at the County Courthouse, Sandersville, GA, microfilmed & digitized with the title, *Census Returns of Washington County Taken by the County, 1890,* to access the digital images, see www.familysearch.org/search/catalog/287607.

2) **Ascension Parish, Louisiana,** originals at the Parish Courthouse, Donaldsonville, LA, with a known microfilm copy at the LA State Archives (not digitized); and indexed in *1890 U.S. Census, Ascension Parish, Louisiana,* publ. 1983, Oracle Press, 256 pages, see
www.familysearch.org/search/catalog/32205.

1890 Union Veterans & Widows Schedules

In addition to the main population schedules, a special census listing was extracted from the 1890 census schedules for surviving Union soldiers, sailors, and marines (or their widows), and a portion of that special census survives.

Of the forty-nine (49) jurisdictions (states, territories, districts) in place in 1890, sixteen (16) of the Union Veterans Schedules jurisdictions were lost. When the National Archives accessioned the surviving schedules in 1943, they were led to believe (by the Census Bureau) that the losses were a result of the same 1921 fire that damaged the population schedules. But upon examination, the National Archives conservators could find no evidence of fire or water damage and did not support that conclusion. The losses were alphabetically from Alabama through Kansas, and about half of the names for Kentucky. Surviving state listings begin with the partial list for Kentucky and are complete from Louisiana through Wyoming.

The *1890 Special Schedules Enumerating Union Veterans and Widows of Union Veterans of the Civil War* were microfilmed on 118 rolls, series M123, beginning with FHL film #338160 (Kentucky). For access to the digital images of each roll, see the FHL catalog page:
https://familysearch.org/search/catalog/230777.

Copies, Microfilming & Digitizing of the 1900-1940 Censuses

The censuses of 1900 through 1940 were each enumerated in one set of schedules; and very few copies were made, if any. For each of these censuses, Congress required any county wanting a copy of their census schedules to pay for the cost of making the copy. Not one county copy has ever been found.

In the 1940s, the problem of storage space became acute for the Census Bureau, part of the Commerce Department in Washington, DC. The original census schedules 1790 through 1880 had already been transferred to the National Archives; but the original schedules from 1900 through 1940 were still stored on several floors of the Commerce Building.

To free up space, the Census Bureau undertook a major project to microfilm the census schedules of 1900 through 1940; and when the microfilming was complete, the original census schedules were destroyed. This was all done with the permission of Congress, who funded the microfilming project, and authorized the destruction of the originals.

In the 1940s, photographic microfilming was still a very new technology with some serious limitations, particularly with the cameras available at the time. It was not until 1972 (the year the 1900 Census was opened to the public) that genealogists discovered that poor microfilming from the 1940s made some of the microfilm images impossible to read. In 1992, when the 1920 Census was released, the microfilm was so bad that companies like Heritage Quest of Bountiful, Utah began an enhancement program to re-photograph the images, just to make them barely readable.

Digitizing of microfilm images began in the late 1990s, and the first generation of scanners were expensive, bulky, and did not improve the microfilm image much. By 2005, however, that technology began to give encouraging results. The original 1940s microfilm was filmed using just a limiting black and white scale – modern digitizing uses a broad grey scale, and brings faint images into focus better. Digitizing has not cured the problem of poor microfilming of the 1940s, but it has improved the images enough to make them usable and mostly readable today.

Soundex Indexes, 1880-1930

When Social Security began in 1935, the first old-age pension system was established for every citizen of the United States of the age of 65 or over. An immediate concern was how to prove an age for a person applying for social security, since not very many people could produce a birth certificate in 1935. Many people who were qualified could not prove their age.

To counter this problem, a special branch of the Census Bureau was created, called the Age Search Group. This group would take a person's application for social security and attempt to find that same person in a census record where a name and age would be given. It was soon determined that indexes would be needed to speed up the work of finding a particular person's name and age listing.

The Census Bureau hired the Rand Corporation to design an indexing system based on phonetic sounds for a name, which become known as "Soundex." Under the supervision of the Age Search Group, the Works Progress Administration (WPA) employed clerical workers to create the indexes to the 1880, 1900, 1920 and 1930 censuses. The WPA workers prepared index cards for heads of household from the 1880 census with children 10 years or younger, as well as the index cards for all heads of household from the 1900 and 1920. The 1930 Soundex was complete for 10 states only, with partial indexes for two more states.

In 1962, the Age Search Group, on their own, undertook a census index of the 1910 census but limited the index to twenty-one states. The 1910 index was the first to employ the use of computers. Two systems for coding the names in the 1910 index were used. The coding used was either the Soundex or Miracode system, but both systems were exactly the same for coding a surname. The index cards for Miracode or Soundex differ only in the citation to a visitation (house) or page number on the full schedules.

Today, all the 1880-1920 Soundex cards prepared by the WPA for the Age Search Group have been microfilmed and made available to genealogists. The computer-generated 1910 Miracode print-outs, and the 1910 Soundex cards were also microfilmed.

Soundex Code

In all cases, a Soundex Code was given at the top of the index card, followed by the name of the head of the household, the names and ages of each member of the family, and a citation to the census schedules on which they appeared. The cards were then arranged by the Soundex codes for each census index, A000-Z600, and after that by the first name of the head of the household.

The code consisted of an alpha character for the surname, removing all vowels and any doubled letters, and coding up to three consonants with similar sounds:
- 1 = b, p, f, v
- 2 = c, s, k, g, j, q, x, z
- 3 = d, t
- 4 = l
- 5 = m, n
- 6 = r

To code the surname MARBUTT, start with the letter M, eliminate vowels and doubled letters, thus, M-R-B-T codes as M613. If less than 3 coded letters use 0's; e.g., LEE would code as L000.

Personal Census Search

The Age Search Group of the Census Bureau is still in operation. The services of this group can be used for a personal census search to locate one person in a census 1910-2010. The request must be for yourself, a deceased ancestor, or for any person alive today who provides written permission. The fee for the search is $65.00 plus $10.00 for a "genealogy" search (which adds the full details for one person on a particular census schedule). The application for a search must be on a Bureau of Census form BC-600. A downloadable form is available, see
www.census.gov/history/pdf/bc-600-2013.pdf.
For a GenealogyBlog article with detailed information, *The U.S. Census Bureau's Age Search Service,* see
www.genealogyblog.com/?p=42239.

County Boundary Changes

When using census records for genealogical research, it is important to understand how the old county boundaries changed over the years. Since the basic census enumeration unit in all censuses, 1790-2010, was a county, understanding the genealogy of counties is part of locating the place where an ancestor lived.

For example, if a genealogist knows that an ancestor lived in Allegheny County, Pennsylvania in 1790, the county courthouse there today is a resource for old deeds, marriages, probates, and other court records, and a place where an ancestor's name may be mentioned. But in 1800, due to the formation of counties taken from Allegheny, there were nine counties covering the same area: Allegheny, Beaver, Butler, Mercer, Crawford, Erie, and parts of Armstrong, Venango, and Warren Counties.

Take the example of county boundary changes in Oregon. Any marriage for a couple in the little town of Linkville in Linn County in 1850 would have been recorded in Albany, the county seat; but in 1860, due to the formation of new counties in Oregon, all marriages performed in Linkville, now in Wasco County, were recorded in The Dalles. In 1870, a marriage performed in Linkville was recorded in Jacksonville, the county seat of Jackson County (but later the county seat was moved to Medford). In 1880, a marriage performed in Linkville was recorded in Lakeview, the county seat of Lake County; and in 1890, for the first time, a marriage performed in Linkville was recorded in the same town since Linkville became the county seat of Klamath County – but then the name Linkville was changed to Klamath Falls. The boundaries of Klamath County have not changed since 1890.

Of course, the town of Linkville never moved. As the settlement of Oregon took place, new counties were created; and earlier county boundaries were changed, placing the town of Linkville-Klamath Falls in five different counties from 1850 through 1890. Therefore, all county records such as deeds, probates, marriages, etc., for a family that lived in Linkville, Oregon, are spread across the state and stored today in five different county courthouses. These examples can be repeated in virtually every state.

Table 3 shows that the number of counties in the United States increased from 292 in 1790 to 3,142 by 2010. It is common that genealogists attempting to identify the places their ancestors lived must first face the reality of changing county boundaries over the years.

Table 3 – Statistics of U.S. Federal Census, 1790-2010

Census Year	U.S. Population	No. of States	No. of Counties	Territories Included in the Census
1790	3,929,214	14	292	Southwest Territory (tally only).
1800	5,308,483	16	419	Northwest, IN, MI & MS Territories.
1810	7,239,881	17	574	IL, IN, MI, MS, LA (MO) & Orleans Territories.
1820	9,638,453	23	759	AR, MI & MO Territories.
1830	12,860,702	24	988	AR, FL & MI Territories.
1840	17,063,353	26	1,279	IA, FL & WI Territories.
1850	23,191,876	31	1,623	MN, NM, OR & UT Territories.
1860	31,443,321	33	2,080	KS, NM, NE, UT, WA, Indian Terr. (Non-Indians only) & Unorg. Dakota
1870	38,558,371	37	2,295	AZ, CO, ID, NM, MT, UT, WA, WY & Dakota Territories.
1880	50,189,209	38	2,570	AK, AZ, ID, NM, MT, UT, WA, WY & Dakota Territories.
1890	62,979,766	44	2,813	AK, AZ, NM, OK & UT Territories
1900	76,212,168	45	2,862	AK, AZ, HI, NM & OK Territories.
1910	92,228,496	46	2,962	AK, AZ, NM, HI & Puerto Rico Territories.
1920	106,021,521	48	3,076	[AK, HI, Guam, Midway, Wake Island, American Samoa, Panama Canal Zone,
1930	123,202,589	48	3,110	Puerto Rico & U.S. Virgin Islands].
1940	132,164,569	48	3,108	Same as above.
1950	151,325,798	48	3,111	Same as above.
1960	179,323,175	50	3,133	[Guam, Midway, Wake Island, American Samoa, Panama Canal Zone,
1970	203,302,031	50	3,142	Puerto Rico & U.S. Virgin Islands].
1980	226,542,199	50	3,137	Same as above.
1990	248,709,873	50	3,141	[Guam, Northern Mariana Islands, Midway, American Samoa, Wake Island,
2000	281,421,906	50	3,141	Puerto Rico & U.S. Virgin Islands]
2010	308,745,538	50	3,142	Same as above.

Table 3 Notes

1. Alaska is the only state without counties. The totals above include the census subdivisions (boroughs) of Alaska.

2. In Louisiana, a parish has the same function as a county in other states.

3. The District of Columbia was included in all censuses, 1800 forward, but was not included in the No. of States column above.

3. Since 1790, there have been 138 counties reported in the censuses that have since been renamed or abolished and subsequently absorbed into other counties.

4. Through 2018, there were 38 cities in Virginia independent of any county. The Census Bureau treats them as "county-equivalents."

5. Any special schedule enumerations were not included above, e.g., Indians, Overseas Military & Naval Forces.

References

Alterman, Hyman, *Counting People: The Census in History,* New York: Harcourt, Brace & World, 1969.

Barrows, Robert C., "The Ninth Federal Census of Indianapolis: A Case in Civic Chauvinism," *Indiana Magazine of History* 73 (1977).

Bureau of the Census, *200 Years of U.S. Census Taking: Population and Housing Questions, 1790-1990,* Washington: GPO, 1989. Reprint, Bountiful, UT: AGLL, 1996.

Davidson, Katherine H. and Charlotte M. Ashby, *Preliminary Inventory of the Records of the Bureau of the Census, National Archives Preliminary Inventory No. 16,* Washington: NARS, 1964. Reprint, 1997.

Dollarhide, William, *Substitutes for the Lost 1890 Federal Census,* Orting, WA: Family Roots Publ. Co., 2019. See
www.familyrootspublishing.com/store/product_view.php?id=3577.

Dollarhide, William, *1790-1940 Census: A Quick Look – A Genealogists' Insta-Guide,* 16 Census years, 4-8 pages each, UV Coated Card Stock, publ. Family Roots Publ. Co., 2018. See
www.familyrootspublishing.com/store/category.php?cat=3443.

Eckler, A. Ross, *The Bureau of the Census,* New York: Praeger, 1972.

Forstall, Richard L., *Population of States and Counties of the United States: 1790-1990.* Washington: U.S. Bureau of the Census, 1996.

Holt, W. Stull, *The Bureau of the Census: Its History, Activities and Organization,* Washington: Brookings Institution, 1929.

Rossiter, W. S., *A Century of Population Growth: From the First Census of the U.S. to the Twelfth, 1790-1920.* Washington: GPO, 1909. Reprint, Orting, WA: Heritage Quest, Press, 1989.

Russell, Donna Valley, ed., *Michigan Censuses, 1710-1830 Under the French, British, and Americans,* Detroit: Detroit Society for Genealogical Research, 1982.

Scott, Ann Herbert. *Census U.S.A.: A Fact Finding for the American People, 1790-1970,* New York: Seabury Press, 1968.

Thorndale, William and William Dollarhide, *Map Guide to the U.S. Federal Census, 1790-1920,* Baltimore: Genealogical Publishing Co., Inc., 1987-2018. 393 census year maps show the changing county boundaries for 3,142 counties, old and current boundaries on the same map, see
www.familyrootspublishing.com/store/product_view.php?id=67.

Wright, Carroll D., *The History and Growth of the United States Census: Prepared for the Senate Committee on the Census,* GPO, Washington, DC, 1900, 967 pages. To access a digital version of this classic, see the FHL catalog page:
www.familysearch.org/search/catalog/1912123.

Census Legislation, 1790-1940

A Census Bureau website identifies the titles and dates of each legislative act authorizing a census, beginning with the 1789 Constitution of the United States, followed by all census acts 1790 to the Present. There is a link to a downloadable PDF for census years, organized as follows:

1789-1820. For the complete 1789 U.S. Constitution, and legislative acts for the 1790, 1800, 1810, and 1820 censuses. see
www.census.gov/history/www/reference/legislation/legislation_1789_-_1820.html.

1830-1900. For the legislative acts for the 1830, 1840, 1850-1860-1870, 1880, 1890, and 1900 censuses, see
www.census.gov/history/www/reference/legislation/legislation_1830_-_1899.html.

1910-1940. For the legislative acts beginning with the *Act to Provide a Permanent Census Office* (March 6, 1902); and for the legislative acts for 1910, 1920, 1930, and 1940 Censuses; plus other census and apportioning acts, see
www.census.gov/history/www/reference/legislation/legislation_1902_-_1941.html.

1790-1940 Census Overviews, U.S. Census Bureau

The Census Bureau has a special website with a link to an overview of each census year from 1790 on. Each overview site has details about the Authorizing Legislation, Enumeration, and Further Information. See the following:

1790 Census Overview, see
www.census.gov/history/www/through_the_decades/overview/1790.html.

1800 Census Overview, see
www.census.gov/history/www/through_the_decades/overview/1800.html.

1810 Census Overview, see
www.census.gov/history/www/through_the_decades/overview/1810.html.

1820 Census Overview, see
www.census.gov/history/www/through_the_decades/overview/1820.html.

1830 Census Overview, see
www.census.gov/history/www/through_the_decades/overview/1830.html.

1840 Census Overview, see
www.census.gov/history/www/through_the_decades/overview/1840.html.

1850 Census Overview, see
www.census.gov/history/www/through_the_decades/overview/1850.html.

1860 Census Overview, see
www.census.gov/history/www/through_the_decades/overview/1860.html.

1870 Census Overview, see
www.census.gov/history/www/through_the_decades/overview/1870.html.

1880 Census Overview, see
www.census.gov/history/www/through_the_decades/overview/1880.html.

1890 Census Overview, see
www.census.gov/history/www/through_the_decades/overview/1890.html.

1900 Census Overview, see
www.census.gov/history/www/through_the_decades/overview/1900.html.

1910 Census Overview, see
www.census.gov/history/www/through_the_decades/overview/1910.html.

1920 Census Overview, see
www.census.gov/history/www/through_the_decades/overview/1920.html.

1930 Census Overview, see
www.census.gov/history/www/through_the_decades/overview/1930.html.

1940 Census Overview, see
www.census.gov/history/www/through_the_decades/overview/1940.html.

1950 Census Overview, see
www.census.gov/history/www/through_the_decades/overview/1950.html.

GenealogyBlog Articles Related to Censuses & Substitutes

Substitute Name Lists for the Lost 1890 Federal Census – Part 1: National & Alabama to Missouri, See www.genealogyblog.com/?p=41927.

Substitute Name Lists for the Lost 1890 Federal Census – Part 2: National & Montana to Wyoming, see www.genealogyblog.com/?p=41997.

Are You Reading the Originals? Reading Federal Census Records, Census Copies, etc., see www.genealogyblog.com/?p=24002.

County Name Changes and Abolished Counties Reflected in the 1790-1920 Censuses, see www.genealogyblog.com/?p=21820.

Census Records and County Boundary Changes, when your ancestors appear to move from county to county, but actually the boundaries moved, not the people, see
www.genealogyblog.com/?p=19203.

Census Mistakes. Things to consider when using census records, and areas where mistakes are prevalent, see
www.genealogyblog.com/?p=18199.

Taking the Census in the Applegate Valley of Oregon. 1950 census taker met by shotgun, see www.genealogyblog.com/?p=19385.

The 1880 Census Short Forms & Where to Find Them. A list of 48 counties holding originals, see www.genealogyblog.com/?p=41858.

Section 2 – Population Schedules

Contents

Table 4: Availability of U.S. Federal Censuses,
        1790-1950..30
First Census of the U.S. – 1790........................31
Second Census of the U.S. – 1800......................35
Third Census of the U.S. – 1810....................... 39
Fourth Census of the U.S. – 1820..........................43
Fifth Census of the U.S. – 1830........................47
Sixth Census of the U.S. – 1840........................51
Seventh Census of the U.S. – 1850......................55
Eighth Census of the U.S. – 1860....................... 61
Ninth Census of the U.S. – 1870........................ 67
Tenth Census of the U.S. – 1880........................ 73
State Censuses Taken in 1885............................ 77
Eleventh Census of the U.S. – 1890....................79
Table 5 – 1884-1896 State Censuses................... 82
Twelfth Census of the U.S. – 1900..................... 83
Thirteenth Census of the U.S. – 1910................... 87
Fourteenth Census of the U.S. – 1920.....................91
Fifteenth Census of the U.S. – 1930.................... 95
Sixteenth Census of the U.S. – 1940................... 99
Seventeenth Census of the U.S. – 1950................103

Table 4 - Availability of U.S. Federal Censuses, 1790-1950

State	Year a Terr	Year a State	1790	1800	1810	1820	1830	1840	1850	1860	1870	1880	1890	1900	1910	1920	1930	1940	1950
Alabama	1817	1819				lost	•	•	•	•	•	•	lost	•	•	•	•	•	•
Alaska (to US 1867)	1912	1959	No census taken, District of Alaska, 1870, 1880, or 1890 →								--	--	--	•	•	•	•	•	•
Arizona	1863	1912									•	•	lost	•	•	•	•	•	•
Arkansas	1819	1836				lost	•	•	•	•	•	•	lost	•	•	•	•	•	•
California (to US 1848)	—	1850							•	•	•	•	lost	•	•	•	•	•	•
Colorado	1861	1876									•	•	lost	•	•	•	•	•	•
Connecticut	—	1788	•	•	•	•	•	•	•	•	•	•	lost	•	•	•	•	•	•
Delaware	—	1787	•	•	•	•	•	•	•	•	•	•	lost	•	•	•	•	•	•
Distr. of Columbia	1801	—		•	•	•	•	•	•	•	•	•	lost	•	•	•	•	•	•
Florida	1822	1845							•	•	•	•	lost	•	•	•	•	•	•
Georgia	—	1788	lost	lost	lost	•	•	•	•	•	•	•	lost	•	•	•	•	•	•
Hawaii (to US 1898)	1900	1959												•	•	•	•	•	•
Idaho	1863	1890									•	•	lost	•	•	•	•	•	•
Illinois	1809	1818			part	•	•	•	•	•	•	•	lost	•	•	•	•	•	•
Indiana	1800	1816		lost	lost	•	•	•	•	•	•	•	lost	•	•	•	•	•	•
Iowa (* part of WI Terr.)	1838	1846						•*	•	•	•	•	lost	•	•	•	•	•	•
Kansas	1854	1861								•	•	•	lost	•	•	•	•	•	•
Kentucky (*Distr. of VA)	—	1791	lost*	lost	•	•	•	•	•	•	•	•	lost	•	•	•	•	•	•
Louisiana (*OrleansTer)	1809	1812			•*	•	•	•	•	•	•	•	lost	•	•	•	•	•	•
Maine (*Distr. of MA)	—	1820	•*	•*	•*	•	•	•	•	•	•	•	lost	•	•	•	•	•	•
Maryland	—	1788	•	•	•	•	•	•	•	•	•	•	lost	•	•	•	•	•	•
Massachusetts	—	1788	•	•	•	•	•	•	•	•	•	•	lost	•	•	•	•	•	•
Michigan	1805	1837			lost	•	•	•	•	•	•	•	lost	•	•	•	•	•	•
Minnesota	1849	1858	MN Terr. had a special federal census in 1857 →							•	•	•	lost	•	•	•	•	•	•
Mississippi	1798	1817			lost	•	•	•	•	•	•	•	lost	•	•	•	•	•	•
Missouri	1805	1821			lost	lost	•	•	•	•	•	•	lost	•	•	•	•	•	•
Montana	1864	1889									•	•	lost	•	•	•	•	•	•
Nebraska	1854	1867								•	•	•	lost	•	•	•	•	•	•
Nevada	1861	1864								•	•	•	lost	•	•	•	•	•	•
New Hampshire	—	1788	•	•	•	•	•	•	•	•	•	•	lost	•	•	•	•	•	•
New Jersey	—	1787	lost	lost	lost	lost	•	•	•	•	•	•	lost	•	•	•	•	•	•
New Mexico	1850	1912							•	•	•	•	lost	•	•	•	•	•	•
New York	—	1788	•	•	•	•	•	•	•	•	•	•	lost	•	•	•	•	•	•
North Carolina	—	1789	•	•	•	•	•	•	•	•	•	•	lost	•	•	•	•	•	•
North Dakota*	1861	1889	*1860, 1870, 1880 as part of Dakota Territory →								•	•	lost	•	•	•	•	•	•
Ohio (*NW Terr.)	1787	1803		* lost	lost	•	•	•	•	•	•	•	lost	•	•	•	•	•	•
Oklahoma	1890	1907	OK Terr. & Indian Terr. had a special federal census in 1907 →										lost	•	•	•	•	•	•
Oregon	1848	1859							•	•	•	•	lost	•	•	•	•	•	•
Pennsylvania	—	1787	•	•	•	•	•	•	•	•	•	•	lost	•	•	•	•	•	•
Rhode Island	—	1790	•	•	•	•	•	•	•	•	•	•	lost	•	•	•	•	•	•
South Carolina	—	1788	•	•	•	•	•	•	•	•	•	•	lost	•	•	•	•	•	•
South Dakota*	1861	1889	*1860, 1870, 1880 as part of Dakota Territory →								•	•	lost	•	•	•	•	•	•
Tennessee (*SW Terr)	1790	1796	* tally	lost	lost	part	•	•	•	•	•	•	lost	•	•	•	•	•	•
Texas (to US 1845)	—	1845							•	•	•	•	lost	•	•	•	•	•	•
Utah	1850	1896							•	•	•	•	lost	•	•	•	•	•	•
Vermont	—	1791	•	•	•	•	•	•	•	•	•	•	lost	•	•	•	•	•	•
Virginia	—	1788	lost	lost	•	•	•	•	•	•	•	•	lost	•	•	•	•	•	•
Washington	1853	1889								•	•	•	lost	•	•	•	•	•	•
West Virginia	—	1863	Part of Virginia, 1790-1860								•	•	lost	•	•	•	•	•	•
Wisconsin	1836	1848						•	•	•	•	•	lost	•	•	•	•	•	•
Wyoming	1868	1890									•	•	lost	•	•	•	•	•	•

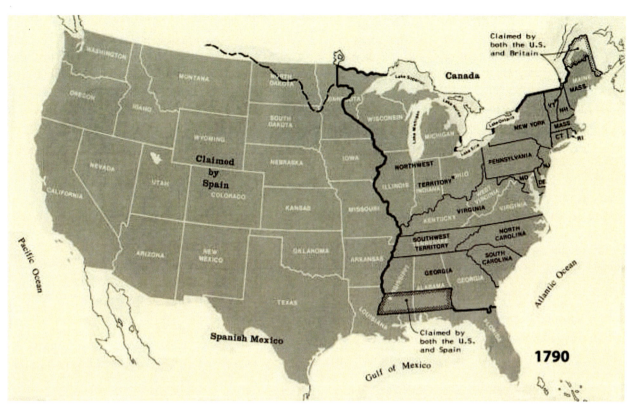

The U.S. in 1790. At the Treaty of Paris in 1783, the U.S. had agreed to meet later with Spain to settle a land dispute in the West Florida region; and also to meet with Great Britain to resolve the issue of the northern border of present Maine with present New Brunswick. Map Source: Page 1, *Map Guide to the U.S. Federal Censuses, 1790-1920* by William Thorndale and William Dollarhide.

First Census of the United States - 1790

Description

Location of Original Records: National Archives, Washington, DC.

U.S. Population: 3.9 million (3.2 free and .7 million slave).

1790 Census Legislative Act: 1 Stat. 101, 1 March 1790.

Responsibility: The President of the United States (George Washington), with authority delegated to the Secretary of State (Thomas Jefferson). Reporting to the Secretary of State, the U.S. Marshal of each U.S. Federal Court District hired and managed Assistant Marshals as the door-to-door census takers within his district. The Assistant Marshals were all political appointees (Mainly people loyal to the Federalist Party).

Census day: the first Monday in August (2 Aug 1790). All of the questions asked by the census taker were related to a person's age or place of residence as of the census day. The original 1790 instructions were issued by Secretary of State Thomas Jefferson:

"...all the questions refer to the day when the enumeration is to commence; the first Monday in August next. Your assistants will thereby understand that they are to insert in their returns all the persons belonging to the family on the first

Monday in August, even those who may be deceased at the time when they take the account; and, on the other hand, that they will not include in it, infants born after that day."

Time Allowed: Nine months. (Except VT had 5 months, and SC had 19 months).

States Included: 14 States. Of the two states late to join the Union, Rhode Island (the last of the 13 states to ratify the Constitution on 29 May 1790), was to be enumerated within the set nine months (1 Stat. 129, 5 July 1790). Vermont entered the Union as the 14th state on 4 Mar 1791, and had a census day of the 1st Monday in April 1791 (4 Apr 1791); the field count due within five months (1 Stat. 197, 2 March 1791). South Carolina's field count was extended to allow completion within nineteen months of the census day (1 Stat. 226, 8 November 1791).

Federal Court Districts: 16 Districts. There were fourteen (14) states at the time of the 1790 census, but the census was enumerated in sixteen (16) federal court districts. The districts lined up with the states, except that Maine was still part of Massachusetts and had its own census because it was a separate federal court district. The same was true of Kentucky, still part of Virginia but was a separate federal court district.

Territories Included: Congress believed there was no need for a census in the Northwest Territory because territories had no voting representation in Congress. But military captains in the Southwest Territory (which became Tennessee in 1796) took a count under the direction of the Governor (See *Censuses in U.S. Territories,* page 13).

Surviving Censuses: Eleven (11) federal court districts: Connecticut, Maine, Maryland, Massachusetts, New Hampshire, New York, North Carolina, Pennsylvania, Rhode Island, South Carolina, and Vermont.

Census Losses: Five (5) federal court districts: Kentucky, Delaware, Georgia, New Jersey, and Virginia. These five states did not return the original 1790-1820 census manuscripts to Washington, DC as was specified in the 1830 law (4 Stat. 430, 28 May 1830).

Content of the Population Schedules: 5 columns. The 1790 format included:
- Name of a head of household
- Number of free white males under 16
- Number of free white males 16 or older
- Number of free white females of any age
- Number of slaves (omitted in places without slaves)

1790 Census Publications with Digital Images

Microfilm of Originals & Digital Capture: The National Archives film for the 1790 census is contained on 12 rolls, series M637, beginning with FHL film #568141 (Connecticut). The microfilm was digitized by FamilySearch International. For a list of roll numbers, contents, and access to the digital images of each roll, see the online FHL catalog page: https://familysearch.org/search/catalog/121535.

Printed Extract & Index: In 1908, the Census Bureau in Washington, DC undertook a project to extract and index the 1790 census name lists, a publication now commonly known as the *1790 Heads of Families.* It included one volume each for twelve of the sixteen federal court districts that were originally enumerated in the 1790 census. Although Virginia's 1790 census originals were lost, Virginia had extant tax lists covering all of its counties for the years immediately preceding 1790. The Census Office's 1908 publication used these tax lists to reconstruct the 1790 name lists for the lost Virginia census. A few 1790 counties of other states were also reconstructed from tax lists, including certain counties in North Carolina and Maryland. This 1790 census extract & index was printed in 1908, one volume per state; later microfilmed by the National Archives on three rolls as series T498. Search the FHL catalog for one of the 12 volumes. Search by: (Name of State) – 1790 Census. See www.familysearch.org/search/catalog/search.

First Census of the U.S. - 1790

As an example, search the Connecticut list of census categories to find the first volume entitled, *Heads of Families of the First Census of the United States Taken in the Year 1790, Connecticut,* Government Printing Office, 1908, 227 pages, FHL book 974.6 X2. To access a digital version of this book, see the FHL catalog page: www.familysearch.org/search/catalog/244344. Repeat this exercise for the other eleven (11) states in this series.

Online Searching - 1790 Census Indexes and Digital Images

The 1790 Census was digitized from the National Archives microfilm, indexed, and made available at the following websites:

- **Ancestry.com**. Subscription site, free database searching. Ancestry and FamilySearch share images and indexes. See www.ancestry.com/search/collections/1790usfedcen.

- **FamilySearch.org**. Free database search, with images by FamilySearch, index by Ancestry. See www.familysearch.org/search/collection/1803959.

- **MyHeritage.com**. A Family Tree subscription site. All U.S. Federal Census Records are available to subscribers with a data plan. See www.myheritage.com/research/collection-10120/1790-united-states-federal-census.

- **Findmypast.com**. Monthly or annual subscriptions. Initial searches to U.S. Federal Censuses are free. See www.findmypast.com/articles/search-the-1790-us-census.

- **GenealogyBank.com**. Subscription site. Initial searches to the U.S. Federal Censuses, 1790-1940 are free. www.genealogybank.com/explore/census/all.

- **HeritageQuestOnline-Subscribers Login**. This is a library subscription service. Check with your local library to see if they subscribe to the HeritageQuest databases. See www.heritagequestonline.com/hqoweb/library/do/login.

Table 1790 – Statewide Census Publications

1790 Jurisdictions Included in Census	Population	Census Extant?	FHL Film Number	Comments, Census Substitutes, etc.
1. Connecticut	237,946	Yes	568141	
2. Delaware	59,096	No	--	Reconstructed name list exists. See Note 1.
3. Georgia	82,548	No	--	Reconstructed name list exists. See Note 2.
4. Kentucky	73,677	No	-	District of Virginia. Reconstructed name list exists. See Note 3.
5. Maine	96,540	Yes	568142	District of Massachusetts.
6. Maryland	319,728	Yes	568143	Includes the town of Georgetown, DC
7. Massachusetts	378,787	Yes	568144	
8. New Hampshire	141,885	Yes	568145	
9. New Jersey	184,139	No	--	Reconstructed name list exists. See Note 4.
10. New York	340,120	Yes	568146	
11. North Carolina	393,751	Yes	568147	
-- Northwest Territory	--	--	--	No Census Taken. Substitute name lists exist. See Note 5.
12. Pennsylvania	434,373	Yes	568148	
13. Rhode Island	68,825	Yes	568150	
14. South Carolina	249,073	Yes	568151	
-- Southwest Territory	35,691 *	--	--	* No name list, tally only. See Note 6.
15. Vermont	85,425	Yes	568152	
16. Virginia	747,610	No	--	Reconstruction exists. See Note 7. Town of Alexandria, DC lost.
U.S. Total:	3,929,214			

Table 1790 Notes

1. See ***Reconstructed 1790 Census of Delaware,*** by Leon DeValinger, Jr., publ. as Special Publications of the National Genealogical Society; No. 10, 1962, 83 pages. For a digital version of this index, see the FHL catalog page:
www.familysearch.org/search/catalog/2792986.

2. See ***The Reconstructed 1790 Census of Georgia: Substitutes for Georgia's Lost 1790 Census,*** by Marie Delamar and Elizabeth Rothstein (Baltimore: GPC, 1985). See the FHL catalog page:
www.familysearch.org/search/catalog/216319.

3. The 1790 Kentucky census names were reconstructed from voters' lists, tax lists, and other sources and published as ***First Census of Kentucky, 1790,*** by Charles Heinemann (Baltimore: GPC, 1965). Filmed as FHL film #1440537, see the FHL catalog page: www.familysearch.org/search/catalog/1006571.

4. An attempt to reconstruct the lost New Jersey 1790 census was included in ***1790 Census Index, Miscellaneous Sources,*** North Salt Lake, UT: Accelerated Indexing Systems, 1990. The name lists from this book were included in Ancestry's database, ***New Jersey, Compiled Census and Census Substitutes Index, 1643-1890,*** see
www.ancestry.com/search/collections/njcen.

5. A partial list of Inhabitants of the Northwest Territory was compiled from tax lists in ***The Index to Early Ohio Tax Records***, Carol Willsey Bell, et al (Akron, OH: Esther Weygandt Powell, 1973, 173 pages), for a digital version of this book, see the FHL catalog: www.familysearch.org/search/catalog/235315. See also ***Michigan Censuses, 1710-1830, Under the French, British, and Americans,*** by Donna Valley Russell (Detroit Society for Genealogical Research, 1982, 291 pages), see the FHL catalog page:
www.familysearch.org/search/catalog/266465.

6. Papers of Governor William Blount of the Southwest Territory relating to a 1790 census of the inhabitants can be found in Clarence E. Carter, ***The Territorial Papers of the United States,*** Vol. 4, *The Territory South of the River Ohio, 1790-1796* (Washington: GPO, 1936), pp 49-50, 52-53, 69-70, 80-81, and 105-106. To access a digital version of all 28 volumes of *The Territorial Papers*, see the FHL catalog page: www.familysearch.org/search/catalog/42234.

7. See ***Heads of Families at the First Census of the United States Taken in the Year 1790, Virginia: Records of the State Enumerations: 1782-1785,*** Bureau of the Census, Washington, DC, GPO, 1908, 189 pages. To access a digital version of this book, see the FHL catalog page:
www.familysearch.org/search/catalog/2135455.

Selected Online Databases from the time of the 1790 Census

1790-1909 U.S. Patent and Trademark Office Patents, digitized and indexed at the Ancestry.com website. The database contains Patent number, Current U.S. Classification, Name of patentee, Patent date, and Patent place. This database has 3,577,054 records. See
www.ancestry.com/search/collections/uspatents.

1791-1906 New England Naturalization Index, digitized and indexed at the FamilySearch.org website. The index consists of 3x5 cards arranged by state and then by name of petitioner. The index uses the Soundex indexing system. This database has 615,903 records. See
https://familysearch.org/search/collection/1840474.

1794-1995 U.S. Naturalization Records Indexes, digitized and indexed at the Ancestry.com website. index cards to naturalization records of various district courts of the U.S. (in several states). This database has 2,494,749 records.
www.ancestry.com/search/collections/usnaturalizationindexes.

1795-1925 Passport Applications, digitized at the FamilySearch.org website. This database has 959,931 images. See
https://familysearch.org/search/collection/2185145.

1795-1972 U.S., Naturalization Records - Original Documents, digitized and indexed at the Ancestry.com website. Includes the original documents of Declaration of Intentions and other naturalization papers.
www.ancestry.com/search/collections/usnaturalizationoriginals.

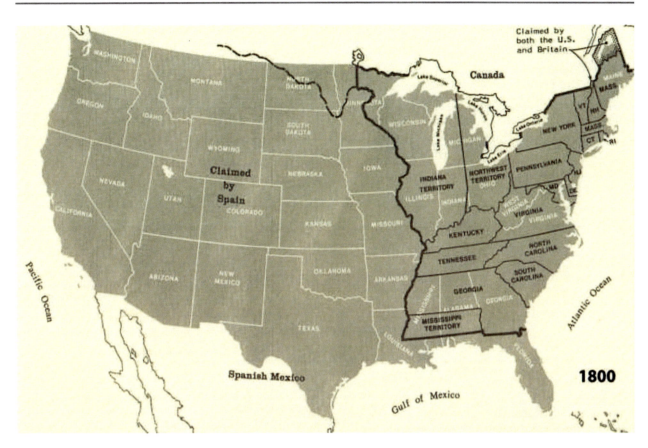

The U.S. in 1800. In the 1796 Treaty of San Lorenzo, the U.S. resolved the Spanish-U.S. disputed area by purchasing the area from Spain. In 1798, the area became Mississippi Territory. Map source: Page 2, *Map Guide to the U.S. Federal Censuses, 1790-1920* by William Thorndale and William Dollarhide.

Second Census of the United States - 1800

Description

Location of Original Records: National Archives, Washington, DC.

U.S. Population: 5.3 million (4.4 million free and .9 million slave).

1800 Census Legislative Act: 2 Stat. 11, 28 February 1800.

Responsibility: The President of the United States (John Adams), with authority delegated to the Secretary of State (Charles Lee). Reporting to the Secretary of State, the U.S. Marshal of each U.S. Federal Court District hired and managed Assistant Marshals as the door-to-door census takers within his district. Territories were enumerated by local militia captains, under the supervision of the Territorial Governor.

Census day: the first Monday in August (4 Aug 1800). All of the questions asked by the census taker were related to a person's age or place of residence as of the census day.

Time Allowed: Nine months.

1800 Jurisdictions: 21. Two new states were admitted to the Union since 1790: Kentucky, admitted in 1792; and Tennessee, previously the "Southwest Territory," admitted in 1796, for a total of 16 states in the Union. Still part of Massachusetts, the federal court district of Maine was enumerated separately from Massachusetts. The District of Columbia was included, separated from Maryland and Virginia.

In addition, three territories were enumerated for the first time: Mississippi Territory, created in 1798 from lands obtained in a treaty with Spain; the Northwest Territory, created in 1787 (but not enumerated in 1790); and Indiana Territory, divided from the old Northwest Territory in early 1800, for a total of 21 jurisdictions.

Surviving Censuses: Thirteen (13) federal court districts: Connecticut, Delaware, District of Columbia (Washington Co DC only), Maine, Maryland, Massachusetts, New Hampshire, New York, North Carolina, Pennsylvania, Rhode Island, South Carolina, and Vermont.

Census Losses: Five (5) state/federal court districts; Georgia, Kentucky, New Jersey, Tennessee, and Virginia; and Three (3) Territories: Indiana Territory, Mississippi Territory, and Northwest Territory. These eight states/territories did not return the original 1790-1820 census manuscripts to Washington as was specified in the 1830 law (4 Stat. 430, 28 May 1830).

Content of the Population Schedules: 13 columns of questions were asked for the Head of Household, on one line, across one page, for the following:
- Name of a head of household
- Number of free white males, 0-9 years old
- Number of free white males, 10-15 years old
- Number of free white males, 16-25 years old
- Number of free white males, 26-44 years old
- Number of free white males, 45 & over
- Number of free white females, 0-9 years old
- Number of free white females, 10-15 years old
- Number of free white females, 16-25 years old
- Number of free white females, 26-44 years old
- Number of free white females, 45 & over
- Number of other free persons
- Number of slaves (omitted in places without slaves)

1800 Census Publications with Digital Images

Microfilm of Originals & Digital Capture: The National Archives film for the 1800 census is contained on 54 rolls, series M32, beginning with FHL film #205618 (Connecticut). The microfilm was digitized by FamilySearch International. For a list of roll numbers, contents, and access to the digital images of each roll, see the online FHL catalog page:
https://familysearch.org/search/catalog/118365.

Online Searching - 1800 Census Indexes and Digital Images

The 1800 Census was digitized from the National Archives microfilm, indexed, and made available at the following websites:

- **Ancestry.com.** Subscription site, free database searching. Ancestry and FamilySearch share images and indexes. See www.ancestry.com/search/collections/1800usfedcenancestry.

- **FamilySearch.org.** Free database search, with images by FamilySearch, index by Ancestry. See https://familysearch.org/search/collection/1804228.

- **MyHeritage.com.** A Family Tree subscription site. All U.S. Federal Census Records are available to subscribers with a data plan. See www.myheritage.com/research/collection-10121/1800-united-states-federal-census.

- **Findmypast.com.** Monthly or annual subscriptions. Initial searches to U.S. Federal Censuses are free. See www.findmypast.com/articles/search-the-1800-us-census.

- **GenealogyBank.com.** Subscription site. Initial searches to the U.S. Federal Censuses, 1790-1940 are free. www.genealogybank.com/explore/census/all.

- **HeritageQuestOnline-Subscribers Login.** This is a library subscription service. Check with your local library to see if they subscribe to the ProQuest & HeritageQuest databases. Many subscribing libraries allow their library card holders remote access. See www.heritagequestonline.com/hqoweb/library/do/login.

Table 1800 – Statewide Census Publications

1800 Jurisdictions Included in Census	Population	Census Extant?	FHL Film Number	Comments, Census Substitutes, etc.
1. Connecticut	251,002	Yes	205618	
2. Delaware	64,273	Yes	6413	
3. District of Columbia	8,144	Yes	6697	Washington Co DC only.
4. Georgia	162,686	No	--	Oglethorpe Co GA exists. See Note 1.
5. Indiana Territory	5,090	No	--	
6. Kentucky	220,955	No	--	Reconstructed from tax lists. See Note 2
7. Maine	151,719	Yes	218676	District of Massachusetts.
8. Maryland	341,548	Yes	193662	
9. Massachusetts	422,845	Yes	205611	
10. Mississippi Territory	7,600	No	--	
11. New Hampshire	183,858	Yes	218679	
12. New Jersey	211,149	No	--	
13. New York	589,051	Yes	193709	
14. North Carolina	478,.103	Yes	337905	
15. Northwest Territory	45,916	No	--	Washington Co exists. See Note 3.
16. Pennsylvania	602,365	Yes	363338	
17. Rhode Island	69,122	Yes	218680	
18. South Carolina	345,591	Yes	181422	
19. Tennessee	105,602	No	--	
20. Vermont	154,465	Yes	2186888	
21. Virginia	886,149	No	--	

U.S. Total: 5,308,483

Table 1800 Notes

1. See *1800 Census of Oglethorpe County, Georgia: The Only Extant Census of 1800 Within the State of Georgia, Transcribed From the Original and Indexed,* by Mary Bondurant Warren, publ. Athens, GA , 1965, 53 pages. See the FHL catalog page: www.familysearch.org/search/catalog/166427.

2. See *Second Census of Kentucky-1800 : A Privately Compiled and Published Enumeration of Tax Payers Appearing in the 79 Manuscript Volumes Extant of Tax Lists of the 42 counties of Kentucky in Existence in 1800,* by G Glen Clift (Baltimore: GPC, 1966). See the FHL catalog page: www.familysearch.org/search/catalog/88524.

3. See *Second Census of the United States, 1800, Population Schedules, Washington County, Territory Northwest of the River Ohio; and Population Census, 1803, Washington County, Ohio* [Microfilm & Digital Capture], These two name lists were part of the original papers of Rufus Putnam's Ohio Company, who kept a copy of the first (1800) federal census taken in Washington County. The 1803 list was the first Quadrennial Enumeration for Washington Co OH, and lists the name of all free males over the age of 21. The area of 1800-1803 Washington County includes the modern counties of Washington, Meigs, Gallia, Lawrence, and Athens counties, Ohio. FHL film #2155491. To access the digital images, See the FHL catalog page: www.familysearch.org/search/catalog/720623.

Selected Online Databases from the time of the 1800 Census

***Search Historical Books* [Online Database],** digitized and indexed at the GenealogyBank.com website, over 14,250 book titles, all published before 1900. See **www.genealogybank.com/gbnk/books.**

***1798-1892 Muster Rolls of the Marine Corps*,** digitized at the FamilySearch.org website. Images of muster rolls of the United States Marine Corps located at the National Archives. The records are arranged chronologically by month, then by post, station or ship. This database has 56,678 images. See **www.familysearch.org/search/collection/1916228.**

***1798-1914 U.S. Army, Register of Enlistments*,** digitized and indexed at the Ancestry.com website. The Regular Army is comprised of career soldiers and maintained through peacetime. Information listed on these records includes: 1) Name of enlistee. 2) Age at time of enlistment. 3) Birthplace. 4) Date of enlistment. 5) Enlistment place. 6) Occupation. 7) Physical description (eye color, hair color, complexion, and height). 8) Rank, company, and regiment. 9) Date and cause of discharge. And 10) Remarks. Some of this information is only viewable at the register image. This database has 1,401,585 records. See
www.familysearch.org/search/collection/1880762.
For the Ancestry.com version of this database, see **www.ancestry.com/search/collections/usarmyenlistments.**

***1798-1958 U.S. Marine Corps Muster Rolls* [Online Database],** digitized and indexed at the Ancestry.com website. Information in the database includes a Name, Rank, Enlistment date, Muster date, and Station. This roll was used as the basis for pay due the marines. Names of commissioned officers were listed first, followed by names of noncommissioned officers and then privates. Shown on the form are the date and place of enlistment of each individual, by whom enrolled and for what period of time. Remarks might contain a "record of events" column describing the activities engaged in by the unit. This database has 39,841,896 records. See
www.ancestry.com/search/collections/marine_muster.

***1800-1900 Revolutionary War Pension Files*,** digitized and indexed at the FamilySearch.org website. This collection includes an estimated 80,000 pension and bounty-land warrant application files based on the participation of American military, naval, and marine officers and enlisted men in the Revolutionary War. The records in this collection include entire pension files for soldiers and sailors who served in the Revolutionary War. The size of the files range from a handful of pages to hundreds of pages. Unlike Selected Records, which were typically chosen subjectively for genealogical content, these records reveal more details about each veteran's history and service, as well as more information about his family, state of health, and life after the war. If you know the state for which a man served, you can locate him through the alphabetical hierarchy in the browse menu. Select the state, the first letter of his last name, then locate his surname, followed by his given name. This database has 6,959,032 records. See
https://familysearch.org/search/collection/1417475.

***U.S., County and Regional Histories and Atlases, 1804-1984* [Online Database],** indexed at the Ancestry.com website. Source: Gale County and Regional Histories and Atlases Collection. Detroit, Michigan: Gale Research Company. This image only database contains more than 2,200 volumes of county and regional histories. In them you'll find history, biographical sketches, maps, business notices, statistics and population numbers, pictures, descriptions of industry and business, stories of early settlement and pioneers, colleges and universities, military history, geography, and plenty of other details. Browse the collection, organized by state, then title of the history book. See
www.ancestry.com/search/collections/uscountyreghist.

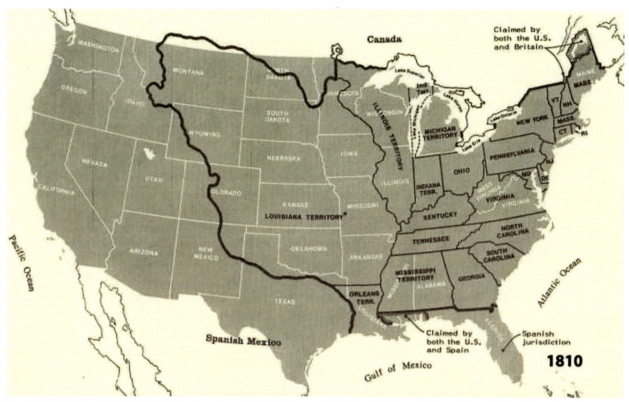

The U.S. in 1810. In 1803, the U.S. had purchased "The drainage of the Mississippi and Missouri Rivers" (Louisiana) from France. In 1804, the Louisiana Purchase was divided into Orleans Territory and Louisiana Territory, as shown on the map. In October 1810, in a proclamation by President James Madison, the U.S. arbitrarily annexed Spain's West Florida from the Mississippi River to the Perdido River. The area included Baton Rouge, Biloxi, and Mobile, but was not organized nor included in the 1810 census. Spain did not recognize the annexation, and continued their claim to West Florida in dispute with the U.S. Map Source: Page 3, *Map Guide to the U.S. Federal Censuses, 1790-1920* by William Thorndale and William Dollarhide.

Third Census of the United States - 1810

Description

Location of Original Records: National Archives, Washington, DC.

U.S. Population: 7.2 million (6.0 million free and .9 million slave).

1810 Census Legislative Act: 2 Stat. 564, 26 March 1810.

Responsibility: The President of the United States (James Madison), with authority delegated to the Secretary of State (Robert Smith). Reporting to the Secretary of State, the U.S. Marshal of each U.S. Federal Court District hired and managed Assistant Marshals as the door-to-door census takers within his district. Territories without a federal court district were enumerated by local militia captains, under the supervision of the Territorial Governor.

Census day: the first Monday in August (6 Aug 1810). All of the questions asked by the census taker were related to a person's age or place of residence as of the census day.

Time Allowed: In the first act, nine months; but extended to ten months (2 Stat. 658, 2 March 1811).

1810 Jurisdictions: 25. The 1810 federal census included one new state, Ohio, admitted in 1803, bringing the total to seventeen (17) states in the Union. The census also included the District of Columbia, the Federal Court District of Maine, and six (6) territories: Mississippi, Louisiana, Orleans, Michigan, Illinois, and Indiana territories, for a total of 25 jurisdictions.

Surviving Censuses & Census Losses: Seventeen (17) States & Territories had all or partial surviving censuses: Connecticut, Delaware, Illinois Territory (1 county only), Kentucky, Maine, Maryland, Massachusetts, New Hampshire, New York, North Carolina, Ohio (1 county only), Orleans Territory, Pennsylvania, Rhode Island, South Carolina, Vermont, and Virginia (about one fourth of VA's 135+ counties/independent cities survive). Eight (8) states, districts, or territories had complete losses: District of Columbia, Georgia, Indiana Territory, Louisiana Territory, Michigan Territory, Mississippi Territory, New Jersey, and Tennessee – the jurisdiction not returning the original 1790-1820 census manuscripts to Washington as was specified in the 1830 law (4 Stat. 430, 28 May 1830).

Content of the Population Schedules: 13 columns of questions were asked for the Head of Household, on one line, across one page, for the following:
- Name of a head of household
- Number of free white males, 0-9 years old
- Number of free white males, 10-15 years old
- Number of free white males, 16-25 years old
- Number of free white males, 26-44 years old
- Number of free white males, 45 & over
- Number of free white females, 0-9 years old
- Number of free white females, 10-15 years old
- Number of free white females, 16-25 years old
- Number of free white females, 26-44 years old
- Number of free white females, 45 & over
- Number of other free persons
- Number of slaves (omitted in places without slaves)

1810 was the first census in which the U.S. Marshals conducted non-population lists: A Census of Manufactures under the direction of the Secretary of the Treasury (Albert Gallatin) was authorized (2 Stat. 605, 1 May 1810). Any extant manufacturing lists are scattered among the population schedules, their page locations given in Katherine H. Davidson and Charlotte M. Ashby, *Preliminary Inventory of the Records of the Bureau of the Census* (Washington: National Archives, 1964), pp. 132-134.

1810 Census Publications with Digital Images

Microfilm of Originals & Digital Capture: The National Archives film for the 1810 census is contained on 72 rolls, series M252, beginning with FHL film #281229 (Connecticut). The microfilm was digitized by FamilySearch International. For a list of roll numbers, contents, and access to the digital images of each roll, see the online FHL catalog page:
https://familysearch.org/search/catalog/118496.

Online Searching - 1810 Census Indexes and Digital Images

The 1810 Census was digitized from the National Archives microfilm, indexed, and made available at the following websites:

- **Ancestry.com.** Subscription site, free database searching. Ancestry and FamilySearch share images and indexes. See
www.ancestry.com/search/collections/1810usfedcenancestry.

- **FamilySearch.org.** Free database search, with images by FamilySearch, index by Ancestry. See
https://familysearch.org/search/collection/1803765.

- **MyHeritage.com.** A Family Tree subscription site. All U.S. Federal Census Records are available to subscribers with a data plan. See
www.myheritage.com/research/collection-10122/1810-united-states-federal-census.

- **Findmypast.com.** Monthly or annual subscriptions. Initial searches to U.S. Federal Censuses are free. See
www.findmypast.com/articles/search-the-1810-us-census.

- **GenealogyBank.com.** Subscription site. Initial searches to the U.S. Federal Censuses, 1790-1940 are free. www.genealogybank.com/explore/census/all.

- **HeritageQuestOnline-Subscribers Login.** This is a library subscription service. Check with your local library to see if they subscribe to the ProQuest & HeritageQuest databases. Many subscribing libraries allow their library card holders remote access. See
www.heritagequestonline.com/hqoweb/library/do/login.

Table 1810 – Statewide Census Publications

1810 Jurisdictions Included in Census	Population	Census Extant?	FHL Film Number	Comments, Census Substitutes, etc.
1. Connecticut	261,942	Yes	281229	
2. Delaware	72,674	Yes	224381	
3. District of Columbia	15,471	No	--	Substitute name lists exist. See Note 1.
4. Georgia	251,407	No	--	Substitute name lists exist. See Note 2.
5. Illinois Territory	12,282	Yes		Randolph Co Only. See Note 3.
6. Indiana Territory	24,520	No	--	1807 IN Territorial census exists. See Note 4.
7. Kentucky	406,511	Yes	181350	
8. Louisiana Territory	19,763	No	--	Renamed Missouri Territory in 1812.
9. Maine	226,705	Yes	218682	District of Massachusetts.
10. Maryland	380,546	Yes	193666	
11. Massachusetts	472,040	Yes	205625	
12. Michigan Territory	4,762	No	--	Substitute name lists exist. See Note 5.
13. Mississippi Territory	40,352	No	--	1808 & 1810 MS Territorial Censuses exit. See Note 6.
14. New Hampshire	214,460	Yes	218684	
15. New Jersey	245,562	No	--	
16. New York	959,049	Yes	181380	
17. North Carolina	556,526	Yes	337911	
18. Ohio	230,760	Yes		Washington Co Only. See Note 7.
19. Orleans Territory	75,556	Yes	218675	Orleans Territory became the State of Louisiana in 1812
20. Pennsylvania	810,091	Yes	193670	
21. Rhode Island	69,122	Yes	281232	
22. South Carolina	415,115	Yes	181419	
23. Tennessee	261,727	Yes	218687	Rutherford County only. See Note 8.
24. Vermont	217,895	Yes	218668	
25. Virginia	983,152	Yes	181426	

U.S. Total: 7,239,881

Table 1810 Notes

1. See *Historical Court Records of Washington, District of Columbia, 1800-1954* [Online Database], digitized and OCR indexed at the Ancestry.com website. Source: Book, same title, by Homer A. Walker, 14 vols., 1,442 pages. The records are organized by types, then alphabetical. See www.ancestry.com/search/collections/genealogy-glh35550663/.

2. See *Georgia Property Tax Digests, 1793-1893* [Online Database]. This digitized and indexed database is the primary census substitute for all of Georgia, which had lost federal censuses for 1790, 1800, 1810, and 1890. Within this database of over 4.8 million records, a search can be done by the name of a taxpayer for the entire span of years. A more precise search can be done by county, see https://search.ancestry.com/search/db.aspx?dbid=1729.

3. See *Illinois Census Returns, 1810 and 1818* [Online Database], from a digitized book, indexed at the Ancestry.com website. See www.ancestry.com/search/collections/flhg-ilcensusreturns1.

See also, *Name Index to Early Illinois Records* [Microfilm & Digital Capture], from 3x5 card indexes at the Illinois State Archives, indexes census records from 1810 to 1855, see www.familysearch.org/search/catalog/40879.

Table 1810 Notes – Continued:

4. See *Census of Indiana Territory for 1807* [Printed Book], a name index to the first four counties (plus two counties now Illinois). See the FHL catalog page: www.familysearch.org/search/catalog/270021.

5. See *Michigan Censuses, 1710-1830, Under the French, British, and Americans*, by Donna Valley Russell (Detroit Society for Genealogical Research, 1982, 291 pages), see the FHL catalog page:
www.familysearch.org/search/catalog/266465.

6. Mississippi Territory's 1810 Federal Census was lost, but the territory took its own census in 1808 and again in 1810. See *Mississippi, State and Territorial Census Collection, 1792-1866* [Online Database], digitized and indexed at the Ancestry.com website. Source: MDAH, Jackson, MS. See www.ancestry.com/search/collections/msstatecen.

7. See *Third Census of the United States, 1810, Population Schedules, Washington County, Ohio* [Microfilm & Digital Capture], from the originals of the Ohio Company, Marietta, Ohio. Lists name of head of the family and age brackets of other members of the family. Arranged in alphabetical order by township. Special microfilm publication by the National Archives, 1994, series M1803, 1 roll, FHL film #2155490. To access the digital images of this roll, see the FHL catalog page:
www.familysearch.org/search/catalog/720620. See also *Ohio 1810 Tax Duplicates Arranged in State-wide Alphabetical List of Names of Taxpayers: With an Index of Names of Original Entries,* by Gerald M. Petty, publ. Columbus, OH, 1976, 221 pages, see FHL film #982373 at the FHL catalog page:
www.familysearch.org/search/catalog/75701.

8. Tennessee's 1810 Federal Census has one surviving county (Rutherford), see *Tennessee, 1810 Thru 1840 Federal Census: Population Schedules* [Microfilm & Digital Capture], FHL film #218687 (Rutherford Co TN). To access the digital images, see the FHL catalog page: www.familysearch.org/search/catalog/745506.

See also *The Reconstructed 1810 Census of Tennessee: 33,000 Long-lost Records From Tax Lists, Court Minutes, Church Records, Wills, Deeds and Other Sources* [Printed Book], by Charles A. Sherrill, published by the author, Mt. Juliet, TN, 2001, 576 pages. Names listed in alphabetical order. FHL book 976.8 X2s.

Selected Online Databases from the time of the 1810 Census

U.S. Military and Naval Academies, Cadet Records and Applications, 1805-1908 **[Online Database],** digitized and indexed at the Ancestry.com website. Source: Application papers and Registers of the US Military Academy, West Point, NY; and US Naval Academy, Annapolis, MD; now at the National Archives. Each index record includes: Name, Year, Volume, Record set, and Location. The document images have more information about a person. This database has 116,318 records. See
www.ancestry.com/search/collections/militaryacademycadets

1806-1916 U.S. Returns from Military Posts **[Online Database],** digitized and indexed at the Ancestry.com website. Army Regulations stipulated that every post was to submit a return to the Adjutant General, usually at monthly intervals. The returns showed the units stationed at each post; the strength of each unit; names and duties of the officers; number of officers present and absent; listing of official communications received, and record of events. While most of the records in this collection consist of monthly post returns, some additional records, such as morning reports, field returns, rosters of officers, and other related papers, have been mixed in. These additional records provide supplemental information or act as substitutes for missing returns. Records are available for military posts in all 50 states, Washington D.C., Cuba, Panama Canal Zone, Philippine Islands, Puerto Rico, Canada, China, and Mexico. See www.ancestry.com/search/collections/usmilitaryposts.

War of 1812 Pension Files **[Online Database],** digitized and indexed at the Fold3.com website. The documents in this collection include full pension application files for soldiers and sailors who served in the War of 1812, as well as for their widows and children, or other heirs. The first applications were filed by servicemen who were disabled as a result of their service, or by widows who lost a husband in the war. See
www.fold3.com/title_761/war_of_1812_pension_files.

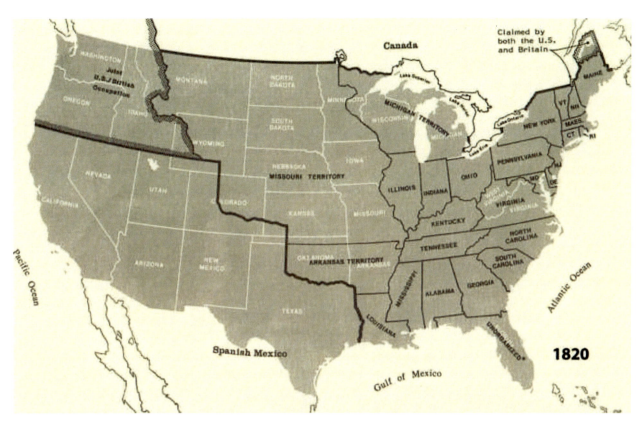

The U.S. in 1820: In the 1818 Anglo-American Convention, the United States and Great Britain agreed to a joint occupation of the Oregon Country/Columbia District. Both parties accepted the area as extending from the Continental Divide to the Pacific Ocean, and from about Latitude 54° in present British Columbia, to the Boundary Mountains (now Siskiyou Mountains) at Latitude 42°. Also in the 1818 treaty, Britain and the U.S. agreed to the 49th parallel as the international boundary from the Lake of the Woods (now Minnesota) to the Continental Divide. In 1819, the Adams-Onis Treaty settled the Purchase of Florida, and set the Western boundary between Spanish and U.S. territory. However, the treaty was not ratified until 1821, and Florida was not a territory until 1822. Map Source: Page 3, *Map Guide to the U.S. Federal Censuses, 1790-1920* by William Thorndale and William Dollarhide.

Fourth Census of the United States - 1820

Description

Location of Original Records: National Archives, Washington, DC.

U.S. Population: 9.6 million (8.1 million free and 1.5 million slave).

1820 Census Legislative Act: 3 Stat. 548, 14 March 1820.

Responsibility: The President of the United States (James Monroe), with authority delegated to the Secretary of State (John Quincy Adams).

Reporting to the Secretary of State, the U.S. Marshal of each U.S. Federal Court District hired and managed Assistant Marshals as the door-to-door census takers within his district. Territories without a federal court district were enumerated by local militia captains, under the supervision of the Territorial Governor.

Census day: the first Monday in August (7 Aug 1820). All of the questions asked by the census taker were related to a person's age or place of residence as of the census day.

Time Allowed: In the first act, six months; but extended to thirteen months (3 Stat. 643, 3 March 1821).

1820 Jurisdictions: 27. Between 1810 and 1820, six (6) new states had been formed bringing the total to twenty-three (23) states in the Union: Orleans Territory became the state of Louisiana in 1812, followed by Indiana in 1816; Mississippi in 1817; Illinois in 1818; Alabama in 1819; and Maine in 1820. Add the District of Columbia and three (3) territories: Louisiana Territory was renamed Missouri Territory in 1812; Michigan Territory spanned the northern portion of the old Northwest Territory north of the states of Ohio, Indiana, and Illinois; and a new Arkansas Territory was created from the southern area of Missouri Territory in 1819; for a total of twenty-seven (27) census jurisdictions.

Surviving Censuses: Twenty Three (23) states & territories: Connecticut, District of Columbia, Delaware, Georgia, Illinois, Indiana, Kentucky, Louisiana, Maine, Maryland, Massachusetts, Michigan Territory, Mississippi Territory, New Hampshire, New York, North Carolina, Ohio, Pennsylvania, Rhode Island, South Carolina, Tennessee (26 counties), Vermont, and Virginia.

Census Losses: Four (4) complete states & territories: Alabama, Arkansas Territory, Missouri Territory, and New Jersey. These states or territories did not return the original 1790-1820 census manuscripts to Washington as was specified in the 1830 law (4 Stat. 430, 28 May 1830). NOTE: In 1820, two federal court districts were in place in Tennessee, one with a U.S. Courthouse in Nashville, the other in Knoxville. The original censuses returned to Washington according to the 1830 law were twenty-six (26) western counties within the 1820 Nashville district only. The twenty (20) eastern counties enumerated within the 1820 Knoxville district were not received in Washington.

Content of the Population Schedules: 33 columns of questions were asked for the Head of Household, on one line, spread over two large pages of census schedules. The hand-drawn census forms had columns in the following order:
- Name of a head of household
- Number of free white males, 0-9 years old
- Number of free white males, 10-15 years old
- Number of free white males, 16-18 years old*
- Number of free white males, 16-25 years old*
- Number of free white males, 26-44 years old
- Number of free white males, 45 years & over
- Number of free white females, 0-9 years old
- Number of free white females, 10-15 years old
- Number of free white females, 16-25 years old
- Number of free white females, 26-44 years old
- Number of foreigners not naturalized
- Number of persons engaged in Agriculture
- Number of persons engaged in Commerce
- Number of persons engaged in Manufacture
- Number of male slaves (4 age categories)
- Number of female slaves (4 age categories)
- Number of free colored males (4 age categories)
- Number of free colored females (4 age cat.)
- Number of all other persons

NOTE: see page 19 for details on the 16-18 & 16-26 columns.

In addition to the Population schedules, the U.S. Marshals conducted a census of Manufactures. See *Records of the 1820 Census of Manufactures* [Microfilm & Digital Capture], filmed by the National Archives, 27 rolls, beginning with FHL film #1024492 (Maine and New Hampshire). For access to the digital images of certain rolls, see the FHL catalog page: www.familysearch.org/search/catalog/280127.

1820 Census Publications with Digital Images

Microfilm of Originals & Digital Capture: The National Archives film for the 1820 census is contained on 142 rolls, series M33, beginning with FHL film #281234 (Connecticut). The microfilm was digitized by FamilySearch International. For a list of roll numbers, contents, and access to the digital images of each roll, see the online FHL catalog page: www.familysearch.org/search/catalog/120949.

Online Searching - 1820 Census Indexes and Digital Images

The 1820 Census was digitized from the National Archives microfilm, indexed, and made available at the following websites:

- **Ancestry.com.** Subscription site, free database searching. Ancestry and FamilySearch share images and indexes. See www.ancestry.com/search/collections/1820usfedcenancestry.

- **FamilySearch.org**. Free database search, with images by FamilySearch, index by Ancestry. See www.familysearch.org/search/collection/1803955.

- **MyHeritage.com**. A Family Tree subscription site. All U.S. Federal Census Records are available to subscribers with a data plan. See www.myheritage.com/research/collection-10123/1820-united-states-federal-census.

- **Findmypast.com**. Monthly or annual subscriptions. Initial searches to U.S. Federal Censuses are free. See www.findmypast.com/articles/search-the-1820-us-census.

- **GenealogyBank.com**. Subscription site. Initial searches to the U.S. Federal Censuses, 1790-1940 are free. www.genealogybank.com/explore/census/all.

- **HeritageQuestOnline-Subscribers Login**. This is a library subscription service. Check with your local library to see if they subscribe to the ProQuest & HeritageQuest databases. Many subscribing libraries allow their library card holders remote access. See www.heritagequestonline.com/hqoweb/library/do/login.

Table 1820 – Statewide Census Publications

1820 Jurisdictions Included in Census	Population	Census Extant?	FHL Film Number	Comments, Census Substitutes, etc.
1. Alabama	127,901	No	--	AL 1820 State Census exists. See Note 1.
2. Arkansas Territory	14,273	No	--	Reconstructed name list & tax lists exist. See Note 2.
3. Connecticut	275,248	Yes	28124	
4. Delaware	72,749	Yes	205610	
5. District of Columbia	25,336	Yes	6698	
6. Georgia	340,989	Yes	175766	
7. Illinois	55,211	Yes	506763	
8. Indiana	147,148	yes	205607	
9. Kentucky	564,317	Yes	186176	
10. Louisiana	153,407	Yes	181356	
11. Maine	298,335	Yes	281237	
12. Maryland	407,350	Yes	193703	
13. Massachusetts	523,287	Yes	193735	
14. Michigan Territory	8,896	Yes	506762	Includes Brown & Crawford Cos, now Wisconsin.
15. Mississippi	75,448	Yes	181359	
16. Missouri Territory	66,586	No	--	Several county name lists exist for 1817-1819. See Note 3.
17. New Hampshire	244,161	Yes	205621	
18. New Jersey	277,575	No	--	Tax Ratable Lists are good substitutes. See Note 4.
19. New York	1,372,812	Yes	193717	
20. North Carolina	556,526	Yes	162796	
21. Ohio	581,434	Yes	18392	
22. Pennsylvania	1,049,458	Yes	181402	
23. Rhode Island	83,059	Yes	281244	
24. South Carolina	502,741	Yes	162021	
25. Tennessee	442,823	Yes	193684	
26. Vermont	235,981	Yes	281247	
27. Virginia	1,075,069	Yes	193688	

U.S. Total: 9,638,453

Table 1820 Notes

1. Alabama's 1820 Federal Census was lost – but Alabama took its own state census in 1820, which survives for several counties. See *Alabama State Censuses* [Online Database], digitized and indexed at the Ancestry.com website. Source: ADAH, Montgomery AL. This database contains state censuses from Alabama for the years 1820, 1850, 1855, and 1866. Each of these censuses recorded the names of the head of households and the members of a household according to gender and age categories. Some years also included race categories and distinguished between individuals who were free and slave. Unfortunately, records do not exist for every county that existed at the time. Below is a list showing what counties are available for each year. **1820:** Baldwin, Conecuh, Dallas, Franklin, Limestone, St.Clair, and Wilcox counties, AL, See
www.ancestry.com/search/collections/alabamacensus.

2. Arkansas Territory was created in 1819, taken from the southern area of Missouri Territory, and included the areas of present Arkansas and Oklahoma. Arkansas Territory's 1820 Federal Census was lost. A reconstruction was compiled from tax lists, voter lists, and other sources. See *1820 Census of the Territory of Arkansas (Reconstructed)* [Printed Book] by James Logan Morgan, published by Arkansas Research, Conway, AR, 1992, 108 pages, FHL book 976.7 X2m 1820. See the FHL catalog page: www.familysearch.org/search/catalog/711126. See also *1814 Missouri Territory, Arkansas County Tax List* [Online Database], from originals at the Missouri State Archives. see
http://files.usgwarchives.net/ar/state/history/terr/1814.txt.
See also *1816 Missouri Territory, Arkansas County Tax List* [Online Database], from originals at the Missouri State Archives. see
http://files.usgwarchives.net/ar/state/history/terr/1816.txt.

3. Missouri Territory's 1820 Federal Census was lost. Several censuses were taken for Missouri Territory, 1812-1819, and the surviving name lists are for St. Charles County in 1817 and 1819, and Cape Girardeau and Ste. Genevieve in 1818. See *Missouri State and Territorial Census Records, 1732-1933* [Online Database], digitized and indexed at the FamilySearch.org website. Source: MO State Archives (MSA) & FHL microfilm. See
https://familysearch.org/search/collection/2075262.

4. New Jersey had more lost federal censuses than any other state, including the lost 1790, 1800, 1810, 1820 and 1890 censuses. From the 1700s through the 1800s, numerous tax lists were prepared at the county level in New Jersey. A person named in one of these assessment lists of county residents was called a "ratable." Many of the original Tax Ratable Lists are now at the NJ state archives and are probably the best chance of finding a lost ancestor in New Jersey. The starting point for finding these tax lists is to search through a guide from the New Jersey State Archives, *Index to Tax Ratables, 1700's-1800's: Listing of Counties and Townships and Years of Taxes* [Microfilm & Digital Capture], 1 roll of microfilm, FHL film #913174. To access the digital images of this roll, see the FHL catalog page:
www.familysearch.org/search/catalog/96527.

Selected Online Databases from the time of the 1820 Census

1821-1916 U.S. Returns from Regular Army Infantry Regiments **[Online Database],** digitized and indexed at the Ancestry.com website. This database primarily contains monthly returns from U.S. Regular Army infantry regiments received by the Adjutant General's Office from June 1821 to December 1916. The Regular Army monthly returns reported on the strength of each regiment, including total numbers of men present, absent, sick, or on extra daily duty, as well as giving a report of officers and some categories of enlisted men by name. Later returns included an accounting of strength in terms of horses and artillery. These records can be searched by name, year, and regiment. They can be browsed by regiment or year. Forms changed several times over the years, so the information recorded about regiments and individuals varies. See
www.ancestry.com/search/collections/returnsregarmyinf.

1822-1995. See *U.S. City Directories, 1822-1995* **[Online Database],** digitized and indexed at the Ancestry.com website. This database is a collection of directories for U.S. cities and counties in various years. The database currently contains directories for all states except Alaska. Each index record includes: Name, Gender, Spouse, and Publication title (and state, city, year of publication). This database has 1,560,284,730 records. (Not a typo…that's 1.56 billion). See
www.ancestry.com/search/collections/usdirectories.

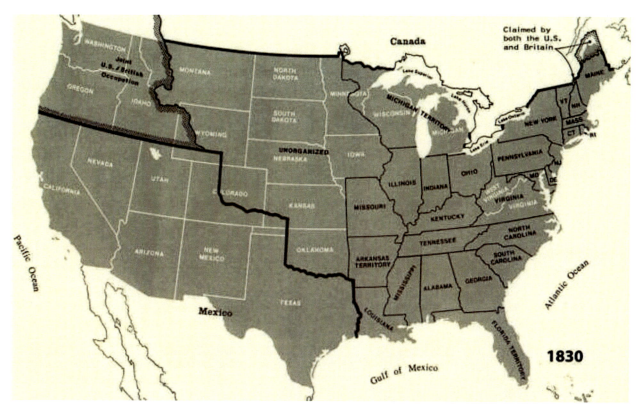

The U.S. in 1830. Missouri became a state in 1821, and Florida Territory was created in 1822. In 1828, Congress set aside specific areas of the Unorganized Territory as "Indian Territory." In doing so, about half of Arkansas Territory plus areas of present-day Kansas were redesignated as exclusive Indian resettlement areas. Indians were specifically excluded from the federal censuses until 1880, when separate schedules were compiled for several tribes. Map Source: Page 5, *Map Guide to the U.S. Federal Censuses, 1790-1920* by William Thorndale and William Dollarhide.

Fifth Census of the United States - 1830

Description

Location of Original Records: National Archives, Washington, DC.

U.S. Population: 12.9 million (10.9 million free and 2.0 million slave).

1830 Census Legislative Act: 4 Stat. 383, 23 March 1830.

Responsibility: The President of the United States (Andrew Jackson), with authority delegated to the Secretary of State (Martin Van Buren). Reporting to the Secretary of State, the U.S. Marshal of each U.S. Federal Court District hired and managed Assistant Marshals as the door-to-door census takers within his district. Territories without a federal court district were enumerated by local militia captains, under the supervision of the Territorial Governor.

Census day: the first Monday in August (7 Aug 1820). All of the questions asked by the census taker were related to a person's age or place of residence as of the census day.

Time Allowed: In the first act, six months; but extended to twelve months (4 Stat. 439, 3 February 1831).

1830 Jurisdictions: 28. Between 1820 and 1830, one (1) new state was admitted to the Union. Missouri became a state in 1821, bringing the total number in the 1830 census to twenty-four (24) states. The treaty with Spain for the purchase of Florida was signed in 1819, but ratification did not occur until 1821. Florida Territory was created in 1822, its first federal census taken in 1830. Add the District of Columbia, Arkansas Territory, and Michigan Territory, for a total of twenty-eight (28) jurisdictions. An area commonly called the "Indian Territory" was created in 1828 from the western part of Arkansas Territory and parts of present-day Kansas, but no federal census was taken in that area until 1860 (for non-Indians only).

Census Losses: There were no statewide census losses for 1830.

The new 1830 Census Law. Congress decided before the 1830 census to ask for the return of all original censuses, 1790-1820, kept at the various Clerk of Court Offices in all Federal Circuit Court Districts. There was a dismal response. The clerks could not return manuscripts for several statewide censuses and for several years. (See Table 1 on page 14 for the extent of census losses).

As a result, a new 1830 Census Law was passed that changed the way the censuses were handled, and to provide for their timely return to Washington, DC. All of the original censuses, 1790-1820, were made in a single copy, and by law, preserved at the District Clerk of Court's office. All losses to the early censuses can therefore be blamed on the Clerks of Court. In 1830, the Clerks were asked to make a complete district-wide copy of all census name lists, suitable for transmission to Washington, DC immediately.

Change in the Census Day. The new 1830 law also changed the census day from the first Monday in August to the first day of June. Since the census days for 1820 and 1830 are not exactly ten years apart, the two-month difference may reveal some surprising results. For example, if a person were born between 1 June 1820 and 7 August 1820, that child would appear in the 1820 census in the "under 5" category. But in 1830, that same person would appear in the "under ten" rather than the "of 10 and under 16" category, since the person had not yet turned 10. Comparing the other age categories for a person appearing ten years later and not in the correct age category may give a clue to a person's date of birth within a two-month period. NOTE: See the *1790-1840 Census Worksheet* on page 242 for a way to visualize the two-month difference in age reporting.

Content of the Population Schedules: 57 columns of questions were asked for the Head of Household, on one line, spread over two large pages of census schedules. The columns were shown in the following order:
• Name of a head of household
• Number of free white males, 0-4 years old
• Number of free white males, 5-9 years old
• Number of free white males, 10-14 years old
• Number of free white males, 15-19 years old
• Number of free white males, 20-29 years old
• Number of free white males, 30-39 years old
• Number of free white males, 40-49 years old
• Number of free white males, 50-59 years old
• Number of free white males, 60-69 years old
• Number of free white males, 70-79 years old
• Number of free white males, 80-89 years old
• Number of free white males, 90-99 years old
• Number of free white males, 100 years & over
• Number of free white females, 0-4 years old
• Number of free white females, 5-9 years old
• Number of free white females, 10-14 years old
• Number of free white females, 15-19 years old
• Number of free white females, 20-29 years old
• Number of free white females, 30-39 years old
• Number of free white females, 40-49 years old
• Number of free white females, 50-59 years old
• Number of free white females, 60-69 years old
• Number of free white females, 70-79 years old
• Number of free white females, 80-89 years old
• Number of free white females, 90-99 years old
• Number of free white females, 100 years & over
• Number of male slaves (6 age categories)
• Number of female slaves (6 age categories)
• Number of free colored males (6 age categories)
• Number of free colored females (6 age cat.)
• Total Number of persons in this family
• Number of white persons who are deaf and dumb (3 age categories)
• Number of white persons who are blind
• Number of white persons who are aliens

NOTE: The 1830 was the first census where the Assistant Marshals received pre-printed forms for recording the names.

1830 Census Publications with Digital Images

Microfilm of Originals & Digital Capture: The National Archives film for the 1830 census is contained on 201 rolls, series M19, beginning with FHL film #2328 (Alabama). The microfilm was digitized by FamilySearch International. For a list of roll numbers, contents, and access to the digital images of each roll, see the online FHL catalog page: www.familysearch.org/search/catalog/119992.

Online Searching - 1830 Census Indexes and Digital Images

The 1830 Census was digitized from the National Archives microfilm, indexed, and made available at the following websites:

- **Ancestry.com.** Subscription site, free database searching. Ancestry and FamilySearch share images and indexes. See www.ancestry.com/search/collections/1830usfedcenancestry.

- **FamilySearch.org.** Free database search, with images by FamilySearch, index by Ancestry. See https://familysearch.org/search/collection/1803958.

- **MyHeritage.com.** A Family Tree subscription site. All U.S. Federal Census Records are available to subscribers with a data plan. See www.myheritage.com/research/collection-10125/1830-united-states-federal-census.

- **Findmypast.com.** Monthly or annual subscriptions. Initial searches to U.S. Federal Censuses are free. See www.findmypast.com/articles/search-the-1830-us-census.

- **GenealogyBank.com.** Subscription site. Initial searches to the U.S. Federal Censuses, 1790-1940 are free. www.genealogybank.com/explore/census/all.

- **HeritageQuestOnline-Subscribers Login.** This is a library subscription service. Check with your local library to see if they subscribe to the ProQuest & HeritageQuest databases. Many subscribing libraries allow their library card holders remote access. See www.heritagequestonline.com/hqoweb/library/do/login.

Table 1830 – Statewide Census Publications

1830 Jurisdictions Included in Census	Population	Census Extant?	FHL Film Number	Comments, Census Substitutes, etc.
1. Alabama	309,527	Yes	2328	
2. Arkansas Territory	30,388	Yes	2473	A part of AR Territory was actually outside the U.S. See Note 1.
3. Connecticut	297,675	Yes	2799	
4. Delaware	76.748	Yes	6414	
5. District of Columbia	30,261	Yes	6699	
6. Florida Territory	34,730	Yes	6711	
7. Georgia	516,823	Yes	7036	Printed index exists. See Note 2.
8. Illinois	157,445	Yes	7647	
9. Indiana	343,031	Yes	7715	Printed index exists. See Note 3.
10. Kentucky	687,917	Yes	7812	
11. Louisiana	215,739	Yes	9686	
12. Maine	399,455	Yes	9700	
13. Maryland	447,040	Yes	13176	Missing 5 counties.
14. Massachusetts	523,287	Yes	337917	Most of Suffolk Co lost.
15. Michigan Territory	16,639	Yes	363348	Includes Wisconsin & Minnesota areas. See Note 4.
16. Mississippi	136,621	Yes	14838	Pike Co lost.
17. Missouri	140,455	Yes	14853	Printed index w/digital version exists. See Note 5.

1830 Jurisdictions Included in Census	Population	Census Extant?	FHL Film Number	Comments, Census Substitutes, etc.
18. New Hampshire	269,328	Yes	337927	
19. New Jersey	277,575	Yes	337932	
20. New York	1,918,608	Yes	17144	
21. North Carolina	737,989	Yes	18084	
22. Ohio	937,903	Yes	337937	OH 1830 printed index exists. See Note 6.
23. Pennsylvania	1,348,233	Yes	20617	
24. Rhode Island	97,199	Yes	22266	
25. South Carolina	581,185	Yes	22503	SC 1829 State Census exists for a few counties. See Note 7.
26. Tennessee	681,904	Yes	24532	TN 1830 printed index/digital version exists. See Note 8.
27. Vermont	280,652	Yes	27449	
28. Virginia	1,220,978	Yes	27454	
U.S. Total:	12,860,702			

Table 1830 Notes

1. Arkansas Territory was reduced in size with the separation of Indian lands in 1828. As a result, the area of old Miller County was now totally south of the Red River and west of the present Arkansas line. The entire area was in Mexican Texas due to Arkansas's misinterpretation of the 1819 treaty line with Spain. This was the only time an American county was completely outside of the U.S. Nevertheless, an 1830 census exits for the residents of old Miller County. FHL film #2473 has the digital images, see the FHL catalog page: **www.familysearch.org/search/catalog/119992**. See also *Census, Arkansas Territory, 1830* [Printed Book], by Mrs. Leister E. Presley, Searcy, AR, 1971, see the FHL catalog page:
www.familysearch.org/search/catalog/180832.

2. See *Index to Heads of Families 1830 Census of Georgia* [Printed Book], publ. Delwyn Associates, Albany, GA, 1974, 323 pages, see the FHL catalog page:
www.familysearch.org/search/catalog/166480.

3.. See *Index, 1830 Federal Population Census for Indiana* [Printed Book], compiled by Leona Tobey Alig, publ. IN Historical Soc., 1991, 245 pages, see the FHL catalog page:
www.familysearch.org/search/catalog/2474689.

4. See *Michigan Censuses, 1710-1830, Under the French, British, and Americans* [Printed Book], by Donna Valley Russell (Detroit Society for Genealogical Research, 1982, 291 pages), see the FHL catalog page:
www.familysearch.org/search/catalog/266465.

See also *Wisconsin Census Index, 1830* [Microfilm], from an index prepared by the Wisconsin State Historical Society, 1970, 1 roll, FHL film #933597. The index is to the two counties of Michigan Territory that became Wisconsin Territory in 1838. (Brown and Crawford Cos). See the FHL catalog page:
www.familysearch.org/search/catalog/282581.

5. See *Heads of Families, 1830 Census of Missouri* [Printed Book & Digital Capture], by Beverly M. Stercula, Genealogems Publications, Sumner, WA, 1966, 143 pages, for access to a digital version of this index, see the FHL catalog page:
www.familysearch.org/search/catalog/1172118?.

6. See *1830 Federal Population Census, Ohio, Index* [Microfilm], from a Census Index prepared by the Ohio Library Foundation in 1964, FHL film #795954, see the FHL catalog page:
www.familysearch.org/search/catalog/84010.

7. South Carolina's 1829 State Census for several counties is part of *South Carolina, State and City Census Records, 1752-1920* [Microfilm & Digital Capture]. To access the digital images, see the FHL catalog page:
www.familysearch.org/search/catalog/2841555.

8. See *United States Census 1830 for Tennessee* [Printed Book & Digital Capture], from a census index by Byron Sistler, 1971, 242 pages. To access the digital images, see the FHL catalog page:
www.familysearch.org/search/catalog/2493364.

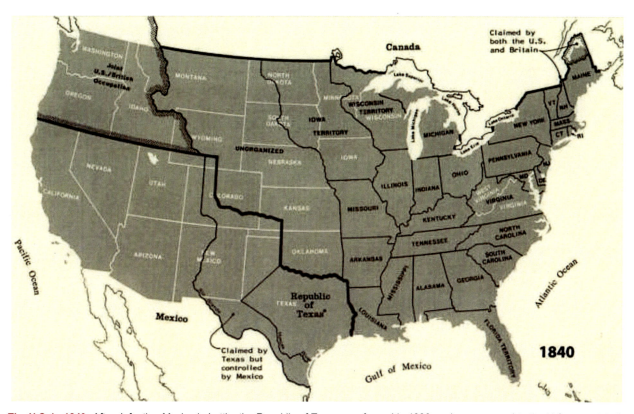

The U.S. in 1840: After defeating Mexico in battle, the Republic of Texas was formed in 1836, and was annexed to the U.S. as a state in 1845. The Republic's claim to lands extended to the Rio Grande, and that claim was to be the basis for the U.S. invasion of Mexico in 1846. Map Source: Page 6, *Map Guide to the U.S. Federal Censuses, 1790-1920,* by William Thorndale and William Dollarhide.

Sixth Census of the United States - 1840

Description

Location of Original Records: National Archives, Washington, DC.

U.S. Population: 17.1 million (14.6 million free and 2.5 million slave).

1840 Census Legislative Act: 5 Stat. 331, 3 March 1840.

Responsibility: The President of the United States (Martin Van Buren), with authority delegated to the Secretary of State (John Forsyth). Reporting to the Secretary of State, the U.S. Marshal of each U.S. Federal Court District hired and managed Assistant Marshals as the door-to-door census takers within his district. Territories without a federal court district were enumerated by local militia captains, under the supervision of the Territorial Governor.

Census day: 1 June 1840. All of the questions asked by the census taker were related to a person's age or place of residence as of the census day.

Time Allowed: In the first act, nine months; but extended to eighteen months (5 Stat. 453, 1 September 1841).

1840 Jurisdictions: 30. As of the census day of 1 June 1840, two new states had been added to the U.S. since the 1830 federal census: Arkansas was admitted in 1836; and Michigan in 1837, bringing the total to Twenty-six (26) states in the Union. Territories added: Florida (created 1821),

Wisconsin Territory (1836) and Iowa Territory (1838). Add the District of Columbia for a total of 30 census jurisdictions in 1840.

1840 Census Copies & Census Losses: A 2nd original copy of the 1840 census name lists was transcribed by the Clerk of the District Court in each district/state/territory. It was usually the clerk's copy that was sent to Washington, DC. There were no census losses for 1840.

Content of the Population Schedules: 66 columns of questions were asked for the Head of Household, spread over two large pages of census schedules. Unique to the 1840 census was an array of questions concerning a person's occupation; including persons engaged in mining, agriculture, commerce, manufacturing and trades; navigation of the ocean, navigation of canals, lakes, and rivers; and learned professionals and engineers. Also unique to the 1840 census was the special listing of any person in a household who was a Revolutionary War or other military pensioner. As a result, the 1840 census was the first to list the name of another person living in a household other than the head of the house. Columns included:
- Name of a head of household / Slave Owner (if slaves indicated).
  - Number of male slaves, in 6 age categories.
  - Number of female slaves, in 6 age categories.
- Name and age of each person receiving Revolutionary War/Military pension.
- Number of free white males, in 13 age categories.
- Number of free white females, in 13 age categories.
- Number of free colored males, in 6 age categories.
- Number of free colored females, in 6 age categories.
- Number of white persons who were deaf & dumb, in 3 age categories.
- Number of white persons who were blind.
- Number of white persons who were aliens (foreigners not naturalized).
- Number of persons engaged in:
  - Mining
  - Agriculture
  - Commerce
  - Manufacturing and Trades
  - Navigation of the Ocean
  - Navigation of Canals, Lakes, and Rivers
- Number of Learned Professionals and Engineers.
- Number of persons attending school.

1840 Census Publications with Digital Images

Microfilm of Originals & Digital Capture: The National Archives film for the 1840 census is contained on 215 rolls, series M704, beginning with FHL film #2532 (Alabama). The microfilm was digitized by FamilySearch International. For a list of roll numbers, contents, and access to the digital images of each roll, see the online FHL catalog page: www.familysearch.org/search/catalog/120333.

Online Searching - 1840 Census Indexes and Digital Images

The 1840 Census was digitized from the National Archives microfilm, indexed, and made available at the following websites:

- **Ancestry.com.** Subscription site, free database searching. Ancestry and FamilySearch share images and indexes. See www.ancestry.com/search/collections/1840usfedcenancestry.

- **FamilySearch.org.** Free database search, with images by FamilySearch, index by Ancestry. See https://familysearch.org/search/collection/1786457.

- **MyHeritage.com.** A Family Tree subscription site. All U.S. Federal Census Records are available to subscribers with a data plan. See www.myheritage.com/research/collection-10124/1840-united-states-federal-census.

- **Findmypast.com.** Monthly or annual subscriptions. Initial searches to U.S. Federal Censuses are free. See www.findmypast.com/articles/search-the-1840-us-census.

- **GenealogyBank.com.** Subscription site. Initial searches to the U.S. Federal Censuses, 1790-1940 are free. www.genealogybank.com/explore/census/all.

- **HeritageQuestOnline-Subscribers Login.** This is a library subscription service. Check with your local library to see if they subscribe to the ProQuest & HeritageQuest databases. Many subscribing libraries allow their library card holders remote access. See www.heritagequestonline.com/hqoweb/library/do/login.

Table 1840 – Statewide Census Publications

1840 Jurisdiction Included in Census	Population	Census Extant?	FHL Film Number	Comments, Census Substitutes, etc.
1. Alabama	590,756	Yes	2332	
2. Arkansas	97,574	Yes	2474	1840 Printed Index/Digital version exists. See Note 1.
3. Connecticut	309,978	Yes	3018	
4. Delaware	78,085	Yes	6434	
5. District of Columbia	33,745	Yes	6700	
6. Florida Territory	54,477	Yes	6712	1840 FL index exists. See Note 2.
7. Georgia	691,392	Yes	7042	2 printed indexes exist for 1840 GA. See Note 3.
8. Illinois	476,183	Yes	7641	IL State Census of 1840 exists. See Note 4.
9. Indiana	685,866	Yes	7722	1840 IN index exists. See Note 5.
10. Iowa Territory	43,112	Yes	7790	1840 IA census index/digital version exists. See Note 6.
11. Kentucky	779,828	Yes	7823	
12. Louisiana	352,411	Yes	9689	
13. Maine	501,793	Yes	9702	
14. Maryland	470,019	Yes	13182	
15. Massachusetts	737,699	Yes	14674	
16. Michigan Territory	212,267	Yes	14795	MI Terr. Index exists. See Note 7.
17. Mississippi	375,651	Yes	14840	MS 1840 Index/digital version exists. See Note 8.
18. Missouri	383,702	Yes	14855	MO 1840 printed index exists. See Note 9.
19. New Hampshire	284,574	Yes	14931	
20. New Jersey	373,306	Yes	16515	
21. New York	2,428,921	Yes	17178	1835 & 1845 NY State censuses exist. See Note 10.
22. North Carolina	753,419	Yes	18092	
23. Ohio	1,519,467	Yes	20158	OH 1840 census index exists. See Note 11.
24. Pennsylvania	1,724,033	Yes	20536	
25. Rhode Island	108,830	Yes	22260	
26. South Carolina	594,398	Yes	22508	
26. Tennessee	829,210	Yes	24542	TN 1840 census index exists. See Note 12.
28. Vermont	291,948	Yes	27438	
29. Virginia	1,249,764	Yes	29683	
30. Wisconsin Territory	30,945	Yes	34498	WI Terr. 1840 census index exists. See Note 13.

U.S. Total: 17,063,353

Table 1840 Notes

1. See *An Index to 1840 United States Census of Arkansas* [Printed Book & Digital Capture], by Bobbie Jones McLane and Inez Halsell Cline, publ. Hot Springs Nat'l Park, AR, 1967, 127 pages. To access a digital version of this index, see the FHL catalog page:
www.familysearch.org/search/catalog/178318.

2. See *1840 Index to Florida Census* [Microfilm], from a printed index by Lucille Simms Mallon, publ. 1975, see the FHL catalog page:
www.familysearch.org/search/catalog/135716.

3. See *Citizens of Georgia, 1840* [Printed Book], publ. 1985, St. Louis, MO, 684 pages, see the FHL catalog:
www.familysearch.org/search/catalog/438191.
See also *1840 Index to Georgia Census* [Printed Book], by Barbara Woods and Eileen Sheffield, publ. 1969, 380 pages, see the FHL Catalog page:
www.familysearch.org/search/catalog/166489.

Table 1840 Notes, Continued:

4. Illinois conducted a state census in 1840, in addition to the 1840 federal census. See *1840 State Census* [Microfilm & Digital Capture], IL Secretary of State, 2 rolls, FHL film #1004694/5. To access the digital images, see the FHL catalog page: www.familysearch.org/search/catalog/270278. IL 1840 was digitized and indexed as part of *Illinois, State Census Collection, 1825-1865* [Online Database], see www.ancestry.com/search/collections/ilstatecen. For the IL 1840 federal census, see *Illinois 1840 Census Index* [Printed Book], by Maxine E. Wormer, publ. Heritage House, Thomson, IL, 1976, 4 volumes, see the FHL catalog page: www.familysearch.org/search/catalog/270405.

5. See *Index, 1840 Federal Population Census, Indiana* [Printed Book], publ. IN Hist. Soc., 1975, 374 pages, see the FHL catalog page: www.familysearch.org/search/catalog/158873.

6. See *The 1840 Iowa Census* [Printed Book & Digital Capture], by Rowene T. Obert, Helen Blumhagen, and Wilma Adkins, publ. Salt Lake City, 1968, 342 pages. To access a digital version of this book, see the FHL catalog page: www.familysearch.org/search/catalog/193563.

7. See *Index to 1840 Federal Population Census of Michigan* [Printed Book], edited by Estelle A. McGlynn, publ. Detroit Soc. for Genealogical Research, 1977, 165 pages, see the FHL catalog page: www.familysearch.org/search/catalog/263561.

8. See *Mississippi, Index to the United States Census of 1840: And Revolutionary Pensioners* [Printed Book & Digital Capture], by Gwen Platt, et al, publ. GAM Publications, Santa Ana, CA, 1970, 2 vols., to access a digital version, see the FHL catalog page: www.familysearch.org/search/catalog/153467. See also: Mississippi took state censuses from 1792 to 1866; including state censuses for 1837 (12 counties extant); 1840 (1 county extant); and 1841 (28 counties extant); all digitized and indexed as part of Ancestry's *Mississippi, State and Territorial Census Collection, 1792-1866,* see www.ancestry.com/search/collections/msstatecen.

9. See *The Index to the Federal Census of Missouri for 1840: A Guide to the County by County Enumeration* [Printed Book], by Frances Nelson and Gwendolyn Irene Brouse, publ. Ancestor's Attic, Riverside, CA, 1977, 3 vols., see the FHL catalog page: www.familysearch.org/search/catalog/148503.

10. See *New York State Censuses & Substitutes* [Printed Book], 2005, 250 pages, by William Dollarhide, an annotated bibliography of state censuses, census substitutes, and selected name lists in print, microform, or online. This identification of state censuses and substitutes is for statewide resources as well as 448 state census originals from New York's 62 counties. The book also includes county boundary maps, 1683-1915; and state census forms, 1825-1925. Available from: www.familyrootspublishing.com/store/product_view.php?id=60.

11. See *Index to 1840 Federal Population Census of Ohio* [Microfilm], from a book by Cleo Goff Wilkens, publ. 1972, 4 vols., see the FHL catalog page: www.familysearch.org/search/catalog/84024.

12. See *1840 Census Tennessee* [Microfilm], from a book by Byron Sistler, publ. Nashville, TN, 1986, 597 pages, see the FHL catalog page: www.familysearch.org/search/catalog/470651.

13. See *Wisconsin Census Index, 1840* [Microfilm], from an index compiled by the State Historical Society of Wisconsin, 1971, see the FHL catalog page: www.familysearch.org/search/catalog/283875.

The U.S. in 1850. In 1842, the U.S. and Britain resolved the location of the northern New Hampshire-Maine border with New Brunswick. After the 1846 settlement of the Oregon Country boundaries with Britain; and the 1848 Mexican Cession, the U.S. land area dramatically increased in size. For the first time, the United States of America now spanned "from Sea to Shining Sea." Map Source: Page 7, *Map Guide to the U.S. Federal Censuses, 1790-1920,* by William Thorndale and William Dollarhide.

Seventh Census of the United States - 1850

Description

Location of Original Records: National Archives, Washington, DC.

U.S. Population: 23.2 million (20.0 million free and 3.2 million slave).

1850-1860-1870 Census Legislative Act: 9 Stat. 428, 23 May 1850.

Responsibility: The 1850 was the first census conducted under the direction of a **Census Office,** a new division under the U.S. Secretary of the Interior. Reporting to the Census Office, U.S. Marshals of the Federal Court Districts hired and managed Assistant Marshals as the door-to-door census takers within their districts. Territories without a federal court district were enumerated by local militia captains, under the supervision of the Territorial Governor.

Census day: 1 June 1850. All of the questions asked by the census taker were related to a person's age or place of residence as of the census day.

Time Allowed: Five months. However, California, Utah Territory, and New Mexico Territory were all given extra time to complete their censuses. Utah Territory's Census Day was moved to April 1, 1851.

1850 Jurisdictions: 36. Between 1840 and 1850 five new states were added to the Union: Florida and Texas, both admitted in 1845; Iowa in 1846; Wisconsin in 1848; and California in 1850, bringing the total to thirty-one (31) states. In addition, four new territories were included:

Oregon Territory, created in 1848; Minnesota Territory in 1849; and New Mexico Territory and Utah Territory, both created in 1850. Add the District of Columbia for a total of thirty-six (36) census jurisdictions.

1850 Census Copies: Three (3) sets of the 1850 census schedules were made: 1) The originals for one county remained at the county courthouse for public display. 2) The Supervising Assistant Marshal for a county made a second copy of each county set to be transmitted to the Secretary of State of the state or territory, and 3) a copy was made by the secretaries of state for transmittal to the Census Office/Secretary of the Interior in Washington, DC. The third copy is referred to as the Federal Copy, the same copy that was later microfilmed and digitized for public use.

Content of the Population Schedules: For the first time, the 1850 census schedules listed the name of every person in a household. Since there were both House Numbers and Family Numbers indicated on the census schedules, when more than one family lived in the same house, the head of each family would be clearly delineated as the first person listed for a family. The categories included a name; age as of the census day; sex; color; birthplace; occupation; value of real estate; whether married within the previous year; whether deaf, dumb, blind, or insane; whether a pauper; whether able to read or speak English; and whether the person attended school within the previous year. **Clues to Relationships:** Although relationships were not given, there can be clues based on the household listing parameters. For example, per the published instructions to the Assistant Marshals, all persons included within a family grouping were listed in a specified order: 1) Head of House, 2) Spouse of head of house, 3) Children of head of house, in order of birth; and 4) Other persons living with the family. Other relatives living with a family are not identified, but their surname and position in the household listing can reveal possible relationships, i.e., in-laws, married siblings, parents, grandparents, etc. Persons with a different surname than the family group may be identified by their occupation (housekeeper, farm hand, laborer, etc.), which might explain their living arrangements.

1850 Census Publications with Digital Images

Microfilm of Originals & Digital Capture: The National Archives film for the 1850 census is contained on 1,013 rolls, series M432, beginning with FHL film #2343 (Alabama). The microfilm was digitized by FamilySearch International. For a list of roll numbers, contents, and access to the digital images of each roll, see the FHL catalog page: https://familysearch.org/search/catalog/121180.

Online Searching - 1850 Census Indexes and Digital Images

The 1850 Census was digitized from the National Archives microfilm, indexed, and made available at the following websites:

- **Ancestry.com.** Subscription site, free database searching. Ancestry and FamilySearch share images and indexes. See www.ancestry.com/search/collections/1850usfedcenancestry.

- **FamilySearch.org.** Free database search, with images by FamilySearch, index by Ancestry. See https://familysearch.org/search/collection/1401638.

- **MyHeritage.com.** A Family Tree subscription site. All U.S. Federal Census Records are available to subscribers with a data plan. See www.myheritage.com/research/collection-10126/1850-united-states-federal-census.

- **Findmypast.com.** Monthly or annual subscriptions. Initial searches to U.S. Federal Censuses are free. See www.findmypast.com/articles/search-the-1850-us-census.

- **GenealogyBank.com.** Subscription site. Initial searches to the U.S. Federal Censuses, 1790-1940 are free. www.genealogybank.com/explore/census/all.

- **HeritageQuestOnline-Subscribers Login.** This is a library subscription service. Check with your local library to see if they subscribe to the ProQuest & HeritageQuest databases. Many subscribing libraries allow their library card holders remote access. See www.heritagequestonline.com/hqoweb/library/do/login.

Table 1850 – Statewide Census Publications

1850 Jurisdictions Included in Census	Population	Census Extant?	FHL Film Number	Comments, Census Substitutes, etc.
1. Alabama	771,623	Yes	2343	
2. Arkansas	209,897	Yes	2479	AR 1850 census index exists. See Note 1.
3. California	92,597	Yes	2490	CA 1850 index & CA 1852 state census exists. See Note 2.
4. Connecticut	370,792	Yes	3065	CT 1850 census index exists. See Note 3.
5. Delaware	91,532	Yes	6436	DE 1850 census index exists. See Note 4.
6. District of Columbia	51,687	Yes	6702	
7. Florida	87,445	Yes	6714	FL 1845 State census & 1850 index exists. See Note 5.
8. Georgia	906,185	Yes	7057	GA tax lists are good census substitutes. See Note 6.
9. Illinois	851,470	Yes	7670	IL 1845 & 1855 state censuses exist. See Note 7.
10. Indiana	988,416	Yes	7748	
11. Iowa	192,214	Yes	7791	
12. Kentucky	982,405	Yes	7843	1850 KY printed index exists. See Note 8.
13. Louisiana	517,762	Yes	9696	
14. Maine	583,034	Yes	9714	ME 1850-1870 census indexes exist. See Note 9.
15. Maryland	583,034	Yes	13194	
16. Massachusetts	994,514	Yes	14697	
17. Michigan	397,654	Yes	14808	MI 1850 index exists. For original county originals, see Note 10.
18. Minnesota Territory	6,077	Yes	14834	MN 1850 index exists. See Note 11.
19. Mississippi	606,526	Yes	14847	MS 1850 index exists. See Note 12.
20. Missouri	682,044	Yes	14871	MO State censuses in 1852 & 1856. See Note 13.
21. New Hampshire	317,976	Yes	14938	
22. New Jersey	489,555	Yes	16529	NJ 1855 State Census exists. See Note 14.
23. New Mexico Territory	61,547	Yes	16603	NM 1850 index exists. See Note 15.
24. New York	3,097,394	Yes	17047	1835 & 1845 NY state censuses exist. See Note 16.
25. North Carolina	869,039	Yes	18105	
26. Ohio	1,980,329	Yes	20205	OH 1850 index exists. See Note 17.
27. Oregon Territory	12,093	Yes	20298	OR 1850 index exists. See Note 18.
28. Pennsylvania	2,311,786	Yes	20594	PA 1852-1854 births index is a good substitute. See Note 19.
29. Rhode Island	147,545	Yes	22264	
30. South Carolina	668,507	Yes	22528	
31. Tennessee	1,002,717	Yes	24560	TN 1850 census index exists. See Note 20.
32. Texas	212,592	Yes	24887	TX tax rolls are good census substitutes. See Note 21.
33. Utah Territory	11,380	Yes	25540	1850 UT census index/digital version exists. See Note 22.
34. Vermont	314,120	Yes	27446	VT Town Clerk records are good substitutes. See Note 23.
35. Virginia	1,421,661	Yes	29707	
36. Wisconsin	305,945	Yes	34508	1847 WI Territorial census exists. See Note 24.

U.S. total: 23,191,876

Table 1850 Notes

1. See *Arkansas Census, 1850 Surname Index* [Printed Book], by Mrs. Leister E. Presley, publ. Searcy, AR, 1974, 318 pages, see the FHL catalog page: **www.familysearch.org/search/catalog/178306**.

2. See *Index to the 1850 Census of the State of California* [Printed Book], by Alan P. Bowman, publ. GPC, Baltimore, MD, 1972, FHL catalog page: **www.familysearch.org/search/catalog/135878**.

For the only state census taken in California, see

California State Census, 1852 [Online Database], digitized and indexed at the FamilySearch.org website, see
www.familysearch.org/search/collection/1771089.

3. See *Index of Connecticut Census Records* [Microfilm & Digital Capture]. The Connecticut State Library prepared index cards for every head of household for Connecticut censuses, 1790-1850. To view the digital images of certain rolls, see the FHL catalog page:
www.familysearch.org/search/catalog/332021.

4. See *Index to the 1850 Census of Delaware* [Printed Book], compiled by Virginia Langham Olmsted (Baltimore: GPC, 1977), FHL Catalog page:
www.familysearch.org/search/catalog/130410.

5. See *Florida Statehood Election Returns, 1845* [Microfilm & Digital Capture]. This name list is Florida's "First state census - 1845." Filmed by the Genealogical Society of Utah, 1990, 1 roll, FHL film #1672587. For access to the digital images for this roll, see the FHL catalog page:
www.familysearch.org/search/catalog/538089.
See also *Index to 1850 Florida Census* [Printed Book], compiled by the Southern Genealogist's Exchange Society, 1976, 131 pages, FHL catalog page: www.familysearch.org/search/catalog/742542.

6. See *Georgia Property Tax Digests, 1793-1893* [Online Database]. This digitized and indexed database is the primary census substitute for all of Georgia, which had lost federal censuses for 1790, 1800, 1810, and 1890. Within this database of over 4.8 million records, a search can be done by the name of a taxpayer for the entire span of years. A more precise search can be done by county, see
www.ancestry.com/search/collections/georgia1890proptaxdigests.

7. Illinois conducted state censuses in 1845 and 1855, both census years digitized and indexed as part of *Illinois, State Census Collection, 1825-1865* [Online Database], see
www.ancestry.com/search/collections/ilstatecen.

8. See *1850 Kentucky Federal Census* [Printed Book], this census index was compiled by Byron Sistler and Associates in 1995, in 14 volumes, see the FHL catalog page:
https://familysearch.org/search/catalog/759293.

9. See *Maine Census Indexes, 1850-1870* [Microfilm], from the original records at the Maine Division of Vital Statistic, Augusta, ME. These card indexes to Maine's federal censuses for 1850, 1860, and 1870 were the first statewide indexes ever done by any state, executed by the Maine Vital Statistics Division in the early 1950s. For a complete list of roll numbers and contents of each roll, see the online FHL catalog page:
https://familysearch.org/search/catalog/78880.

10. See *Index to the 1850 Federal Population Census of Michigan* [Printed Index], compiled and published by the DAR, Lansing, MI, 1976, 463 pages, see the FHL catalog page:
www.familysearch.org/search/catalog/267203.
See also *Michigan Censuses & Substitute Name Lists, 1700-2015 - 2nd Edition* [Printed Book & eBook], by Wm. Dollarhide, publ. 2018, Family Roots Publishing Co., 117 pages. Michigan is one of just a few states where original state copies of censuses exist. For 1850 there are five MI counties with county/state originals on microfilm or digital captures: Eaton, Barry, Kent, Montcalm, and Washtenaw counties. See page 33 for details. This book is available at
www.familyrootspublishing.com/store/product_view.php?id=3068.

11. See *Minnesota Territorial Census, 1850* [Printed Book], by Patricia C. Harpole and Mary D. Nagle, publ. MN Hist. Soc., 1972, 115 pages. FHL catalog page: www.familysearch.org/search/catalog/200411.

12. See *Mississippi 1850 Census, Surname Index* [Printed Book], compiled by Irene S. Gillis, publ. Shreveport, LA, 1972., 521 pages, FHL catalog page:
www.familysearch.org/search/catalog/153435.

13. See *Missouri State and Territorial Census Records, 1732-1933* [Online Database], digitized and indexed at the FamilySearch.org website. Missouri took state censuses in 1852 and 1856. See
https://familysearch.org/search/collection/2075262.
For a list of all extant MO censuses by county, see the MO State Archives Digital Heritage webpage:
www.sos.mo.gov/records/archives/census/pages/territorial.

14. See *New Jersey, State Census, 1855* [Online Database], digitized and indexed at the Family-Search.org website. See
www.familysearch.org/search/collection/2469955.

15. See *New Mexico 1850 Territorial Census* [Printed Book], compiled by Margaret L. Windham (New Mexico Genealogical Society, 1976). The index includes the area which became Arizona Territory, see the FHL catalog page:
www.familysearch.org/search/catalog/157862.

16. See *New York State Census, 1855* [Online Database], digitized and indexed at the FamilySearch.org website, see
www.familysearch.org/search/collection/1937366.

17. See *Index to the 1850 Federal Population Census of Ohio* [Printed Book], compiled by the Ohio Family Historians, publ. 1972, 1,098 pages, FHL catalog page: www.familysearch.org/search/catalog/84020.

18. See *1850 Oregon Territorial Census* [Printed Book & Digital Capture], by Elsie Youngberg, End of Trail Researchers, Lebanon, OR, 1970, 310 pages, to access a digital version of this book, see the FHL catalog page:
www.familysearch.org/search/catalog/149145.

19. See *Pennsylvania, Births, 1852-1854* [Online Database], indexed at the Ancestry.com website. Source: PA State Archives. Includes registers of birth from 39 Pennsylvania counties, with names, dates, and other details. See
www.ancestry.com/search/collections/pabirths.

20. See *1850 Census, Tennessee* [Printed Book], a complete extraction and index, 8 volumes, compiled by Byron and Barbara Sistler, publ. Natchez, TN, 1976, see the FHL catalog page:
www.familysearch.org/search/catalog/170353.

21. See *The State of Texas Federal Population Schedules, Seventh Census of the United States, 1850* [Printed Book & Digital Capture], by Mrs. V. K. Carpenter, publ. Century Enterprises, 1969, 5 vols., see a digital version at the FHL catalog page:
www.familysearch.org/search/catalog/190137.
See also, *1837-1910 Texas, County Tax Rolls,* digitized and indexed from 424 microfilm rolls at the TX State Archives, with 4,575,333 records. see https://familysearch.org/search/collection/1827575.

22. The 1850 census for Utah Territory had a census day of 1 April 1851. See *1851 Census of Utah* [Printed Book & Digital Capture], by William Bowen, publ. 1972, Salt Lake City, 1972, 228 pages. To access a digital version of this index, see the FHL catalog page:
www.familysearch.org/search/catalog/186877.

23. See *Vermont, Town Clerk, Vital and Town Records, 1732-2005* [Online Database], this is the main census substitute for Vermont. There are name lists from every county and every town of Vermont, see www.familysearch.org/search/collection/1987653.

24. See *Wisconsin Territory Census for 1847* [Microfilm & Digital Capture], from the originals at the WI State Hist. Soc, Madison, WI. To access the digital images, see the FHL catalog page:
www.familysearch.org/search/catalog/235251,
See also *Index to 1850 Federal Census of Wisconsin* [Microfilm], from the original State Copy, located at the State Historical Society of Wisconsin, see the FHL catalog page:
www.familysearch.org/search/catalog/283885.

Selected Online Databases from the time of the 1850 Census

Ellis Island and Other New York Passenger Lists, 1820-1957 [Online Database], digitized and indexed at the MyHeritage.com website. During the 19th and 20th centuries millions of immigrants came to the United States. This collection contains millions of records of individuals arriving at the port of New York between 1820 and 1957. This includes individuals who arrived at three well-known immigrant processing stations: Castle Garden (1855-1890), the Barge Office (1890-1892), and Ellis Island (1892-1957). This database has 113,439,615 records, see www.myheritage.com/research/collection-10512/ellis-island-other-new-york-passenger-lists-1820-1957.

1834-1897 Russians to America Index [Online Database], digitized and indexed at the FamilySearch.org website. These are records of passengers, mostly arriving at the Port of New York, but some arriving at the Ports of Baltimore, Boston, New Orleans, and Philadelphia. Each of the passenger records may include a name, age, town of last residence, destination, and codes for passenger's sex, occupation, literacy, country of origin, transit and/or travel compartment, the name of the ship, the port of departure, date of arrival, and the port of arrival. This database has 527,394 passengers who arrived in the U.S. between 1834 and 1897 and identified their country of origin as Armenia, Finland, Galicia, Lithuania, Poland, Russia, Russian Poles, or Ukraine. See https://familysearch.org/search/collection/2110813.

United States Mexican War Index and Service Records, 1846-1848 **[Online Database]**, indexed at the FamilySearch.org website. Military service records for the Mexican War (1846-1848) are comprised of cards created from muster, pay, receipt and other rolls for soldiers and sailors who served in the war. The information includes name, service dates, terms of service, monthly pay, where they served, and notes. This database has 211,909 images. See
https://familysearch.org/search/collection/1987567.

1846-1851 Famine Irish Passenger Index **[Online Database]**, digitized and indexed at the FamilySearch.org website. Records for passengers who arrived at the Port of New York during the Irish Famine 1846-1851. Created by the Balch Institute for Ethnic Studies, Center for Immigration Research. This database has 604,596 records. See
www.familysearch.org/search/collection/2110821.

1850-1897 Germans to America Index **[Online Database]**, digitized and indexed at the FamilySearch.org website. These are records of the Center for Immigration Research, identifying passenger arrival records of Germans, mostly for arrivals at the Port of New York, although there are some records from the ports of Baltimore, Boston, New Orleans, and Philadelphia. Each of the passenger records may include name, age, town of last residence, destination, and codes for passenger's sex, occupation, literacy, country of origin, transit and/or travel compartment, the name of the ship, the port of departure, date of arrival, and other places. This database has 4,048,907 passengers who arrived in the U.S. between 1850 and 1897. See
www.familysearch.org/search/collection/2110801.

U.S., Department of Veterans Affairs BIRLS Death File, 1850-2010 **[Online Database]**, indexed at the Ancestry.com website. Original data: Beneficiary Identification Records Locator Subsystem (BIRLS) Death File. Washington, D.C.: U.S. Department of Veterans Affairs. This index contains birth and death dates for more than 14 million veterans and VA beneficiaries who died between the years 1850 and 2010. The majority of information in the index comes from the BIRLS Death File. However, the veteran's name has been added by cross-referencing the Social Security Number in the BIRLS Death File with the Social Security Death Index. This database has 14,465,014 records. See
www.ancestry.com/search/collections/vadeaths.

Historical Newspapers, Birth, Marriage, & Death Announcements, 1851-2003 **[Online Database]**, digitized and indexed at the Ancestry.com website. This database is a collection of birth, marriage, and death announcements for the following years and major newspapers:
- *The New York Times* (1851-2003)
- *The Los Angeles Times* (1881-1985)
- *The Boston Globe* (1872-1923)
- *The Chicago Defender* (Big Weekend and National Editions) (1921-1975)
- *The Chicago Tribune* (1850-1985)
- *The Hartford Courant* (1791-1942)
- *The Washington Post* (1877-1990)
- *The Atlanta Constitution* (1869-1929)

The newspaper announcements were digitized by ProQuest, then indexed with an OCR index. This database has 1,582,938 records. See
www.ancestry.com/search/collections/proquestnews.

1855-1891 Naval Enlistment Rendezvous **[Online Database]**, digitized and indexed at the FamilySearch website. This database consists of enlistment registers of men who enlisted in the United States Navy from January 6, 1855 to August 8, 1891. The registers include name of naval rendezvous, name of sailor, date and term of enlistment, rating, previous naval service, place of birth, age, occupation and personal description. Taken from the National Archives, Record Group 24, records of the Bureau of Naval Personnel. This database has 262,742 records. See
https://familysearch.org/search/collection/1825347.

1855-1900 Italians to America Index **[Online Database]**, digitized and indexed at the FamilySearch.org website. These are records of the Center for Immigration Research, identifying passenger arrival records of Italians, mostly for arrivals at the Port of New York. Records may include name, age, town of last residence, destination, and codes for passenger's sex, occupation, literacy, country of origin, transit and/or travel. There are some records from the ports of Baltimore, Boston, New Orleans, and Philadelphia. All records include the name of the ship, the port of departure, date of arrival, and other places visited. This database has 845,368 passengers who arrived in the U.S. between 1855 and 1900. See
www.familysearch.org/search/collection/2110811.

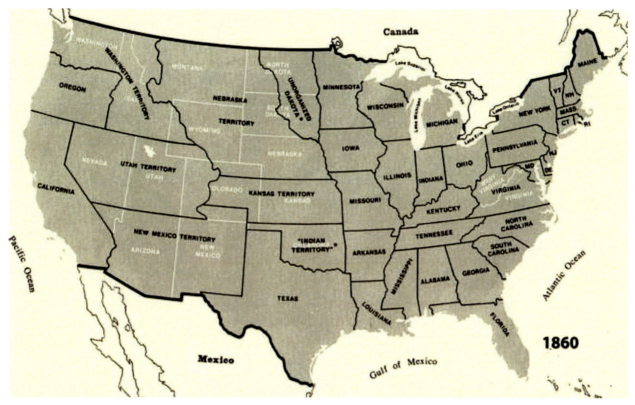

The U.S. in 1860. In a treaty ratified in 1854, the U.S. purchased a 45,000 square mile tract of land from Mexico, called the Gadsden Purchase. As the only benefactor of the tract, New Mexico Territory created Arizona County in the newly acquired area.
Map Source: Page 8, *Map Guide to the U.S. Federal Censuses, 1790-1920,* by William Thorndale and William Dollarhide.

Eighth Census of the United States - 1860

Description

Location of Original Records: National Archives, Washington, DC.

U.S. Population: 31.5 million (27.5 million free and 4.0 million slave).

1850-1860-1870 Census Legislative Act: Section 23, 9 Stat. 432, 23 May 1850.

Responsibility / Copies: The 1860 census was conducted under the direction of a **Census Office,** a division under the U.S. Secretary of the Interior. Reporting to the Census Office, U.S. Marshals of the Federal Court Districts hired and managed Assistant Marshals as the door-to-door census takers within their districts. Territories without a federal court district were enumerated by local militia captains, under the supervision of the Territorial Governor.
Mandated Copies: Three (3) sets, to the county courthouse, the secretary of state of the territory or state, and the Census Office/U.S. Secretary of the Interior.

Census day: 1 June 1860. All of the questions asked by the census taker were related to a person's age or place of residence as of the census day.

Time Allowed: Five months.

1860 Jurisdictions: 40. Between 1850 and 1860, two (2) new states were added to the Union: Minnesota was admitted in 1858, and Oregon in 1859, for a total of thirty-three (33) states at the time of the 1860 federal census. Add the District of Columbia and five (5) territories:

New Mexico, Utah, Washington, Nebraska, and Kansas territories. And, add one (1) more area between the Red River of the North and the Missouri River, enumerated as *Unorganized Dakota* (a name invented by the Census Office); for a total of 40 jurisdictions. The name lists for non-Indians in the unorganized "Indian Territory" were incorporated into the Arkansas schedules.

Content of the Population Schedules: The 1860 census schedule format had 14 columns, each person on one line, spread across a single schedule page, numbered as follows:
1. Dwelling houses numbered in the order of visitation.
2. Families numbered in the order of visitation.
3. The name of every person whose usual place of abode on the first day of June, 1860, was in this family.
4. Age.
5. Sex.
6. Color: White, Black, or Mulatto.
7. Profession, Occupation, or Trade of each person, male and female, over 15 years of age.
8. Value of Real Estate.
9. Value of Personal Estate.
10. Place of Birth, Naming the State, Territory, or Country
11. Married within the year.
12. Attended School within the year.
13. Persons over 20 years of age who cannot read or write.
14. Whether deaf and dumb, blind, insane, idiotic, pauper or convict.

Slave States vs Free States to 1860. The slavery issue in America was a dividing political force, often causing new states to be admitted to the Union in pairs, one a free state, the other a slave state. For example, in 1800 there were 8 slave and 8 free states. By the time of the 1840 federal census, there were 13 slave states and 13 free states. Texas was annexed to the U.S. as a slave state in 1845, bringing a balance of 15 slave and 15 free states. But, when the free state of California was admitted to the Union in 1850, the balance shifted to the Free state side. As it turned out, Texas was the last slave state to enter the Union. With the addition of the free states of Minnesota in 1858, and Oregon in 1859, the free states now numbered 18 vs 15 slave.

In November 1860, Abraham Lincoln was elected President of the United States, with a platform of extreme opposition to slavery. Lincoln's election set in motion the secession of southern states, starting with South Carolina in December 1860, one month after Lincoln's election win.

1860 Census and the Civil War Era. Name lists from the 1860 federal census can be used to find any soldier as a civilian just prior to his service. It may be possible to identify every future Union or Confederate soldier and their families about ten months before the Civil War began on 12 April 1861. Start a search in a major online database indexed at the National Park Service website. The *Civil War Soldiers and Sailors Database* contains information about the men who served in both the Union and Confederate armies during the Civil War. Other information at this website includes histories of Union and Confederate regiments, links to descriptions of significant battles, selected lists of prisoner-of-war records, and cemetery records. This database has 6.3 million records. See www.nps.gov/civilwar/soldiers-and-sailors-database.htm.

1860 Census Publications with Digital Images

Microfilm of Originals & Digital Capture: The National Archives film for the 1860 census is contained on 1,013 rolls, series M432, beginning with FHL film #803001 (Alabama). The microfilm was digitized by FamilySearch International. For a list of roll numbers, contents, and access to the digital images of each roll, see the FHL catalog page: https://familysearch.org/search/catalog/121214.

Online Searching - 1860 Census Indexes and Digital Images

The 1860 Census was digitized from the National Archives microfilm, indexed, and made available at the following websites:

• **Ancestry.com.** Subscription site, free database searching. Ancestry and FamilySearch share images and indexes. See www.ancestry.com/search/collections/1860usfedcenancestry.

Eighth Census of the U.S. - 1860

- **FamilySearch.org**. Free database search, with images by FamilySearch, index by Ancestry. See https://familysearch.org/search/collection/1473181.

- **MyHeritage.com**. A Family Tree subscription site. All U.S. Federal Census Records are available to subscribers with a data plan. See www.myheritage.com/research/collection-10127/1860-united-states-federal-census.

- **Findmypast.com**. Monthly or annual subscriptions. Initial searches to U.S. Federal Censuses are free. See www.findmypast.com/articles/search-the-1860-us-census.

- **GenealogyBank.com**. Subscription site. Initial searches to the U.S. Federal Censuses, 1790-1940 are free. www.genealogybank.com/explore/census/all.

- **HeritageQuestOnline-Subscribers Login**. This is a library subscription service. Check with your local library to see if they subscribe to the ProQuest & HeritageQuest databases. Many subscribing libraries allow their library card holders remote access. See www.heritagequestonline.com/hqoweb/library/do/login.

Table 1860 – Statewide Census Publications

1860 Jurisdictions Included in Census	Population	Census Extant?	FHL Film Number	Comments, Census Substitutes, etc.
1. Alabama	996,992	Yes	803001	AL 1855 & 1866 state censuses exist. See Note 1.
2. Arkansas	435,450	Yes	803037	Includes Non-Indians in the Indian Territory. See Note 2.
3. California	379,994	Yes	803055	CA 1860 index exists. See Note 3.
4. Connecticut	460,147	Yes	803073	CT 1860 index exists. See Note 4.
5. Dakota-Unorganized	4,837	Yes	803094	1860 Unorg. Dakota name lists exist. See Note 5.
6. Delaware	61,073	Yes	803095	DE 1860 index exists. See Note 6.
7. District of Columbia	75,080	Yes	803101	DC 1860 index exists. See Note 7.
8. Florida	140,424	Yes	803106	FL 1860 index exists. See Note 8.
9. Georgia	1,057,286	Yes	803111	GA 1860 index exists. See Note 9.
10. Illinois	1,711,951	Yes	803154	IL 1855 & 1865 state censuses exist. See Note 10.
11. Indiana	1,350,428	Yes	803242	IN 1860 index exists. See Note 11.
12. Iowa	674,913	Yes	803310	IA 1859 state census exists. See Note 12.
13. Kansas Territory	107,206	Yes	803346	1855-1859 KS Terr. & 1865 KS state census. See Note 13.
14. Kentucky	1,155,684	Yes	803353	
15. Louisiana	708,002	Yes	803407	
16. Maine	628,279	Yes	803432	1850-1870 ME census indexes exist. See Note 14.
17. Maryland	687,049	Yes	803456	MD 1862-1865 federal tax lists/substitutes. See Note 15.
18. Massachusetts	1,231,066	Yes	803486	MA 1855 & 1865 state censuses exist. See Note 16.
19. Michigan	749,113	Yes	803535	Several substitute name lists exist. See Note 17.
20. Minnesota	172,023	Yes	803567	MN 1855, 1857 Terr. & 1865 state exist. See Note 18.
21. Mississippi	791,305	Yes	803577	MS 1853, 1860, & 1866 state censuses exist. See Note 19.
22. Missouri	1,182,012	Yes	803605	MO 1857-1858 state censuses. See Note 20.
23. Nebraska Territory	28,841	Yes	803665	NE 1854, 1855, 1856 Terr. censuses. See Note 21.
24. New Hampshire	326,073	Yes	803666	
25. New Jersey	489,555	Yes	803682	NJ 1865 state census. See Note 22.
26. New Mexico Territory	93,516	Yes	803712	
27. New York	3,880,735	Yes	803717	NY 1855 & 1865 state census. See Note 23.

1860 Jurisdictions Included in Census	Population	Census Extant?	FHL Film Number	Comments, Census Substitutes, etc.
28. North Carolina	992,622	Yes	803886	
29. Ohio	2,339,511	Yes	803928	
30. Oregon	52,465	Yes	805055	OR Hist. Records Index – all censuses. See Note 24.
31. Pennsylvania	2,906,215	Yes	805057	
32. Rhode Island	174,260	Yes	805202	RI 1865 state census online. See Note 25.
33. South Carolina	703,708	Yes	805212	
34. Tennessee	1,109,801	Yes	805239	
35. Texas	604,215	Yes	805287	TX county tax rolls - best census substitutes. See Note 26.
36. Utah Territory	40,273	Yes	805313	UT 1856 Terr. census exists. See Note 27.
37. Vermont	315,098	Yes	805315	
38. Virginia	1,596,318	Yes	805330	
39. Washington Territory	11,594	Yes	805398	WA 1857 Terr. census exists. See Note 28.
40. Wisconsin	775,881	Yes	805399	WI 1855 & 1865 state censuses exist. See Note 29.
U.S. Total:	31,443,321			

Table 1860 Notes

1. See *Alabama State Census, 1855* [Online Database], digitized and indexed at the FamilySearch.org website, see www.familysearch.org/search/collection/1915984.
See also *Alabama State Census, 1866* [Online Database], digitized and indexed at the FamilySearch.org website, see www.familysearch.org/search/collection/1915987.

2. See *Arkansas 1860 U.S. Census Index* [Printed Book], abstracted and indexed by Kathryn Rose Bonner, publ. 1984, 239 pages, see the FHL catalog page: www.familysearch.org/search/catalog/348327.

3. See *California 1860 Census Index* [Printed Book], originally prepared by Index Publishing, publ. by Heritage Quest, 1999, 2 vols., see the FHL catalog page: www.familysearch.org/search/catalog/1062781.
NOTE: This index is included in the HeritageQuestOnline databases noted in the Online Searching category above.

4. See *1860 Connecticut Census Index* [Printed Book], compiled by Bryan Lee Dilts, publ. Index Publishing Co., Salt Lake City, 1985, 707 pages, see the FHL catalog page:
www.familysearch.org/search/catalog/52263.

5. See *Dakota Territory 1860* [Printed Book], edited by Ronald Vern Jackson, publ. Accelerated Indexing Systems, North Salt Lake, UT, 1980, 72 pages, (the title should be *Unorganized Dakota*), see the FHL catalog page:
www.familysearch.org/search/catalog/967817. See also

1860 Federal Census Images (Unorganized Dakota) [Online Database], digitized 1860 census pages, organized by post office, town, or area descriptions, such as "between Red River and Big Sioux." The images are the actual census forms, where the *County of* and *State* were replaced with *Unorganized Dakota*. See www.usgwarchives.net/sd/census/1860images.html.
ADDED NOTE: *Unorganized Dakota* was an area enumerated by the U.S. Census Office. Included were the communities of Medary, Sioux Falls, Vermillion, and Yankton Agency (now South Dakota). In addition, several military forts along the Missouri River were enumerated, most of which were on the west side of the river, and therefore, technically in Nebraska Territory. The standard 1860 forms were used, but the line "Assistant Marshal" crossed out and written over with "Census Agent." A minor detail, perhaps, but this was the first time the U.S. Census Office hired their own enumerators to conduct a door-to-door census. It was because the area had population without any jurisdiction – the area had been part of old Dakotah County, Minnesota Territory, but was orphaned when Minnesota became a state in 1858. A legal jurisdictional parent was restored to the area with the creation of the official Dakota Territory in 1861.

6. See *1860 Delaware Census Index* [Printed Book], compiled by Bryan Lee Dilts, publ. Index Publishing Co., Salt Lake City, 1985, 153 pages, see the FHL catalog page:
www.familysearch.org/search/catalog/216465.

Eighth Census of the U.S. - 1860

7. See *1860 District of Columbia Census Index* [Printed Book], compiled by Bryan Lee Dilts, publ. Index Publishing Co., Salt Lake City, 1983, 109 pages, see the FHL catalog page: www.familysearch.org/search/catalog/216474.

8. See *1860 Florida Census Index* [Printed Book], compiled by Bryan Lee Dilts, publ. Index Publishing Co., Salt Lake City, 1984, see the FHL catalog page: www.familysearch.org/search/catalog/456070.

9. See *An Index for the 1860 Federal Census of Georgia* [Printed Book], compiled by Artis Acord, Martha S. Anderson & Others, publ. Family Tree, LaGrange, GA, 1986, 1,024 pages, FHL catalog page: www.familysearch.org/search/catalog/526999.

10. See *Illinois, State Census Collection, 1825-1865* [Online Database], digitized and indexed at the Ancestry.com website, includes the IL 1855 and IL 1865 state censuses, see www.ancestry.com/search/collections/ilstatecen.

11. See *1860 Indiana Census Index: Every Name Listing* [Printed Book], by the IN Hist. Soc., publ. 1990, see the FHL catalog page: www.familysearch.org/search/catalog/409321.

12. See *Census of Iowa, 1859* [Microfilm & Digital Capture], from the originals at the Iowa State Historical Society, Des Moines, IA, to access the digital images, see the FHL catalog page: www.familysearch.org/search/catalog/3720.
See also *Iowa, State Census Collection, 1836-1925* [Online Database], includes the 1856 IA State Census, digitized and indexed at the Ancestry.com website, see www.ancestry.com/search/collections/iastatecen.

13. See *Kansas State Census Collection, 1855-1925* [Online Database], includes the KS 1855, 1856, 1857, 1858, 1859 territorial, and 1865 state censuses; digitized and indexed at the Ancestry.com website, see www.ancestry.com/search/collections/ksstatecen.

14. See *Maine Census Indexes, 1850-1870* [Microfilm], from the original records at the Maine Division of Vital Statistic, Augusta, ME. These card indexes to Maine's federal censuses for 1850, 1860, and 1870 were the first statewide indexes ever done by any state, executed by the Maine Vital Statistics Division in the early 1950s. See the FHL catalog page: https://familysearch.org/search/catalog/78880.

15. See **1862-1866** *Internal Revenue Assessment Lists for Maryland* [Microfilm & Online Database], from the originals at the National Archives, Washington, DC. These are name lists of taxpayers taken during the Civil War Era in Maryland. Most are arranged by year or month, then division of district and then alphabetically. See the online FHL catalog page: https://familysearch.org/search/catalog/88651.
To access the online Internal Revenue Assessment Lists for the entire U.S., see
https://familysearch.org/search/collection/2075263.

16. See *Massachusetts State Census, 1855-1865* [Microfilm & Digital Capture], from the originals at the MA State Archives. 1855 and 1865 were filmed together, to access the digital images, see the FHL catalog page:
www.familysearch.org/search/catalog/293408.
See also *Records of Massachusetts, State Census, 1855* [Online Database], digitized and indexed at the FamilySearch.org website, see
www.familysearch.org/search/collection/1459985.
See also *Records of Massachusetts, State Census, 1865* [Online Database], digitized and indexed at the FamilySearch.org website, see
www.familysearch.org/search/collection/1410399.

17. **Michigan Census Substitutes.** There are county copies of the 1860 federal census for Eaton, Barry, Bay, Clinton, Houghton, Kent, and Montcalm counties. There are also city directories available from the period 1855-1865 for larger Michigan cities, as well as county-wide tax lists, and state-wide vital records for the time of the 1860 census. For details, see pp 34-38, *Michigan Census & Substitute Name Lists,* see
www.familyrootspublishing.com/store/product_view.php?id=3068.

18. See *Minnesota, Territorial and State Censuses, 1849-1905* [Online Database], digitized and indexed at the Ancestry.com website. Included are the MN 1855 and 1857 Terr., and the MN 1865 State Census, see www.ancestry.com/search/collections/mnstatecen.
See also *Index to the 1860 Federal Census Schedules for Minnesota* [Microfilm], from index cards at the MN Historical Society Library in St. Paul. This index is to the state's original copy, not the federal copy, so the page numbers do not always match up with the federal copy. See the FHL catalog page: www.familysearch.org/search/catalog/276458.

19. See *Mississippi, State and Territorial Census Collection, 1792-1866* [Online Database], digitized and indexed at the Ancestry.com website. Included are the MS state censuses of 1853 (17 counties), 1860 (2 counties), and 1866 (11 counties). See www.ancestry.com/search/collections/msstatecen. See also *Mississippi 1860 U.S Census Index* [Printed Book], by Kathryn Bonner, publ. Marianna, AR, 1983, 3 vols., FHL catalog page:
www.familysearch.org/search/catalog/403637.

20. See *Missouri, State Census Collection, 1844-1881* [Online Database], digitized and indexed at the Ancestry.com website. Only St. Louis has a census in this database from the time period (1857-1858), see www.ancestry.com/search/collections/mo_state_census.

21. See *Nebraska, Compiled Census Index, 1854-1870* [Online Database], indexed at the Ancestry.com website. The 1854, 1855, and 1856 NE Territorial Census name lists were added to the 1860 NE Territory Federal Census. No 1870 names could be found in this database. See
www.ancestry.com/search/collections/necen.

22. See *New Jersey, State Census, 1865* [Online Database], digitized at the FamilySearch.org website, see https://familysearch.org/search/collection/2475024.

23. See *New York State Census, 1855* [Online Database], digitized and indexed at the FamilySearch.org website, see
www.familysearch.org/search/collection/1937366.
See also *New York State Census, 1865* [Online Database], digitized and indexed at the Ancestry.com website, see
www.ancestry.com/search/collections/general-7218.

24. See *Oregon Historical Records Index* [Online Database], indexed city / county / state records at the Oregon State Archives website. Included are the names from all territorial censuses, 1849-1859; all state censuses, 1865-1905; and all OR federal censuses 1850-1940. See
http://sos.oregon.gov/archives/Pages/records/genealogy/about-historical-records.aspx.

25. See *Rhode Island State Censuses* [Online Database], digitized and indexed at the Ancestry.com website. This collection includes the 1865, 1875, 1885, 1915, 1925, and 1935 state censuses, see www.ancestry.com/search/collections/ricensus.

26. See *1837-1910 Texas, County Tax Rolls* [Online Database], digitized and indexed from 424 microfilm rolls at the TX State Archives, with 4,575,333 records. see https://familysearch.org/search/collection/1827575.

27. See *Utah, Compiled Census and Census Substitutes Index, 1850-1890* [Online Database], indexed at the Ancestry.com website. Source: Accelerated Indexing Systems, Salt Lake City, UT, 1999. This collection contains the following indexes: 1850 Federal Census Index; 1856 State Census Index; 1859 Tax List; 1860 Federal Census Index; 1870 Federal Census Index; 1880 Federal Census Index; 1890 Veterans Schedule. See
www.ancestry.com/search/collections/utcen.

28. See *Washington State and Territorial Censuses, 1857-1892* [Online Database], digitized and indexed at the Ancestry.com website. In addition to the 1857 territorial census, there are six (6) counties with original county copies of their 1860 federal census included in the index, see
www.ancestry.com/search/collections/washterrcen.

29. See *Index to the 1860 Federal Census of Wisconsin (State Copy)* [Microfilm], from the original index cards at the WI Hist, Soc. Library, Madison, WI. See the FHL catalog page:
https://familysearch.org/search/catalog/283919.
See also *Wisconsin, State Censuses, 1855-1905* [Online Database], digitized and indexed at the Ancestry.com website. Includes 1855 but not 1865. See www.ancestry.com/search/collections/wistatecen.
See also, *Wisconsin State Census, 1865* [Online Database], digitized and index at the FamilySearch.org website, see
www.familysearch.org/search/collection/2058670.

The U.S. in 1870. The huge tract of land known as Russian America was purchased by the U.S. in 1867. Congress renamed the area the Department of Alaska. (Not Shown on map). No federal census was taken in Alaska until 1900. Note that the map shows the area of Dakota Territory, which was divided into the states of North Dakota and South Dakota in 1889. Also shown is the unorganized "Indian Territory," the same area that became the State of Oklahoma in 1907. Map Source: Page 9, *Map Guide to the U.S. Federal Censuses, 1790-1920,* by William Thorndale and William Dollarhide.

Ninth Census of the United States - 1870

Description

Location of Original Records: National Archives, Washington, DC.

U.S. Population: 38.6 million.

1850-1860-1870 Census Legislative Act: Section 23, 9 Stat. 432, 23 May 1850.

Responsibility / Copies: The 1870 census was conducted under the direction of a **Census Office,** a division under the U.S. Secretary of the Interior. Reporting to the Census Office, U.S. Marshals of the Federal Court Districts hired and managed Assistant Marshals as the door-to-door census takers within their districts. Territories without a federal court district were enumerated by local militia captains, under the supervision of the Territorial Governor.

Mandated Copies: Three (3) sets, to the county courthouse, the secretary of state of the territory or state, and the Census Office/U.S. Secretary of the Interior.

Census day: 1 June 1870. All of the questions asked by the census taker were related to a person's age or place of residence as of the census day.

Time Allowed: Five months.

1870 Jurisdictions: 47. Between 1860 and 1870, the decade of the Civil War, four (4) new states were added to the Union for a total of Thirty-seven (37) states: Kansas became a state in 1861, West Virginia in 1863, Nevada in 1864, and Nebraska in 1867. Add the District of Columbia, New Mexico Territory, Washington Territory, and Utah Territory; and add six (6) new territories: Dakota Territory and Colorado Territory in 1861; Arizona Territory and Idaho Territory in 1863; Montana Territory in 1864; and Wyoming Territory in 1868, for a total of forty-seven (47) jurisdictions. Left out of the 1870 Census was the Department of Alaska, acquired by the U.S. in 1867; and the "Indian Territory," also not enumerated in 1870.

Content of the Population Schedules. The 1870 format had 20 columns, each person on one line, spread across a single schedule page, as follows:

1. Dwelling houses – numbered in the order of visitation.
2. Families, numbered in the order of visitation.
3. The name of every person whose place of abode on the first day of June, 1870, was in this family.
4. Age at last birthday. If under 1 year; give number in fractions, thus 9/12.
5. Sex – Male (M) Female (F)
6.. Color – White (W.), Black (B.), Mulatto (M.), Chinese (C.), Indian (I.)
7. Profession, Occupation, or Trade of each person, male and female.
8. Value of Real Estate.
9. Value of Personal Estate.
10. Place of Birth, Naming the State or Territory of U.S., or the Country, if of foreign birth.
11. Father of foreign birth.
12. Mother of foreign birth.
13. If born within the year, state month (Jan, Feb, &c)
14. If married with the year, state month (Jan, Feb, &c)
15. Attended school within the year.
16. Cannot read.
17. Cannot write.
18. Whether deaf and dumb, blind, insane, or idiotic.
19. Male Citizens of the U.S. of 21 years of age and up.
20. Male Citizens of the U.S. whose right to vote was denied.

Accuracy of the 1870 Census. After the Civil War, northern carpetbaggers were often used as census takers in the former Confederate states. They were not particularly interested in an accurate count of the southern population. Undercounting in the southern states was later estimated to be as much as 10-15 per cent of the population; while undercounting in the northern states was no more than 3-5 percent. In terms of completeness and accuracy, the 1870 Federal Census is now considered the worst one ever taken.

1870 Census Publications with Digital Images

Microfilm of Originals & Digital Capture: The National Archives film for the 1870 census is contained on 2,322 rolls, series M593, beginning with FHL film #545500 (Alabama). The microfilm was digitized by FamilySearch International. For a list of roll numbers, contents, and access to the digital images of each roll, see the FHL catalog page: https://familysearch.org/search/catalog/122118.

Online Searching - 1870 Census Indexes and Digital Images

The 1870 Census was digitized from the National Archives microfilm, indexed, and made available at the following websites:

● **Ancestry.com.** Subscription site, free database searching. Ancestry and FamilySearch share images and indexes. See www.ancestry.com/search/collections/1870usfedcen.

● **FamilySearch.org.** Free database search, with images by FamilySearch, index by Ancestry. See https://familysearch.org/search/collection/1438024.

● **MyHeritage.com.** A Family Tree subscription site. All U.S. Federal Census Records are available to subscribers with a data plan. See www.myheritage.com/research/collection-10128/1870-united-states-federal-census.

● **Findmypast.com.** Monthly or annual subscriptions. Initial searches to U.S. Federal Censuses are free. See www.findmypast.com/articles/search-the-1870-us-census.

● **GenealogyBank.com.** Subscription site. Initial searches to the U.S. Federal Censuses, 1790-1940 are free. www.genealogybank.com/explore/census/all.

● **HeritageQuestOnline-Subscribers Login.** This is a library subscription service. Check with your local library to see if they subscribe to the ProQuest & HeritageQuest databases. Many subscribing libraries allow their library card holders remote access. See www.heritagequestonline.com/hqoweb/library/do/login.

Ninth Census of the U.S. - 1870

Table 1870 – Statewide Census Publications

1870 Jurisdictions Included in Census	Population	Census Extant?	FHL Film Number	Comments, Census Substitutes, etc.
1. Alabama	996,992	Yes	545500	AL 1866 state census exists. See Note 1.
- Alaska, Department of	--	--	--	Several AK villages have 1870 name lists. See Note 2.
2. Arizona Territory	9,658	Yes	545545	AZ Terr. censuses taken in 1864 & 1866. See Note 3.
3. Arkansas	484,471	Yes	545546	
4. California	560,247	Yes	545567	CA Great Registers are the best census substitutes. See Note 4.
5. Colorado Territory	39,864	Yes	545593	CO 1870 (Territory's Copy) exists. See Note 5.
6. Connecticut	537,464	Yes	545595	
7. Dakota Territory	14,181	Yes	545617	
8. Delaware	125,015	Yes	545618	
9.. District of Columbia	131,700	Yes	545622	
10. Florida	187,784	Yes	545627	FL 1867 state census exists. See Note 6.
11. Georgia	1,184,109	Yes	545633	1867-1869 GA voter lists exist. See Note 7.
12. Idaho Territory	14,999	Yes	545684	1867-1874 ID Terr. IRS name lists exist. See Note 8.
13. Illinois	2,539,891	Yes	545685	IL 1865 state census exists. See Note 9.
14. Indiana	1,680,637	Yes	545795	IN state digital archives databases, see note 10.
15. Iowa	1,194,020	Yes	545873	IA 1865-1875 census substitutes exist. See note 11.
16. Kansas	364,399	Yes	545927	KS 1865 state census exists. See Note 12.
17. Kentucky	1,321,011	Yes	545943	KY 1865-1875 census substitutes exist. See note 13.
18. Louisiana	726,915	Yes	552004	LA 1867-1875 voter & tax lists exist. See Note 14.
19. Maine	626,915	Yes	552035	ME 1850-1870 census indexes exist. See Note 15.
20. Maryland	780,894	Yes	552065	
21. Massachusetts	1,457,351	Yes	552099	MA 1865 state census exists. See Note 16.
22. Michigan	1,184,059	Yes	552159	MI 1864 & 1874 state censuses exist. See Note 17.
23. Minnesota	430,706	Yes	830421	MN 1865 & 1875 state censuses exist. See Note 18.
24. Mississippi	827,922	Yes	552219	MS 1866 state census exists. See Note 19.
25. Missouri	1,721,295	Yes	552254	MO 1876 state census exists. See Note 20.
26. Montana Territory	20,595	Yes	552326	MT 1865-1875 census substitutes exist. See Note 21.
27. Nebraska	122,993	Yes	552327	NE 1865 terr. & 1869 state censuses exist. See Note 22.
28. Nevada	42,941	Yes	552333	NV 1868-1869 directory & 1875 state census exist. See Note 23.
29. New Hampshire	316,300	Yes	552335	
30. New Jersey	906,096	Yes	552350	NJ 1865 state censuses exist. See Note 24.
31. New Mexico Territory	91,874	Yes	552392	1865-1875 NM Terr. census substitutes exist. See Note 25.
32. New York	4,382,759	Yes	552397	NY 1865 & 1875 state censuses exist. See Note 26.
33. North Carolina	1,071,361	Yes	552620	
34. Ohio	2,665,260	Yes	552666	
35. Oregon	90,923	Yes	552784	OR Hist. Records Index – all censuses. See Note 27.
36. Pennsylvania	3,521,951	Yes	552788	
37. Rhode Island	217,353	Yes	552970	RI 1865 & 1875 state censuses exist. See Note 28.
38. South Carolina	705,606	Yes	552980	SC 1869 state census exists. See Note 29.
39. Tennessee	1,258,520	Yes	553012	
40. Texas	818,579	Yes	553072	TX tax lists exists for the period 1865-1875. See Note 30.
41. Utah Territory	86,786	Yes	25542	
42. Vermont	330,551	Yes	27758	VT vital records index exists for the period 1871-1908. See Note 31.
43. Virginia	1,225,163	Yes	29724	VA 1870 (State Copy) exists. See Note 32.
44. Washington Territory	23,955	Yes	295687	WA 1871 Terr. census exists. See Note 33.
45. West Virginia	442,014	Yes	338016	
46. Wisconsin	1,054,670	Yes	295688	WI 1865 & 1875 state censuses exist. See Note 34.
47. Wyoming Territory	9,118	Yes	34519	WY 1869 Terr. Census exists. See Note 35.

U.S. total: 38,558,371

Table 1870 Notes

1. See *1866 Alabama State Census,* included with *Alabama State Censuses, 1820-1866* [Online Database], digitized and indexed at the Ancestry.com website, see
www.ancestry.com/search/collections/alabamacensus.
See also, *1866 Alabama State Census Index* [Online Database], indexed at the FamilySearch.org website. This database has 243,781 records, see
https://familysearch.org/search/collection/1915987.
See also *1867 Alabama Voter Registrations* [Online Database], digitized and indexed at the Ancestry.com website, see
www.ancestry.com/search/collections/alabama1867voterreg.
See also *1870 Census Index to Selected Alabama Counties* [Microfilm], from a card index located at the ADAH, Montgomery, AL. This was a WPA project to index Alabama's state copy of the 1870 federal census. Not all counties have survived, and not all of those that did survive were included, but what was done is a valuable alternative index to Alabama in 1870, see the FHL catalog page:
www.familysearch.org/search/catalog/410510.

2. No federal census for 1870 was conducted for the Department of Alaska. But, local censuses exist for Sitka, St. Paul Island, Unalaska, and a few Aleutian Villages, part of the U.S. Government surveys of the seal and fishing industries. See *Alaska, Compiled Census and Census Substitutes Index, 1870-1907* [Online Database], indexed at the Ancestry.com website, see
www.ancestry.com/search/collections/akcen.

3. See *Arizona, Territorial Census Records, 1864-1882* [Online Database], includes AZ 1864 and 1866, the only two territory-wide censuses taken. The database adds county censuses for 1867, 1869, 1874, and 1882 with one or two counties in each. See
www.ancestry.com/search/collections/azterrcensus.

4. See *California Great Registers, 1866-1898* [Online Database], digitized and indexed at the Ancestry.com website. This database of county voters has 3,682,235 records, see
www.ancestry.com/search/collections/cagreatregisters.

5. See *1870 Colorado Territory Federal Census (Territory's Copy)* [Microfilm & Online Database], digitized and indexed, along with 160 other databases at the Colorado State Archives website, see
www.colorado.gov/pacific/archives/archives-search.

6. See *Florida State Censuses, 1867-1945* [Online Database], digitized and indexed at the Ancestry.com website. Includes the 1867 FL State Census (Hernando, Madison, Orange, and Santa Rosa counties only) and the 1875 FL State Census (Alachua county only). The state censuses for 1885, 1935, and 1945 are mostly complete. See
www.ancestry.com/search/collections/floridastatecen1867.

7. See *Georgia, Returns of Qualified Voters and Reconstruction Oath Books, 1867-1869* [Online Database], digitized and indexed at the Ancestry.com website. The returns provide: date of registration, name, number and page number of the county's registration oath book with the voter's oath of allegiance, race, time of residence in state, county, and precinct within a year, nativity by state or county, and remarks. This database has 390,373 records. See
www.ancestry.com/search/collections/ga1867votersoathbooks.

8. See *Internal Revenue Assessment Lists for the Territory of Idaho, 1867-1874* [Microfilm & Digital Capture], to access the digital images, see the FHL catalog page:
www.familysearch.org/search/catalog/577988.

9. See *Illinois State Census, 1865* [Online Database], digitized and indexed at the FamilySearch.org website. This database has 380,262 records, including Chicago, see
www.familysearch.org/search/collection/1803971.

10. See *Indiana State Digital Archives* [Online Database], with over 3 million names from death records, Institution Records, Military Records, Miscellaneous Historical Records, or Naturalization records, see www.indianadigitalarchives.org.

11. See *Iowa Censuses & Substitute Name Lists, 1833-2008* [Printed Book & eBook], includes a listing of a number of census substitutes for the period 1865-1875, see
www.familyrootspublishing.com/store/product_view.php?id=2827.

12. See *Kansas State Census Collection, 1855-1925* [Online Database], digitized and indexed at the Ancestry.com website. Includes the 1865 KS state census as part of a combined database with 8,238,557 records. See
www.ancestry.com/search/collections/ksstatecen.

13. See ***Kentucky Censuses & Substitute Name Lists, 1773-2000*** [Printed Book & eBook], includes a listing of a number of census substitutes for the period 1865-1875, see
www.familyrootspublishing.com/store/product_view.php?id=2927.

14. See ***Louisiana Censuses & Substitute Name Lists, 1679-2017*** [Printed Book & eBook], includes a listing of voter lists, tax lists, and other census substitutes for the period 1867-1875, see
www.familyrootspublishing.com/store/product_view.php?id=2939.

15. See ***Maine Census Indexes, 1850-1870*** [Microfilm], from the original records at the Maine Division of Vital Statistic, Augusta, ME. These card indexes to Maine's federal censuses for 1850, 1860, and 1870 were the first statewide indexes ever done by any state, executed by the Maine Vital Statistics Division in the early 1950s. See the FHL catalog page: https://familysearch.org/search/catalog/78880.

16. See ***Records of Massachusetts, State Census, 1865*** [Online Database], digitized and indexed at the FamilySearch.org website, see
www.familysearch.org/search/collection/1410399.

17. **Michigan Censuses & Substitute Names Lists** [Printed Book & eBook], includes details about the thirteen original county copies of the 1870 federal census, and several counties extant for the MI 1864 state census, as well as the 1874 state census, see
www.familyrootspublishing.com/store/product_view.php?id=3068.

18. See ***Minnesota State Census, 1865*** [Online Database], indexed at the FamilySearch.org website. Apparent family members are listed with surnames and given names, but since no relationships or ages are given, it is difficult to predict the family positions of a spouse or child, except by the order they are listed. This database has 246,591 records. See
https://familysearch.org/search/collection/1503054.
See also, ***Minnesota State Census, 1875*** [Online Database], indexed at the FamilySearch.org website. This database has 612,847 records. See
https://familysearch.org/search/collection/1503053.

19. See ***Mississippi, State and Territorial Census Collection, 1792-1866*** [Online Database], digitized and indexed at the Ancestry.com website. Includes the MS state census of 1866 (Bolivar, Holmes, Jasper, Leake, Simpson, Wayne, Claiborne, Issaquena, Jefferson, Marion, and Smith counties, MS. See
www.ancestry.com/search/collections/msstatecen.

20. See ***Missouri State and Territorial Census Records, 1732-1933*** [Online Database], digitized and indexed at the FamilySearch.org website. The 1876 state census was the most complete. The FamilySearch.org website has a list of census years and counties included, see
https://familysearch.org/search/collection/2075262.
ADDED NOTE: The FamilySearch list of counties does not agree with a list at the MO State Archives website. To see a table of extant MO state & territorial censuses, visit the MO State Archives Digital Heritage webpage. See
www.sos.mo.gov/records/archives/census/pages/territorial.

21. See ***Montana Censuses & Substitute Name Lists, 1860-2014*** [Printed Book & eBook], includes a listing of voter lists, tax lists, and other census substitutes for the period 1865-1875, see
www.familyrootspublishing.com/store/product_view.php?id=3261.

22. See ***Census Records of Nebraska*** [Online Database] Extant lists for 1854, 1855, 1856, 1865 (Territorial), and 1869 were extracted and published in *Nebraska & Midwest Genealogical Records* (N&MGR), a past publication of the Nebraska Genealogical Society. The USGenWeb site for Nebraska has put all of the census articles from the N&MGR online. See
www.usgennet.org/usa/ne/topic/resources/OLLibrary/Journals/NMGR/censindx.html.

23. See ***Nevada Directory 1868-1869*** [Online Database], indexed at the Ancestry.com website. Each index record includes: Given name, Surname, Location (Place in Nevada, includes "boards with"), and Occupation, see
www.ancestry.com/search/collections/nvdir1868. See also ***Nevada State Census, 1875*** [Online Database], indexed at the Ancestry.com website, the only state census ever taken in Nevada. Counties included: Churchill, Douglas, Elko, Esmeralda, Eureka, Landon, Lincoln, Lyon, Nye, Ormsby, Storey, Washoe, and White Pine counties. For each index entry, the Person's given name, Surname, Age, Sex, Race, Occupation, Place of birth, Status as head of household, and Place of residence is given. This database has 51,506 records:
www.ancestry.com/search/collections/nvcen1875.

24. See *New Jersey, State Census, 1865* [Online Database], digitized at the FamilySearch.org website. Census image contents: Name of head of household and number of males and females in each household by category: white, colored, native, foreign and children ages 5 to 16. For some places, the name of each person in the household is listed, or at least the name of the adults. Per NJ State Archives: "No records exist for the following counties: Cape May, Mercer, Morris, Ocean, Somerset and Warren. Several others are incomplete." This database has 2,488 images. See
https://familysearch.org/search/collection/2475024.

25. See *New Mexico Censuses & Substitute Name Lists, 1600-2010* [Printed Book & eBook], includes a listing of tax lists, probates, and other census substitutes for the period 1865-1875, see
www.familyrootspublishing.com/store/product_view.php?id=3267.

26. See *New York State Census, 1865* [Online Database], digitized and indexed at the FamilySearch.org website. The most detailed state census taken by any state, includes every name, relationships, etc. This database has 2,623,218 records. See
https://familysearch.org/search/collection/1491284.
This database also available at Ancestry.com, see www.ancestry.com/search/collections/general-7218. See also See *New York State Census, 1875* [Online Database], indexed at the FamilySearch.org website. This database has 3,125,090 records. See
https://familysearch.org/search/collection/1918735.
This database also available at Ancestry.com, see www.ancestry.com/search/collections/nystatecen1875.

27. See *Oregon Historical Records Index* [Online Database], indexed city / county / state records at the Oregon State Archives website. Included are the names from all territorial censuses, 1849-1859; all state censuses, 1865-1905; and all OR federal censuses 1850-1940. See
http://sos.oregon.gov/archives/Pages/records/genealogy/about-historical-records.aspx.

28. See *Rhode Island, State Censuses, 1865-1935* [Online Database], digitized and indexed at the Ancestry.com website. Includes 1865 and 1875 state censuses, see
www.ancestry.com/search/collections/ricensus.

29. See *South Carolina State Population Census Schedules, 1869* [Microfilm & Digital Capture], from the originals at the SC Dept. of Archives & History, 6 rolls, beginning with FHL film #2453275 (Abbeville-Beaufort counties). For access to the digital images, see the FHL catalog page:
www.familysearch.org/search/catalog/2047647.

30. See *1837-1910 Texas, County Tax Rolls* [Online Database], digitized and indexed from 424 microfilm rolls at the TX State Archives, with 4,575,333 records. see https://familysearch.org/search/collection/1827575.

31. See *General Index to Vital Records of Vermont, 1871-1908* [Microfilm & Digital Capture], includes births, deaths and marriages. 122 rolls, beginning with FHL film #540051 (Aabin, Louise – Albee, William Taylor). For access to the digital images, see the FHL catalog page:
https://familysearch.org/search/catalog/313352.

32. See *Virginia Inhabitants County by County in 1870* [Microfilm & Digital Capture], from the original state copy of the 1870 federal census at the VA State Library, Richmond. To access the digital images, see the FHL library catalog page:
www.familysearch.org/search/catalog/394443.

33. See *Washington State and Territorial Censuses, 1857-1892* [Online Database], digitized and indexed at the Ancestry.com website. There are number of counties extant from the 1871 territorial census. for details, see
www.ancestry.com/search/collections/washterrcen.

34. See *Wisconsin State Census, 1865* [Online Database], digitized and indexed at the FamilySearch.org website. Six counties only, 21,162 records, see
https://familysearch.org/search/collection/2058670.
See also *Wisconsin State Census, 1875* [Online Database], digitized and indexed at the FamilySearch.org website. Complete for all WI counties, 295,899 records, see
https://familysearch.org/search/collection/1443778.

35. See *Wyoming Territory 1869 Census* [Microfilm], from the originals at the WY State Archives, 1 roll, FHL film #2261365 (Entire territory), see the FHL catalog page:
www.familysearch.org/search/catalog/958477.

The U.S. in 1880. Note that the map shows the area of **Dakota Territory,** which was divided into North Dakota and South Dakota in 1889. Also shown is the so-called **"Indian Territory,"** the same area that became the State of Oklahoma in 1907. **Map Source:** Page 9, *Map Guide to the U.S. Federal Censuses, 1790-1920,* by William Thorndale and William Dollarhide.

Tenth Census of the United States - 1880

Description

Location of Original Records: In 1956, the National Archives transferred the original 1880 census volumes to state archives, state libraries, universities, or other repositories. These were the only population schedules handled in this way. For a review and state-by-state guide, see the GenealogyBlog article, *Repositories Holding 1880 Federal Census Originals*. See www.genealogyblog.com/?p=22977. The federal copies of the 1880 non-population schedules were also distributed to various non-federal repositories. For details, see Section 3 - Non-Population Schedules.

U.S. Population: 50.2 million.

1880 Census Legislative Act: 20 Stat. 473, 3 March 1879, as amended by 21 Stat. 75, 20 April 1880.

Responsibility / Schedules / Copies: The 1880 census was conducted under the direction of the Superintendent of the Census (Census Office, U.S. Department of the Interior). For the first time, the Census Office hired and managed their own door-to-door enumerators for each state/territory. **Schedules:** Population, Mortality, Agriculture, and Industry. **Mandated Copies:** Two (2) sets, an abbreviated version (Short Form) to the county courthouse, and the original, full version to the Census Office/Secretary of the Interior. NOTE: For details on the 1880 Short Form, see page 22.

Census day: 1 June 1880. All of the questions asked by the census taker were related to a person's age or place of residence as of the census day.

Time Allowed: field count due within 30 days, except communities over 10,000 in population due within two weeks.

1880 Jurisdictions: 47. Colorado was added to the Union in 1876, bringing the total to thirty-eight (38) states at the time of the 1880 census. Add the District of Columbia, and the territories of Arizona, Dakota, Idaho, Montana, New Mexico, Utah, Washington, and Wyoming Territory, for a total of forty-seven (47) jurisdictions. The population of the Department of Alaska was tallied, but no name list could be found. The Indian Territory was not enumerated. However, certain Indian Reservations were enumerated, e.g., Sisseton and Wahpeton Reservations, Dakota Territory.

Content of the Population Schedules. The census schedules listed the name of every person in a household with a census day of 1 June 1880. The categories included the following for each person: name and age as of the census day; month of birth if born during the year; relationship to the head of house; name of street and number of house; sex; color; birthplace; occupation; marital status; whether married within the previous year; whether temporarily or permanently disabled; whether crippled, maimed, or deformed; time unemployed during the census year; whether deaf, dumb, blind, or insane; whether able to read or write; birthplace of father and mother; and whether the person attended school within the previous year.

The 1880 Soundex Index. Soon after the creation of the Social Security Administration in 1935, clerical workers from the Works Progress Administration (WPA) were called upon to create an index to the 1880 census. A special system of coding names was created, called "Soundex." 3x5 index cards were prepared for each household which included children ten years of age or younger. The information on the Soundex index cards was extracted from the full census schedules and included the full name, age, and birthplace for a head of household, and included any other person living in the household, regardless of their age. Each head of household's surname was given a Soundex code, and the cards were then arranged in alphabetical order by the Soundex code number (A001-Z001) and after that by the first name of the head of the household. (See page 24 for more information about the 1880-1930 Soundex Indexes).

1880 Census Publications with Digital Images

Microfilm of Originals & Digital Capture: The National Archives film for the 1880 census is contained on 1,458 rolls, series T9, beginning with FHL film #1254001 (Alabama). The microfilm was digitized by FamilySearch International. For a list of roll numbers, contents, and access to the digital images of each roll, see the FHL catalog page:
https://familysearch.org/search/catalog/1417529. For the 1880 Soundex Index, see
https://familysearch.org/search/catalog/70449.

Online Searching – 1880 Census Indexes and Digital Images

The 1880 Census was digitized from the National Archives microfilm, indexed, and made available at the following websites:

- **Ancestry.com.** Subscription site, free database searching. Ancestry and FamilySearch share images and indexes. See
www.ancestry.com/search/collections/1880usfedcen.

- **FamilySearch.org.** Free database search, with images by FamilySearch, index by Ancestry. See
https://familysearch.org/search/collection/1417683.

- **MyHeritage.com.** A Family Tree subscription site. All U.S. Federal Census Records are available to subscribers with a data plan. See
www.myheritage.com/research/collection-10129/1880-united-states-federal-census.

- **Findmypast.com.** Monthly or annual subscriptions. Initial searches to U.S. Federal Censuses are free. See
www.findmypast.com/articles/search-the-1880-us-census.

- **GenealogyBank.com.** Subscription site. Initial searches to the U.S. Federal Censuses, 1790-1940 are free. www.genealogybank.com/explore/census/all.

- **HeritageQuestOnline-Subscribers Login.** This is a library subscription service. Check with your local library to see if they subscribe to the ProQuest & HeritageQuest databases. Many subscribing libraries allow their library card holders remote access. See
www.heritagequestonline.com/hqoweb/library/do/login.

Table 1880 – Statewide Census Publications

1880 Jurisdictions Included in Census	Population	Census Extant?	FHL Film Numbers Schedules	FHL Film Numbers Soundex	Comments, Census Substitutes, etc.
1. Alabama	1,262,505	Yes	1254001	445330	
- Alaska, Department of	33,426	--	--	--	AK 1878, 1880, & 1881 local censuses. See Note 1.
2. Arizona Territory	40,440	Yes	1254036	445404	AZ Great Registers exist for 1875-1885. See Note 2.
3. Arkansas	802,525	Yes	1254038	445406	
4. California	864,694	Yes	1254061	445454	CA Great Registers exist for 1878-1882. See Note 3.
5. Colorado	194,327	Yes	1254087	377999	See Table 1885. For CO State Archives search, see Note 4.
6. Connecticut	622,700	Yes	1254094	445488	
7. Dakota Territory	135,177	Yes	1254111	445513	See Table 1885.
8. Delaware	146,608	Yes	1254116	445519	
9. District of Columbia	177,624	Yes	1254121	445528	
10. Florida	269,493	Yes	1254125	445537	See Table 1885.
11. Georgia	1,542,180	Yes	1254133	445553	GA Tax Lists are good census substitutes. See Note 5.
12. Idaho Territory	32,610	Yes	1254173	378006	
13. Illinois	3,077,871	Yes	1254174	446678	
14. Indiana	1,978,301	Yes	1254263	446821	IN state digital archives databases, see Note 6.
15. Iowa	1,624,615	Yes	1254325	446919	See Table 1885.
16. Kansas	996,096	Yes	1254372	446997	See Table 1885.
17. Kentucky	1,648,690	Yes	1254401	447040	
18. Louisiana	939,943	Yes	1254447	447123	
19. Maine	648,936	Yes	1254475	447186	
20. Maryland	934,946	Yes	1254493	447215	
21. Massachusetts	1,783,085	Yes	1254549	447262	
22. Michigan	1,636,937	Yes	1254569	447332	See Table 1885. (Includes MI 1884 state census)
23. Minnesota	780,773	Yes	1254615	287547	See Table 1885.
24. Mississippi	1,131,597	Yes	1254639	287584	
25. Missouri	2,168,380	Yes	1254671	287653	St. Louis was enumerated twice.
26. Montana Territory	39,159	Yes	1254742	287767	
27. Nebraska	452,402	Yes	1254743	287769	See Table 1885.
28. Nevada	62,266	Yes	1254758	378008	
29. New Hampshire	346,991	Yes	1254760	287791	
30. New Jersey	1,131,116	Yes	1254770	287804	See Table 1885.
31. New Mexico Territory	119,565	Yes	1254802	287853	See Table 1885.
32. New York	5,082,871	Yes	1254805	287859	
33. North Carolina	1,399,750	Yes	1254950	448290	
34. Ohio	3,198,062	Yes	1254989	448369	
35. Oregon	174,768	Yes	1255080	448512	See Table 1885.
36. Pennsylvania	4,282,891	Yes	1255085	448520	
37. Rhode Island	276,531	Yes	1255209	448688	See Table 1885.
38. South Carolina	995,577	Yes	1255217	448699	
39. Tennessee	1,542,359	Yes	1255244	448755	
40. Texas	1,591,749	Yes	1255288	448841	
41. Utah Territory	143,963	Yes	1255335	378011	
42. Vermont	332,286	Yes	1255340	448918	VT vital records index exists for 1871-1908. See Note 7.
43. Virginia	1,512,565	Yes	1255351	448933	
44. Washington Territory	75,116	Yes	1255396	449015	See Table 1885.
45. West Virginia	618,457	Yes	1255399	449019	
46. Wisconsin	1,315,497	Yes	1255417	449051	See Table 1885.
47. Wyoming Territory	20,789	Yes	1255454	449101	

U.S. total: 50,189,209

1. See *Census of Unalaska and Aleutian Villages, Alaska, 1878* [Microfilm & Digital Capture], to access the digital images, see the FHL catalog page www.familysearch.org/search/catalog/214871. See also *Census of Sitka, Alaska Taken April 25, 1880* [Microfilm], see the FHL catalog page: www.familysearch.org/search/catalog/47626. See also *Sitka, Alaska, 1881 Census* [Microfilm], see the FHL catalog page: www.familysearch.org/search/catalog/627469.

2. See *Arizona Censuses & Substitute Name Lists, 1684-2008* [Printed Book & eBook], identifies countywide Great Registers (Voter lists) for most AZ counties, 1875-1885. See www.familyrootspublishing.com/store/product_view.php?id=2525.

3. See *California Great Registers, 1866-1898* [Online Database], digitized and indexed at the Ancestry.com website. Review the list of CA counties and years available, see www.ancestry.com/search/collections/cagreatregisters.

4. See *Historical Records Index – Colorado State Archives* [Online Database], digitized and indexed records from 160 state & county databases (vitals, probates, pensions, courts, etc.), see www.colorado.gov/pacific/archives/archives-search.

5. See *Georgia Property Tax Digests, 1793-1893* [Online Database]. This digitized and indexed database is the primary census substitute for all of Georgia, which had lost federal censuses for 1790, 1800, 1810, and 1890. Within this database of over 4.8 million records, a search can be done by the name of a taxpayer for the entire span of years. A more precise search can be done by county, see www.ancestry.com/search/collections/georgia1890proptaxdigests.

6. See *Indiana State Digital Archives* [Online Database], with over 3 million names from death records, Institution Records, Military Records, Miscellaneous Historical Records, or Naturalization records, see www.indianadigitalarchives.org.

7. See *General Index to Vital Records of Vermont, 1871-1908* [Microfilm & Digital Capture], includes births, deaths and marriages. 122 rolls, beginning with FHL film #540051 (Aabin, Louise – Albee, William Taylor). For access to the digital images, see the FHL catalog page:
https://familysearch.org/search/catalog/313352.

Selected Online Databases from the time of the 1880 Census

See *U.S., Evangelical Lutheran Church of America, Records, 1781-1969* [Online Database], digitized and indexed at the Ancestry.com website. Source: Births, Marriages, Deaths, ELCA, Chicago, IL. This collection contains images and an index to baptism, confirmation, marriage, and burial records from more than 2,000 Evangelical Lutheran Churches in America (ELCA) congregations. Search the indexes, or browse through the collection, organized by state, then city of a church. This database has 8,094,994 records. See www.ancestry.com/search/collections/elcabmd.

See *Headstones Provided for Deceased Union Civil War Veterans, 1861-1904* [Online Database], from the original records at the National Archives, digitized and indexed by Ancestry.com. The searchable digitized cards have the following for each soldier: Name, rank, company, and regiment; burial place (cemetery, town, county, state); grave number, if applicable; death date; name of contractor that supplied the headstone; and date of contract in which the headstone was provided. The card records are mostly for private cemeteries, see www.ancestry.com/search/collections/civilwarheadstones. This database is also available at the FamilySearch.org website, see www.familysearch.org/search/collection/1913388.

See *List of Pensioners on the Roll, January 1, 1883, Vols. 1-5* [Online Database], digitized and indexed at the Ancestry.com website. Includes the name of each pensioner, the cause for which pensioned, the post-office address, the rate of pension per month, and the date of original allowance. See www.ancestry.com/search/collections/flhmilitary_090312_090316.

The U.S. in 1885. There were a total of 14 states with 1885 state censuses: Colorado, Dakota Territory, Florida, Iowa, Kansas, Michigan (1884), Minnesota, Nebraska, New Jersey, New Mexico Territory, Oregon, Rhode Island, Washington Territory, and Wisconsin. Note that the map shows the so-called **"Indian Territory,"** the same area that became the State of Oklahoma in 1907. **Map Source:** Page 9, *Map Guide to the U.S. Federal Censuses, 1790-1920,* by William Thorndale and William Dollarhide.

State Censuses Taken in 1885

The 1890 federal census was mostly lost due to a 1921 fire in the Commerce Building in Washington, DC. To fill in the lost names, researchers need substitute name lists from the 1885-1895 period. There are many substitute name lists available, such as statewide tax lists, voter lists, etc. A recent publication has an annotated list of over 1,200 substitute name list databases from the period 1885-1895, see **Substitutes for the Lost 1890 Federal Census,** by William Dollarhide (publ. 2019, Family Roots Publishing Co., 103 pages). See www.familyrootspublishing.com/store/product_view.php?id=3577.

Perhaps the best substitutes are the state censuses taken five years before the 1890 disaster. A total of fourteen (14) states/territories conducted a state census in 1885. Five (5) of the states/territories had a census taken with federal assistance. The census act authorizing the 1880 census pledged the federal government to pay half the cost of a census taken by any state or territory in June or July 1885, if the format followed the same federal census form as 1880, and if a copy of all schedules were sent to Washington (Section 22, 20 Stat. 480, 3 March 1879). The five states/territories that took up the government's offer were as follows: 1) Colorado, 2) Dakota Territory, 3) Florida, 4) Nebraska, and 5) New Mexico Territory. These five were combined in a single printed index by the National Archives, with the title, *The 1885 Census*, see the FHL catalog page:
www.familysearch.org/search/catalog/2686600.

Another nine (9) states/territories conducted an 1885 state census on their own, all done without federal assistance. These nine were as follows:
1) Iowa, 2) Kansas, 3) Michigan (taken in 1884), 4) Minnesota, 5) New Jersey, 6) Oregon, 7) Rhode Island, 8) Washington Territory, and 9) Wisconsin.

The five (5) states/territories done with federal assistance all followed the format of the 1880 federal census form; but the nine (9) state censuses done without federal assistance were all conducted separately and with a design unique to that state/territory. Some list the names of the Heads of Household only; while others are an every-name listing similar to the federal layout.

There are some lost counties in the 1885 state censuses, but in general, they provide a good substitute for the lost 1890 census in 14 states.

Table 1885 – State Census Publications

States/Territories with an 1885 State Census	No. of Records or Images*	FHL Film No.	URL of Online Database or FHL catalog page for access to Digital Images
Taken with Federal Assistance:			
1. Colorado[1] - state copy	234,383	929067	www.familysearch.org/search/catalog/60816.
Colorado[1] - federal copy	195,979	498503-	www.familysearch.org/search/collection/1807096.
2. Dakota Territory North[2]	151,500	--	https://library.ndsu.edu/db/census.
Dakota Territory South[2]	76,472	1405268	www.familysearch.org/search/catalog/361027.
3. Florida[3] - federal copy	309,323	888962	www.familysearch.org/search/catalog/82520.
Florida[3] - state copy (lost)	--	--	
4. Nebraska[4] - federal copy	747,367	499529	https://familysearch.org/search/collection/1810728.
Nebraska[4] - state copy (lost)	--	--	
5. New MexicoTerr.[5] - state copy	100,000 +/-	16610	www.familysearch.org/search/catalog/179492.
New Mexico Terr.[5] - Fed. copy	798*	--	www.familysearch.org/search/collection/2110742.
Without Federal Assistance:			
1. Iowa	1,737,228	1021316	https://familysearch.org/search/collection/1803643.
2. Kansas	94,071*	975699	www.familysearch.org/search/collection/1825188
3. Michigan (1884)	62,000*	--	http://seekingmichigan.org/discover/state-census-1884-1894.
4. Minnesota	1,133,198	56733	https://familysearch.org/search/collection/1503044.
5. New Jersey	1,294,279	865499	www.familysearch.org/search/collection/1803972.
6. Oregon (Linn & Umatilla counties only)	--	--	Umatilla Co included in the Oregon Historical Records Index, see http://sos.oregon.gov/archives/Pages/records/aids-census_osa.aspx.
7. Rhode Island	321,999	953910	www.familysearch.org/search/collection/1794115.
8. Washington Territory	100,000 +/-	1841781	Indexed by county, part of the Washington State Archives – Digital Archives, see www.digitalarchives.wa.gov/Collections#RSID:3.
9. Wisconsin	407,138	1032695	https://familysearch.org/search/collection/1443713.

Table 1885 Notes:
1. Colorado's 1885 federal copy is missing Fremont and Garfield counties, while the state copy has Fremont, but is missing Garfield and eighteen other counties.

2. The Dakota Territory 1885 census survives for 17 ND counties, and 20 SD counties. No federal copy of the Dakota Territory 1885 exists. The National Archives included only the SD portion as part of their printed index.

3. Florida's state copy of the 1885 census was lost. The federal copy is missing 4 counties.

4. Nebraska's 1885 state copy was lost. The federal copy of the Nebraska 1885 is missing one county.

5. New Mexico Territory's federal copy of the 1885 census is complete for all counties. The territorial copy is missing 4 counties.

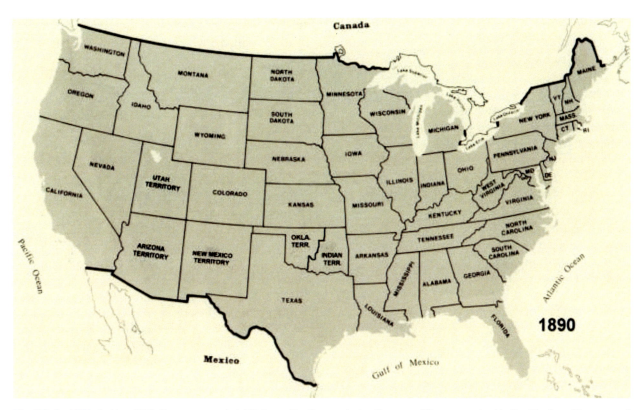

The U.S. in 1890. In May 1890, Congress created Oklahoma Territory, reducing the area of the unorganized Indian Territory. The areas of the two territories were merged in 1907 to become the State of Oklahoma. Idaho Territory became the state of Idaho on 3 July 1890, 3 days after the completion of the 1890 enumeration. And, Wyoming Territory became the state of Wyoming on 10 July 1890, 10 days after the 1890 enumeration. **Map Source:** Page 9, *Map Guide to the U.S. Federal Censuses, 1790-1920,* by William Thorndale and William Dollarhide.

Eleventh Census of the United States - 1890

Loss of the Original Records: The original 1890 census population schedules (the name lists) were involved in a 1921 fire that took place in the Commerce Building in Washington, DC. The fire was contained to the basement storage area that held the entire collection of the 1890 federal census originals (the only copy). Fragments of the schedules that survived the 1921 fire are together on one roll of microfilm, all indexed, listing 6,160 persons out of the entire 1890 population of 63 million people. More of the bound volumes may have been harmed by water damage during the attempts to put out the fire, than were actually burned to ashes. There was some controversy about the handling of the remaining schedules, but several years after the fire, Congress permitted the Census Bureau to destroy the damaged remnants.

U.S. Population: 63.0 million.

1890 Census Legislative Act: 26 Stat. 760, 1 March 1890.

Responsibility / Schedules / Copies: The 1890 census was conducted under the direction of the Superintendent of the Census (Census Office, U.S. Department of the Interior). **Schedules:** Population, Mortality, Agriculture, Manufactures, Indians, and Union Veterans. **Mandated Copies:** One copy, to the Census Office/Secretary of the Interior. Counties could buy a Short Form copy of their schedules at cost. NOTE: For details on the 1890 Short Form, see page 23.

Census day: 1 June 1890. All of the questions asked by the census taker were related to a person's age or place of residence as of the census day.

Time Allowed: field count due within 30 days, except communities over 10,000 in population, due within two weeks.

1890 Jurisdictions: 49. Between 1880 and 1890, six states were added to the Union: Montana, North Dakota, South Dakota, and Washington in 1889; Idaho and Wyoming in 1890, for a total of forty-four (44) states at the time of the 1890 census. Also enumerated: District of Columbia, Arizona Territory, New Mexico Territory, Oklahoma Territory, and Utah Territory, for a total of forty-nine (49) jurisdictions. Not enumerated: District of Alaska (statistics only), Indian Territory (some Indians were enumerated by tribe/nation), and Hawaii (not annexed to the U.S. until 1898).

Content of the Population Schedules. In 1890, the Census Office created a completely different method of recording the census enumeration, one that was unique to the 1890 census and never repeated. Up to 10 persons in one household were enumerated on both sides of one sheet of paper. The detailed information captured for every household was extensive, including the address of the house; the number of persons in the household; each individual by name; whether a soldier, sailor, or marine during the Civil War and whether Union or Confederate, or whether the widow of a veteran; relationship to head of family; race; sex; age; marital status; whether married during the previous year; if a mother, mother of how many children, and how many living; place of birth of the individual and his/her father and mother; if foreign born, how many years in the U.S.; whether naturalized or in the process of naturalization; a profession, trade, or occupation; the number of months unemployed during the previous year; ability to read and write; ability to speak English, if not, language or dialect spoken; whether suffering from an acute or chronic disease, if so, name of disease and length of time afflicted; whether defective in mind, sight, hearing, or speech, or whether crippled, maimed, or deformed, with the name of defect; whether a prisoner, convict, homeless child, or pauper; whether the home was rented or owned by the head or other member of the family, and whether it was mortgaged; whether a farmer, and if so, whether the farm was rented or owned; and if mortgaged, the post office address of the owner.

Microfilm of Originals & Digital Capture: The surviving fragments from the fire consist of a few names each from Perry Co Alabama, the District of Columbia, Muscogee Co Georgia, McDonough Co Illinois, Wright Co Minnesota, Hudson Co New Jersey, Westchester and Suffolk Co New York, Cleveland and Gaston Co North Carolina, Hamilton Co Ohio, Union Co South Dakota, and Ellis, Hood, Kaufman, Rusk and Trinity Co Texas. The remnants were filmed by the National Archives, 1962, Series M407, 6 rolls, beginning with FHL film #926497. To access the digital images, see the FHL catalog page:
https://familysearch.org/search/catalog/231212.

1890 Union Veterans and Widows Schedules. In addition to the main population schedules, a special census listing was extracted from the 1890 population schedules for surviving Union soldiers, sailors, and marines (or their widows), and a portion of that special census survives. Census losses: Of the forty-nine (49) jurisdictions (states, territories, districts) in place in 1890, sixteen (16) of the Union Veterans Schedules jurisdictions were lost. The losses were alphabetically from Alabama through Kansas, and about half of the names for Kentucky. Surviving state listings begin with the partial list for Kentucky and are complete from Louisiana through Wyoming. Microfilm: *1890 Special Schedules Enumerating Union Veterans, and Widows of Union Veterans of the Civil War,* microfilmed on 118 rolls, series M123, beginning with FHL film #338160 (Kentucky). For access to the digital images of each roll, see the FHL catalog page:
https://familysearch.org/search/catalog/230777.

Content of the 1890 Veterans Schedules. The 1890 veterans format had 12 numbered columns, with space for up to 12 veterans per page. The top half of the format was as follows:
1. House No. (from Population Schedule)
2. Family No. (from Population Schedule)
3. Names of Surviving Soldiers, Sailors, Marines, & Widows. (This column had 2 lines: a widow's name, if applicable, on the top line, and a veteran's name on the bottom line).
4. Rank.
5. Company.
6. Name of Regiment or Vessel.
7. Date of Enlistment (day/month/year)
8. Date of Discharge (day/month/year)
9. Length of Service (Years/Months/Days)

The bottom half of the format was as follows:
10. Post Office Address.
11. Disability Incurred.
12. Remarks.

1890 Veterans Online Images and Indexes. This database has 990,276 records, see www.ancestry.com/search/collections/1890veterans. For the FamilySearch.org version, see www.familysearch.org/search/collection/1877095.

Online Searching – 1890 Census Indexes and Digital Images

The surviving fragments of the 1890 Census population schedules were digitized from the National Archives microfilm, indexed, and made available at the following websites:

- **Ancestry.com.** Subscription site, free database searching. Ancestry and FamilySearch share images and indexes. See www.ancestry.com/search/collections/1890orgcen.

- **FamilySearch.org.** Free database search, with images by FamilySearch, index by Ancestry. See https://familysearch.org/search/collection/1610551.

- **MyHeritage.com.** A Family Tree subscription site. All U.S. Federal Census Records are available to subscribers with a data plan. See www.myheritage.com/research/collection-10130/1890-united-states-federal-census.

- **GenealogyBank.com.** Subscription site. Initial searches to the U.S. Federal Censuses, 1790-1940 are free. www.genealogybank.com/explore/census/all.

- **HeritageQuestOnline-Subscribers Login.** This is a library subscription service. Check with your local library to see if they subscribe to the ProQuest & HeritageQuest databases. Many subscribing libraries allow their library card holders remote access. See www.heritagequestonline.com/hqoweb/library/do/login.

Related 1890 Resources Available

- *Censuses & Substitute Name Lists,* 52 books, Alabama to Wyoming, plus DC & U.S. Territories, publ. Family Roots Publ. Co., Orting, WA 2017-2018, www.familyrootspublishing.com/store/category.php?cat=3347.

- *Substitutes for the Lost 1890 Federal Census,* by William Dollarhide, publ. Family Roots Publ. Co., Orting, WA, 2019, 103 pages. This book continues the  concept of the 52 books, *Censuses & Substitute Name Lists,* with bibliographic listings of databases with large numbers of names/events during the period 1885 to 1895. This book is the most comprehensive review of substitutes for the lost 1890 Census ever published, e.g., there are over 1,200 nationwide and statewide databases identified. Also, this new guidebook is abundantly and colorfully illustrated with actual database images, screen prints, and maps. See www.familyrootspublishing.com/store/product_view.php?id=3577.

- *First in the Path of the Firemen: The Fate of the 1890 Population Census, Part 1,* in *Prologue Magazine,* an online publication of the National Archives. See www.archives.gov/publications/prologue/1996/spring/1890-census-1.html.

- *First in the Path of the Firemen: The Fate of the 1890 Population Census, Part 2.* in *Prologue Magazine,* an online publication of the National Archives. See www.archives.gov/publications/prologue/1996/spring/1890-census-2.html.

Table 5: 1884-1896 State Censuses: Substitutes for the Lost 1890 Census

State	Year a Terr.	Year a State	1884	1885	1890	1891	1892	1894	1895	1896	Notes
Alabama	1817	1819									
Alaska	1912	1959									
Arizona	1863	1912									
Arkansas	1819	1836									
California	—	1850									
Colorado	**1861**	**1876**		●							
Connecticut	—	1788									
Delaware	—	1787									
Distr. of Columbia	—	1791									
Florida	**1822**	**1845**		●					●		
Georgia	—	1788									
Hawaii	**1900**	**1959**			●				●		Kingdom of Hawaii
Idaho	1863	1890									
Illinois	1809	1818									
Indiana	1800	1816									
Iowa	**1838**	**1846**		●					●		
Kansas	**1854**	**1861**		●					●		
Kentucky	—	1791									
Louisiana	1809	1812									
Maine	—	1820									
Maryland	—	1788									
Massachusetts	—	1788									
Michigan	**1805**	**1837**	●					●			
Minnesota	**1849**	**1858**		●					●		
Mississippi	1798	1817									
Missouri	1805	1821									
Montana	1864	1889									
Nebraska	**1854**	**1867**		●							
Nevada	1861	1864									
New Hampshire	—	1788									
New Jersey	**—**	**1787**		●					●		
New Mexico	**1850**	**1912**		●							
New York	**—**	**1788**					●				
North Carolina	—	1789									
North Dakota	**1861**	**1889**		●							1885 Dakota Terr. - 17 cos.
Ohio	1787	1803									
Oklahoma	**1890**	**1907**			●						1890 Oklahoma Territory
Indian Territory	**--**	**--**			●						1890 Cherokee Nation
Oregon	**1848**	**1859**		●					●		1885 2 Counties. 1895 4 Cos.
Pennsylvania	—	1787									
Rhode Island	**—**	**1790**		●							
South Carolina	—	1788									
South Dakota	**1861**	**1889**		●					●		1885 Dakota Terr. - 20 Cos
Tennessee	**1790**	**1796**				●					
Texas	—	1845									
Utah	1850	1896									
Vermont	—	1791									
Virginia	—	1788									
Washington	**1853**	**1889**		●							
West Virginia	—	1863									
Wisconsin	**1836**	**1848**		●					●		
Wyoming	1868	1890									
Total Number of States			1	14	3	1	1	1	8	1	
			1884	1885	1890	1891	1892	1894	1895	1896	

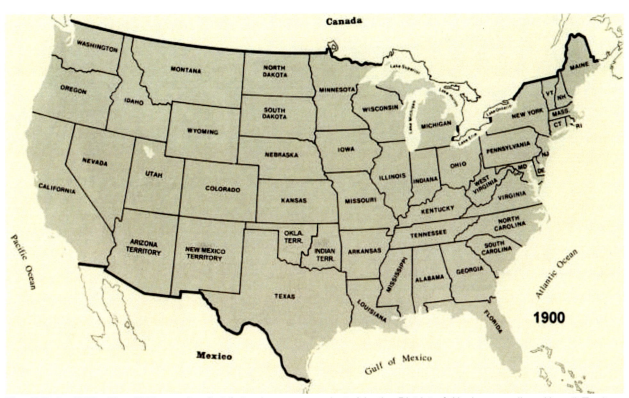

The U.S. in 1900. The 1900 was the first federal census conducted in the District of Alaska as well as Hawaii Territory (neither are shown on the map). The areas of Oklahoma Territory and Indian Territory were merged in 1907 to become the state of Oklahoma. Both Arizona Territory and New Mexico Territory became states in 1912. **Map Source:** Page 9, *Map Guide to the U.S. Federal Censuses, 1790-1920,* by William Thorndale and William Dollarhide.

Twelfth Census of the United States - 1900

Destruction of the Original Records: By the mid 1940s, the early original census schedules from 1790 through 1880 had already been transferred from the Census Bureau to the National Archives; but the original schedules from 1900 through 1940 were still stored on several floors of the Commerce Building.

To free up space, the Census Bureau undertook a major project to microfilm the census schedules of 1900 through 1940; and when the microfilming was complete, the original census schedules were destroyed. This was all done with the permission of Congress, who funded the microfilming project, and authorized the destruction of the originals.

U.S. Population: 76.2 million.

1900 Census Legislative Act: 30 Stat. 1014, 3 March 1899.

Responsibility / Schedules / Copies: The 1900 census was conducted under the direction of the Director of the Census (Census Office, U.S. Department of the Interior). **Schedules:** Population, Mortality, Agriculture, Manufactures, Indians, and Military & Naval. **Mandated Copies:** One copy, to the Census Office/Secretary of the Interior. Counties could buy a copy of their schedules at cost. (None did).

Census day: 1 June 1900. All of the questions asked by the census taker were related to a person's age or place of residence as of the census day.

Time Allowed: field count due within 30 days, except communities over 10,000 in population, due within two weeks.

1900 Jurisdictions: 52. Utah was admitted to the Union in 1896, bringing the number to forty-five stars on the U.S. Flag. Seven more jurisdictions were enumerated: the District of Alaska, the District of Columbia, Arizona Territory, Hawaii Territory, Indian Territory, New Mexico Territory, and Oklahoma Territory. American Indians were enumerated within their tribal affiliations on *Indian Population* schedules. Non-Indians living within the bounds of any Indian Nation/Reservation were enumerated on standard *Schedule 1 - Population* forms.

Content of the Population Schedules. The 1900 census schedules listed every person in a household and included a name; relationship to the head of house; name of street and number of house; sex; color; the person's age, plus the exact month and year of birth; birthplace; if female, number of children, and number of children alive in 1900; occupation; marital status, and if married, number of years; number of years in the U.S.; birthplace of father and mother; whether parents were of foreign birth; whether able to read or write; whether a person could speak English; and whether the person attended school the previous year.

The 1900 Soundex Index. Soon after the creation of the Social Security Administration in 1935, clerical workers from the Works Progress Administration (WPA) were called upon to create an index to the 1900 census. A special system of coding names was created, called "Soundex." 3x5 index cards were prepared for each household in the U.S. The information on the Soundex index cards was extracted from the full census schedules and included the full name, age, and birthplace for a head of household, and included any other person living in the household, regardless of their age. Each head of household's surname was given a Soundex code, and the cards were then arranged in alphabetical order by the Soundex code number (A001-Z001) and after that by the first name of the head of the household. (See page 24 for more information about the 1880-1930 Soundex Indexes).

1900 Census Publications with Digital Images

Microfilm of Originals & Digital Capture: The National Archives film for the 1900 census is contained on 1,854 rolls, series T623, beginning with FHL film #1240001 (Alabama). The microfilm was digitized by FamilySearch International. For a list of roll numbers, contents, and access to the digital images of each roll, see the FHL catalog page: https://familysearch.org/search/catalog/26038. At this writing, the digitizing project for the **1900 Soundex** microfilm was still in progress. Check the catalog list for the rolls digitized and available to date, see https://familysearch.org/search/catalog/33540.

Online Searching – 1900 Census Indexes and Digital Images

The 1900 Census was digitized from the National Archives microfilm, indexed, and made available at the following websites:

• **Ancestry.com.** Subscription site, free database searching. Ancestry and FamilySearch share images and indexes. See
www.ancestry.com/search/collections/1900usfedcen.

• **FamilySearch.org.** Free database search, with images by FamilySearch, index by Ancestry. See www.familysearch.org/search/collection/1325221.

• **MyHeritage.com.** A Family Tree subscription site. All U.S. Federal Census Records are available to subscribers with a data plan. See www.myheritage.com/research/collection-10131/1900-united-states-federal-census.

• **Findmypast.com.** Monthly or annual subscriptions. Initial searches to U.S. Federal Censuses are free. See https://search.findmypast.com/search-world-Records/us-census-1900.

• **GenealogyBank.com.** Subscription site. Initial searches to the U.S. Federal Censuses, 1790-1940 are free. www.genealogybank.com/explore/census/all.

• **HeritageQuestOnline-Subscribers Login.** This is a library subscription service. Check with your local library to see if they subscribe to the ProQuest & HeritageQuest databases. Many subscribing libraries allow their library card holders remote access. See www.heritagequestonline.com/hqoweb/library/do/login.

Twelfth Census of the U.S. - 1900

Table 1900 – Statewide Census Publications

1900 Jurisdictions Included in Census	Population	Census Extant?	FHL Film Numbers Schedules	Soundex	Comments, Census Substitutes, etc.
1. Alabama	1,828,697	Yes	1240001	1241855	1899 Confederate Veterans lists exist. See Note 1.
2. Alaska, District of	63,592	Yes	1241828	1242032	Names of Alaska-Yukon gold rush people exists. See Note 2.
3. Arizona Territory	122,931	Yes	1240045	1242047	
4. Arkansas	1,311,564	Yes	1240049	1242069	AR Confederate pension records exist for 1901-1929. See Note 3.
5. California	1,485,053	Yes	1240081	1242202	CA Great Registers (Voter Lists) exist for 1900-1968. See Note 4.
6. Colorado	539,700	Yes	1240117	1242399	
7. Connecticut	908,420	Yes	1240131	1242468	
8. Delaware	184,735	Yes	1240153	1242574	
9. District of Columbia	278,718	Yes	1240158	1242595	
10. Florida	528,542	Yes	1240165	1242637	
11. Georgia	2,216,331	Yes	1241828	1242699	
12. Hawaii Territory	154,001	Yes	1241833	1242932	HI Kingdom 1896 census exists. See Note 5.
13. Idaho	161,772	Yes	1240231	1242913	
14. Illinois	4,821,550	Yes	1240235	1242962	
15. Indiana	2,516,462	Yes	1240357	1243437	
16. Iowa	2,231,853	Yes	1240415	1243691	IA 1895 state census exists. See Note 6.
17. Kansas	1,470,495	Yes	1240469	1243904	KS 1895 state census exists. See Note 7.
18. Kentucky	2,147,174	Yes	1240506	1244052	
19. Louisiana	1,381,625	Yes	1240556	1244251	
20. Maine	694,466	Yes	1240587	1244397	
21. Maryland	1,188,044	Yes	1240604	1244477	
22. Massachusetts	2,805,346	Yes	1240631	1244604	
23. Michigan	2,420,982	Yes	1240698	1244920	MI 1894 state census exists. See Note 8.
24. Minnesota	1,751,394	Yes	1240756	1245177	MN 1895 state census exists. See Note 9.
25. Mississippi	1,551,270	Yes	1240799	1245357	
26. Missouri	3,106,665	Yes	1240836	1245513	
27. Montana	243,329	Yes	1240909	1245812	
28. Nebraska	1,066,300	Yes	1240916	1245852	
29. Nevada	42,335	Yes	1240943	1245959	
30. New Hampshire	411,588	Yes	1240944	1245966	
31. New Jersey	1,883,669	Yes	1240953	1246018	NJ 1895 state census exists. See Note 10.
32. New Mexico Territory	195,310	Yes	1240999	1246222	
33. New York	7,268,894	Yes	1241004	1246245	NY 1905 state census exists. See Note 11.
34. North Carolina	1,896,810	Yes	1241180	1247013	
35. North Dakota	319,146	Yes	1241226	1247180	
36. Ohio	4,157,545	Yes	1241235	1247216	
37. Oklahoma Territory	790,391	Yes	1241335	1247615	
38. Oregon	413,536	Yes	1241345	1247657	
39. Pennsylvania	6,302,115	Yes	1241354	1247711	
40. Rhode Island	428,556	Yes	1241504	1248321	
41. South Carolina	1,340,316	Yes	1241514	1248370	
42. South Dakota	401,570	Yes	1241546	1248494	SD 1895 state census exists. See Note 12.
43. Tennessee	2,020,616	Yes	1241557	1248538	
44. Texas	3,048,710	Yes	1241607	1248726	
45. Utah	276,749	Yes	1241682	1249012	
46. Vermont	343,641	Yes	1241689	1249041	
47. Virginia	1,854,184	Yes	1241697	1249082	
48. Washington	518,103	Yes	1241741	1249256	
49. West Virginia	958,800	Yes	1241755	1249325	
50. Wisconsin	2,069,042	Yes	1241777	1249418	WI 1895 & 1905 state censuses exist. See Note 13.
51. Wyoming	92,631	Yes	1241826	1249607	
52. Indian Territory	350,000 +/-	Yes	1241813	1249653	Includes all Indian Nations of the Indian Territory. See Note 14.
- Military and Naval	200,000 +/-	Yes	1241838	1249622	Includes participants in the Filipino-American War. See Note 15.

U.S. Total: 76,212,168

Table 1900 Notes:

1. See *Alabama Confederate Pensions and Service Records* [Online Database], includes 1899 vets added due to a new law extending pensions to all confederate veterans living in Alabama. This database has 1,929,298 records, see www.ancestry.com/search/collections/31335_alconfedpension.

2. See The *Alaska-Yukon Gold Book: A Roster of the Progressive Men and Women Who Were the Argonauts of the Klondike Gold Stampede (1897-1900)* [Printed Book & Microfilm], see the FHL catalog page: www.familysearch.org/search/catalog/254555.

3. See *Arkansas Confederate Pensions, 1901-1929* [Online Database], digitized at the FamilySearch website. Images of applications for pension (in alphabetical order) filed by Confederate veterans and widows living in the state of Arkansas. This database has 159,626 images. See www.familysearch.org/search/collection/1837922.
This database is also available at the Ancestry.com website. See www.ancestry.com/search/collections/fs1arconfederatepensions.

4. See *California Voter Registrations 1900-1968* [Online Database], digitized and indexed at the Ancestry.com website with 67.3 million records, see www.ancestry.com/search/collections/cavoterrosetta.

5. See *Kingdom of Hawaii Census Records, 1878-1896* [Microfilm & Digital Capture], from originals at the Archives of Hawaii, Honolulu. Includes censuses taken in 1878, 1890, and 1896, see www.familysearch.org/search/catalog/421797.

6. See *Iowa, State Census Collection, 1836-1925* [Online Database], digitized and indexed at the Ancestry.com website. Includes IA 1895 state census, www.ancestry.com/search/collections/iastatecen.

7. See *Kansas State Census Collection, 1855-1925* [Online Database], digitized and indexed at the Ancestry.com website. Includes the 1895 KS state census, see www.ancestry.com/search/collections/ksstatecen.

See also *1895 Kansas State Census* [Online Database], indexed at the KS Hist. Society website, see www.kshs.org/p/kansas-censuses-1855-1930/10961.

8. See *Michigan State Census, 1884-1894* [Online Database], indexed at the *Seeking Michigan* website: http://seekingmichigan.org/discover/state-census-1884-1894.

9. See *Minnesota State Census, 1895* [Online Database], indexed at the FamilySearch.org website. This database has 1,570,739 records. See https://familysearch.org/search/collection/1503031.

10. See *New Jersey State Census, 1895* [Online Database], indexed at the Ancestry.com website, with 1,560,521 records, see www.ancestry.com/search/collections/njstatecen.

11. See *New York State Census, 1905* [Online Database], indexed at the FamilySearch.org website. This database has 7.5 million records, see https://familysearch.org/search/collection/1463113.

12. See *South Dakota State Census, 1895* [Online Database], digitized and indexed at the Ancestry.com website. This database has 21,007 records, see www.ancestry.com/search/collections/sd1895.

14. *Wisconsin, State Censuses, 1895 and 1905* [Online Database], indexed at the Ancestry.com website. This database has 2,690,489 records. See www.ancestry.com/search/collections/wistatecen.

14. **Indian Territory.** The 1900 populations recorded in the Indian Territory included Indians, listed by name on the *Indian Population* form; as well as non-Indians using the standard *Schedule 1 – Population* form. The microfilm/digital images containing the Indian Nations of the Indian Territory are organized in this order: Cherokee, Chickasaw, Choctaw, Creek, Peoria, Quapaw, Seneca, Wyandotte, Seminole, Modoc, Ottawa, and Shawnee Nations.

15. **Military and Naval** personnel on duty outside of the U.S. were enumerated on *Military and Naval Population* forms. Interspersed are the standard *Schedule 1 – Population* forms for civilians living at a foreign military post. A large number of the persons listed were participants in the Filipino-American War (1899-1902).

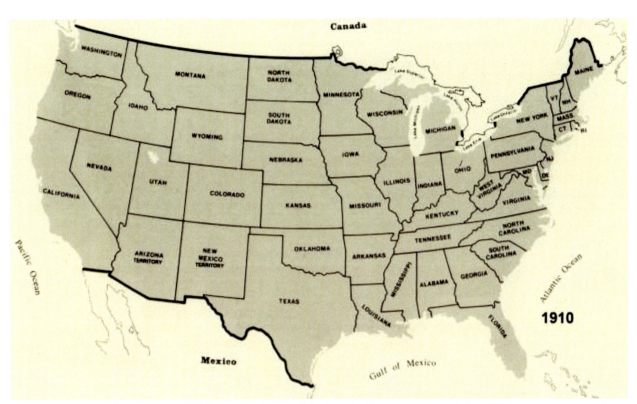

The U.S. in 1910. The areas of Oklahoma Territory and Indian Territory were merged in 1907 to become the state of Oklahoma. Jurisdictions enumerated in 1910 but not shown on the map: the District of Alaska, Hawaii Territory, and the Territory of Puerto Rico. **Map Source:** Page 9, *Map Guide to the U.S. Federal Censuses, 1790-1920.*

Thirteenth Census of the United States - 1910

Destruction of the Original Records: By the mid 1940s, the original census schedules from 1790 through 1880 had already been transferred from the Census Bureau to the National Archives; but the original schedules from 1900 through 1940 were still stored on several floors of the Commerce Building.

To free up space, the Census Bureau undertook a major project to microfilm the census schedules of 1900 through 1940; and when the microfilming was complete, the original census schedules were destroyed. This was all done with the permission of Congress, who funded the microfilming project, and authorized the destruction of the originals.

U.S. Population: 92.2 million.

1910 Census Legislative Act: 36 Stat. 1, 2 July 1909.

Responsibility / Schedules / Copies: The 1910 census was conducted under the direction of the Director of the Census (Census Bureau, U.S. Department of Commerce and Labor). **Schedules:** Population, Agriculture, Manufactures, and Military & Naval. **Mandated Copies:** One copy, to the Director of the Census. Counties could buy a copy of their schedules at cost. (None did).

Census day: 15 April 1910. All of the questions asked by the census taker were related to a person's age or place of residence as of the census day.

Time Allowed: field count due within 30 days, except communities over 5,000 in population, due within two weeks.

1910 Jurisdictions: 52. The areas of Oklahoma Territory and Indian Territory were merged in 1907 to become the state of Oklahoma – the 46th state in the Union. Also enumerated in 1910 were the District of Alaska, District of Columbia; and the territories of Arizona, Hawaii, New Mexico, and Puerto Rico.

Content of the Population Schedules. The 1910 census schedules listed every person in a household and included the name of a street, house number; and the name and age of each person; relationship to the head of house; sex; color; if female, the number of children, and number of children still living in 1910; marital status, and if married, number of years; year of immigration to the U.S.; whether a naturalized citizen, alien, or papers pending; language spoken; trade or profession, type of business, and whether an employee, employer, or working on one's own account; whether out of work, and if so, the number weeks out; birthplace of father and mother; whether able to read or write; whether the person attended school within the previous year; whether a person owned or rented a house; whether the house was mortgaged or mortgage free; whether a farm or a home; whether the person was a veteran; and whether the person was blind or deaf.

1910 Soundex & Miracode Indexes. The 1910 Soundex/Miracode indexes were compiled in 1962 for twenty-one (21) states by the staff of the Census Age Search section of the Bureau of the Census. The Soundex indexes were done on hand-entered index cards, similar to all of the other Soundex indexes; while the Miracode indexes were done using computers. The two systems are identical except for the citation to a page number (Miracode) or to a house number (Soundex).

1910 Soundex States: Alabama, Georgia, Louisiana (except Shreveport and New Orleans), Mississippi, South Carolina, Tennessee, and Texas.

1910 Miracode States: Arkansas, California, Florida, Illinois, Kansas, Kentucky, Louisiana (Shreveport and New Orleans only), Michigan, Missouri, North Carolina, Ohio, Oklahoma, Pennsylvania, Virginia, and West Virginia.

1910 Census Publications with Digital Images

Microfilm of Originals & Digital Capture: The National Archives film for the 1910 census is contained on 1,784 rolls, series T624, beginning with FHL film #1374014 (Alabama). The microfilm was digitized by FamilySearch International. For a list of roll numbers, contents, and access to the digital images of each roll, see the FHL catalog page: https://familysearch.org/search/catalog/297155. At this writing, the digitizing project for the **1910 Soundex & Miracode** microfilm for all 21 states was still in progress. Check the catalog list for the rolls digitized and available to date, see
https://familysearch.org/search/catalog/297271.

Online Searching – 1910 Census Indexes and Digital Images

The 1910 Census was digitized from the National Archives microfilm, indexed, and made available at the following websites:

- **Ancestry.com.** Subscription site, free database searching. Ancestry and FamilySearch share images and indexes. See
www.ancestry.com/search/collections/1910uscenindex.

- **FamilySearch.org.** Free database search, with images by FamilySearch, index by Ancestry. See
https://familysearch.org/search/collection/1727033.

- **MyHeritage.com.** A Family Tree subscription site. All U.S. Federal Census Records are available to subscribers with a data plan. See
www.myheritage.com/research/collection-10132/1910-united-states-federal-census.

- **Findmypast.com.** Monthly or annual subscriptions. Initial searches to U.S. Federal Censuses are free. See
www.findmypast.com/articles/search-the-1910-us-census.

- **GenealogyBank.com.** Subscription site. Initial searches to the U.S. Federal Censuses, 1790-1940 are free. www.genealogybank.com/explore/census/all.

- **HeritageQuestOnline-Subscribers Login.** This is a library subscription service. Check with your local library to see if they subscribe to the ProQuest & HeritageQuest databases. Many subscribing libraries allow their library card holders remote access. See
www.heritagequestonline.com/hqoweb/library/do/login.

Thirteenth Census of the U.S. - 1910

Table 1910 – Statewide Census Publications

1910 Jurisdictions Included in Census	Population	Census Extant?	FHL Film Numbers Schedules	Soundex Miracode*	Comments, Census Substitutes, etc.
1. Alabama	2,138,093	Yes	1374014	1369119	AL 1907 census of Confederate soldiers exists. See Note 1.
2. Alaska, District of	64,356	Yes	1375761	--	
3. Arizona Territory	204,354	Yes	1374051	--	
4. Arkansas	1,574,449	Yes	1374056	1369141*	
5. California	2,377,549	Yes	1374082	1369280*	CA Great Registers (Voter Lists) exist for 1900-1968. See Note 2.
6. Colorado	799,024	Yes	1374125	--	
7. Connecticut	1,114,756	Yes	1374140	--	
8. Delaware	202,322	Yes	1374158	--	
9. District of Columbia	331,069	Yes	1374162	--	
10. Florida	752,619	Yes	1374169	1369552*	
11. Georgia	2,609,121	Yes	1374183	1369784	
12. Hawaii Territory	191,874	Yes	1375764	--	Midway Island was included with Honolulu Co HI
13. Idaho	325,594	Yes	1374234	--	
14. Illinois	5,638,591	Yes	1374242	1369810*	
15. Indiana	2,700,876	Yes	1374351	--	
16. Iowa	2,224,771	Yes	1374403	--	IA 1905 & 1915 state censuses exist. See Note 3.
17. Kansas	1,690,949	Yes	1374444	1369141*	KS 1905 & 1915 state censuses exist. See Note 4.
18. Kentucky	2,289,905	Yes	1374475	1370446*	
19. Louisiana	1,656,388	Yes	1374520	1370718*	LA (Soundex) except New Orleans & Shreveport (Miracode*)
20. Maine	742,371	Yes	1374549	--	
21. Maryland	1,295,346	Yes	1374562	--	
22. Massachusetts	3,366,416	Yes	1374584	--	
23. Michigan	2,810,173	Yes	1374647	1370772*	
24. Minnesota	2,075,708	Yes	1374702	--	MN 1905 state census exists. See Note 5.
25. Mississippi	1,797,114	Yes	1374744	1371025	
26. Missouri	3,293,335	Yes	1374779	1371143*	
27. Montana	376,053	Yes	1374842	--	
28. Nebraska	1,192,214	Yes	1374851	--	
29. Nevada	81,875	Yes	1374871	--	
30. New Hampshire	430,572	Yes	1374873	--	
31. New Jersey	2,537,167	Yes	1374880	--	NJ 1905 & 1915 state censuses exist. See Note 6.
32. New Mexico Territory	327,301	Yes	1374926	--	
33. New York	9,113,614	Yes	1374933	--	NY 1905 & 1915 state censuses exist. See Note 7.
34. North Carolina	2,206,287	Yes	1375108	1371428*	
35. North Dakota	577,056	Yes	1375151	--	ND 1915 state census exists. See Note 8.
36. Ohio	4,767,121	Yes	1375163	1371606*	
37. Oklahoma	1,657,155	Yes	1375255	1372024*	OK Terr. 1907 Census exists, Seminole Co only. See Note 9.
38. Oregon	672,765	Yes	1375291	--	
39. Pennsylvania	7,665,111	Yes	1375305	1372167*	
40. Puerto Rico Territory	1,118,012	Yes	1375769	--	Population Schedules in Spanish
41. Rhode Island	542,610	Yes	1375449	--	RI 1905 & 1915 state censuses exist. See Note 10.
42. South Carolina	1,515,400	Yes	1375458	1372855	SC State Archives Online Index exists. See Note 11.
43. South Dakota	583,888	Yes	1375488	--	SD 1905 & 1915 state censuses exist. See Note 12.
44. Tennessee	2,184,789	Yes	1375503	1373059	
45. Texas	3,896,542	Yes	1375540	1373090	
46. Utah	373,351	Yes	1375615	--	
47. Vermont	355,956	Yes	1375625	--	
48. Virginia	2,061,612	Yes	1375632	1373352*	
49. Washington	1,141,990	Yes	1375666	--	
50. West Virginia	1,221,119	Yes	1375689	1373535*	
51. Wisconsin	2,333,860	Yes	1375713	--	WI 1905 state census exists. See Note 13.
52. Wyoming	145,965	Yes	1375758	--	
- Military and Naval	35,000 +/-	Yes	1375797	--	Organized by Philippines, Hospitals, Ships, and Stations.

U.S. Total: 92,228,496

Table 1910 Notes:

1. See *Alabama, Census of Confederate Veterans, 1907, 1921, 1927* [Online Database], digitized at the FamilySearch.org website. Any indexes were digitized along with the records. This database has 13,710 images, see
https://familysearch.org/search/collection/2487274.

2. See *California Voter Registrations 1900-1968* [Online Database], digitized and indexed at the Ancestry.com website with 67.3 million records, see
www.ancestry.com/search/collections/cavoterrosetta.

3. *Iowa, State Census, 1905* [Online Database], digitized and indexed at the FamilySearch.org website. Each individual was recorded on a single card which includes name, age, and place of birth. This database has 2,171,125 records. See
https://familysearch.org/search/collection/2126961.
See also *Iowa State Census, 1915* [Online Database], digitized and indexed at the FamilySearch.org website. This database has 2,574,691 records. See
www.familysearch.org/search/collection/2240483.

4. See *Kansas State Census Collection, 1855-1925* [Online Database], digitized and indexed at the Ancestry.com website. Included in this collection are the 1905 and 1915 KS state censuses, see
www.ancestry.com/search/collections/ksstatecen.

5. See *Minnesota State Census, 1905* [Online Database], indexed at the FamilySearch.org website. This database has 1,973,884 records. See
https://familysearch.org/search/collection/1503056.

6. See *New Jersey State Census, 1905* [Online Database], indexed at the FamilySearch.org website. This database has 2,146,861 records. See
https://familysearch.org/search/collection/1928107.
See also *New Jersey State Census, 1915* [Online Database], indexed at the FamilySearch.org website. Source: This database has 2,785,409 records. See
https://familysearch.org/search/collection/2061544.

7. See *New York State Census, 1905* [Online Database], indexed at the FamilySearch.org website. This database has 7,513,232 records. See
https://familysearch.org/search/collection/1463113.
See also *New York State Census, 1915* [Online Database], indexed at the FamilySearch.org website. This database has 9,742,867 records. See
https://familysearch.org/search/collection/1937454.

8. See *North Dakota Census, 1915* [Online Database], digitized and indexed at the FamilySearch.org website. Source: State Historical Society of North Dakota, Bismarck. The index record includes: Name Birth, Parents, Spouse, Children, Other (names living in the household), and Residence. More details can be viewed on the digitized census page. This database has 619,486 records. See
https://familysearch.org/search/collection/2346284.

9. See *Oklahoma, Territorial Census, 1890 and 1907* [Online Database], digitized and indexed at the Ancestry.com website. In June 1890 a territorial census of Oklahoma was taken. It enumerated the following seven counties: Beaver, Canadian, Cleveland, Kingfisher, Logan, Oklahoma, and Payne Co OK Territory. In 1907 a census of Indian and Oklahoma territories, comprising the proposed state of Oklahoma, was also taken. However, only the schedules for Seminole County exist. See
www.ancestry.com/search/collections/okcensus1890.

10. See *Rhode Island State Census, 1905* [Online Database]. Indexed at the FamilySearch.org website. This database has 950,314 images. See
https://familysearch.org/search/collection/1542866.
See also *Rhode Island State Census, 1915* [Online Database], digitized and indexed at the FamilySearch.org website. This database has 540,589 records. See
https://familysearch.org/search/collection/1532188.

11. See *South Carolina State Archives – Online Records Index* [Online Database], includes several databases from the period 1905-1915. See
www.archivesindex.sc.gov.

12. See *South Dakota State Census, 1905* [Online Database], digitized and indexed at the FamilySearch.org website. This database has 472,575 records. See
https://familysearch.org/search/collection/1477737.
See also *South Dakota State Census, 1915* [Online Database], indexed at the FamilySearch.org website. This database has 613,769 records. See
https://familysearch.org/search/collection/1476041.

13. See *Wisconsin State Census, 1905* [Online Database], indexed at the FamilySearch.org website. This database has 2,228,391 records. See
https://familysearch.org/search/collection/1443899.

The U.S. in 1920. Arizona and New Mexico both became states in 1912 bringing the total number to forty-eight (48) states at the time of the 1920 Census. Add eight (8) jurisdictions: The District of Columbia, Hawaii Territory and Alaska Territory; plus the insular territories of Guam, American Samoa, the Panama Canal Zone, Puerto Rico, and the U.S. Virgin Islands, for a total of 56 jurisdictions. The population of the U.S. Territory of the Philippines was not enumerated except for U.S. Military & Naval personnel stationed there. The population of the U.S. Territory of Wake Island was mostly military or civilians working for the military, thus part of the Military & Naval enumeration. For convenience, the U.S. Territory of Midway Atoll was enumerated as part of Honolulu Co HI. **Map source:** *National Atlas of the United States,* 1997-2014 edition.

Fourteenth Census of the United States - 1920

Destruction of the Original Records: In the 1940s, the Census Bureau undertook a major project to microfilm the census schedules of 1900 through 1940; and when the microfilming was complete, the original census schedules were destroyed. This was all done with the permission of Congress, who funded the microfilming project, and authorized the destruction of the originals.

U.S. Population: 106.0 million.

1920 Census Legislative Act: 40 Stat. 1291, 3 March 1919.

Responsibility / Schedules / Copies: The 1920 census was conducted under the direction of the Director of the Census (Census Bureau, U.S. Department of Commerce). **Schedules:** Population, Agriculture, Manufactures, and Military & Naval Forces. **Mandated Copies:** One copy, to the Director of the Census. Counties could buy a copy of their schedules at cost. (None did).

Census day: 1 January 1920. All of the questions asked by the census taker were related to a person's age or place of residence as of the census day.

Time Allowed: field count due within 30 days, except communities over 2,500 in population, due within two weeks.

Content of the 1920 Population Schedules: The 1920 Census Form had 29 numbered columns, labeled as follows: 1) Street Address, 2) House Number or Farm, 3) Dwelling Number in order of visitation, 4) Family Number in order of Visitation, 5) Name of Person whose place of abode on January 1, 1920, was in this Family 6) Relationship to the Head of House, 7) Home Owned or Rented, 8) If Owned, free or mortgaged, 9) Sex, 10) Color or Race, 11) Age at last birthday, 12) Marital Status: single, marriage, widowed, or divorced, 13) Year of Immigration to the U.S., 14) Naturalized or Alien, 15) Year Naturalized, 16) Attended School (in the past Six months), 17) Can Read, 18) Can Write, 19) Place of Birth of Person, 20) Mother Tongue of Person , 21) Place of Birth of Father, 22) Mother Tongue of Father, 23) Place of Birth of Mother, 24) Mother Tongue of Mother, 25) Can Speak English, 26) Trade or Profession, 27) Type of Business, 28) Employer, Employee, or Works on Own Account, and 29) No. of Farm Schedule.

1920 Soundex Index. The original records were microfilmed in the early 1940s and subsequently destroyed by the Census Bureau. The microfilm was later transferred to the National Archives, Washington, DC. Before the originals were destroyed, clerical workers from the Works Progress Administration (WPA) were called upon to create a comprehensive index to the 1920 census. The index was completed for every household in America. A special system of coding names was created, called "Soundex." 3x5 index cards were prepared for each household in the U.S. The information on the Soundex index cards was extracted from the full census schedules and included the full name, age, and birthplace for a head of household, and included any other person living in the household, regardless of their age. Each head of household's surname was given a Soundex code, and the cards were then arranged in alphabetical order by the Soundex code number (A001-Z001) and after that by the first name of the head of the household. (See page 24 for more information about the 1880-1930 Soundex Indexes).

1920 Census Publications with Digital Images

Microfilm of Originals & Digital Capture: The National Archives film for the 1920 census is contained on 2,076 rolls, series T625, beginning with FHL film #1820001 (Alabama). The microfilm was digitized by FamilySearch International. For a list of roll numbers, contents, and access to the digital images of each roll, see the FHL catalog page: **https://familysearch.org/search/catalog/489386.**
At this writing, the digitizing project for the **1920 Soundex** microfilm was still in progress. Check the catalog list for the rolls digitized and available to date, see **https://familysearch.org/search/catalog/489383.**

Online Searching – 1920 Census Indexes and Digital Images

The 1920 Census was digitized from the National Archives microfilm, indexed, and made available at the following websites:

- **Ancestry.com.** Subscription site, free database searching. Ancestry and FamilySearch share images and indexes. See
www.ancestry.com/search/collections/1920usfedcen.

- **FamilySearch.org.** Free database search, with images by FamilySearch, index by Ancestry. See
https://familysearch.org/search/collection/1488411.

- **MyHeritage.com.** A Family Tree subscription site. All U.S. Federal Census Records are available to subscribers with a data plan. See
www.myheritage.com/research/collection-10133/1920-united-states-federal-census.

- **Findmypast.com.** Monthly or annual subscriptions. Initial searches to U.S. Federal Censuses are free. See
www.findmypast.com/articles/search-the-1920-us-census.

- **GenealogyBank.com.** Subscription site. Initial searches to the U.S. Federal Censuses, 1790-1940 are free. www.genealogybank.com/explore/census/all.

- **HeritageQuestOnline-Subscribers Login.** This is a library subscription service. Check with your local library to see if they subscribe to the ProQuest & HeritageQuest databases. Many subscribing libraries allow their library card holders remote access. See
www.heritagequestonline.com/hqoweb/library/do/login.

Table 1920 – Statewide Census Publications

1920 Jurisdictions Included in Census	Population	Census Extant?	FHL Film Numbers Schedules	Soundex	Comments, Census Substitutes, etc.
1. Alabama	2,348,174	Yes	1820001	1823076	AL Census of Confederate Veterans exists. See Note 1.
2. Alaska Territory	55,036	Yes	1822030	1831443	
3. Arizona	334,162	Yes	1820046	1823235	
4. Arkansas	1,752,204	Yes	1820053	1823265	
5. California	3,426,861	Yes	1820087	1823396	
6. Colorado	939,629	Yes	1820155	1823724	
7. Connecticut	1,380,631	Yes	1820174	1823803	CT 1917 military census exists. See Note 2.
8. Delaware	223,003	Yes	1820200	1823914	
9. District of Columbia	437,571	Yes	1820205	1823934	
10. Florida	968,470	Yes	1820214	1823983	
11. Guam Territory	13,275	Yes	1822032	1831659	
12. Georgia	2,895,832	Yes	1820233	1824057	
13. Hawaii Territory	255,881	Yes	1822033	1831449	Includes Midway Atoll with Honolulu Co HI
14. Idaho	431,866	Yes	1820287	1831659	
15. Illinois	6,485,280	Yes	1820296	1824290	
16. Indiana	2,930,390	Yes	1820420	1824800	
17. Iowa	2,404,021	Yes	1820476	1825030	IA 1915 & 1925 state censuses exist. See Note 3.
18. Kansas	1,769,257	Yes	1820522	1823265	KS 1915 & 1925 state censuses exist. See Note 4.
19. Kentucky	2,416,630	Yes	1820557	1825340	
20. Louisiana	1,798,509	Yes	1820603	1825520	
21. Maine	768,014	Yes	1820637	1825655	
22. Maryland	1,449,661	Yes	1820652	1825722	
23. Massachusetts	3,852,356	Yes	1820679	1825848	
24. Michigan	3,668,412	Yes	1820753	1826174	
25. Minnesota	2,387,125	Yes	1820822	1826465	
26. Mississippi	1,790,618	Yes	1820072	1826639	
27. Missouri	3,404,055	Yes	1820902	1826762	
28. Montana	548,889	Yes	1820967	1827032	
29. Nebraska	1,296,372	Yes	1820979	1827078	
30. Nevada	77,407	Yes	1821004	1827174	
31. New Hampshire	443,083	Yes	1821006	1827183	
32. New Jersey	3,155,900	Yes	1821015	1827223	NJ 1915 state census exists. See Note 5.
33. New Mexico	360,350	Yes	1821074	1827476	
34. New York	10,385,227	Yes	1821081	1827507	NY 1915 & 1925 state censuses exist. See Note 6.
35. North Carolina	2,559,123	Yes	1821282	1828392	
36. North Dakota	646,872	Yes	1821330	1828558	ND 1915 & 1925 state censuses exist. See Note 7.
37. Ohio	5,759,394	Yes	1821344	1828606	
38. Oklahoma	2,028,283	Yes	1821451	1829082	
39. Oregon	783,389	Yes	1821491	1829237	
40. Panama Canal Zone	22,858	Yes	1822042	1831475	
41. Pennsylvania	8,720,017	Yes	1821507	1829306	
42. Puerto Rico Territory	1,299,809	Yes	1822043	1831496	
43. Rhode Island	604,397	Yes	1821670	1830022	RI 1915 & 1925 state censuses exist. See Note 8.
44. Samoa Territory	8,056	Yes	1822032	1831660	
45. South Carolina	1,683,724	Yes	1821682	1830075	
46. South Dakota	636,547	Yes	1821714	1830187	SD 1915 & 1925 state censuses exist. See Note 9.
47. Tennessee	2,337,885	Yes	1821728	1830225	
48. Texas	4,663,228	Yes	1821772	1830397	
49. Utah	449,396	Yes	1821861	1830770	
50. Vermont	352,428	Yes	1821870	1830803	
51. Virgin Islands of the U.S.	26,051	Yes	1822076	1831662	First U.S. Census taken in 1917, included with U.S.1920.
52. Virginia	2,309,187	Yes	1821877	1830835	
53. Washington	1,356,621	Yes	1821920	1831003	
54. West Virginia	1,463,701	Yes	1821947	1831121	
55. Wisconsin	2,632,067	Yes	1821975	1831230	
56. Wyoming	194,402	Yes	1822025	1831426	
- Military and Naval	450,000 +/-	Yes	1822040	1831476	
- Institutions, Vessels, Misc.	20,000 +/-	Yes	-	1831665	See Note 10.

U.S. Total: 106,021,537

Table 1920 Notes:

1. See *Alabama, Census of Confederate Veterans, 1907, 1921, 1927* [Online Database], digitized at the FamilySearch.org website. Any indexes were digitized along with the records. This database has 13,710 images, see
https://familysearch.org/search/collection/2487274.

2. See *Connecticut, Military Census, 1917* [Online Database], indexed at the Ancestry.com website. This database has 442,226 records. See
www.ancestry.com/search/collections/ctmilitarycensus.

3. See *Iowa State Census, 1915* [Online Database], digitized and indexed at the FamilySearch.org website. This database has 2,574,691 records. See
www.familysearch.org/search/collection/2240483.
See also *1925 Iowa State Census* [Online Database], digitized and indexed at the FamilySearch.org website. This database has 2,487,170 records. See
www.familysearch.org/search/collection/2224537.

4. See *Kansas State Census, 1915* [Online Database], digitized at the FamilySearch.org website. This is an image-only database, with 301,658 records. Browse through the images, organized first by county, then by township. See
www.familysearch.org/search/collection/2640442.
See also *1925 Kansas State Census* [Microfilm], from the originals at the KS Hist. Soc., Topeka. For information about the microfilmed indexes, see
www.kshs.org/p/kansas-1925-state-census/10957.

5. See *New Jersey State Census, 1915* [Online Database], indexed at the FamilySearch.org website. Source: NJ State Archives microfilm. This database has 2,785,409 records. See
https://familysearch.org/search/collection/2061544.

6. See *New York State Census, 1915* [Online Database], indexed at the FamilySearch.org website. This database has 9,742,867 records. See
https://familysearch.org/search/collection/1937454.
See also *New York State Census, 1925* [Online Database], indexed at the FamilySearch.org website. Source: NY State Archives. This database has 11,117,922 records. See
https://familysearch.org/search/collection/1937489.

7. See *North Dakota Census, 1915* [Online Database], digitized and indexed at the FamilySearch.org website. This database has 619,486 records. See
https://familysearch.org/search/collection/2346284.

See also *North Dakota Census, 1925* [Online Database], indexed at the FamilySearch.org website. This database has 678,504 records. See
https://familysearch.org/search/collection/2351024.

8. See *Rhode Island State Census, 1915* [Online Database], digitized and indexed at the FamilySearch.org website. This database has 540,589 records. See
https://familysearch.org/search/collection/1532188.
See also *Rhode Island State Census, 1925* [Online Database], digitized and indexed at the FamilySearch.org website. This database has 684,447 records. See
https://familysearch.org/search/collection/1532195.

9. See *South Dakota State Census, 1915* [Online Database], indexed at the FamilySearch.org website. This database has 613,769 records. See
https://familysearch.org/search/collection/1476041.
See also *South Dakota State Census, 1925* [Online Database], indexed at the FamilySearch.org website. This database has 705,319 records. See
https://familysearch.org/search/collection/1476077.

10. FHL microfilm title: *Institutions, 1920 Federal Census Soundex and Population Schedules,* but this title was included with the U.S. Soundex listings only. The film note states: "Soundex: Various Institutions, Vessels and persons with no reported surname for the states of: Alabama, Florida, Georgia, Louisiana, Mississippi, North Carolina, South Carolina, Tennessee and Virginia."

Census Substitute Available

See *World War I Draft Registration Cards, 1917-1918* [Online Database], digitized and indexed at the FamilySearch.org website. Name index and images of draft registration cards for World War I. Three registrations occurred between 1917 and 1918. The 1st was held 5 Jun 1917 for men ages 21-31. The 2nd was held 5 Jun 1918 for men who turned 21 since the 1st registration. The 3rd started 12 Sep 1918 for men ages 18-45. The collection includes cards for 24 million men. The cards are arranged by state, by city or county, by local draft board, then alphabetical by surname. The draft registration cards are part of Record Group 163, Records of the Selective Service System (WWI), 1917-1939, and is National Archives Microfilm publication M1509. This database has 24,867,345 records. See
www.familysearch.org/search/collection/1968530.

Fifteenth Census of the U.S. - 1930

The U.S. in 1930. There were a total of forty-eight (48) states at the time of the 1930 Census. Add eight (8) jurisdictions: The District of Columbia, Hawaii Territory and Alaska Territory; plus the insular territories of Guam, American Samoa, the Panama Canal Zone, Puerto Rico, and the U.S. Virgin Islands, for a total of 56 jurisdictions. The population of the U.S. Territory of the Philippines was not enumerated. For convenience, the U.S. Territory of Midway Atoll was enumerated as part of Honolulu Co HI. Added to the insular territories was an enumeration of U.S. citizens employed at Consular Services around the world (e.g., Acapulco, Mexico to Darien, Manchuria; and Danzig, Poland to Zurich, Switzerland). **Map source:** *National Atlas of the United States,* 1997-2014 edition.

Fifteenth Census of the United States - 1930

Destruction of the Original Records: In the 1940s, the Census Bureau undertook a major project to microfilm the census schedules of 1900 through 1940; and when the microfilming was complete, the original census schedules were destroyed. This was all done with the permission of Congress, who funded the microfilming project, and authorized the destruction of the originals.

U.S. Population: 122.7 million.

1930 Census Legislative Act: 46 Stat. 21, 18 June 1929.

Responsibility / Schedules / Copies: The 1930 census was conducted under the direction of the Director of the Census (Census Bureau, U.S. Department of Commerce). **Schedules:** Population, Agriculture, Unemployment, and Mines. **Mandated Copies:** One copy, to the Director of the Census. Counties could buy a copy of their schedules at cost. (None did).

Census day: 1 April 1930. All of the questions asked by the census taker were related to a person's age or place of residence as of the census day.

Time Allowed: field count due within 30 days, except communities over 2,500 in population, due within two weeks.

Content of the 1930 Population Schedules: The 1930 Census Form had 32 numbered columns, labeled as follows: 1) Street Address, 2) House number (in cities or towns), 3) Dwelling Number in order of visitation, 4) Family Number in order of Visitation, 5) Name of person whose placed of abode on April 1, 1930, was in this family 6) Relationship to the Head of House, 7) Home owned or rented, 8) Value of home if owned, or monthly rental if rented, 9) R=Radio set, 10) Live on a farm? 11) Sex, 12) Color or race, 13) Age at last birthday, 14) Marital status (S, M, Wd, D), 15) Age at first marriage, 16) Attended school (in the past 6 months), 17) Can Read and write, 18) Person's birthplace, 19) Father's birthplace, 20) Mother's birthplace, 21) Language spoken before coming to U.S., 22) Year of immigration to U.S., 23) Naturalization (Na=Naturalized, Pa=First Papers, Al=Alien) 24) Can speak English 25) Occupation, 26) Industry, 27) Class of worker (E=Employer, W=Wage or salary worker, O=Working on own account, NP=Unpaid worker, member of the family), 28) At work yesterday? 29) If not, Line No. on Unemployment schedule, 30) Veteran? 30) What War? and 32) No. of Farm Schedule.

1930 Soundex Index. The original population schedules were microfilmed in the 1940s and subsequently destroyed by the Census Bureau. The microfilm was later transferred to the National Archives, Washington, DC. Before the originals were destroyed, clerical workers from the Works Progress Administration (WPA) were called upon to create a partial index to the 1930 census. The 1930 Soundex index was completed for the southern states of Alabama, Arkansas, Florida, Georgia, Louisiana, Mississippi, North Carolina, South Carolina, Tennessee, and Virginia, plus seven counties in Kentucky and seven more in West Virginia. The information on the Soundex index cards was extracted from the full census schedules and included the full name, age, and birthplace for a head of household and included any other person living in the household, with the person's relationship to the head of household. Persons in a household with a different surname than the head of household were given another separate card and included in Soundex code order.

1930 Census Publications with Digital Images

Microfilm of Originals & Digital Capture: The National Archives film for the 1930 census is contained on 2,667 rolls, series T626, beginning with FHL film #2339736 (Alabama). The microfilm was digitized by FamilySearch International. For a list of roll numbers, contents, and access to the digital images of each roll, see the FHL catalog page: https://familysearch.org/search/catalog/1037623.

At this writing, the digitizing project for the **1930 Soundex** microfilm was still in progress. Check the catalog list for the rolls digitized and available to date, see https://familysearch.org/search/catalog/1037621.

Online Searching – 1930 Census Indexes and Digital Images

The 1930 Census was digitized from the National Archives microfilm, indexed, and made available at the following websites:

- **Ancestry.com.** Subscription site, free database searching. Ancestry and FamilySearch share images and indexes. See www.ancestry.com/search/collections/1930usfedcen.

- **FamilySearch.org.** Free database search, with images by FamilySearch, index by Ancestry. See https://familysearch.org/search/collection/1810731.

- **MyHeritage.com.** A Family Tree subscription site. All U.S. Federal Census Records are available to subscribers with a data plan. See www.myheritage.com/research/collection-10134/1930-united-states-federal-census.

- **Findmypast.com.** Monthly or annual subscriptions. Initial searches to U.S. Federal Censuses are free. See www.findmypast.com/articles/search-the-1930-us-census.

- **GenealogyBank.com.** Subscription site. Initial searches to the U.S. Federal Censuses, 1790-1940 are free. www.genealogybank.com/explore/census/all.

- **HeritageQuestOnline-Subscribers Login.** This is a library subscription service. Check with your local library to see if they subscribe to the ProQuest & HeritageQuest databases. Many subscribing libraries allow their library card holders remote access. See www.heritagequestonline.com/hqoweb/library/do/login.

Fifteenth Census of the U.S. - 1930

Table 1930 – Statewide Census Publications

1930 Jurisdictions Included in Census	Population	Census Extant?	FHL Film Numbers Schedules	Soundex	Comments, Census Substitutes, etc.
1. Alabama	2,646,248	Yes	2339736	2338000	AL 1927 Widows of Confederate Soldiers. See Note 1.
2. Alaska Territory	59,278	Yes	2342360	--	
3. Arizona	435,573	Yes	2339790	--	
4. Arkansas	1,854,482	Yes	2339799	2338195	AR 1933-1939 Marriage Index exists. See Note 2.
5. California	5,677,251	Yes	2339835	--	
6. Colorado	1,035,791	Yes	2339964	--	
7. Connecticut	1,606,903	Yes	2339988	--	
8. Delaware	238,380	Yes	2340021	--	
9. District of Columbia	486,869	Yes	2340027	--	
10. Florida	1,468,211	Yes	2340041	2338295	FL 1935 state census exists. See Note 3.
11. Guam Territory	18,500	Yes	2342363	--	
12. Georgia	2,908,506	Yes	2340071	2338393	GA 1928-1940 Deaths Index exists. See Note 4.
13. Hawaii Territory	368,336	Yes	2342365	--	
14. Idaho	445,032	Yes	2340130	--	ID 1931 Old Age Pension Index exists. See Note 5.
15. Illinois	7,630,654	Yes	2340140	--	
16. Indiana	3,238,503	Yes	2340310	--	
17. Iowa	2,470,939	Yes	2340375	--	IA 1925 state census exists. See Note 6.
18. Kansas	1,880,999	Yes	2340427	--	KS 1925 state census exists. See Note 7.
19. Kentucky	2,614,589	Yes	2340466	2338646	KY Soundex, 7 counties only. See Note 8.
20. Louisiana	2,101,593	Yes	2340517	2338670	
21. Maine	797,423	Yes	2340562	--	
22. Maryland	1,631,526	Yes	2340578	--	
23. Massachusetts	4,249,614	Yes	2340618	--	
24. Michigan	4,842,325	Yes	2340707	--	
25. Minnesota	2,563,953	Yes	2340813	--	
26. Mississippi	2,009,821	Yes	2340872	2338816	
27. Missouri	3,629,367	Yes	2340909	--	
28. Montana	537,606	Yes	2340987	--	
29. Nebraska	1,377,963	Yes	2341000	--	
30. Nevada	91,058	Yes	2341031	--	
31. New Hampshire	465,293	Yes	2341033	--	
32. New Jersey	4,041,334	Yes	2341043	--	
33. New Mexico	423,317	Yes	2341127	--	
34. New York	12,588,066	Yes	2341136	--	NY 1925 state census exists. See Note 9.
35. North Carolina	3,170,276	Yes	2341405	2338974	
36. North Dakota	680,845	Yes	2341465	--	ND 1925 state census exists. See Note 10.
37. Ohio	6,646,697	Yes	2341480	--	
38. Oklahoma	2,396,040	Yes	2341626	--	
39. Oregon	953,786	Yes	2340950	--	
40. Panama Canal Zone	30,407	Yes	2342372	--	
41. Pennsylvania	9,631,350	Yes	2341693	--	
42. Puerto Rico Territory	1,543,018	Yes	2342373	--	
43. Rhode Island	687,497	Yes	2341902	--	RI 1925 & 1935 state censuses exist. See Note 11.
44. Samoa Territory	10,055	Yes	2342363	--	
45. South Carolina	1,738,765	Yes	2341918	2339143	
46. South Dakota	692,849	Yes	2341951	--	SD 1925 & 1935 state censuses exist. See Note 12.
47. Tennessee	2,616,556	Yes	2341967	2339252	
48. Texas	5,824,715	Yes	2342021	--	
49. Utah	507,847	Yes	2342148	--	
50. Vermont	359,611	Yes	2342160	--	
51. Virgin Islands of the U.S.	22,012	Yes	2342402	--	
52. Virginia	2,421,851	Yes	2342167	2339421	
53. Washington	1,563,396	Yes	2342218	--	
54. West Virginia	1,729,205	Yes	2342260	2339548	WV Soundex, 7 counties only, plus Institutions. See Note 13.
55. Wisconsin	2,939,006	Yes	2342294	--	
56. Wyoming	225,565	Yes	2342355	--	
- Consular Services	5,000 +/-	Yes	2342372	--	

U.S. Total: 122,775,046

Table 1930 Notes:

1. *Alabama, Questionnaires of Widows of Confederate Soldiers, 1927* [Online Database], indexed at the Ancestry.com website. The documents can include a wide variety of details on both the widow and the veteran, see
www.ancestry.com/search/collections/alconfedwidows.

2. See *Arkansas, Marriage Index, 1933-1939* [Online Database], from the Arkansas Department of Health, digitized and indexed at the FamilySearch.org website. Information that may be found in this database for each entry includes groom's full name, bride's full name, their marriage date, license date, county of marriage, marriage certificate number, and the volume number in which the certificate is located. This database has 421,079 records. See
www.familysearch.org/search/collection/1940215.
This database is also available at the Ancestry.com website. See
www.ancestry.com/search/collections/armarriageindex.

3. See *Florida State Census, 1935* [Online Database], digitized and indexed at the FamilySearch.org website. The records are organized alphabetically by county, then election precinct. All Florida counties are represented, although there are a few missing election precincts. This database has 1,599,085 records. See
https://familysearch.org/search/collection/1457856.

4. See *Georgia Deaths, 1928-1940* [Online Database], digitized and indexed at the FamilySearch.org website. From FHL microfilm of the Department of Health and Vital Statistics, Atlanta, GA. This database has 462,877 records. See
https://familysearch.org/search/collection/1385727.

5. See *Idaho State Archives Old Age Pension Index* [Online Database]. In 1931, the State of Idaho introduced an Old Age Pension Act, which provided a monthly payment of $25.00 to qualified residents of Idaho. This database was later produced in Microsoft Excel format, which can be downloaded for printing, sorting, etc. See
https://docs.google.com/spreadsheets/d/1Hvg8mmA4WOuZjgRUI0BoVXzB6DL55WWOE9H-kejFq7k/edit#gid=1572461861.

6. See *Iowa State Census, 1925* [Online Database], digitized & indexed at the FamilySearch.org website. This database has 2,487,170 records. See
www.familysearch.org/search/collection/2224537.

7. See *1925 Kansas State Census* [Microfilm], from the originals at the KS Hist. Soc., Topeka. For information about the microfilmed indexes, see www.kshs.org/p/kansas-1925-state-census/10957.

8. The Kentucky counties of Bell, Floyd, Harlan, Kenton, Muhlenberg, Perry, and Pike were the only ones with a 1930 Soundex index. See
https://familysearch.org/search/catalog/1037621.

9. See *New York State Census, 1925* [Online Database], indexed at the FamilySearch.org website. Source: NY State Archives. This database has 11,117,922 records. See
https://familysearch.org/search/collection/1937489.

10. See *North Dakota Census, 1925* [Online Database], indexed at the FamilySearch.org website. This database has 678,504 records. See
https://familysearch.org/search/collection/2351024.

11. See *Rhode Island State Census, 1925* [Online Database], digitized and indexed at the FamilySearch.org website. This database has 684,447 records. See
https://familysearch.org/search/collection/1532195.
See also *Rhode Island State Census, 1935* [Online Database], digitized and indexed at the FamilySearch.org website. This database has 693,472 records. See
https://familysearch.org/search/collection/1529126.

12. See *South Dakota State Census, 1925* [Online Database], indexed at the FamilySearch.org website. This database has 705,319 records. See
https://familysearch.org/search/collection/1476077.
See also *South Dakota State Census, 1935* [Online Database], indexed at the FamilySearch.org website. This database has 673,322 records. See
https://familysearch.org/search/collection/1614831.

13. The West Virginia counties of Fayette, Harrison, Kanawha, Logan, McDowell, Mercer, and Raleigh were the only ones with a 1930 Soundex index. See
https://familysearch.org/search/catalog/1037621.

The U.S. in 1940. There were a total of forty-eight (48) states at the time of the 1940 Census. Add eight (8) jurisdictions: The District of Columbia, Hawaii Territory and Alaska Territory; plus the insular territories of Guam, American Samoa, the Panama Canal Zone, Puerto Rico, and the U.S. Virgin Islands, for a total of 56 jurisdictions. The population of the U.S. Territory of the Philippines was not enumerated. **Map source:** *National Atlas of the United States,* 1997-2014 edition.

Sixteenth Census of the United States - 1940

Destruction of the Original Records: In the 1940s, the Census Bureau undertook a major project to microfilm the census schedules of 1900 through 1940; and when the microfilming was complete, the original census schedules were destroyed. This was all done with the permission of Congress, who funded the microfilming project, and authorized the destruction of the originals.

U.S. Population: 132.1 million.

1940 Census Legislative Act: 46 Stat. 21, 18 June 1929; as amended by 54 Stat. 162, 25 April 1940.

Responsibility / Schedules / Copies: The 1940 census was conducted under the direction of the Director of the Census (Census Bureau, U.S. Dept. of Commerce). **Schedules:** Population, Agriculture, Manufactures, Housing, Businesses, Mines. **Mandated Copies:** One copy, to the Director of the Census. Counties could buy a copy of their schedules at cost.

Census day: 1 April 1940. All of the questions asked by the census taker were related to a person's age or place of residence as of the census day.

Time Allowed: field count due within 30 days, except communities over 2,500 in population, due within two weeks.

Content of the 1940 Population Schedules: The 1940 Census Form had 34 numbered columns, labeled as follows: **Location:** 1) Street, avenue, road, etc., 2) House number. **Household Data:** 3) No. of household in order of visitation, 4) Home owned

(O) or rented (R), 5) Value of Home or Monthly rental if rented, 6) Farm? Yes or No. 7) **Name** of each person whose usual place of residence on April 1, 1940, was in the household *[Be sure to include: 1. Persons temporarily absent from household. Write "Ab" after names of such persons. 2. Children under 1 year of age. Write "Infant" if child has not been give a first name. Enter ☒ after name of person furnishing information]*. **Relation:** 8) Relation of the person to the head of household, as wife, daughter, father, mother-in-law, grandson, lodger, lodger's wife, servant, hired hand, etc., **Personal Description:** 9) Sex, 10) Color or Race, 11) Age at last birthday, 12) Marital status. **Education:** 13) Attended school or college at any time since March 1, 1940? 14) Highest grade of school completed. **Place of Birth:** 15) If born in U.S. give state, territory or possession. If foreign born, give country in which birthplace was situated on Jan. 1, 1937. **Citizenship:** 16) Citizenship of the foreign born. **Residence, April 1, 1935:** 17) City-Town-Village, 18) County, 19) State-Territory-Country, 20) On a Farm? Y or N. **Employment Status** (Persons 14 years old and over): 21) At work for pay last week? 22) If not, assigned to WPA, CCC, etc.? 23) Seeking work (Y or N), 24) Have a job, business, etc.? (Y or N), 25) Engaged in home housework (H), in School (S), Unable to work (U), or Other (Ot), 26) Number of hours worked last week, 27) Duration of unemployment in weeks, 28) Occupation, 29) Industry, 30) Class of worker, 31) No. of weeks worked in 1939, 32) Amount of money, wages, salary, or commissions received, 33) Did this person receive income of $50.00 or more from money wages or salary (Y or N), 34) No. of Farm schedule.

1940 Census Extraction Form. A 2-page PDF file is available at the National Archives website. The 1940 format was designed to fit on a standard legal size sheet of paper (8-1/2" x 14"). Side 1 of the form has columns 1 to 34. Side 2 has Supplementary Questions for Persons Enumerated on Lines 14 and 29 (columns 35 to 50); Side 2 also has a key to Symbols and Explanatory Notes. To access the webpage and download the form, see www.archives.gov/files/research/census/1940/1940.pdf.

1940 Census Publications with Digital Images

Digital Capture: Just prior to the 1 April 2012 opening date of the 1940 population schedules, approximately 4,400 rolls of microfilm were digitized for the National Archives by FamilySearch International. The images were made available to other interested websites for shared indexing. Upon the opening date, FamilySearch.org's 3.84 million digitized images of the 1940 census were made accessible to the public online. For the No. of Rolls, Film/DGS numbers, and the URL to access the digital images for each state/territory, see *Table 1940*.

Online Searching – 1940 Census Indexes and Digital Images

The 1940 Census was digitized and indexed at the following websites:

- **Ancestry.com.** Subscription site, free access to indexes and images. See www.ancestry.com/search/collections/1940usfedcen.

- **FamilySearch.org.** Free access to images and indexes. See https://familysearch.org/1940census.

- **MyHeritage.com.** A Family Tree subscription site. Free access to images and indexes. See www.myheritage.com/research/collection-10053/1940-united-states-federal-census.

- **Findmypast.com.** Monthly or annual subscriptions. Free access to images and indexes. See www.findmypast.com/articles/world-records/full-list-of-united-states-records/census-land-and-substitutes/us-census-1940-free-access?rc=1.

- **GenealogyBank.com.** Subscription site. Initial searches to the U.S. Federal Censuses, 1790-1940 are free. www.genealogybank.com/explore/census/all.

- **HeritageQuestOnline-Subscribers Login.** This is a library subscription service. Check with your local library to see if they subscribe to the ProQuest & HeritageQuest databases. Many subscribing libraries allow their library card holders remote access. See www.heritagequestonline.com/hqoweb/library/do/login.

Sixteenth Census of the U.S. - 1940

Table 1940 – Statewide Census Publications

1940 Jurisdictions Included in Census	Population	Approx. Rolls of Film	Starting Film/DGS Number	URL of the FHL Catalog Page with Access to the Digital Images	Remarks
1. Alabama	2,832,961	90	5454693	www.familysearch.org/search/catalog/2034309.	
2. Alaska Territory	72,524	4	5460001	www.familysearch.org/search/catalog/2052180.	
3. Arizona	499,261	17	5461855	www.familysearch.org/search/catalog/2057740.	
4. Arkansas	1,949,387	68	5461490	www.familysearch.org/search/catalog/2057742.	
5. California	6,907,387	286	5455010	www.familysearch.org/search/catalog/2057743.	
6. Colorado	1,123,296	39	5449352	www.familysearch.org/search/catalog/2057744.	
7. Connecticut	1,709,242	50	5461383	www.familysearch.org/search/catalog/2057745.	
8. Delaware	266,505	9	5449024	www.familysearch.org/search/catalog/2057746.	
9. District of Columbia	663,091	20	5461938	www.familysearch.org/search/catalog/2057747.	
10. Florida	1,897,414	63	5449564	www.familysearch.org/search/catalog/2057748.	
11. Georgia	3,123,723	99	5460961	www.familysearch.org/search/catalog/2057749.	
12. Guam Territory	22,290	1	5462183	www.familysearch.org/search/catalog/2057750.	Unorg. Terr. of Guam / U.S. Navy Govt.
13. Hawaii Territory	423,330	11	5460005	www.familysearch.org/search/catalog/2057751.	
14. Idaho	524,873	21	5460520	www.familysearch.org/search/catalog/2057752.	
15. Illinois	7,897,241	283	5459497	www.familysearch.org/search/catalog/2057801.	
16. Indiana	3,427,796	110	5459780	www.familysearch.org/search/catalog/2057753.	
17. Iowa	2,538,268	82	5461433	www.familysearch.org/search/catalog/2057755.	Some IA counties were digitized twice.
18. Kansas	1,801,028	58	5449123	www.familysearch.org/search/catalog/2057756.	
19. Kentucky	2,845,627	131	5460582	www.familysearch.org/search/catalog/2057757.	
20. Louisiana	2,363,880	68	5454613	www.familysearch.org/search/catalog/2057758.	
21. Maine	847,226	29	5462013	www.familysearch.org/search/catalog/2057759.	
22. Maryland	1,821,244	67	5461060	www.familysearch.org/search/catalog/2057760.	
23. Massachusetts	4,316,721	155	5460837	www.familysearch.org/search/catalog/2057761.	
24. Michigan	5,256,106	183	5461556	www.familysearch.org/search/catalog/2057762.	
25. Minnesota	2,792,300	102	5454892	www.familysearch.org/search/catalog/2057765.	
26. Mississippi	2,183,796	76	5449627	www.familysearch.org/search/catalog/2057766.	
27. Missouri	3,784,664	134	5460016	www.familysearch.org/search/catalog/2057767.	
28. Montana	559,456	23	5461680	www.familysearch.org/search/catalog/2057768.	
29. Nebraska	1,315,834	41	5460541	www.familysearch.org/search/catalog/2057769.	
30. Nevada	110,247	7	5461127	www.familysearch.org/search/catalog/2057770.	
31. New Hampshire	491,524	17	5454893	www.familysearch.org/search/catalog/2057771.	
32. New Jersey	4,160,165	140	5461958	www.familysearch.org/search/catalog/2057772.	
33. New Mexico	531,818	18	5461734	www.familysearch.org/search/catalog/2057774.	
34. New York	13,479,142	412	5458123	www.familysearch.org/search/catalog/2057775.	
35. North Carolina	3,571,623	175	5460199	www.familysearch.org/search/catalog/2057776.	
36. North Dakota	641,935	27	5462042	www.familysearch.org/search/catalog/2057778.	
37. Ohio	6,907,612	383	5460421	www.familysearch.org/search/catalog/2057779.	
38. Oklahoma	2,336,434	78	5454569	www.familysearch.org/search/catalog/2057781.	
39. Oregon	1,089,684	43	5449181	www.familysearch.org/search/catalog/2057782.	
40. Panama Canal Zone	51,827	1	5461826	www.familysearch.org/search/catalog/2057783.	Mil. Governor/Canal Commission
41. Pennsylvania	9,900,180	607	5456535	www.familysearch.org/search/catalog/2057784.	
42. Puerto Rico Territory	1,869,255	51	5462242	www.familysearch.org/search/catalog/2057785.	Organized Territory of Puerto Rico
43. Rhode Island	713,346	25	5461752	www.familysearch.org/search/catalog/2057786.	
44. Samoa Territory	12,908	1	5462184	www.familysearch.org/search/catalog/2052181.	Unorg. Territory of American Samoa
45. South Carolina	1,899,804	66	5461872	www.familysearch.org/search/catalog/2057788.	
46. South Dakota	642,961	24	5462069	www.familysearch.org/search/catalog/2057789.	
47. Tennessee	2,915,841	96	5461277	www.familysearch.org/search/catalog/2057790.	
48. Texas	6,414,824	327	5456897	www.familysearch.org/search/catalog/2057791.	
49. Utah	550,310	19	5459982	www.familysearch.org/search/catalog/2057793.	
50. Vermont	359,231	13	5461776	www.familysearch.org/search/catalog/2057794.	
51. Virgin Islands	24,889	1	5461827	www.familysearch.org/search/catalog/2057795.	Unorg. Terr., Virgin Islands of the U.S.
52. Virginia	2,677,773	90	5449033	www.familysearch.org/search/catalog/2057796.	
53. Washington	1,736,191	61	5460323	www.familysearch.org/search/catalog/2057797.	
54. West Virginia	1,961,974	64	5462119	www.familysearch.org/search/catalog/2057798.	
55. Wisconsin	3,137,587	114	5461166	www.familysearch.org/search/catalog/2057799.	
56. Wyoming	250,742	10	5461789	www.familysearch.org/search/catalog/2057800.	

U.S. Total: 132,164,569

Selected Online Databases from the time of the 1940 Census

U.S., Social Security Applications and Claims Index, 1936-2007 [Online Database], indexed at the Ancestry.com website. Source: Social Security Administration. This database includes information filed with the Social Security Administration through the application or claims process. Each index record includes: Applicant's full name, Social Security Number (SSN), Gender, Race, Birth date, Birth place, Father, Mother, Type of claim, and Notes. This database has 117,554,105 records. See www.ancestry.com/search/collections/numident.

Associated Press, Stories and News Features, 1937-1985 [Online Database], indexed at the Ancestry.com website. Source: Associated Press Corporate Archives, New York, NY. This collection includes AP news stories of over 700 reels of microfilm. This database has 704,997 records. See www.ancestry.com/search/collections/apmicrofilm. See also ***Associated Press, Subject Card Index to AP Stories, 1937–1985*** [Online Database], indexed at the Ancestry.com website. This database has 493,916 records. See www.ancestry.com/search/collections/apsubjectcardindexes.

1938-1946 World War II Army Enlistment Records [Online Database], digitized and indexed at the FamilySearch.org website. Name index to Army Serial Number Enlistment Card Records, excluding officers, in the United States Army including the Women's Army Auxiliary Corps and the Enlisted Reserve Corps circa 1938-1946. This database has 9,038,855 records. See www.familysearch.org/search/collection/2028680.

1938-1949 U.S. World War II Navy Muster Rolls [Online Database], is a searchable database at the Ancestry.com website. Includes Name of enlistee, Rating (Occupation/Specialty), Service number, Date reported for particular duty or on board, Date of enlistment, Name of ship, station, or activity, Ship number or other numeric designation, and date of muster roll. This database has 33,037,784 images. See http://search.ancestry.com/search/db.aspx?dbid=1143.

1939-1945 U.S. Rosters of World War II Dead [Online Database], digitized and indexed at the Ancestry.com website. This database contains the names of those who died in World War II from all U.S. armed services. Names are listed in alphabetical order according to surname. Information available in this database includes (listed in order as it appears on the image from left to right): 1) Name of permanent interment site. 2) Name. 3) Rank. 4) Service Number. 5) Name of temporary interment site. 6) Religion. 7) Race. And 8) Disposition. See www.ancestry.com/search/collections/rosterswwiidead.

1941-1945 World War II Prisoners of War of the Japanese [Online Database], indexed at the FamilySearch.org website. The index includes name, rank, service number, branch of service, source of information, unit information as available from parent unit to subordinate unit and notes. This database has 29,879 records. See https://familysearch.org/search/collection/2127320.

1941-1945 World War II Navy, Marine Corps, and Coast Guard Casualties [Online Database], digitized and indexed at the Ancestry.com website. includes: Name of military personnel, Rank of military personnel, Name, address, and relationship of next-of-kin. The records are arranged first by state. then by casualty type, then alphabetically by surname of personnel. This database has 150,715 records. See www.ancestry.com/search/collections/wwiicasualties.

1942 World War II Draft Registration Cards [Online Database], digitized and indexed at the FamilySearch.org website. Includes a name index and images of cards for men, age 45-64 (born 1877-1897), This database contains 11,096,106 records. See https://familysearch.org/search/collection/1339071.

1942-1946 Japanese Americans Relocated During World War II [Online Database], indexed at the FamilySearch.org website. Includes a name index of Japanese Americans living in Washington, Oregon, and California who were relocated during World War II. This database has 109,368 records. See https://familysearch.org/search/collection/2043779.

1942-1948 U.S., World War II Cadet Nursing Corps Card Files [Online Database], digitized and indexed at the Ancestry.com website. National Archives, Records of the Public Health Service. Each index record includes: Name, Age, Birth date, Issue date, Educational institution, and School location. The images of the membership cards contains more details. This database has 390,020 records. See www.ancestry.com/search/collections/wwiinursingcorps.

Seventeenth Census of the U.S. - 1950

The 1950 census encompassed the 48 states (and DC) of the continental United States, plus the Territories of Alaska, Hawaii, American Samoa, Panama Canal Zone, Guam, Puerto Rico, and the U.S. Virgin Islands. The 1950 census also made special provisions/schedules for the enumeration of American citizens living abroad (and their dependents), including the armed forces of the United States, employees of the United States Government, and the crews of vessels in the American Merchant Marine at sea or in foreign ports. Also enumerated were any American citizens living on small islands claimed by the U.S., such as the Corn Islands, Midway Atoll, Wake Island, Canton Island, and Johnston Atoll. Also in 1950, the Trust Territory of the United States (1947-1986) was enumerated. (The Trust Territory included the main Micronesian island groups of the Northern Mariana Islands (later a U.S. Commonwealth Territory), the Marshall Islands (later the main population of the Federated States of Micronesia); and Palau, the western chain of the Caroline Islands (later the Republic of Palau). **Map source:** *National Atlas of the United States,* 1997-2014 edition.

Seventeenth Census of the United States - 1950

Destruction of the Original Records: After microfilming, the Census Bureau destroyed the original schedules of the 1950 census. This was all done with the permission of Congress, who funded the microfilming project, and authorized the destruction of the originals. All the related microfilm and original published materials of the 1950 census were transferred to the National Archives in the year 2000.

U.S. Population: 150.7 million.

1950 Census Legislative Act: 46 Stat. 21, 18 June 1929; as amended by an act dd 7 September 1950 to add or exclude certain schedules.

Responsibility / Copies: The 1950 census was conducted under the direction of the Director of the Census (Census Bureau, U.S. Department of Commerce). **Mandated Copies:** One copy, to the Director of the Census.

Census day: 1 April 1950. All of the questions asked by the census taker were related to a person's age or place of residence as of the census day.

Time Allowed: field count due within 30 days, except communities over 2,500 in population, due within two weeks.

Content of the 1950 Population Schedules: The 1950 census questionnaire had 20 numbered columns, labeled as follows:
For Head of Household: 1) Name of street, avenue, or road. 2) House (and apartment) number. 3) Serial number of dwelling unit. 4) Is this house on a farm (or ranch)? (Yes or No). 5) If No in item 4 – Is this house on a place of three or more acres? (Yes or No).
6) Agriculture Questionnaire Number. **For All Persons:** 7) **Name:** What is the name of the head of this household? What are the names of all other persons who live here? List in this order: The Head, His wife, Unmarried sons and daughters (in order of age), Married sons and daughters and their families, Other relatives, Other persons, such as lodgers, roomers, maids or hired hands who live in, and their relatives. 8) **Relationship** of person to head of household, as Head, Wife, Daughter, Grandson, Mother-in-law, Lodger, Lodger's wife, Maid, Hired Hand, Patient, etc. 9) **Race:** White (W), Negro (Neg), American Indian (Ind), Japanese (Jap), Chinese (Chi), Filipino (Fil), Other race-spell out. 10) **Sex:** Male (M), Female (F), 11) How old was he on his last birthday? (If under one year of age, enter month of birth as April, May, Dec., etc.). 12) **Marital Status:** Is he now married, widowed, divorced, separated, or never married (Mar, Wd, D, Sep, Nev). 13) **Place of Birth:** What State (or foreign country) was he born in? If born outside Continental United States, enter name of Territory, possession, or foreign country. Distinguish Canada-French from Canada-other. 14) If foreign born – Is he naturalized? (Yes, No, or AP for born abroad of American Parents).
For Persons 14 years of Age and Over: 15) What was this person doing most of last week – working, keeping house, or something else? (Wk, H, Ot, or U for unable to work). 16) If H or Ot in Item 15 – Did this person do any work at all last week, not counting work around the house? (Include work for pay, in own business, profession, or farm, or un-paid family work (Yes or No). 17) If No in Item 16 – Was this person looking for work? (Yes or No). 18) If No in Item 17 – does he have a job or business? (Yes or No).
19) If Wk in Item 15 or Yes in item 16 – How many hours did he work last week? (Number of hours).
20a (Occupation): What kind of work was he doing?
20b (Industry): What kind of business or industry was he working in? 20c) Class of Worker: Private (P), Government (G), Own business (O), Without pay (family or farm business) (NP).

1950 Census Publications

Digital Capture: Prior to the April 2022 opening date of the 1950 population schedules, approximately 5,000 rolls of microfilm will be digitized for the National Archives. The images will be made available to several interested websites for shared indexing. Soon after the opening, expect FamilySearch.org's digitized images of the 1950 census to be made accessible online. To find the images, start with a FamilySearch.org catalog search, see **www.familysearch.org/search/catalog/search**. For the "Place" use "United States," then click on *Search*. At the list of categories, look for "United States – Census – 1950."

Online Searching – 1950 Census Indexes and Digital Images

The 1950 Census will be digitized from the National Archives microfilm; indexed, then made available in April 2022 at the following websites:

• **Ancestry.com**. Subscription site, free database searching. See www.ancestry.com/search/places/usa.

• **FamilySearch.org**. Free database and index search. See www.familysearch.org/search/collection/location/1.

• **MyHeritage.com**. A Family Tree subscription site. All U.S. Federal Census Records are available to subscribers with a data plan. See www.myheritage.com/research/category-1100/us-census.

• **Findmypast.com**. Monthly or annual subscriptions. Initial searches to U.S. Federal Censuses are free. See https://search.findmypast.com/search-world-records-in-census-land-and-substitutes.

• **GenealogyBank.com**. Subscription site. Initial searches to the U.S. Federal Censuses, 1790-1950 will be free. www.genealogybank.com/explore/census/all.

• **HeritageQuestOnline-Subscribers Login.** This is a library subscription service. Check with your local library to see if they subscribe to the ProQuest & HeritageQuest databases. Many subscribing libraries allow their library card holders remote access. See www.heritagequestonline.com/hqoweb/library/do/login.

Table 1950 – Statewide Census Publications

1950 Jurisdictions Included in Census	Population	Approx. Rolls of Film	Starting Film/DGS Number	URL of the FHL Catalog Page with Access to the Digital Images	Remarks
1. Alabama	3,060,000				
2. Alaska Territory	138,000				
3. Arizona	756,000				
4. Arkansas	1,906,000				
5. California	10,586,223				
6. Colorado	1,337,000				
7. Connecticut	2,007,280				
8. Delaware	321,000				
9. District of Columbia	814,000				
10. Florida	2,821,000				
11. Georgia	3,451,000				
12. Guam Territory	59,498				Unorg. Territory of Guam
13. Hawaii Territory	491,000				
14. Idaho	592,000				
15. Illinois	8,712,176				
16. Indiana	3,952,000				
17. Iowa	2,621,000				
18. Kansas	1,915,000				
19. Kentucky	2,957,000				
20. Louisiana	2,701,000				
21. Maine	911,000				
22. Maryland	2,376,000				
23. Massachusetts	4,690,000				
24. Michigan	6,421,000				
25. Minnesota	2,995,000				
26. Mississippi	2,169,000				
27. Missouri	3,946,000				
28. Montana	598,000				
29. Nebraska	1,324,000				
30. Nevada	162,000				
31. New Hampshire	531,000				
32. New Jersey	4,860,000				
33. New Mexico	687,000				
34. New York	14,830,192				
35. North Carolina	4,060,000				
36. North Dakota	616,000				
37. Ohio	7,946,627				
38. Oklahoma	2,193,000				
39. Oregon	1,532,000				
40. Panama Canal Zone	52,300				Mil. Gov. / Canal Commission Govt.
41. Pennsylvania	10,498,012				
42. Puerto Rico Territory	2,218,000				Organized Territory of Puerto Rico
43. Rhode Island	779,000				Unorg. Territory of American Samoa
44. Samoa Territory	19,550				
45. South Carolina	2,119,000				
46. South Dakota	652,000				
47. Tennessee	3,304,000				
48. Texas	7,748,000				
49. Utah	696,000				
50. Vermont	377,000				
51. Virgin Islands of the U.S.	26,654				Unorg. Terr., Virgin Islands of the U.S.
52. Virginia	3,262,000				
53. Washington	2,386,000				
54. West Virginia	2,006,000				
55. Wisconsin	3,449,000				
56. Wyoming	292,000				
-- Americans living abroad	487,545				
-- Small Islands of the U.S.	2,923				
-- Trust Territory of the U.S.	54,843				

U.S. Total: 150,697,361

Selected Online Databases from the time of the 1950 Census

1950 Census Substitute [Online Database], digitized and OCR indexed at the Ancestry.com website. This is Ancestry's extraction of city directory entries from the period c1940-1995, to include persons possibly alive at the time of the U.S. Federal Census conducted in April 1950. See www.ancestry.com/search/categories/1950census/#collections.

U.S. City Directories, 1822-1995 [Online Database], digitized and OCR indexed at the Ancestry.com website. This is the source of the names in the above 1950 database. This larger database covers the period 1822-1995. The same search elements are available, including keyword, year of residence, name, location, etc., plus this main database allows a *Browse This Collection* by State, City or County, Year, or Directory Title. This main city directory database has 1.56 billion records, see
www.ancestry.com/search/collections/usdirectories.

American Prisoners of War During the Korean War, 1950-1953 [Online Database], indexed at the FamilySearch.org website. Name index of American prisoners of war during the Korean War, compiled by the Army Staff. This database has 4,714 records. See
https://familysearch.org/search/collection/2043777.

Korean War Dead and Army Wounded, 1950-1953 [Online Database], indexed at the FamilySearch.org website. Includes an index to the casualties of Army personnel during the Korean War. Includes dead, missing, wounded or captured soldiers. This database has 109,961 records. See
https://familysearch.org/search/collection/2127897.

Korean War Repatriated Prisoners of War, 1950-1953 [Online Database], indexed at the FamilySearch.org website. Includes an index to Korean War former prisoners of war. The event date is the date of release and event place is the prisoner of war camp. This database has 4,447 records. See
https://familysearch.org/search/collection/2127902.

Korean War Battle Deaths, 1950-1957 [Online Database], indexed at the FamilySearch.org website. Includes an Index of military personnel who died (battle deaths) during the Korean War. The event date is the date died or declared dead. This database has 33,642 records. See
https://familysearch.org/search/collection/2127893.

U.S. Public Records Index, 1950-1993, Volume 1, [Online Database], indexed at the Ancestry.com website. Source: Voter Registration Lists, Public Record Filings, Historical Residential Records, and Other Household Database Listings. This Index is a compilation of various public records spanning all 50 states in the United States, including White pages, Directory assistance records, Marketing lists, Postal change-of-address forms, Public record filings, and Historical residential records. Each index record may include: A person's first name, middle name or initial and last name, A street or mailing address, A telephone number, A birth date or birth year, and an age. This database has 418,687,293 records. See
www.ancestry.com/search/collections/uspublicrecords3.

See also ***U.S. Public Records Index, 1950-1993, Volume 2*** [Online Database], indexed at the Ancestry.com website. Volume 2 has a continuation of the same compilations as Volume 1. This database has 402,469,185 records. See
www.ancestry.com/search/collections/uspublicrecords2.

National Register of Scientific and Technical Personnel Files, 1954-1970 [Online Database], indexed at the FamilySearch.org website. Includes a name index from registers of specialized personnel from the National Science Foundation. It includes professionals in the field of biology, chemistry, economics, geology, mathematics, psychology, meteorology, physics, anthropology, political science, and sociology. This database has 125,530 records. See
https://familysearch.org/search/collection/2126719.

Section 3 – Non-Population Schedules

Contents

Table 6: Availability of Non-Population Schedules 108

Descriptions of the Non-Population Schedules, 1820-1885 & 1929-1935
- Industry/Manufactures, 1820, 1850, 1860, 1870 & 1880 109
- Agricultural Schedules, 1850-1880 109
- Mortality Schedules, 1850-1880 110
- Slave Schedules, 1850-1860 110
- Social Statistics Schedules, 1850-1870 110
- 1880 Defective/Dependent/Delinquent 111
- 1885 Non-Population Schedules 112
- 1929-1930 Agriculture (Territories) 112
- 1935 Business Schedules/1935 Puerto Rico ... 112

State Availability Tables
Alabama 113
Alaska 114
American Samoa 114
Arizona 114
Arkansas 115
California 115
Colorado 116
Connecticut 117
Dakota Territory (1861-1889) 117
Delaware 118
District of Columbia 118
Florida 119
Georgia 120
Guam 121
Hawaii 121
Idaho 121
Illinois 122
Indiana 122
Iowa 123
Kansas 124
Kentucky 124
Louisiana 125
Maine 126
Maryland 126
Massachusetts 127
Michigan 128
Minnesota 129
Mississippi 129
Missouri 130
Montana 131
Nebraska 131
Nevada 132
New Hampshire 132
New Jersey 133
New Mexico 133
New York 134
North Carolina 135
North Dakota (1889-1935) 135
Ohio 136
Oklahoma 136
Oregon 136
Pennsylvania 137
Puerto Rico 138
Rhode Island 138
South Carolina 138
South Dakota (1889-1935) 139
Tennessee 139
Texas 140
Utah 141
Vermont 141
Virgin Islands of the U.S. 142
Virginia 142
Washington 143
West Virginia 144
Wisconsin 144
Wyoming 145

Table 6. Availability of Non-Population Schedules

State / Territory	Year a Terr.	Year a State	Industry/Manufactures 1820	1850	1860	1870	1880	1885	Agriculture Schedules 1850	1860	1870	1880	1885	Mortality Schedules 1850	1860	1870	1880	1885	Slaves 1850	1860	Social Statistics 1850	1860	1870	1880 DDD	Misc. Cens.	1930 Terr.	1935 Cens.
Alabama	1817	1819	•	•	•	•	•		•	•	•	•		•	•	•	•		•	•				•			•
Alaska	1912	1959																									•	
American Samoa	1899	--																									•	
Arizona	1861	1912													•	•												•
Arkansas	1819	1836	•			•			•	•	•			•	•	•	•		•	•				•			•
California	--	1850		•	•	•	•		•	•	•	•		•	•	•	•				•	•	•	•			•
Colorado	1861	1876					•		•	•	•	•	•		•	•	•						•	•			•
Connecticut	--	1788	•	•	•	•	•		•	•	•	•		•	•	•	•							•			•
Dakota Territory	1861	--				•	•			•	•	•			•		•	•						•		1		
Delaware	--	1787	•	•	•	•	•		•	•	•	•		•	•	•	•		•	•	•	•		•			•
Distr. of Columbia	1801	--	•	•	•	•	•		•	•	•	•		•	•	•	•		•	•				•			•
Florida	1822	1845		•	•	•	•	•	•	•	•	•	•	•	•	•	•	•	•	•		•	•	•			•
Georgia	--	1788	•			•			•	•	•	•		•	•	•	•		•	•		•	•	•			•
Guam	1898	--																									•	
Hawaii	1900	1959																									•	
Idaho	1863	1890			•	•				•	•				•	•								•	•			•
Illinois	1809	1818	•		•	•			•	•	•			•	•	•	•				•		•					•
Indiana	1800	1816	•	•	•	•	•		•	•	•	•		•	•	•	•				•	•	•	•			•
Iowa	1838	1846		•	•	•	•		•	•	•	•		•	•	•	•				•	•	•	•			•
Kansas	1854	1861			•	•	•			•	•	•			•	•	•						•	•			•
Kentucky	--	1791	•	•	•	•	•		•	•	•	•		•	•	•	•		•	•		•	•	•			•
Louisiana	1809	1812	•			•			•	•	•	•		•	•	•	•		•	•	•	•	•	•			•
Maine	--	1820	•	•	•	•	•		•	•	•	•		•	•	•	•				•	•	•	•			•
Maryland	--	1788	•	•	•	•	•		•	•	•	•		•	•	•	•		•	•	•	•	•	•			•
Massachusetts	--	1788	•	•	•	•	•		•	•	•	•		•	•	•	•				•	•	•	•			•
Michigan	1805	1837	•	•	•	•	•		•	•	•	•		•	•	•	•				•	•	•	•			•
Minnesota	1849	1858		•	•	•	•		•	•	•	•		•	•	•	•				•	•	•	•			•
Mississippi	1798	1817	•	•	•	•	•		•	•	•	•		•	•	•	•		•	•	•	•	•	•			•
Missouri	1805	1821	•	•	•	•	•		•	•	•	•		•	•	•	•		•	•	•	•	•	•			•
Montana	1864	1889			•	•					•	•				•	•						•	•			•
Nebraska	1854	1867			•	•	•	•		•	•	•	•		•	•	•	•					•	•			•
Nevada	1861	1864			•					•					•									•				•
New Hampshire	--	1788	•	•	•	•	•		•	•	•	•		•	•	•											•
New Jersey	--	1787	•	•	•	•	•		•	•	•	•		•	•	•	•		•		•	•	•	•			•
New Mexico	1850	1912					•					•					•										•
New York	--	1788	•	•	•	•	•		•	•	•	•		•	•	•	•				•	•	•	•			•
North Carolina	--	1789	•	•	•	•	•		•	•	•	•		•	•	•	•		•	•	•	•	•	•			•
North Dakota	--	1889																										•
Ohio	1787	1803	•	•	•	•	•		•	•	•	•		•	•	•								•			•
Oklahoma	1890	1897																										•
Oregon	1848	1859		•	•	•	•		•	•	•	•		•	•	•	•				•	•	•	•			•
Pennsylvania	--	1787	•	•	•	•	•		•	•	•	•		•	•	•	•				•	•	•	•			•
Puerto Rico	1898	--																									•	•
Rhode Island	--	1790	•			•				•					•								•					•
South Carolina	--	1788	•	•	•	•	•		•	•	•	•		•	•	•	•		•	•	•	•	•	•			•
South Dakota	--	1889																										•
Tennessee	1790	1796	•	•	•	•	•		•	•	•	•		•	•	•	•		•	•	•	•	•	•			•
Texas	--	1845		•	•	•	•		•	•	•	•		•	•	•	•		•	•	•	•	•	•			•
Utah	1850	1896			•	•				•	•	•			•	•						•	•					•
Vermont	--	1791	•	•	•	•	•		•	•	•	•		•	•	•	•				•	•	•	•			•
Virgin Islands	1917	--																								2	•	
Virginia	--	1788	•	•	•	•	•		•	•	•	•		•	•	•	•		•	•	•	•	•	•			•
Washington	1853	1889			•	•				•	•				•	•							•	•				•
West Virginia	--	1863			•	•			•	•	•			•	•	•								•				•
Wisconsin	1836	1848	•	•	•	•			•	•	•	•		•	•	•	•				•	•	•	•			•
Wyoming	1868	1890				•																						•

Note 1: **Dakota Territory** had an **1885** Union Soldiers Schedule.   Note 2: The **Virgin Islands of the U.S.** had a **1917** Agriculture Schedule.

Descriptions of the Non-Population Schedules, 1820-1885 & 1929-1935

Amateur genealogists are devoted users of the *Population Schedules* of the U.S. federal censuses. Yet, there are many underused census schedules available, i.e., the special *Non-Population Schedules*.

There were separate Non-Population schedules recorded as part of every federal census, 1820-2010. However, there were Non-Population schedules that did not survive the World War II era, when the Census Bureau was given permission by Congress to destroy the original 1900-1940 census schedules. The Population Schedules had all been microfilmed, but most of the Non-Population schedules for 1900-1940 had not been microfilmed – they were included in the destruction of original records and were lost forever. Thus, this review has a gap between 1885 and 1929.

The work to identify all of the surviving Non-Population Schedules could not have been done without the help of these standard references:
1) Caroll D. Wright, "Non-Population Census Forms and Instructions Before 1900," in ***History and Growth of the United States Census*** (Washington, DC: Government Printing Office, 1900); and for Non-Population schedules after 1900, 2) Claire Prechtel-Kluskens, "The Nonpopulation Census Schedules," ***The Record***, Vol. 2, No. 1, pp. 9 & 25 (Sept. 1995); and 3) NARA's ***Nonpopulation Census Records***, see www.archives.gov/research/census/nonpopulation.

This section identifies all known surviving copies of the following special census schedules:
- **Industry and Manufacturing Schedules** for 1820, 1850, 1860, 1870, and 1880 censuses.
- **Agricultural Schedules** for 1850, 1860, 1870, and 1880.
- **Mortality Schedules** for 1850, 1860, 1870, and 1880.
- **Slave Schedules** for 1850 and 1860.
- **Social Statistics Schedules** for 1850, 1860, and 1870.
- **1880 Defective, Dependent, Delinquent Classes.**
- **1885 Non-population Schedules** (for five states & territories with a federally-assisted 1885 census).
- **1929-1930 Agricultural schedules** (for Territories).
- **1935 Business Schedules** & the **1935 Puerto Rico Census.**

Industry and Manufacturing Schedules

The **1810 Manufactures** lists were actually the first Non-Population statistics recorded, but the 1810 lists are not included here because the schedules were integrated into the population schedules (added to the end of each county's name list). The only exception was for New York, where selected pages from ten counties were filmed separately. (See the NY Statewide Availability Table; page 134 – NY1).

The ***1820 Manufactures;*** and the ***1850, 1860, and 1870 Products of Industry Schedules*** each had special lists of manufactured products and other statistics about businesses producing articles valued at $500 or more per year. Typical questions included: Name of the business owner, or agent; Name of business; Capital invested in the business; Raw materials used; Kind of motive power used; Average number of hands employed, Average monthly cost for male wages, Average monthly cost for female wages, and Annual product: quantities, kind, and values.

The ***1880 Manufactures Schedules*** added special lists by the category of the business, including 1) Boot and shoe factories; leather and tanning-curing works; 2) Flouring and grist mills; cheese or butter processing plants; salt works. 3) Lumber mills, sawmills; brickyards, tile works, and coal mines; and 4) agricultural implement works, and quarries.

Agricultural Schedules

For the 1850, 1860, 1870, and 1880 censuses, a separate schedule was prepared listing the production of all farms in America. (The Virgin Islands had an Agriculture Schedule taken in 1917). All of these schedules show the name of a farm owner, agent, or manager, along with details about his livestock and produce. The types of questions on the 1850 form are shown below. Each of the other census years had a similar layout:
- Name of owner, agent, or manager of a farm.
- Number of improved/unimproved acres.
- Cash value of a farm.
- Value of farming implements and machinery.
- Number of horses, milk cows, working oxen, other cattle, sheep, and swine.

- Value of livestock
- Bushels produced during the census year ending June 1, of wheat, rye, Indian corn, oats, rice, tobacco, clover seed, other grass seed, hops, flax seed, and hemp.
- Pounds produced during the census year ending June 1, of butter, cheese, flax, cane sugar, maple sugar, beeswax, and honey.
- Value of orchard products, in dollars.
- Wine produced, in gallons.
- Hay produced, in tons.
- Gallons of molasses.
- Value of homemade manufactures.
- Value of slaughtered animals.

Mortality Schedules

These special lists were prepared for the 1850, 1860, 1870, and 1880 censuses. The mortality schedules were taken separately from the population schedules and list the names of any person who died within one year before the census day, e.g., the 1850 mortality schedule lists the name of any person who died between 1 June 1849 and 31 May 1850.

The *1850 and 1860 Mortality Schedules* included the following information:
- Name of deceased.
- Age.
- Sex.
- Color.
- Free or slave.
- Married or widowed.
- Birthplace.
- Month of death.
- Occupation.
- Disease or cause of death.
- Number of days ill.

The *1870 Mortality Schedule* included the following information:
- Name of deceased.
- Age, last birthday.
- Sex.
- Color.
- Married or widowed.
- Birthplace.
- Whether father of foreign birth.
- Whether mother of foreign birth.
- Month of death.
- Occupation.
- Disease or cause of death.

The *1880 Mortality Schedule* included the following information:
- Page number (from population schedule).
- Family Number (from population schedule).
- Name of deceased.
- Age.
- Sex.
- Color.
- Whether single, married, widowed, or divorced.
- Birthplace of deceased.
- Birthplace of deceased's father.
- Birthplace of deceased's mother.
- Occupation.
- Month of death.
- Disease or cause of death.
- Months in county.
- Place disease contracted.
- Name of attending physician.

Slave Schedules

Slave Schedules were produced only for the 1850 and 1860 censuses. In all cases, the schedules list the name of a slave owner and numbers of slaves held by that slave owner. Virtually all of the original manuscripts for all applicable states were retained by the National Archives and all surviving schedules were microfilmed by the National Archives. The information listed on the *1850 and 1860 Slave Schedules* was as follows:
- City, town, or sub-district of slave owner.
- Name of slave owner.
- Number of slaves, listed by age, sex, and color.
- Whether a fugitive.
- Whether manumitted (granted freedom).
- Whether deaf, dumb, insane, or idiotic.

NOTE: Most of the countywide slave schedules list the names of slave owners only; however, some enumerators chose to list the first names of individual slaves on their lists. A researcher must view each countywide slave schedules to see if the names of slaves are shown or not.

Social Statistics Schedules

For the 1850, 1860, and 1870 censuses, a special set of forms was used to gather statistics concerning a particular geographic area within a county. The divisions are described on each schedule page, such as "North Half Fulton County," and the divisions in rural areas do not follow any strict rules. Most divisions are easily identified as townships, towns, cities, or parts of a county. As an example of the type of statistics gathered, the listings for the 1850 Social Statistic Schedules are shown below:
- Total value of real estate for the division.
- Total value of personal property for the division.
- Names and numbers of colleges, academies, and schools in the division; the number of pupils and

number of teachers; and facts about endowments, taxation, etc.
- Names and number of libraries in the division.
- Names and number of newspapers in the division, with description, publication dates, and circulation.
- Poor Houses (pauperism) with a count of the number of native / foreign paupers, and the support cost.
- Number of criminals in the division, native and foreign.
- Average monthly wage for a farmhand in the division.
- Average monthly wage for a day laborer in the division.
- Average monthly wage for a carpenter in the division.
- Average weekly wage for a male domestic.
- Average weekly wage for a female domestic.
- Average price of board to a laboring man for a week.

Defective, Dependent, and Delinquent (1880 census only)

A total of seven supplementary schedules under the title ***Defective, Dependent, and Delinquent Classes*** were prepared for the 1880 census as they applied to each county's census enumeration. The supplementary schedules were: 1) Insane Inhabitants, 2) Idiots, 3) Deaf-mutes, 4) Blind, 5) Homeless Children, 6) Inhabitants in Prison, and 7) Pauper and Indigent Inhabitants:

1. Insane Inhabitants. This supplemental schedule lists the following information:
- Page number (from population schedule).
- Line number (from population schedule).
- Name of insane person.
- City or town of residence.
- County of residence.
- Whether an inmate of an institution or a day patient.
- Form of disease.
- Duration of current attack.
- Number of attacks.
- Age at first attack.
- Whether person must be kept in a cell.
- Whether person must be restrained.
- Whether person is an inmate in a hospital or asylum.
- Total length of time in institution.
- Date of discharge.
- Whether the person is epileptic.
- Whether the person is suicidal.
- Whether the person is homicidal.

2. Idiots. (In 1880, an idiot was the common term for someone who was mentally deficient.) The supplemental schedule listed the following information for each person:
- Page number (from population schedule).
- Line number (from population schedule).
- Name of person.
- City or town of residence.
- County of residence.
- Whether person is self-supporting or partly so.
- Age at which idiocy occurred.
- Supposed cause of idiocy.
- Size of person's head (large, small, or normal).
- Whether person ever in training school. If yes, name of school.
- Time spent during life in training school.
- Year of discharge from training school.
- Whether the person is also insane.
- Whether the person is also blind.
- Whether the person is also deaf.
- Whether the person is also epileptic.
- Whether the person is paralyzed. On left or right side?

3. Deaf-mutes. This schedule listed the following information:
- Page number (from population schedules).
- Line number (from population schedules).
- Name of person.
- City or town of residence.
- County of residence.
- Whether person is self-supporting, or partly so.
- Supposed cause of deafness, if known.
- Age at which deafness occurred.
- Whether person is semi-mute.
- Whether person is semi-deaf.
- Whether person was ever in an institution for deaf-mutes.
- Total length of time in an institution.
- Year of discharge.
- Whether person is also insane.
- Whether person is also idiotic.
- Whether person is also blind.

4. Blind Inhabitants. This schedule listed the following information:
- Page number (from population schedule).
- Line number (from population schedule).
- Name of person.
- City or town of residence.
- County of residence.
- Whether person is self-supporting or partly so.
- Age at which blindness occurred.
- Form of blindness.
- Supposed cause of blindness, if known.
- Whether totally blind.
- Whether semi-blind.
- Whether an inmate at an institution for the blind. If so, name of institution.
- Total length of time in such an institution.
- Year of discharge.
- Whether this person is also insane.
- Whether this person is also idiotic.
- Whether this person is also deaf-mute.

5. Homeless Children. This schedule listed the following information:
- Page number (from population schedule).
- Line number (from population schedule).
- Name of person.
- City or town of residence.
- County of residence.
- Whether child's father is deceased.
- Whether child's mother is deceased.
- Whether the child was abandoned by his/her parents.
- Whether the child was surrendered to an institution by parents.
- Whether the child was born in an institution.
- Year admitted to an institution.
- Whether the child is illegitimate.
- Whether the child is separated from his/her mother.
- Whether the child was arrested. If so, for what offense?
- Whether the child was convicted or sentenced.
- Whether the origin of the child was respectable.
- Whether the child was removed from criminal surroundings.
- Whether the child is blind.
- Whether the child is deaf-mute.
- Whether the child is an idiot.

6. Inhabitants in Prison. This schedule listed the following information:
- Line number (from population schedules).
- Name of person.
- City or town of residence.
- County of residence.
- Place of imprisonment.
- Whether imprisoned by U.S., State, or City.
- Whether person is awaiting trail.
- Whether person is serving a term of imprisonment.
- Whether person is serving out a fine.
- Whether person is awaiting execution (death).
- Whether person sentenced to higher prison and awaiting transfer.
- Whether person is held as a witness.
- Whether imprisoned for debt.
- Whether imprisoned for insanity.
- Date incarcerated.
- Alleged offense.
- Amount of fine imposed.
- Number of days in jail or workhouse.
- Number of years in penitentiary.
- Whether at hard labor. If yes, what kind of work.
- If at hard labor, inside or outside work.
- If at hard labor, whether labor contracted out.

7. Pauper and Indigent Inhabitants in Institutions. This schedule listed the following information:
- Page number (from population schedules).
- Line number (from population schedules).
- Name of person.
- City or town of residence.
- County of residence.
- Supported at cost of city or town.
- Supported at cost of county.
- Supported at cost of state.
- Supported at cost of institution.
- Whether person is able-bodied.
- Whether person is habitually intemperate (alcoholic).
- Whether person is epileptic.
- Whether person ever convicted of a crime.
- Whether person disabled. If so, describe disability.
- Whether person was born in an institution.
- Date of admission to institution.
- Whether husband is also in this establishment.
- Whether wife is also in this establishment.
- Whether mother is also in this establishment.
- Whether father is also in this establishment.
- Whether sons in this establishment. If so, how many?
- Whether daughters in this establishment. If so, how many?
- Whether brothers in this establishment. If so, how many?
- Whether sisters in this establishment. If so, how many?
- Whether person is also blind.
- Whether person is also deaf and dumb.
- Whether person is also insane.

1885 Non-population Census Schedules

The states and territories that took an 1885 census with federal assistance were Colorado, Dakota Territory, Florida, Nebraska, and New Mexico Territory. The 1885 was patterned after the 1880 census format, and included similar Manufactures, Agriculture, and Mortality schedules. For details of surviving 1885 Non-Population schedules, see the State Availability Tables for the five states/territories.

1929-1930 Agricultural Schedules - Territories

Taken only in the territories of Alaska, American Samoa, Guam, Hawaii, Puerto Rico, and the Virgin Island of the U.S. For details, see the Availability Table for each territory.

1935 Business & 1935 Puerto Rico Censuses

In 1935, the first national business census was conducted. It had statistics under six categories: Advertising, Banking, Miscellaneous Enterprises, Trucking, Warehousing, and Radio Stations.

Also in 1935, a full census was taken for the Territory of Puerto Rico. For details, see the State Availability Tables.

State Availability Tables – Alabama to Wyoming
Non-Population Schedules, 1820-1935

The following tables show the Non-Population Schedules available for each state or territory. Each table has four columns: 1) Non-Population Schedules - Year & Type of Schedule. 2) National Archives & Records Administration (NARA) Microfilm Series Number & Number of Rolls. 3) Family History Library (FHL) Film Number (for an original schedule or index on microfilm), and 4) the Repository/Location of Originals (O), and URL (for online databases, indexes, digital images, or info pages). See the state **Notes** for the locations of originals or remarks.

Fifteen (15) states had all of their Non-Population schedules digitized and indexed, then combined into a single National database (still in progress). Also, the Mortality Schedules and Slave Schedules for all states were each gathered together, digitized, and indexed as national databases. These databases, plus those states with another set of digital images are all noted in the State Availability tables below.

Use the Family History Library (FHL) online catalog to search for a microfilm number. Go to www.familysearch.org/search/catalog/search. Click on *Film/Fiche Number* for a dialog box to enter a film number. At any catalog title page, a list of microfilm roll numbers and the contents of each roll will also indicate whether the microfilm was digitized yet (if so, click on the camera icon 📷 to access the images). **NOTE:** All FHL roll microfilms are expected to be digitized and accessible online by 2025.

Alabama

Non-Population Schedules Year & Type of Schedule	NARA Series, No. of Rolls	FHL Film No.	(O) Location of Originals (See Notes) URL: online database, digital images, or info page.
1820 Manufactures	M279, 1 roll	1024518	(O) NARA (AL-1)
1850 Industry	--	6002862	(O) ADAH (AL-2)
1860 Industry	--	--	(O) ADAH (AL-2)
1870 Industry	--	--	(O) ADAH (AL-2)
1880 Manufactures	--	--	(O) ADAH (AL-2)
1850 Agricultural	--	6002862	(O) ADAH (AL-2)
1860 Agricultural	--	--	(O) ADAH (AL-2).
1870 Agricultural	--	--	(O) ADAH (AL-2)
1880 Agricultural	--	--	(O) ADAH (AL-2).
1850 Mortality	--	--	(O) ADAH (AL-2)
1860 Mortality	--	1533724	(O) ADAH (AL-2) Digital images: www.familysearch.org/search/catalog/632406.
1870 Mortality	--	1405189	(O) ADAH (AL-2) Digital images: www.familysearch.org/search/catalog/306345.
1880 Mortality	--	1405191	(O) ADAH (AL-2) Digital images: www.familysearch.org/search/catalog/372488.
1880 Def/Dep/Del Classes	--	--	(O) ADAH (AL-2) See www.ancestry.com/search/collections/1880uscensusddd.
1850 Slave	M432, 8 rolls	--	(O) NARA See www.ancestry.com/search/collections/1850slaveschedules.
1860 Slave	M653, 10 rolls	--	(O) NARA www.ancestry.com/search/collections/1860slaveschedules.
1935 Business-Advertising	M1797, 1 roll.	--	(O) Info: www.archives.gov/research/census/nonpopulation/alabama.html.
1935 Business-Banking	M2066, 8 rolls	--	(O) Info: www.archives.gov/research/census/nonpopulation/alabama.html.
1935 Business-Misc.Enter.	M2067, 1 roll	--	(O) Info: www.archives.gov/research/census/nonpopulation/alabama.html.
1935 Business-Trucking	M2068, 2 rolls	--	(O) Info: www.archives.gov/research/census/nonpopulation/alabama.html.
1935 Business-Warehousing	M2069, 1 roll	--	(O) Info: www.archives.gov/research/census/nonpopulation/alabama.html.
1935 Business-Radio Sta.	M2070, 1 roll	--	(O) Info: www.archives.gov/research/census/nonpopulation/alabama.html.

Alabama Notes:

AL-1. The ***Records of the 1820 Census of Manufactures*** (NARA series M279, 27 rolls). Roll 27 contains the Western District of Tennessee, Illinois, and pages from *Digest of Manufacturing Establishments in the United States and of their Manufactures* (Washington, DC: Gales & Seaton, 1823) for Alabama, Louisiana, Missouri, Michigan, and Arkansas. See the FHL catalog page: **www.familysearch.org/search/catalog/280127**.

AL-2. Alabama's 1850-1880 Non-Population originals are all located at the Alabama Department of Archives & History (ADAH), Montgomery, AL. Alabama is included in ***U.S., Selected Federal Census Non-Population Schedules, 1850-1880*** [Online Database], digitized and indexed at the Ancestry.com website. See **www.ancestry.com/search/collections/nonpopcensus**.

Alaska

Non-Population Schedules Year & Type of Schedule	NARA Series, No. of Rolls	FHL Film No.	(O) Location of Originals (See Notes) URL: online database, digital images, or info page.
1929 Agriculture-Series 1	M1871, 1 roll	--	(O) NARA (AK-1)
1929 Agriculture-Series 2	M1871, 1 roll	--	(O) NARA (AK-1)

Alaska Notes:
AL-1. NARA microfilm publication M1871, *Nonpopulation Census Schedules for Alaska, 1929: Agriculture* (1 roll) has general agricultural and livestock schedules reporting farm products in Alaska during the year ending October 1, 1929. For info, see
www.archives.gov/research/census/nonpopulation/alaska.html.

American Samoa

Non-Population Schedules Year & Type of Schedule	NARA Series, No. of Rolls	FHL Film No.	(O) Location of Originals (See Notes) URL: online database, digital images, or info page.
1930 Agriculture-Series 1	M1874, 1 roll	--	(O) NARA (AS-1)
1930 Agriculture-Series 2	M1874, 1 roll	--	(O) NARA (AS-1)

American Samoa Notes:
AS-1. NARA microfilm publication M1874, *Nonpopulation Census Schedules for American Samoa, 1930: Agriculture* (1 roll) has general agricultural and livestock schedules reporting farm products grown or owned in American Samoa during 1929-1930. For info, see
www.archives.gov/research/census/nonpopulation/american-samoa.html.

Arizona

Non-Population Schedules Year & Type of Schedule	NARA Series, No. of Rolls	FHL Film No.	(O) Location of Originals (See Notes) URL: online database, digital images, or info page.
1870 Mortality	T655, 1 roll	422410	(O) NARA (AZ-1)
1880 Mortality	T655, 1 roll	422410	(O) ADAH (AZ-1)
1935 Business-Advertising	M1797, 1 roll.	--	(O) Info: www.archives.gov/research/census/nonpopulation/arizona.html.
1935 Business-Banking	M2066, 1 roll	--	(O) Info: www.archives.gov/research/census/nonpopulation/arizona.html.
1935 Business-Misc. Enterprises	M2067, 1 roll	--	(O) Info: www.archives.gov/research/census/nonpopulation/arizona.html.
1935 Business-Trucking	M2068, 1 roll	--	(O) Info: www.archives.gov/research/census/nonpopulation/arizona.html.
1935 Business-Warehousing	M2069, 1 roll	--	(O) Info: www.archives.gov/research/census/nonpopulation/arizona.html.
1935 Business-Radio Sta.	M2070, 1 roll	--	(O) Info: www.archives.gov/research/census/nonpopulation/arizona.html.

Arizona Notes:
AZ-1. See *U.S., Federal Census Mortality Schedules Index, 1850-1880* [Online Database], indexed at the Ancestry.com website (includes Arizona). This combined index to the 1850, 1860, 1870, and 1880 Mortality Schedules was taken from a printed index, same title, Jackson, Ron V., Accelerated Indexing Systems, 1999. See www.ancestry.com/search/collections/mortalitycen. See also *U.S. Federal Census Mortality Schedules, 1850-1885* **(Includes Arizona)** [Online Database], digitized and indexed at the Ancestry.com website. See **www.ancestry.com/search/collections/usmortality.**

Arkansas

Non-Population Schedules Year & Type of Schedule	NARA Series, No. of Rolls	FHL Film No.	(O) Location of Originals (See Notes) URL: online database, digital images, or info page.
1820 Manufactures	M279, 1 roll	1024518	(O) NARA (AR-1)
1880 Manufactures	--	--	(O) UofAR (AR-2)
1850 Agricultural	--	--	(O) UofAR (AR-2)
1860 Agricultural	--	--	(O) UofAR (AR-2)
1870 Agricultural	--	--	(O) UofAR (AR-2)
1850 Mortality	--	--	(O) UofAR (AR-2) Online DB: www.familysearch.org/search/collection/1420441.
1860 Mortality	--	1549729	(O) UofAR (AR-2) Digitized Index: www.familysearch.org/search/catalog/177906.
1870 Mortality	--	1549730	(O) UofAR (AR-2) Digital Images: www.familysearch.org/search/catalog/620295.
1880 Mortality	--	1405191	(O) UofAR (AR-2) Digital Images: www.familysearch.org/search/catalog/620295.
1880 Def/Dep/Del Classes	--	--	(O) UofAR (AR-2) See www.ancestry.com/search/collections/1880uscensusddd.
1850 Slave	M432, 1 rolls	--	(O) NARA See www.ancestry.com/search/collections/1850slaveschedules.
1860 Slave	M653, 2 rolls	--	(O) NARA See www.ancestry.com/search/collections/1860slaveschedules.
1935 Business-Advertising	M1797, 1 roll.	--	(O) Info: www.archives.gov/research/census/nonpopulation/arkansas.html.
1935 Business-Banking	M2066, 6 rolls	--	(O) Info: www.archives.gov/research/census/nonpopulation/arkansas.html .
1935 Business-Misc.Enterprises	M2067, 1 roll	--	(O) Info: www.archives.gov/research/census/nonpopulation/arkansas.html.
1935 Business-Trucking	M2068, 2 rolls	--	(O) Info: www.archives.gov/research/census/nonpopulation/arkansas.html.
1935 Business-Warehousing	M2069, 1 roll	--	(O) Info: www.archives.gov/research/census/nonpopulation/alabama.html.
1935 Business-Radio Stations	M2070, 1 roll	--	(O) Info: www.archives.gov/research/census/nonpopulation/arkansas.html.

Arkansas Notes:

AR-1. The *Records of the 1820 Census of Manufactures* (NARA series M279, 27 rolls). Roll 27 contains the Western District of Tennessee, Illinois, and pages from *Digest of Manufacturing Establishments in the United States and of their Manufactures* (Washington, DC: Gales & Seaton, 1823) for Alabama, Louisiana, Missouri, Michigan, and Arkansas. See the FHL catalog page: www.familysearch.org/search/catalog/280127.

AR-2. The 1850-1880 AR Agricultural Schedules originals; 1880 Manufactures originals; 1850-1880 Mortality originals; and the 1880 Defective/Dependent/Delinquent originals are all located at the University of Arkansas, Fayetteville, AR. See
https://libraries.uark.edu/specialcollections/research/guides/genealogy.asp. Microfilm also available at the Arkansas State Archives, Little Rock. See http://archives.arkansas.gov/research/search-records.aspx.

California

Non-Population Schedules Year & Type of Schedule	NARA Series, No. of Rolls	FHL Film No.	(O) Location of Originals (See Notes) URL: online database, digital images, or info page.
1850 Industry	--	--	(O) UofCalif. (CA-1)
1860 Industry	--	--	(O) UofCalif. (CA-1)
1870 Industry	--	--	(O) UofCalif. (CA-1)
1880 Manufactures	--	--	(O) UofCalif. (CA-1)
1850 Agricultural	--	--	(O) UofCalif. (CA-1)
1860 Agricultural	--	--	(O) UofCalif. (CA-1)
1870 Agricultural	--	--	(O) UofCalif. (CA-1)
1880 Agricultural	--	--	(O) UofCalif. (CA-1)
1850 Mortality	--	--	(O) UofCalif. (CA-1) (CA-2)
1860 Mortality	--	--	(O) UofCalif. (CA-1) (CA-2)
1870 Mortality	--	--	(O) UofCalif. (CA-1) (CA-2)
1880 Mortality	--	--	(O) UofCalif. (CA-1) (CA-2)
1850 Social Statistics	--	--	(O) UofCalif. (CA-1)
1860 Social Statistics	--	--	(O) UofCalif. (CA-1)
1870 Social Statistics	--	--	(O) UofCalif. (CA-1)
1880 Def/Dep/Del Classes	--	--	(O) UCalif.(CA-1) online: www.ancestry.com/search/collections/1880uscensusddd.

California, Cont'd

Non-Population Schedules Year & Type of Schedule	NARA Series, No. of Rolls	FHL Film No.	(O) Location of Originals (See Notes) URL: online database, digital images, or info page.
1935 Business-Advertising	M1797, 1 roll.	--	(O) Info: www.archives.gov/research/census/nonpopulation/california.html.
1935 Business-Banking	M2066, 9 rolls	--	(O) Info: www.archives.gov/research/census/nonpopulation/california.html.
1935 Business-Misc.Enterprises	M2067, 5 roll	--	(O) Info: www.archives.gov/research/census/nonpopulation/california.html.
1935 Business-Trucking	M2068, 3 rolls	--	(O) Info: www.archives.gov/research/census/nonpopulation/california.html.
1935 Business-Warehousing	M2069, 2 roll	--	(O) Info: www.archives.gov/research/census/nonpopulation/california.html.
1935 Business-Radio Stations	M2070, 1 roll	--	(O) Info: www.archives.gov/research/census/nonpopulation/california.html.

California Notes:

CA-1. The original Non-Population schedules, 1850-1880 are all located at the University of California-Berkley. See **www.lib.berkeley.edu**. California is included in *U.S., Selected Federal Census Non-Population Schedules, 1850-1880* [Online Database], digitized and indexed at the Ancestry.com website. See www.ancestry.com/search/collections/nonpopcensus.

CA-2. California is included in the *U.S. Federal Census Mortality Schedules, 1850-1885* [Online Database], digitized and indexed at the Ancestry.com website. See www.ancestry.com/search/collections/usmortality.

Colorado

Non-Population Schedules Year & Type of Schedule	NARA Series, No. of Rolls	FHL Film No.	(O) Location of Originals (See Notes) URL: online database, digital images, or info page.
1870 Industry	--	--	(O) Duke Univ. (CO-1)
1880 Manufactures	--	--	(O) Duke Univ. (CO-1)
1885 Manufactures	--	--	(O) Duke Univ. (CO-1)
1870 Agriculture	--	--	(O) Duke Univ. (CO-1)
1880 Agriculture	--	--	(O) Duke Univ. (CO-1)
1885 Agriculture	--	--	(O) Duke Univ. (CO-1)
1870 Agriculture	--	--	(O) Duke Univ. (CO-1)
1870 Mortality	T655, 1 roll	422411	(O) NARA (CO-2) (CO-3)
1880 Mortality	T655, 1 roll	422411	(O) NARA (CO-2) (CO-3)
1885 Mortality	--	--	(O) Duke Univ. (CO-1)
1870 Social Statistics	--	--	(O) Duke Univ. (CO-1)
1880 Def/Dep/Del Classes	--	--	(O) Duke Univ. (CO-1)
1935 Business-Advertising	M1797, 1 roll.	--	(O) Info: www.archives.gov/research/census/nonpopulation/colorado.html.
1935 Business-Banking	M2066, 9 rolls	--	(O) Info: www.archives.gov/research/census/nonpopulation/colorado.html.
1935 Business-Misc.Enterprises	M2067, 5 roll	--	(O) Info: www.archives.gov/research/census/nonpopulation/colorado.html.
1935 Business-Trucking	M2068, 3 rolls	--	(O) Info: www.archives.gov/research/census/nonpopulation/colorado.html.
1935 Business-Warehousing	M2069, 2 roll	--	(O) Info: www.archives.gov/research/census/nonpopulation/colorado.html.
1935 Business-Radio Stations	M2070, 1 roll	--	(O) Info: www.archives.gov/research/census/nonpopulation/colorado.html.

Colorado Notes:

CO-1. Originals located at Rubenstein Library-Library Service Center, Manuscripts, Duke University, Durham, NC. Search for "non-population" at the search dialog box, see **https://library.duke.edu**.

CO-2. Colorado 1870 & 1880 Mortality Schedules included in the national database, *U.S. Federal Census Mortality Schedules, 1850-1885* [Online Database], digitized and indexed at the Ancestry.com website. See www.ancestry.com/search/collections/usmortality.

CO-3. Colorado's original 1870 and 1880 Mortality Schedules spent some time at the DAR Library in Washington, DC, but were later returned to the National Archives. While there, the DAR undertook a full index to the names from both census years. The NARA microfilm includes the index (as does the FHL film).

Connecticut

Non-Population Schedules Year & Type of Schedule	NARA Series, No. of Rolls	FHL Film No.	(O) Location of Originals (See Notes) URL: online database, digital images, or info page.
1820 Manufactures	M279, 1 roll	1024495	(O) See www.familysearch.org/search/catalog/280127. Digitized.
1850 Industry	--	--	(O) CT St. Lib. (CT-1)
1860 Industry	--	--	(O) CT St. Lib. (CT-1)
1870 Industry	--	--	(O) CT St. Lib. (CT-1)
1880 Manufactures	--	--	(O) CT St. Lib. (CT-1)
1850 Agriculture	--	--	(O) CT St. Lib. (CT-1)
1860 Agriculture	--	--	(O) CT St. Lib. (CT-1)
1870 Agriculture	--	--	(O) CT St. Lib. (CT-1)
1880 Agriculture	--	--	(O) CT St. Lib. (CT-1)
1850 Mortality	--	234536	(O) CT St. Lib. (CT-1) (CT-2) FHL: www.familysearch.org/search/catalog/759730.
1860 Mortality	--	234536	(O) CT St. Lib. (CT-1) (CT-2) FHL: www.familysearch.org/search/catalog/759738.
1870 Mortality	--	234536	(O) CT St. Lib. (CT-1) (CT-2) FHL: www.familysearch.org/search/catalog/41227.
1880 Mortality	--	234537	(O) CT St. Lib. (CT-1) (CT-2) FHL: www.familysearch.org/search/catalog/229789.
1880 Def/Dep/Del Classes	--	--	(O) CT St. Lib. Online: www.ancestry.com/search/collections/1880uscensusddd.
1935 Business-Advertising	M1797, 1 roll.	--	(O) Info: www.archives.gov/research/census/nonpopulation/connecticut.html.
1935 Business-Banking	M2066, 8 rolls	--	(O) Info: www.archives.gov/research/census/nonpopulation/connecticut.html.
1935 Business-Misc.Enterprises	M2067, 2 roll	--	(O) Info: www.archives.gov/research/census/nonpopulation/connecticut.html.
1935 Business-Trucking	M2068, 2 rolls	--	(O) Info: www.archives.gov/research/census/nonpopulation/connecticut.html.
1935 Business-Warehousing	M2069, 1 roll	--	(O) Info: www.archives.gov/research/census/nonpopulation/connecticut.html.
1935 Business-Radio Stations	M2070, 1 roll	--	(O) Info: www.archives.gov/research/census/nonpopulation/connecticut.html.

Connecticut Notes:
CT-1. All 1850-1880 Non-Population originals are located at the Connecticut State Library/Archives, Hartford, CT. Search for "census schedules" at **https://ctstatelibrary.org/combined-site-search/#**. Connecticut is included in *U.S., Selected Federal Census Non-Population Schedules, 1850-1880* [Online Database], digitized and indexed at the Ancestry.com website. See **www.ancestry.com/search/collections/nonpopcensus**.

CT-2. Connecticut's 1850-1880 Mortality Schedules are included in the national database, *U.S. Federal Census Mortality Schedules, 1850-1885* [Online Database], digitized and indexed at the Ancestry.com website. See **www.ancestry.com/search/collections/usmortality**. Also, digital images of the CT 1850, 1860, 1870 & 1880 Mortality Schedules are available at the FHL catalog page, URL for each year noted above.

Dakota Territory (1861-1889) – See both North Dakota & South Dakota for later schedules).

Non-Population Schedules Year & Type of Schedule	NARA Series, No. of Rolls	FHL Film No.	(O) Location of Originals (See Notes) URL: online database, index, digital images, or info page.
1880 Manufactures	--	--	SD Hist.Soc. (DT-1)
1885 Manufactures	GR27, 1 roll	--	SD Hist.Soc. (DT-1)
1870 Agricultural	--	--	SD Hist.Soc. (DT-1) Index: https://history.sd.gov/archives/data/1870census/default.aspx.
1880 Agricultural	--	--	SD Hist.Soc. (DT-1)
1885 Agricultural	--	--	SD Hist.Soc. (DT-1)
1860 Mortality	--	--	SD Hist.Soc. (DT-1)
1880 Mortality	--	--	SD Hist.Soc. (DT-1)
1885 Mortality	GR27, 2 rolls	--	SD Hist.Soc. (DT-1)
1885 Union Soldiers	GR27, 2 rolls	--	SD Hist.Soc. (DT-1)
1880 Def/Dep/Del Classes	--	--	SD Hist.Soc. (DT-1)
1870 Social Statistics	--	--	SD Hist.Soc. (DT-1)
1885 Social Statistics	GR27, 1 roll	--	SD Hist.Soc. (DT-1)

Dakota Territory Notes:
DT-1. The original 1870, 1880, & 1885 Non-population schedules for old Dakota Territory all ended up at the South Dakota State Historical Society (SDSHS) in Pierre, SD. The original Population schedules, however, were split into the 17 North Dakota counties (to NDSHS) and the 20 South Dakota counties (to SDSHS). The 1885 Union Soldiers schedules were unique to Dakota Territory.

Delaware

Non-Population Schedules Year & Type of Schedule	NARA Series, No. of Rolls	FHL Film No.	(O) Location of Originals (See Notes) URL: online database, digital images, or info page.
1820 Manufactures	M279, 1 roll.	1024505	(O) NARA (DE-1)
1850 Industry	--	--	(O) DE Public Archives. (DE-2)
1860 Industry	--	--	(O) DE Public Archives. (DE-2)
1870 Industry	--	--	(O) DE Public Archives. (DE-2)
1880 Manufactures	--	--	(O) DE Public Archives. (DE-2)
1850 Agriculture	--	--	(O) DE Public Archives.(DE-2)
1860 Agriculture	--	--	(O) DE Public Archives. (DE-2)
1870 Agriculture	--	--	(O) DE Public Archives. (DE-2)
1880 Agriculture	--	--	(O) DE Public Archives. (DE-2)
1850 Mortality	--	--	(O) DE Public Archives. (DE-2) (DE-3)
1860 Mortality	--	--	(O) DE Public Archives. (DE-2) (DE-3)
1870 Mortality	--	--	(O) DE Public Archives. (DE-2) (DE-3)
1880 Mortality	--	--	(O) DE Public Archives. (DE-2) (DE-3)
1850 Social Statistics	--	--	(O) DE Public Archives. (DE-2) (DE-3)
1860 Social Statistics	--	--	(O) DE Public Archives. (DE-2)
1850 Slave	M432, 1 roll	--	(O) NARA See www.ancestry.com/search/collections/1850slaveschedules.
1860 Slave	M653, 1 roll.	--	(O) NARA See www.ancestry.com/search/collections/1860slaveschedules.
1880 Def/Dep/Del Classes	--	--	(O) DE Public Archives. (DE-2)
1935 Business-Advertising	M1797, 1 roll.	--	(O) Info: www.archives.gov/research/census/nonpopulation/delaware.html.
1935 Business-Banking	M2066, 6 rolls.	--	(O) Info: www.archives.gov/research/census/nonpopulation/delaware.html.
1935 Business-Misc.Enterprises	M2067, 1 roll.	--	(O) Info: www.archives.gov/research/census/nonpopulation/delaware.html.
1935 Business-Trucking	M2068, 2 rolls.	--	(O) Info: www.archives.gov/research/census/nonpopulation/delaware.html.
1935 Business-Warehousing	M2069, 1 roll.	--	(O) Info: www.archives.gov/research/census/nonpopulation/delaware.html.
1935 Business-Radio Stations	M2070, 1 roll.	--	(O) Info: www.archives.gov/research/census/nonpopulation/delaware.html.

Delaware Notes:
DE-1. The *Records of the 1820 Census of Manufactures* (NARA series M279, 27 rolls). Roll 17 contains New Jersey, Delaware, and the District of Columbia. See the FHL catalog page:
www.familysearch.org/search/catalog/280127.

DE-2. The original Non-Population schedules, 1850-1880 (Agriculture, Industry/Manufactures, Mortality, Social Statistics, and Defective/Dependent/Deficient) are all located at the Delaware Public Archives in Dover. See https://archives.delaware.gov/guide-to-census-records.

DE-3. See U.*S. Federal Census Mortality Schedules, 1850-1885* **(Includes Delaware)** [Online Database], digitized and indexed at the Ancestry.com website. See
www.ancestry.com/search/collections/usmortality.

District of Columbia

Non-Population Schedules Year & Type of Schedule	NARA Series, No. of Rolls	FHL Film No.	(O) Location of Originals (See Notes) URL: online database, digital images, or info page.
1820 Manufactures	M279, 1 roll	1024508	NARA. (DC-1)
1850 Industry	M1793, 1 roll	--	(O) Duke Univ. (DC-2)
1860 Industry	M1793, 1 roll	--	(O) Duke Univ. (DC-2)
1870 Industry	M1793, 1 roll	--	(O) Duke Univ. (DC-2)
1880 Manufactures	M1795, 1 roll	--	(O) Duke Univ. (DC-2)
1850 Agriculture	M1793, 1 roll	--	(O) Duke Univ. (DC-2)
1860 Agriculture	M1793, 1 roll	--	(O) Duke Univ. (DC-2)
1870 Agriculture	M1793, 1 roll	--	(O) Duke Univ. (DC-2)
1880 Agriculture	M1794, 1 roll	--	(O) Duke Univ. (DC-2)

District of Columbia, Cont'd

Non-Population Schedules Year & Type of Schedule	NARA Series, No. of Rolls	FHL Film No.	(O) Location of Originals (See Notes) URL: online database, digital images, or info page.
1850 Mortality	T655, 2 rolls	--	(O) NARA Online DB: www.ancestry.com/search/collections/usmortality.
1860 Mortality	T655, 2 rolls	--	(O) NARA Online DB: www.ancestry.com/search/collections/usmortality.
1870 Mortality	T655, 2 rolls	--	(O) NARA Online DB: www.ancestry.com/search/collections/usmortality.
1880 Mortality	T655, 2 rolls	--	(O) NARA Online DB: www.ancestry.com/search/collections/usmortality.
1850 Social Statistics	M1793, 1 roll	--	(O) Duke Univ. (DC-2)
1860 Social Statistics	M1793, 1 roll	--	(O) Duke Univ. (DC-2)
1850 Slave	M432, 1 roll	--	(O) NARA See www.ancestry.com/search/collections/1850slaveschedules.
1860 Slave	M653, 1 roll	--	(O) NARA See www.ancestry.com/search/collections/1860slaveschedules.
1880 Def/Dep/Del Classes	M1795, 1 roll	--	(O) Duke Univ. (DC-2)
1935 Business-Advertising	M1797, 1 roll	--	(O) Info: www.archives.gov/research/census/nonpopulation/dc.html.
1935 Business-Banking	M2066, 6 rolls	--	(O) Info: www.archives.gov/research/census/nonpopulation/dc.html.
1935 Business-Misc. Enterprises	M2067, 1 roll	--	(O) Info: www.archives.gov/research/census/nonpopulation/dc.html.
1935 Business-Trucking	M2068, 1 roll	--	(O) Info: www.archives.gov/research/census/nonpopulation/dc.html.
1935 Business-Warehousing	M2069, 1 roll	--	(O) Info: www.archives.gov/research/census/nonpopulation/dc.html.
1935 Business-Radio Stations	M2070, 1 roll	--	(O) Info: www.archives.gov/research/census/nonpopulation/dc.html.

District of Columbia Notes:

DC-1. The *Records of the 1820 Census of Manufactures* (NARA series M279, 27 rolls). Roll 17 contains New Jersey, Delaware, and the District of Columbia. See the FHL catalog page: **www.familysearch.org/search/catalog/280127.**

DC-2. Originals located at Rubenstein Library-Library Service Center, Manuscripts, Duke University, Durham, NC. Search for "non-population" at the search dialog box, see **https://library.duke.edu**.

Florida

Non-Population Schedules Year & Type of Schedule	NARA Series, No. of Rolls	FHL Film No.	(O) Location of Originals (See Notes) URL: online database, digital images, or info page.
1850 Industry	T1168, 1 roll	--	(O) FSU (FL-1)
1860 Industry	T1168, 1 roll	1550796	(O) FSU (FL-1)
1870 Industry	T1168, 1 roll	--	(O) FSU (FL-1)
1880 Manufactures	T1168, 1 roll	1550797	(O) FSU (FL-1)
1885 Manufactures	M845, 13 rolls	--	(O) NARA (FL-2)
1850 Agriculture	T1168, 1 roll	--	(O) FSU (FL-1)
1860 Agriculture	--	1550796	(O) FSU (FL-1)
1870 Agriculture	--	--	(O) FSU (FL-1)
1880 Agriculture	T1168, 1 roll	--	(O) FSU (FL-1)
1850 Mortality	--	--	(O) NARA Online DB: www.ancestry.com/search/collections/usmortality.
1860 Mortality	--	1550796	(O) NARA Online DB: www.ancestry.com/search/collections/usmortality.
1870 Mortality	--	--	(O) NARA Online DB: www.ancestry.com/search/collections/usmortality.
1880 Mortality	--	1550797	(O) NARA Online DB: www.ancestry.com/search/collections/usmortality.
1885 Mortality	M845, 13 rolls	--	(O) NARA Online DB: www.ancestry.com/search/collections/usmortality.
1850 Social Statistics	--	--	(O) FSU (FL-1)
1860 Social Statistics	--	--	(O) FSU (FL-1)
1870 Social Statistics	--	--	(O) FSU (FL-1)
1880 Def/Dep/Del Classes	--	--	(O) FSU (FL-1). Printed index available: see FHL book 975.9 X28m
1850 Slave	M432, 1 roll	--	(O) NARA Online DB: https://search.ancestry.com/search/db.aspx?dbid=8055.
1860 Slave	M653, 1 roll	--	(O) NARA Online DB: https://search.ancestry.com/search/db.aspx?dbid=7668.
1935 Business-Advertising	M1797, 1 roll	--	(O) Info: www.archives.gov/research/census/nonpopulation/florida.html.
1935 Business-Banking	M2066, 9 rolls	--	(O) Info: www.archives.gov/research/census/nonpopulation/florida.html.
1935 Business-Misc.Enterprises	M2067, 2 rolls	--	(O) Info: www.archives.gov/research/census/nonpopulation/florida.html.
1935 Business-Trucking	M2068, 1 roll	--	(O) Info: www.archives.gov/research/census/nonpopulation/florida.html.
1935 Business-Warehousing	M2069, 1 roll	--	(O) Info: www.archives.gov/research/census/nonpopulation/florida.html.
1935 Business-Radio Stations	M2070, 1 roll	--	(O) Info: www.archives.gov/research/census/nonpopulation/florida.html.

Florida Notes:

FL-1. The originals of all of Florida's non-population schedules are located at Florida State University in Tallahassee, FL. FSU does not allow non-member access to their online library catalog. Fortunately, NARA microfilmed most of the schedules before transferring them to FSU.

FL-2. Florida's 1885 state census was lost. NARA's copy exists, and was microfilmed as series M845, 13 rolls, which included the FL 1885 Population schedules as well as the 1885 Agriculture, Manufacturing, and Mortality schedules, as noted above. For the roll list and counties, see
www.archives.gov/research/census/nonpopulation/florida.html.

Georgia

Non-Population Schedules Year & Type of Schedule	NARA Series, No. of Rolls	FHL Film No.	(O) Location of Originals (See Notes) URL: online database, digital images, or info page.
1820 Manufactures	M279, 1 roll	1024510	NARA (GA-1)
1880 Manufactures	T1137, 1 roll	--	(O) Duke Univ. (GA-2)
1850 Agriculture	T1137, 3 rolls	--	(O) Duke Univ. (GA-2)
1860 Agriculture	T1137, 3 rolls	--	(O) Duke Univ. (GA-2)
1870 Agriculture	T1137, 3 rolls	--	(O) Duke Univ. (GA-2)
1880 Agriculture	T1137, 12 rolls	--	(O) Duke Univ. (GA-2)
1850 Mortality	T655, 1 roll	(GA-3)	(O) NARA Online DB: www.ancestry.com/search/collections/usmortality.
1860 Mortality	T655, 1 roll	(GA-3)	(O) NARA Online DB: www.ancestry.com/search/collections/usmortality.
1870 Mortality	T655, 1 roll	(GA-3)	(O) NARA Online DB: www.ancestry.com/search/collections/usmortality.
1880 Mortality	T655, 3 rolls	(GA-3)	(O) NARA Online DB: www.ancestry.com/search/collections/usmortality.
1850 Slave	M432, 1 roll	--	(O) NARA See www.ancestry.com/search/collections/1850slaveschedules.
1860 Slave	M653, 1 roll	--	(O) NARA See www.ancestry.com/search/collections/1860slaveschedules.
1850 Social Statistics	T1137, 1 roll	--	(O) Duke Univ. (GA-2)
1860 Social Statistics	T1137, 1 roll	--	(O) Duke Univ. (GA-2)
1870 Social Statistics	T1137, 1 roll	--	(O) Duke Univ. (GA-2)
1880 Def/Dep/Del Classes	T1137, 1 roll	--	(O) Duke U. Online: www.ancestry.com/search/collections/1880uscensusddd.
1935 Business-Advertising	M1797, 1 rolls	--	(O) Info: www.archives.gov/research/census/nonpopulation/georgia.html.
1935 Business-Banking	M2066, 10 rolls	--	(O) Info: www.archives.gov/research/census/nonpopulation/georgia.html.
1935 Business-Misc. Enterprises	M2067, 1 roll	--	(O) Info: www.archives.gov/research/census/nonpopulation/georgia.html.
1935 Business-Trucking	M2068, 3 rolls	--	(O) Info: www.archives.gov/research/census/nonpopulation/georgia.html.
1935 Business-Warehousing	M2069, 2 rolls	--	(O) Info: www.archives.gov/research/census/nonpopulation/georgia.html.
1935 Business-Radio Stations	M2070, 1 roll	--	(O) Info: www.archives.gov/research/census/nonpopulation/georgia.html.

Georgia Notes:
GA-1. The *Records of the 1820 Census of Manufactures* (NARA series M279, 27 rolls). Roll 19 contains North Carolina, South Carolina, and Georgia. See the FHL catalog page:
www.familysearch.org/search/catalog/280127.

GA-2. Georgia's Non-Population originals are located at Rubenstein Library - Library Service Center, Manuscripts, Duke University, Durham, NC. Search for "non-population" at the search dialog box, see **https://library.duke.edu**. Georgia is included in *U.S., Selected Federal Census Non-Population Schedules, 1850-1880* [Online Database], digitized and indexed at the Ancestry.com website. See
www.ancestry.com/search/collections/nonpopcensus.

GA-3. Georgia's original 1850, 1860, 1870 and 1880 Mortality Schedules spent some time at the DAR Library in Washington, DC, but were later returned to the National Archives. While there, the DAR undertook a full index to the names from all census years. The NARA microfilm (T655, 6 rolls) includes the indexes. The FHL obtained the NARA film, gave them their own film numbers (#422413-422418), and to date, has digitized the first two rolls (1850 & 1860). To access the digital images, see the FHL catalog page:
www.familysearch.org/search/catalog/783149.

Guam

Non-Population Schedules Year & Type of Schedule	NARA Series, No. of Rolls	FHL Film No.	(O) Location of Originals (See Notes) URL: online database, digital images, or info page.
1930 Agriculture-Series 1	M1874, 2 rolls	--	(O) NARA (GU-1) . Series 1: Form 15-28, Cultivated Crops Schedule-Guam
1930 Agriculture-Series 2	M1874, 1 roll	--	(O) NARA (GU-1) . Series 2: Form 15-41, Livestock Schedule-Guam

Guam Notes:
GU-1. NARA microfilm publication M1874, ***Nonpopulation Census Schedules for Guam, 1930: Agriculture*** (3 rolls) has general agricultural and livestock schedules reporting farm products grown or owned in Guam during 1929-1930. For info, see
www.archives.gov/research/census/nonpopulation/guam.html.

Hawaii

Non-Population Schedules Year & Type of Schedule	NARA Series, No. of Rolls	FHL Film No.	(O) Location of Originals (See Notes) URL: online database, digital images, or info page.
1930 Agriculture-Series 1	M1876, 11 rolls	--	(O) NARA (HI-1) . Crops Schedule-Hawaii
1930 Agriculture-Series 2	M1890, 1 roll	--	(O) NARA (HI-1) . Livestock Schedule-Hawaii

Hawaii Notes:
HI-1. NARA microfilm publication M1876, ***Nonpopulation Census Schedules for Guam, 1930: Agriculture*** (3 rolls) has general agricultural and livestock schedules reporting farm products grown or owned in Hawaii during 1929-1930. For info, see
www.archives.gov/research/census/nonpopulation/guam.html.

Idaho

Non-Population Schedules Year & Type of Schedule	NARA Series, No. of Rolls	FHL Film No.	(O) Location of Originals (See Notes) URL: online database, digital images, or info page.
1870 Industry	--	--	(O) ID Hist. Soc. (ID-1). Digitized and indexed.
1880 Manufactures	--	--	(O) ID Hist. Soc. (ID-1). Digitized and indexed.
1870 Agriculture	--	--	(O) ID Hist. Soc. (ID-1). Digitized and indexed.
1880 Agriculture	--	--	(O) ID Hist. Soc. (ID-1). Digitized and indexed.
1870 Mortality	T655, 1 roll	(ID-2)	(O) NARA Online DB: www.ancestry.com/search/collections/usmortality.
1880 Mortality	T655, 3 rolls	(ID-2)	(O) NARA Online DB: www.ancestry.com/search/collections/usmortality.
1870 Social Statistics	--	--	(O) ID Hist. Soc. (ID-1). Digitized and indexed.
1880 Def/Dep/Del Classes	--	--	(O) ID Hist. Soc. (ID-1). Digitized and indexed.
1935 Business-Advertising	M1797, 1 rolls	--	(O) Info: www.archives.gov/research/census/nonpopulation/idaho.html.
1935 Business-Banking	M2066, 6 rolls	--	(O) Info: www.archives.gov/research/census/nonpopulation/idaho.html.
1935 Business-Misc. Enterprises	M2067, 2 roll	--	(O) Info: www.archives.gov/research/census/nonpopulation/idaho.html.
1935 Business-Trucking	M2068, 1 rolls	--	(O) Info: www.archives.gov/research/census/nonpopulation/idaho.html.
1935 Business-Warehousing	M2069, 1 rolls	--	(O) Info: www.archives.gov/research/census/nonpopulation/idaho.html.
1935 Business-Radio Stations	M2070, 1 roll	--	(O) Info: www.archives.gov/research/census/nonpopulation/idaho.html.

Idaho Notes:
ID-1. The originals for the 1870 and 1880 Non-Population schedules are located at the Idaho Historical Society/Archives, Boise, ID. To access the digitized databases online, see **https://history.idaho.gov/search-results/?q=census.**

ID-2. See ***Idaho Territory Population Schedules and Mortality Schedules, 1870*** [Printed Book], publ. ID Hist. Society. Digital version, see www.familysearch.org/search/catalog/201347. See also ***Idaho Territory Federal Population Schedules and Mortality Schedules, 1880*** [Printed Book], for a digital version, see
www.familysearch.org/search/catalog/201177.

Illinois

Non-Population Schedules Year & Type of Schedule	NARA Series, No. of Rolls	FHL Film No.	(O) Location of Originals (See Notes) URL: online database, digital images, or info page.
1820 Manufactures	M279, 1 roll	1024518	(O) NARA. (IL-1)
1860 Industry	T1133, 1 roll	(IL-3)	(O) IL St. Archives (IL-2)
1870 Industry	T1133, 2 rolls	(IL-3)	(O) IL St. Archives (IL-2)
1880 Manufactures	T1133, 6 rolls	(IL-3)	(O) IL St. Archives (IL-2)
1850 Agriculture	T1133, 4 rolls	(IL-3)	(O) IL St. Archives (IL-2)
1860 Agriculture	T1133, 7 rolls	(IL-3)	(O) IL St. Archives (IL-2)
1865 Agriculture	T1133, 2 rolls	(IL-3)	(O) IL St. Archives (IL-2)
1870 Agriculture	T1133, 11 rolls	(IL-3)	(O) IL St. Archives (IL-2)
1880 Agriculture	T1133, 25 rolls	(IL-3)	(O) IL St. Archives (IL-2)
1850 Mortality	T655, 1 roll	--	(O) NARA Online DB: www.ancestry.com/search/collections/usmortality.
1860 Mortality	T655, 1 roll	--	(O) NARA Online DB: www.ancestry.com/search/collections/usmortality.
1870 Mortality	T655, 1 roll	--	(O) NARA Online DB: www.ancestry.com/search/collections/usmortality.
1880 Mortality	T655, 3 rolls	--	(O) NARA Online DB: www.ancestry.com/search/collections/usmortality.
1860 Social Statistics	T1133, 1 roll	(IL-3)	(O) IL St. Archives (IL-2)
1880 Def/Dep/Del	--	--	(O) NY St. Lib. Online: www.ancestry.com/search/collections/1880uscensusddd.
1935 Business-Advertising	M1797, 1 roll	--	(O) Info: www.archives.gov/research/census/nonpopulation/illinois.html.
1935 Business-Banking	M2066, 9 rolls	--	(O) Info: www.archives.gov/research/census/nonpopulation/illinois.html.
1935 Business-Misc.Enterprises	M2067, 3 roll	--	(O) Info: www.archives.gov/research/census/nonpopulation/illinois.html.
1935 Business-Trucking	M2068, 6 rolls	--	(O) Info: www.archives.gov/research/census/nonpopulation/illinois.html.
1935 Business-Warehousing	M2069, 1 roll	--	(O) Info: www.archives.gov/research/census/nonpopulation/illinois.html.
1935 Business-Radio Stations	M2070, 1 roll	--	(O) Info: www.archives.gov/research/census/nonpopulation/illinois.html.

Illinois Notes:

IL-1. The *Records of the 1820 Census of Manufactures* (NARA series M279, 27 rolls). Roll 27 contains the Western District of Tennessee and Illinois. See the FHL catalog page: **www.familysearch.org/search/catalog/280127.**

IL-2. The Illinois State Archives, Springfield, IL, holds the original Non-Population schedules, microfilmed by NARA as T1133 (64 rolls). For information, see **www.cyberdriveillinois.com/publications/pdf_publications/ard123.pdf.** Illinois is included in *U.S., Selected Federal Census Non-Population Schedules, 1850-1880* [Online Database], digitized and indexed at the Ancestry.com website. See **www.ancestry.com/search/collections/nonpopcensus.**

IL-3. All of the IL Non-Population schedules, Series T1133 (64 rolls) were digitized by FamilySearch International. See the FHL catalog page: **www.familysearch.org/search/catalog/2287447.**

Indiana

Non-Population Schedules Year & Type of Schedule	NARA Series, No. of Rolls	FHL Film No.	(O) Location of Originals (See Notes) URL: online database, digital images, or info page.
1820 Manufactures	M279, 1 roll	1024504	(O) NARA (IN-1)
1850 Industry	--	--	(O) IN St. Archives (IN-2)
1860 Industry	--	--	(O) IN St. Archives (IN-2)
1870 Industry	--	--	(O) IN St. Archives (IN-2)
1880 Manufactures	--	--	(O) IN St. Archives. (IN-2)
1850 Agriculture	--	--	(O) IN St. Archives (IN-2)
1860 Agriculture	--	--	(O) IN St. Archives (IN-2)
1870 Agriculture	--	--	(O) IN St. Archives (IN-2)
1880 Agriculture	--	--	(O) IN St. Archives (IN-2)
1850 Mortality	T655, 1 roll	--	(O) IN St. Lib. Online DB: www.ancestry.com/search/collections/usmortality.
1860 Mortality	T655, 1 roll	(IN-4)	(O) IN St. Lib. Online DB: www.ancestry.com/search/collections/usmortality.
1870 Mortality	T655, 1 roll	(IN-4)	(O) IN St. Lib. Online DB: www.ancestry.com/search/collections/usmortality.
1880 Mortality	T655, 3 rolls	(IN-4)	(O) IN St. Lib. Online DB: www.ancestry.com/search/collections/usmortality.
1850 Social Statistics	--	--	(O) IN St. Archives (IN-2)
1860 Social Statistics	--	--	(O) IN St. Archives (IN-2)
1870 Social Statistics	--	--	(O) IN St. Archives (IN-2)

Indiana, Cont'd

Non-Population Schedules Year & Type of Schedule	NARA Series, No. of Rolls	FHL Film No.	(O) Location of Originals (See Notes) URL: online database, digital images, or info page.
1880 Def/Dep/Del Classes	--	--	(O) IN St. Archives (IN-2)
1935 Business-Advertising	M1797, 1 roll	--	(O) Info: www.archives.gov/research/census/nonpopulation/indiana.html.
1935 Business-Banking	M2066, 6 rolls	--	(O) Info: www.archives.gov/research/census/nonpopulation/indiana.html.
1935 Business-Misc.Enterprises	M2067, 2 rolls	--	(O) Info: www.archives.gov/research/census/nonpopulation/indiana.html.
1935 Business-Trucking	M2068, 7 rolls	--	(O) Info: www.archives.gov/research/census/nonpopulation/indiana.html.
1935 Business-Warehousing	M2069, 1 roll	--	(O) Info: www.archives.gov/research/census/nonpopulation/indiana.html.
1935 Business-Radio Stations	M2070, 1 roll	--	(O) Info: www.archives.gov/research/census/nonpopulation/indiana.html.

Indiana Notes:

IN-1. The *Records of the 1820 Census of Manufactures* (NARA series M279, 27 rolls). Roll 20 contains Kentucky and Indiana. See the FHL catalog page: **www.familysearch.org/search/catalog/280127**.

IN-2. The Indiana State Archives holds the original Non-Population schedules (Industry, Agriculture, and Social Statistics). To search the Research Indiana Catalog, see **www.in.gov/iara**.

IN-3. The Indiana State Library holds the original 1850, 1860, 1870, and 1880 Mortality Schedules, microfilmed by NARA as Series T655, 6 rolls. To contact the IN State Library, see **www.in.gov/library**.

IN-4. See *Census of Indiana Mortality, 1860* [Microfilm & Digital Capture]. To access the digital images, see the FHL catalog page: **www.familysearch.org/search/catalog/1180237**. Also digitized, *Census of Indiana Mortality, 1870,* see **www.familysearch.org/search/catalog/1180241**. Also digitized, *Census of Indiana Mortality, 1880,* see **www.familysearch.org/search/catalog/1180288**.

Iowa

Non-Population Schedules Year & Type of Schedule	NARA Series, No. of Rolls	FHL Film No.	(O) Location of Originals (See Notes) URL: online database, digital images, or info page.
1850 Industry	T1156, 1 roll	--	(O) IA St.Hist.Soc. (IA-1). Digitized.
1860 Industry	T1156, 1 roll	--	(O) IA St.Hist.Soc. (IA-1). Digitized.
1870 Industry	T1156, 3 rolls	--	(O) IA St.Hist.Soc. (IA-1). Digitized.
1880 Manufactures	T1156, 4 rolls	--	(O) IA St.Hist.Soc. (IA-1). Digitized.
1850 Agriculture	T1156, 1 roll	--	(O) IA St.Hist.Soc. (IA-1). Digitized.
1860 Agriculture	T1156, 4 rolls	--	(O) IA St.Hist.Soc. (IA-1). Digitized.
1870 Agriculture	T1156, 9 rolls	--	(O) IA St.Hist.Soc. (IA-1). Digitized.
1880 Agriculture	T1156, 22 rolls	--	(O) IA St.Hist.Soc. (IA-1). Digitized.
1850 Mortality	T1156, 1 roll	--	(O) IA St.Hist.Soc. Online: https://search.ancestry.com/search/db.aspx?dbid=8756.
1860 Mortality	T1156, 1 roll	--	(O) IA St.Hist.Soc. Online: https://search.ancestry.com/search/db.aspx?dbid=8756.
1870 Mortality	T1156, 3 rolls	--	(O) IA St.Hist.Soc. Online: https://search.ancestry.com/search/db.aspx?dbid=8756.
1880 Mortality	T1156, 4 rolls	--	(O) IA St.Hist.Soc. Online: https://search.ancestry.com/search/db.aspx?dbid=8756.
1850 Social Statistics	T1156, 1 roll	--	(O) IA St.Hist.Soc. (IA-1). Digitized.
1860 Social Statistics	T1156, 2 rolls	--	(O) IA St.Hist.Soc. (IA-1). Digitized.
1870 Social Statistics	T1156, 1 roll	--	(O) IA St.Hist.Soc. (IA-1). Digitized.
1880 Def/Dep/Del Classes	T1156, 4 rolls	--	(O) IA St.Hist.Soc. (IA-1). Digitized.
1935 Business-Advertising	M1797, 1 roll	--	(O) NARA Info: www.archives.gov/research/census/nonpopulation/iowa.html.
1935 Business-Banking	M2066, 9 rolls	--	(O) NARA Info: www.archives.gov/research/census/nonpopulation/iowa.html.
1935 Business-Misc.Enterprises	M2067, 3 rolls	--	(O) NARA Info: www.archives.gov/research/census/nonpopulation/iowa.html.
1935 Business-Trucking	M2068, 6 rolls	--	(O) NARA Info: www.archives.gov/research/census/nonpopulation/iowa.html.
1935 Business-Warehousing	M2069, 1 roll	--	(O) NARA Info: www.archives.gov/research/census/nonpopulation/iowa.html.
1935 Business-Radio Stations	M2070, 1 roll.	--	(O) NARA Info: www.archives.gov/research/census/nonpopulation/iowa.html.

Iowa Notes:

IA-1. The State Historical Society of Iowa in Des Moines, IA, holds all original Non-Population schedules, 1850-1880. Digitized by FamilySearch International. To access the digital images, see the FHL catalog page: **www.familysearch.org/search/catalog/2274801**. Iowa is included in ***U.S., Selected Federal Census Non-Population Schedules, 1850-1880*** [Online Database], digitized and indexed at the Ancestry.com website. See **www.ancestry.com/search/collections/nonpopcensus**.

Kansas

Non-Population Schedules Year & Type of Schedule	NARA Series, No. of Rolls	FHL Film No.	(O) Location of Originals (See Notes) URL: online database, digital images, or info page.
1860 Industry/Mortality/Agri/Soc	T1130, 1 roll	--	(O) KS Hist. Soc. (KS-1)
1865 KS St.Cens-Soc.Statistics	T1130, 1 roll	--	(O) KS Hist. Soc. (KS-1)
1870 Industry/Agriculture	T1130, 3 rolls	--	(O) KS Hist. Soc. (KS-1)
1880 Manufactures	T1130, 3 rolls	--	(O) KS Hist. Soc. (KS-1)
1870 Agriculture	T1130, 5 rolls	--	(O) KS Hist. Soc. (KS-1)
1880 Agriculture	T1130, 26 rolls	--	(O) KS Hist. Soc. (KS-1)
1870 Mortality	T1130, 1 roll	(KS-2)	(O) KS Hist. Soc. Online: www.ancestry.com/search/collections/usmortality.
1880 Mortality	T1130, 2 rolls	(KS-2)	(O) KS Hist. Soc. Online: www.ancestry.com/search/collections/usmortality.
1870 Social Statistics/Mortality	T1130, 1 roll	--	(O) KS Hist. Soc. (KS-1)
1880 Def/Dep/Del Classes	T1130, 4 rolls	--	(O) KS H. Soc. Online: www.ancestry.com/search/collections/1880uscensusddd.
1935 Business-Advertising	M1797, 1 roll	--	(O) NARA Info: www.archives.gov/research/census/nonpopulation/kansas.html.
1935 Business-Banking	M2066, 9 rolls.	--	(O) NARA Info: www.archives.gov/research/census/nonpopulation/kansas.html.
1935 Business-Misc.Enterprises	M2067, 3 rolls	--	(O) NARA Info: www.archives.gov/research/census/nonpopulation/kansas.html.
1935 Business-Trucking	M2068, 6 rolls.	--	(O) NARA Info: www.archives.gov/research/census/nonpopulation/kansas.html.
1935 Business-Warehousing	M2069, 1 roll.	--	(O) NARA Info: www.archives.gov/research/census/nonpopulation/kansas.html.
1935 Business-Radio Stations	M2070, 1 roll.	--	(O) NARA Info: www.archives.gov/research/census/nonpopulation/kansas.html.

Kansas Notes:

KS-1. The Kansas Historical Society in Topeka, KS, holds all Non-Population schedules originals, 1860-1880, microfilmed by NARA (series T1130, 48 rolls). Kansas is included in ***U.S., Selected Federal Census Non-Population Schedules, 1850-1880*** [Online Database], digitized and indexed at the Ancestry.com website. See **www.ancestry.com/search/collections/nonpopcensus**.

KS-2. See ***1870 Mortality Schedule of Kansas*** [Microfilm & Digital Capture], by the Topeka Genealogical Society. To access the digital version of this index, see **www.familysearch.org/search/catalog/174737**. See also ***1880 Mortality Schedules of Kansas*** [Microfilm & Digital Capture], by the Topeka Genealogical Society. To access the digital versions, all 40 vols., see **www.familysearch.org/search/catalog/174881**.

Kentucky

Non-Population Schedules Year & Type of Schedule	NARA Series, No. of Rolls	FHL Film No.	(O) Location of Originals (See Notes) URL: online database, digital images, or info page.
1820 Manufactures	M279, 1 roll	1024511	(O) NARA. (KY-1)
1850 Industry	M1528, 3 rolls	--	(O) KY St. Hist. Soc. (KY-2). Digitized.
1860 Industry	M1528, 1 roll	--	(O) KY St. Hist. Soc. (KY-2). Digitized.
1870 Industry	M1528, 1 roll	--	(O) KY St. Hist. Soc. (KY-2). Digitized.
1880 Manufactures	M1528, 1 roll	--	(O) KY St. Hist. Soc. (KY-2). Digitized.
1850 Agriculture	M1528, 5 rolls	--	(O) KY St. Hist. Soc. (KY-2). Digitized.
1860 Agriculture	M1528, 4 rolls	--	(O) KY St. Hist. Soc. (KY-2). Digitized.
1870 Agriculture	M1528, 5 rolls	--	(O) KY St. Hist. Soc. (KY-2). Digitized.
1880 Agriculture	M1528, 14 rolls	--	(O) KY St. Hist. Soc. (KY-2). Digitized.
1850 Mortality	T655, 1 roll	422419	(O) NARA (KY-3) Online: www.ancestry.com/search/collections/usmortality.
1860 Mortality	T655, 1 roll	422420	(O) NARA (KY-3) Online: www.ancestry.com/search/collections/usmortality.
1870 Mortality	T655, 2 rolls	422421	(O) NARA (KY-3) Online: www.ancestry.com/search/collections/usmortality.
1880 Mortality	T655, 5 rolls	422423	(O) NARA (KY-3) Online: www.ancestry.com/search/collections/usmortality.
1850 Slave	M432, 1 roll	--	(O) NARA See www.ancestry.com/search/collections/1850slaveschedules.
1860 Slave	M653, 1 roll	--	(O) NARA See www.ancestry.com/search/collections/1860slaveschedules.
1860 Social Statistics	M1528, 1 roll	--	(O) KY St. Hist. Soc. (KY-2). Digitized.
1870 Social Statistics	M1528, 1 roll	--	(O) KY St. Hist. Soc. (KY-2). Digitized.

Kentucky, Cont'd

1880 Def/Dep/Del Classes	M1528, 2 rolls	--	(O) KY St. Hist. Soc. (KY-2). Digitized.
1935 Business-Advertising	M1797, 1 roll	--	(O) Info: www.archives.gov/research/census/nonpopulation/kentucky.html.
1935 Business-Banking	M2066, 9 rolls	--	(O) Info: www.archives.gov/research/census/nonpopulation/kentucky.html.
1935 Business-Misc.Enterprises	M2067, 3 roll	--	(O) Info: www.archives.gov/research/census/nonpopulation/kentucky.html.
1935 Business-Trucking	M2068, 6 rolls	--	(O) Info: www.archives.gov/research/census/nonpopulation/kentucky.html.
1935 Business-Warehousing	M2069, 1 roll	--	(O) Info: www.archives.gov/research/census/nonpopulation/kentucky.html.
1935 Business-Radio Stations	M2070, 1 roll	--	(O) Info: www.archives.gov/research/census/nonpopulation/kentucky.html.

Kentucky Notes:

IL-1. The *Records of the 1820 Census of Manufactures* (NARA series M279, 27 rolls). Roll 20 contains Kentucky and Indiana. See the FHL catalog page: **www.familysearch.org/search/catalog/280127**.

KY-2. The Kentucky State Historical Society, Frankfort, KY, holds the original Non-Population schedules, 1850-1880, microfilmed by NARA (Series M1528, 27 rolls); digitized by FamilySearch International. To access the digital images, see the FHL catalog page: **www.familysearch.org/search/catalog/2822772**.

KY-3. Kentucky's original 1850, 1860, 1870 and 1880 Mortality Schedules spent some time at the DAR Library in Washington, DC, but were later returned to the National Archives. While there, the DAR undertook a full index to the names from all census years. The NARA microfilm (Series T655, 8 rolls) includes the index (as does the FHL film). To access the digital images of FHL films #422419 through #422427, see the FHL catalog page: **www.familysearch.org/search/catalog/783162**.

Louisiana

Non-Population Schedules Year & Type of Schedule	NARA Series, No. of Rolls	FHL Film No.	(O) Location of Originals (See Notes) URL: online database, digital images, or info page.
1820 Manufactures	M279, 1 roll	1024518	(O) NARA (LA-1)
1880 Manufactures	T1136, 1 roll	1549565	(O) Duke Univ. (LA-2).
1850 Agriculture	T1136, 1 roll	1549555	(O) Duke Univ. (LA-2). Digitized.
1860 Agriculture	T1136, 1 roll	1549556	(O) Duke Univ. (LA-2). Digitized.
1870 Agriculture	T1136, 3 rolls	1549557	(O) Duke Univ. (LA-2). Digitized.
1880 Agriculture	T1136, 5 rolls	1549565	(O) Duke Univ. (LA-2).
1850 Mortality	T655, 1 roll	1421004	(O) NARA (KY-3) Online: www.ancestry.com/search/collections/usmortality.
1860 Mortality	T655, 1 roll	422429	(O) NARA (KY-3) Online: www.ancestry.com/search/collections/usmortality.
1870 Mortality	T655, 2 roll	422430	(O) NARA (KY-3) Online: www.ancestry.com/search/collections/usmortality.
1880 Mortality	T655, 5 rolls	422431	(O) NARA (KY-3) Online: www.ancestry.com/search/collections/usmortality.
1850 Slave	M432, 1 roll	--	(O) NARA See www.ancestry.com/search/collections/1850slaveschedules.
1860 Slave	M653, 1 roll	--	(O) NARA See www.ancestry.com/search/collections/1860slaveschedules.
1850 Social Statistics	T1136, 1 roll	1549551	(O) Duke Univ. (LA-2).
1860 Social Statistics	T1136, 1 roll	1549552	(O) Duke Univ. (LA-2).
1870 Social Statistics	T1136, 1 roll	1549553	(O) Duke Univ. (LA-2).
1880 Def/Dep/Del Classes	T1136, 1 roll	1549554	(O) Duke Univ. (LA-2).
1935 Business-Advertising	M1797, 1 roll	--	(O) Info: www.archives.gov/research/census/nonpopulation/louisiana.html.
1935 Business-Banking	M2066, 8 rolls	--	(O) Info: www.archives.gov/research/census/nonpopulation/louisiana.html.
1935 Business-Misc.Enterprises	M2067, 3 rolls	--	(O) Info: www.archives.gov/research/census/nonpopulation/louisiana.html.
1935 Business-Trucking	M2068, 2 rolls	--	(O) Info: www.archives.gov/research/census/nonpopulation/louisiana.html.
1935 Business-Warehousing	M2069, 1 roll	--	(O) Info: www.archives.gov/research/census/nonpopulation/louisiana.html.
1935 Business-Radio Stations	M2070, 1 roll	--	(O) Info: www.archives.gov/research/census/nonpopulation/louisiana.html.

Louisiana Notes:

LA-1. See *Records of the 1820 Census of Manufactures* (NARA series M279, 27 rolls), contains pages from *Digest of Manufacturing Establishments in the United States and of their Manufactures* (Washington, DC: Gales & Seaton, 1823) for Alabama, Louisiana, Missouri, Michigan, and Arkansas. See the FHL catalog page: **www.familysearch.org/search/catalog/280127**.

Louisiana Notes, Cont'd:

LA-2. Louisiana's Non-Population originals are located at Rubenstein Library - Library Service Center, Manuscripts, Duke University, Durham, NC. Search for "non-population" at the search dialog box, see **https://library.duke.edu**. Microfilmed by NARA (Series T1136, 15 rolls), digitizing in progress by FamilySearch International. To access the digital images of certain rolls, see the FHL catalog page: **www.familysearch.org/search/catalog/589491**.

LA-3. Louisiana's original 1850, 1860, 1870 and 1880 Mortality Schedules spent some time at the DAR Library. While there, the DAR undertook a full index to the names from all census years. The NARA microfilm (Series T655, 7 rolls) includes the index (as does the FHL film). To access the digital images, see the FHL catalog page: **www.familysearch.org/search/catalog/783169**.

Maine

Non-Population Schedules Year & Type of Schedule	NARA Series, No. of Rolls	FHL Film No.	(O) Location of Originals (See Notes) URL: online database, digital images, or info page.
1820 Manufactures	M279, 1 roll	1024492	(O) NARA (ME-1). FHL film Digitized.
1850 Industry	--	--	(O) ME St. Archives. (ME-2)
1860 Industry	--	--	(O) ME St. Archives. (ME-2)
1870 Industry	--	--	(O) ME St. Archives. (ME-2)
1880 Manufactures	--	--	(O) ME St. Archives. (ME-2)
1850 Agriculture	--	--	(O) ME St. Archives. (ME-2)
1860 Agriculture	--	--	(O) ME St. Archives. (ME-2)
1870 Agriculture	--	--	(O) ME St. Archives. (ME-2)
1880 Agriculture	--	--	(O) ME St. Archives. (ME-2)
1850 Mortality	T655	--	(O) NARA See www.ancestry.com/search/collections/usmortality.
1860 Mortality	T655	--	(O) NARA See www.ancestry.com/search/collections/usmortality.
1870 Mortality	T655	--	(O) NARA See www.ancestry.com/search/collections/usmortality.
1880 Mortality	T655	--	(O) NARA See www.ancestry.com/search/collections/usmortality.
1850 Social Statistics	--	--	(O) ME St. Archives. (ME-2)
1860 Social Statistics	--	--	(O) ME St. Archives. (ME-2)
1870 Social Statistics	--	--	(O) ME St. Archives. (ME-2)
1880 Def/Dep/Del Classes	--	--	(O) ME St. Arc. Online: www.ancestry.com/search/collections/1880uscensusddd.
1935 Business-Advertising	M1797, 1 roll	--	(O) NARA Info: www.archives.gov/research/census/nonpopulation/maine.html.
1935 Business-Banking	M2066, 7 rolls	--	(O) NARA Info: www.archives.gov/research/census/nonpopulation/maine.html.
1935 Business-Misc.Enterprises	M2067, 2 rolls	--	(O) NARA Info: www.archives.gov/research/census/nonpopulation/maine.html.
1935 Business-Trucking	M2068, 2 rolls	--	(O) NARA Info: www.archives.gov/research/census/nonpopulation/maine.html.
1935 Business-Warehousing	M2069, 1 roll	--	(O) NARA Info: www.archives.gov/research/census/nonpopulation/maine.html.
1935 Business-Radio Stations	M2070, 1 roll	--	(O) NARA Info: www.archives.gov/research/census/nonpopulation/maine.html.

Maine Notes:

ME-1. NARA holds *Records of the 1820 Census of Manufactures* (Series M279, 27 rolls). Roll 1 contains Maine and New Hampshire. See the FHL catalog page: **www.familysearch.org/search/catalog/280127**.

ME-2. The Maine State Archives in Augusta, ME holds the Non-Population originals, 1850-1880. Maine is included in *U.S., Selected Federal Census Non-Population Schedules, 1850-1880* [Online Database], digitized and indexed at the Ancestry.com website. See **www.ancestry.com/search/collections/nonpopcensus**.

Maryland

Non-Population Schedules Year & Type of Schedule	NARA Series, No. of Rolls	FHL Film No.	(O) Location of Originals (See Notes) URL: online database, digital images, or info page.
1820 Manufactures	M279, 1 roll	1024507	(O) NARA (MD-1)
1850 Industry	--	--	(O) MD St. Archives (MD-2)
1860 Industry	M1799, 1 roll	--	(O) MD St. Archives (MD-2)
1870 Industry	--	--	(O) MD St. Archives (MD-2)
1880 Manufactures	M1799, 1 roll	--	(O) MD St. Archives (MD-2)
1850 Agriculture	M1799, 1 roll	--	(O) MD St. Archives (MD-2)
1860 Agriculture	M1799, 1 roll	--	(O) MD St. Archives (MD-2)

Maryland, Cont'd

Non-Population Schedules Year & Type of Schedule	NARA Series, No. of Rolls	FHL Film No.	(O) Location of Originals (See Notes) URL: online database, digital images, or info page.
1870 Agriculture	--	--	(O) MD St. Archives. (MD-2)
1880 Agriculture	--	--	(O) MD St. Archives. (MD-2)
1850 Mortality	T655	1429789	(O) NARA See www.ancestry.com/search/collections/usmortality.
1860 Mortality	T655	1429789	(O) NARA See www.ancestry.com/search/collections/usmortality.
1870 Mortality	T655	1429790	(O) MD St. Arch Online: www.ancestry.com/search/collections/usmortality.
1880 Mortality	T655	1429790	(O) MD St. Arch. Online: www.ancestry.com/search/collections/usmortality.
1850 Slave	M432, 2 rolls	--	(O) NARA See www.ancestry.com/search/collections/1850slaveschedules.
1860 Slave	M653, 2 rolls	--	(O) NARA See www.ancestry.com/search/collections/1860slaveschedules.
1850 Social Statistics	M1793, 1 roll	--	(O) MD St. Archives. (MD-2)
1860 Social Statistics	M1793, 1 roll	--	(O) MD St. Archives. (MD-2)
1870 Social Statistics	M1793, 1 roll	--	(O) MD St. Archives. (MD-2)
1935 Business-Advertising	M1797, 1 roll	--	(O) Info: www.archives.gov/research/census/nonpopulation/maryland.html.
1935 Business-Banking	M2066, 9 rolls	--	(O) Info: www.archives.gov/research/census/nonpopulation/maryland.html.
1935 Business-Misc.Enterprises	M2067, 2 rolls	--	(O) Info: www.archives.gov/research/census/nonpopulation/maryland.html.
1935 Business-Trucking	M2068, 2 rolls	--	(O) Info: www.archives.gov/research/census/nonpopulation/maryland.html.
1935 Business-Warehousing	M2069, 1 roll	--	(O) Info: www.archives.gov/research/census/nonpopulation/maryland.html.
1935 Business-Radio Stations	M2070, 1 roll	--	(O) Info: www.archives.gov/research/census/nonpopulation/maryland.html.

Maryland Notes:

MD-1. See *Records of the 1820 Census of Manufactures* (Series, M279, 27 rolls). Roll 16 contains Maryland. See the FHL catalog page: **www.familysearch.org/search/catalog/280127.**

MD-2. Maryland's original Non-Population schedules, 1850-1880 are located at the Maryland State Archives, Annapolis, MD (some may be at the branch archives in Baltimore). See **http://guide.msa.maryland.gov/pages/viewer.aspx?page=census.**

Massachusetts

Non-Population Schedules Year & Type of Schedule	NARA Series, No. of Rolls	FHL Film No.	(O) Location of Originals (See Notes) URL: online database, digital images, or info page.
1820 Manufactures	M279, 1 roll	8479666	(O) NARA (MA-1). FHL film Digitized.
1850 Industry	T1204, 2 rolls	--	(O) MA Archives. (MA-2)
1860 Industry	T1204, 1 roll	--	(O) MA Archives. (MA-2)
1870 Industry	T1204, 1 roll	--	(O) MA Archives. (MA-2)
1880 Manufactures	T1204, 3 rolls	--	(O) MA Archives. (MA-2)
1850 Agriculture	T1204, 4 rolls	--	(O) MA Archives. (MA-2)
1860 Agriculture	T1204, 4 rolls	--	(O) MA Archives. (MA-2)
1870 Agriculture	T1204, 3 rolls	--	(O) MA Archives. (MA-2)
1880 Agriculture	T1204, 6 rolls	--	(O) MA Archives. (MA-2)
1850 Mortality	T1204, 2 rolls	1421015	(O) MA Archives. Online: www.ancestry.com/search/collections/usmortality.
1860 Mortality	T1204, 1 roll	1421017	(O) MA Archives. Online: www.ancestry.com/search/collections/usmortality.
1870 Mortality	T1204, 2 rolls	1421018	(O) MA Archives. Online: www.ancestry.com/search/collections/usmortality.
1880 Mortality	T1204, 4 rolls	1421020	(O) MA Archives. Online: www.ancestry.com/search/collections/usmortality.
1850 Social Statistics	T1204, 2 rolls	--	(O) MA Archives. (MA-2)
1860 Social Statistics	T1204, 1 roll	--	(O) MA Archives. (MA-2)
1870 Social Statistics	T1204, 1 roll	1421018	(O) MA Archives. (MA-2)
1880 Def/Dep/Del Classes	T1204, 4 rolls	--	(O) MA Archives. Online: www.ancestry.com/search/collections/1880uscensusddd.
1935 Business-Advertising	M1797, 1 roll	--	(O) NARA www.archives.gov/research/census/nonpopulation/massachusetts.html.
1935 Business-Banking	M2066, 7 rolls	--	(O) NARA www.archives.gov/research/census/nonpopulation/massachusetts.html.
1935 Business-Misc.Enterprises	M2067, 2 rolls	--	(O) NARA www.archives.gov/research/census/nonpopulation/massachusetts.html.
1935 Business-Trucking	M2068, 2 rolls	--	(O) NARA: www.archives.gov/research/census/nonpopulation/massachusetts.html.
1935 Business-Warehousing	M2069, 3 rolls	--	(O) NARA www.archives.gov/research/census/nonpopulation/massachusetts.html.
1935 Business-Radio Stations	M2070, 1 roll	--	(O) NARA www.archives.gov/research/census/nonpopulation/massachusetts.html.

Massachusetts Notes:

ME-1. NARA holds *Records of the 1820 Census of Manufactures* (Series M279, 27 rolls). Roll 2 contains Massachusetts and Rhode Island. See the FHL catalog page: www.familysearch.org/search/catalog/280127.

ME-2. The Massachusetts Archives in Boston, MA holds the Non-Population originals, 1850-1880 (Series T1204, 40 rolls). Massachusetts is included in *U.S., Selected Federal Census Non-Population Schedules, 1850-1880* [Online Database], digitized and indexed at the Ancestry.com website. See www.ancestry.com/search/collections/nonpopcensus.

Michigan

Non-Population Schedules Year & Type of Schedule	NARA Series, No. of Rolls	FHL Film No.	(O) Location of Originals (See Notes) URL: online database, digital images, or info page.
1820 Manufactures	M279, 1 roll	1024518	(O) NARA (MI-1)
1850 Industry	T1164, 1 roll	--	(O) MI St. Archives (MI-2)
1860 Industry	T1164, 1 roll	--	(O) MI St. Archives (MI-2)
1870 Industry	T1164, 2 rolls	--	(O) MI St. Archives (MI-2)
1880 Manufactures	T1164, 5 rolls	--	(O) MI St. Archives (MI-2)
1850 Agriculture	T1164, 4 rolls	--	(O) MI St. Archives (MI-2)
1860 Agriculture	T1164, 6 rolls	--	(O) MI St. Archives (MI-2)
1870 Agriculture	T1164, 8 rolls	--	(O) MI St. Archives (MI-2)
1880 Agriculture	T1164, 36 rolls	--	(O) MI St. Archives (MI-2)
1850 Mortality	T1163, 1 roll	--	(O) OH St. Lib. Online: www.ancestry.com/search/collections/usmortality.
1860 Mortality	T1164, 1 roll	--	(O) MI St. Archives. see www.ancestry.com/search/collections/usmortality.
1870 Mortality	T1164, 2 rolls	--	(O) MI St. Archives. see www.ancestry.com/search/collections/usmortality.
1880 Mortality	T1164, 4 rolls	--	(O) MI St. Archives. see www.ancestry.com/search/collections/usmortality.
1850 Social Statistics	T1164, 1 roll	--	(O) MI St. Archives (MI-2)
1860 Social Statistics	T1164, 1 roll	--	(O) MI St. Archives (MI-2)
1870 Social Statistics	T1164, 1 roll	--	(O) MI St. Archives (MI-2)
1880 Def/Dep/Del Classes	T1164, 5 rolls	--	(O) MI St. Archives (MI-2)
1935 Business-Advertising	M1797, 1 roll	--	(O) NARA Info: www.archives.gov/research/census/nonpopulation/michigan.html.
1935 Business-Banking	M2066, 6 rolls	--	(O) NARA. Info: www.archives.gov/research/census/nonpopulation/michigan.html.
1935 Business-Misc.Enterprises	M2067, 2 rolls	--	(O) NARA Info: www.archives.gov/research/census/nonpopulation/michigan.html.
1935 Business-Trucking	M2068, 3 rolls	--	(O) NARA Info: www.archives.gov/research/census/nonpopulation/michigan.html.
1935 Business-Warehousing	M2069, 1 roll	--	(O) NARA Info: www.archives.gov/research/census/nonpopulation/michigan.html.
1935 Business-Radio Stations	M2070, 1 roll	--	(O) NARA Info: www.archives.gov/research/census/nonpopulation/michigan.html.

Michigan Notes:

MI-1. The *Records of the 1820 Census of Manufactures* (NARA series M279, 27 rolls). Roll 27 contains the Western District of Tennessee, Illinois, and pages from *Digest of Manufacturing Establishments in the United States and of their Manufactures* (Washington, DC: Gales & Seaton, 1823) for Alabama, Louisiana, Missouri, Michigan, and Arkansas. See the FHL catalog page: www.familysearch.org/search/catalog/280127.

MI-2. Michigan's original Non-Population schedules are located at the Michigan State Archives, Ann Arbor, MI. (Filmed by NARA, series T1164, 71 rolls), with the exception of the MI 1850 Mortality Schedule, located at the Ohio State Library, Columbus, OH. (Series T1163, 1 roll). Michigan is included in *U.S., Selected Federal Census Non-Population Schedules, 1850-1880* [Online Database], digitized and indexed at the Ancestry.com website. See www.ancestry.com/search/collections/nonpopcensus.

Minnesota

Non-Population Schedules Year & Type of Schedule	NARA Series, No. of Rolls	FHL Film No.	(O) Location of Originals (See Notes) URL: online database, digital images, or info page.
1850 Industry	--	--	(O) MN St. Hist. Soc. (MN-1)
1860 Industry	--	--	(O) MN St. Hist. Soc. (MN-1)
1870 Industry	--	--	(O) MN St. Hist. Soc. (MN-1)
1880 Manufactures	--	--	(O) MN St. Hist. Soc. (MN-1)
1850 Agriculture	--	--	(O) MN St. Hist. Soc. (MN-1)
1860 Agriculture	M1802, 1 roll	--	(O) MN St. Hist. Soc. (MN-1)
1870 Agriculture	--	--	(O) MN St. Hist. Soc. (MN-1)
1880 Agriculture	--	--	(O) MN St. Hist. Soc. (MN-1)
1850 Mortality	--	(MN-2)	(O) MM St. HS. Online: www.ancestry.com/search/collections/usmortality.
1860 Mortality	--	(MN-2)	(O) MN St. HS . Online: www.ancestry.com/search/collections/usmortality.
1870 Mortality	--	(MN-2)	(O) MN St. HS. Online: www.ancestry.com/search/collections/usmortality.
1880 Mortality	--	(MN-2)	(O) MN St. HS. Online: www.ancestry.com/search/collections/usmortality.
1850 Social Statistics	--	--	(O) MN St. Hist. Soc. (MN-1)
1860 Social Statistics	M1164, 1 roll	--	(O) MN St. Hist. Soc. (MN-1)
1870 Social Statistics	--	--	(O) MN St. Hist. Soc. (MN-1)
1880 Def/Dep/Del Classes	--	--	(O) MN St. Hist. Soc. (MN-1)
1935 Business-Advertising	M1797, 1 roll	--	(O) Info: www.archives.gov/research/census/nonpopulation/minnesota.html.
1935 Business-Banking	M2066, 9 rolls	--	(O) Info: www.archives.gov/research/census/nonpopulation/minnesota.html.
1935 Business-Misc.Enterprises	M2067, 3 roll	--	(O) Info: www.archives.gov/research/census/nonpopulation/minnesota.html.
1935 Business-Trucking	M2068, 6 rolls	--	(O) Info: www.archives.gov/research/census/nonpopulation/minnesota.html.
1935 Business-Warehousing	M2069, 1 roll	--	(O) Info: www.archives.gov/research/census/nonpopulation/minnesota.html.
1935 Business-Radio Stations	M2070, 1 roll	--	(O) Info: www.archives.gov/research/census/nonpopulation/minnesota.html.

Minnesota Notes:

MN-1. Minnesota's original Non-Population schedules, 1850-1880 are located at the Minnesota State Historical Society, St. Paul, MN See http://libguides.mnhs.org/census/nonpop.

MN-2. See *Mortality Census Schedules, Minnesota, 1860-1880* [Microfilm & Digital Capture], filmed by the MN Historical Society, 2 rolls, FHL film #485345 & #485346. Digitized by FamlySearch International, to access the digital images, see the FHL catalog page: www.familysearch.org/search/catalog/98340.

Mississippi

Non-Population Schedules Year & Type of Schedule	NARA Series, No. of Rolls	FHL Film No.	(O) Location of Originals (See Notes) URL: online database, digital images, or info page.
1850 Industry	--	--	(O) MDAH (MS-1)
1860 Industry	--	--	(O) MDAH (MS-1)
1870 Industry	--	--	(O) MDAH (MS-1)
1880 Manufactures	--	--	(O) MDAH (MS-1)
1850 Agriculture	--	--	(O) MDAH (MS-1)
1860 Agriculture	--	--	(O) MDAH (MS-1)
1870 Agriculture	--	--	(O) MDAH (MS-1)
1880 Agriculture	--	--	(O) MDAH (MS-1)
1850 Mortality	T655, 1 roll	(MS-2)	(O) MDAH Online: www.ancestry.com/search/collections/usmortality.
1860 Mortality	T655, 1 roll	(MS-2)	(O) MDAH Online: www.ancestry.com/search/collections/usmortality.
1870 Mortality	T655, 3 rolls	(MS-2)	(O) MDAH Online: www.ancestry.com/search/collections/usmortality.
1880 Mortality	T655, 2 rolls	(MS-2)	(O) MDAH Online: www.ancestry.com/search/collections/usmortality.
1850 Slaves	M432, 5 rolls	--	(O) NARA See www.ancestry.com/search/collections/1850slaveschedules.
1860 Slaves	M653, 7 rolls	--	(O) NARA See www.ancestry.com/search/collections/1860slaveschedules.
1850 Social Statistics	--	--	(O) MDAH (MS-1)
1860 Social Statistics	--	--	(O) MDAH (MS-1)
1870 Social Statistics	--	--	(O) MDAH (MS-1)
1880 Def/Dep/Del Classes	--	--	(O) MDAH (MS-1)

Mississippi, Cont'd

Non-Population Schedules Year & Type of Schedule	NARA Series, No. of Rolls	FHL Film No.	(O) Location of Originals (See Notes) URL: online database, digital images, or info page.
1935 Business-Advertising	M1797, 1 roll	--	(O) Info: www.archives.gov/research/census/nonpopulation/mississippi.html.
1935 Business-Banking	M2066, 8 rolls	--	(O) Info: www.archives.gov/research/census/nonpopulation/mississippi.html.
1935 Business-Misc.Enterprises	M2067, 1 roll	--	(O) Info: www.archives.gov/research/census/nonpopulation/mississippi.html.
1935 Business-Trucking	M2068, 3 rolls	--	(O) Info: www.archives.gov/research/census/nonpopulation/mississippi.html.
1935 Business-Warehousing	M2069, 1 roll	--	(O) Info: www.archives.gov/research/census/nonpopulation/mississippi.html.
1935 Business-Radio Stations	M2070, 1 roll	--	(O) Info: www.archives.gov/research/census/nonpopulation/mississippi.html.

Mississippi Notes:

MS-1. The Mississippi Department of Archives and History (MDAH), Jackson, MS, holds the original MS Non-Population schedules, 1850-1880. See **www.mdah.ms.gov/new/research/genealogy.**

MS-2. See *Mississippi Mortality Schedule for 1850, 1860, 1870, and 1880* [Microfilm & Digital Capture], filmed by NARA, series M655, 3 rolls, FHL film #1550803-1550805. Digitized by FamilySearch International. To access the digital images, see the FHL catalog page: **www.familysearch.org/search/catalog/422723.**

Missouri

Non-Population Schedules Year & Type of Schedule	NARA Series, No. of Rolls	FHL Film No.	(O) Location of Originals (See Notes) URL: online database, digital images, or info page.
1820 Manufactures	M279, 1 roll	1024518	(O) NARA. (MO-1)
1850 Industry	--	--	(O) MO St. Hist. Soc. (MO-2)
1860 Industry	--	--	(O) MO St. Hist. Soc. (MO-2)
1870 Industry	--	--	(O) MO St. Hist. Soc. (MO-2)
1880 Manufactures	--	--	(O) MO St. Hist. Soc. (MO-2)
1850 Agriculture	--	--	(O) MO St. Hist. Soc. (MO-2)
1860 Agriculture	--	--	(O) MO St. Hist. Soc. (MO-2)
1870 Agriculture	--	--	(O) MO St. Hist. Soc. (MO-2)
1880 Agriculture	--	--	(O) MO St. Hist. Soc. (MO-2)
1850 Mortality	T655, 1 roll	1404274	(O) NARA Online DB: https://search.ancestry.com/search/db.aspx?dbid=8756.
1860 Mortality	T655, 1 roll	1404275	(O) NARA Online DB: https://search.ancestry.com/search/db.aspx?dbid=8756.
1870 Mortality	T655, 2 rolls	1404276	(O) NARA Online DB: https://search.ancestry.com/search/db.aspx?dbid=8756.
1880 Mortality	T655, 4 rolls	1404278	(O) NARA Online DB: https://search.ancestry.com/search/db.aspx?dbid=8756.
1850 Slave	M432, 1 roll	--	(O) NARA See www.ancestry.com/search/collections/1850slaveschedules.
1860 Slave	M653, 1 roll	--	(O) NARA See www.ancestry.com/search/collections/1860slaveschedules.
1850 Social Statistics	--	--	(O) MO St. Hist. Soc. (MO-2)
1860 Social Statistics	--	--	(O) MO St. Hist. Soc. (MO-2)
1870 Social Statistics	--	--	(O) MO St. Hist. Soc. (MO-2)
1880 Def/Dep/Del Classes	--	--	(O) MO St. Hist. Soc. (MO-2)
1935 Business-Advertising	M1797, 1 roll	--	(O) Info: www.archives.gov/research/census/nonpopulation/missouri.html.
1935 Business-Banking	M2066, 8 rolls	--	(O) Info: www.archives.gov/research/census/nonpopulation/missouri.html.
1935 Business-Misc.Enterprises	M2067, 3 rolls	--	(O) Info: www.archives.gov/research/census/nonpopulation/missouri.html.
1935 Business-Trucking	M2068, 2 rolls	--	(O) Info: www.archives.gov/research/census/nonpopulation/missouri.html.
1935 Business-Warehousing	M2069, 1 roll	--	(O) Info: www.archives.gov/research/census/nonpopulation/missouri.html.
1935 Business-Radio Stations	M2070, 1 roll	--	(O) Info: www.archives.gov/research/census/nonpopulation/missouri.html.

Missouri Notes:

MO-1. See *Records of the 1820 Census of Manufactures* (NARA Series M279, 27 rolls). Roll 27 contains Western District of Tennessee, Illinois, and pages from *Digest of Manufacturing Establishments in the United States and of their Manufactures* (Washington, DC: Gales & Seaton, 1823) for Alabama, Louisiana, Missouri, Michigan, and Arkansas. See the FHL catalog page: **www.familysearch.org/search/catalog/280127.**

MO-2. The State Historical Society of Missouri, Columbia, MO, holds the original Non-population schedules for Missouri, 1850-1880. There is a Census Page at their website, see **https://shsmo.org/census.**

Montana

Non-Population Schedules Year & Type of Schedule	NARA Series, No. of Rolls	FHL Film No.	(O) Location of Originals (See Notes) URL: online database, digital images, or info page.
1870 Industry	M1806, 1 roll	1550813	(O) MT Hist. Soc. (MT-1)
1880 Manufactures	M1806, 1 roll	1550813	(O) MT Hist. Soc. (MT-1)
1870 Agriculture	M1806, 1 roll	1550813	(O) MT Hist. Soc. (MT-1)
1880 Agriculture	M1806, 1 roll	1550813	(O) MT Hist. Soc. (MT-1). Another copy at NARA, series M1794, 1 roll.
1870 Mortality	M1806, 1 roll	1550813	(O) MT HS. Online: www.ancestry.com/search/collections/usmortality.
1880 Mortality	M1806, 1 roll	1550813	(O) MT HS. Online: www.ancestry.com/search/collections/usmortality.
1870 Social Statistics	M1806, 1 roll	1550813	(O) MT Hist. Soc. (MT-1)
1880 Def/Dep/Del Classes	M1806, 1 roll	1550813	(O) MT Hist. Soc. (MT-1)
1935 Business-Advertising	M1797, 1 roll	--	(O) Info: www.archives.gov/research/census/nonpopulation/montana.html.
1935 Business-Banking	M2066, 8 rolls	--	(O) Info: www.archives.gov/research/census/nonpopulation/montana.html.
1935 Business-Misc.Enterprises	M2067, 2 rolls	--	(O) Info: www.archives.gov/research/census/nonpopulation/montana.html.
1935 Business-Trucking	M2068, 2 rolls	--	(O) Info: www.archives.gov/research/census/nonpopulation/montana.html.
1935 Business-Warehousing	M2069, 1 roll	--	(O) Info: www.archives.gov/research/census/nonpopulation/montana.html.
1935 Business-Radio Stations	M2070, 1 roll	--	(O) Info: www.archives.gov/research/census/nonpopulation/montana.html.

Montana Notes:
MT-1. Montana's original Non-Population schedules, 1870-1880, are located at the Montana Historical Society, Helena, MT. See **https://mhs.mt.gov**.

Nebraska

Non-Population Schedules Year & Type of Schedule	NARA Series, No. of Rolls	FHL Film No.	(O) Location of Originals (See Notes) URL: online database, digital images, or info page.
1860 Industry	T1128, 1 roll	1025171	(O) NE St. Hist. Soc. (NE-1). FHL copy digitized.
1870 Industry	T1128, 1 roll	1025174	(O) NE St. Hist. Soc. (NE-1)
1880 Manufactures	T1128, 1 roll	1025183	(O) NE St. Hist. Soc. (NE-1)
1885 Manufactures	M352, 1 roll	-	(O) NARA (NE-2). Online DB: www.familysearch.org/search/collection/1810728.
1860 Agriculture	T1128, 1 roll	1025171	(O) NE St. Hist. Soc. (NE-1). FHL copy digitized.
1870 Agriculture	T1128, 2 rolls	1025173	(O) NE St. Hist. Soc. (NE-1).
1880 Agriculture	T1128, 8 rolls	1025175	(O) NE St. Hist. Soc. (NE-1)
1885 Agriculture	M352, 8 rolls		(O) NARA (NE-2). Online DB: www.familysearch.org/search/collection/1810728.
1860 Mortality	T655, 1 roll	1025171	(O) NARA Online DB: www.ancestry.com/search/collections/usmortality.
1870 Mortality	T655, 2 rolls	1025173	(O) NARA Online DB: www.ancestry.com/search/collections/usmortality.
1880 Mortality	T655, 4 rolls	1025184	(O) NARA Online DB: www.ancestry.com/search/collections/usmortality.
1885 Mortality	M352, 4 rolls		(O) NARA (NE-2). Online: www.ancestry.com/search/collections/usmortality.
1860 Social Statistics	T1128, 1 roll	1025171	(O) NE St. Hist. Soc. (NE-1). FHL copy digitized.
1870 Social Statistics	T1128, 1 roll	1025174	(O) NE St. Hist. Soc. (NE-1)
1880 Def/Dep/Del Classes	T1128, 1 roll	1025186	(O) NE St. Hist. Soc. (NE-1)
1935 Business-Advertising	M1797, 1 roll	--	(O) Info: www.archives.gov/research/census/nonpopulation/nebraska.html.
1935 Business-Banking	M2066, 8 rolls	--	(O) Info: www.archives.gov/research/census/nonpopulation/nebraska.html.
1935 Business-Misc.Enterprises	M2067, 3 rolls	--	(O) Info: www.archives.gov/research/census/nonpopulation/nebraska.html.
1935 Business-Trucking	M2068, 2 rolls	--	(O) Info: www.archives.gov/research/census/nonpopulation/nebraska.html.
1935 Business-Warehousing	M2069, 1 roll	--	(O) Info: www.archives.gov/research/census/nonpopulation/nebraska.html.
1935 Business-Radio Stations	M2070, 1 roll	--	(O) Info: www.archives.gov/research/census/nonpopulation/nebraska.html.

Nebraska Notes:
NE-1. Nebraska's original 1860-1880 Non-Population schedules are located at the Nebraska State Historical Society, Lincoln, NE, filmed by NARA (series T1128, 16 rolls). Nebraska is included in *U.S., Selected Federal Census Non-Population Schedules, 1850-1880* [Online Database], digitized and indexed at the Ancestry.com website. See **www.ancestry.com/search/collections/nonpopcensus**.
NE-2. Nebraska's 1885 state census was lost. NARA's copy exists, and was microfilmed as series M352, 56 rolls, which included the NE 1885 Population schedules as well as the 1885 Non-Population schedules, as noted above. M352 was digitized and indexed online by FamilySearch.org, as noted above.

Nevada

Non-Population Schedules Year & Type of Schedule	NARA Series, No. of Rolls	FHL Film No.	(O) Location of Originals (See Notes) URL: online database, digital images, or info page.
1880 Manufactures	M1794, 1 roll	--	(O) NV Hist. Soc. (NV-1)
1880 Agriculture	M1794, 1 roll	--	(O) MV Hist. Soc. (NV-1)
1880 Mortality	M1794, 1 roll	--	(O) NV HS. Online: https://search.ancestry.com/search/db.aspx?dbid=8756.
1880 Def/Dep/Del Classes	M1794, 1 roll	--	(O) NV Hist. Soc. (NV-1)
1935 Business-Advertising	M1797, 1 roll	--	(O) Info: www.archives.gov/research/census/nonpopulation/nevada.html.
1935 Business-Banking	M2066, 7 rolls	--	(O) Info: www.archives.gov/research/census/nonpopulation/nevada.html.
1935 Business-Misc.Enterprises	M2067, 1 roll	--	(O) Info: www.archives.gov/research/census/nonpopulation/nevada.html.
1935 Business-Trucking	M2068, 2 rolls	--	(O) Info: www.archives.gov/research/census/nonpopulation/nevada.html.
1935 Business-Warehousing	M2069, 1 roll	--	(O) Info: www.archives.gov/research/census/nonpopulation/nevada.html.
1935 Business-Radio Stations	M2070, 1 roll	--	(O) Info: www.archives.gov/research/census/nonpopulation/nevada.html.

Nevada Notes:
NV-1. Nevada's original Non-Population schedules, 1880, are located at the Nevada Historical Society, Reno, NV. See **http://nvculture.org/historicalsociety**.

New Hampshire

Non-Population Schedules Year & Type of Schedule	NARA Series, No. of Rolls	FHL Film No.	(O) Location of Originals (See Notes) URL: online database, digital images, or info page.
1820 Manufactures	M279, 1 roll	1024492	(O) NARA (NH-1). FHL film Digitized.
1850 Industry	--	--	(O) NH Archives (NH-2)
1860 Industry	--	--	(O) NH Archives (NH-2)
1870 Industry	--	--	(O) NH Archives (NH-2)
1880 Manufactures	--	--	(O) NH Archives (NH-2)
1850 Agriculture	--	--	(O) NH Archives (NH-2)
1860 Agriculture	--	--	(O) NH Archives (NH-2)
1870 Agriculture	--	--	(O) NH Archives (NH-2)
1880 Agriculture	--	--	(O) NH Archives (NH-2)
1850 Mortality	T655, 1 roll	15580	(O) NH Archives. Online: www.ancestry.com/search/collections/usmortality.
1860 Mortality	T655, 1 roll	15580	(O) NH Archives. Online: www.ancestry.com/search/collections/usmortality.
1870 Mortality	T655, 1 roll	15580	(O) NH Archives. Online: www.ancestry.com/search/collections/usmortality.
1880 Mortality	T655, 1 roll	15581	(O) NH Archives. Online: www.ancestry.com/search/collections/usmortality.
1850 Social Statistics	--	--	(O) NH Archives (NH-2)
1860 Social Statistics	--	--	(O) NH Archives (NH-2)
1870 Social Statistics	--	--	(O) NH Archives (NH-2)
1880 Def/Dep/Del Classes	--	--	(O) NH Archives (NH-2)
1935 Business-Advertising	M1797, 1 roll	--	(O) Info: www.archives.gov/research/census/nonpopulation/new-hampshire.html.
1935 Business-Banking	M2066, 6 rolls	--	(O) Info: www.archives.gov/research/census/nonpopulation/new-hampshire.html.
1935 Business-Misc.Enterprises	M2067, 1 roll	--	(O) Info: www.archives.gov/research/census/nonpopulation/new-hampshire.html.
1935 Business-Trucking	M2068, 1 roll	--	(O) Info: www.archives.gov/research/census/nonpopulation/new-hampshire.html.
1935 Business-Warehousing	M2069, 1 roll	--	(O) Info: www.archives.gov/research/census/nonpopulation/new-hampshire.html.
1935 Business-Radio Stations	M2070, 1 roll	--	(O) Info: www.archives.gov/research/census/nonpopulation/new-hampshire.html.

New Hampshire Notes:
NH-1. See *Records of the 1820 Census of Manufactures* (NARA Series M279, 27 rolls). Roll 1 contains Maine and New Hampshire. See the FHL catalog page: **www.familysearch.org/search/catalog/280127**.

NH-2. New Hampshire's original Non-Population schedules are located at the New Hampshire Division of Archives & Records Management, Concord, NH, see **http://sos.nh.gov/Arch_Rec_Mgmt.aspx**. Microfilm copies of the Non-Population schedules are located at the New Hampshire State Library, Concord, NH, see **www.nh.gov/nhsl**.

New Jersey

Non-Population Schedules Year & Type of Schedule	NARA Series, No. of Rolls	FHL Film No.	(O) Location of Originals (See Notes) URL: online database, digital images, or info page.
1820 Manufactures	M279, 1 roll	1024508	(O) NARA (NJ-1)
1850 Industry	--	--	(O) NJ St. Lib. (NJ-2)
1860 Industry	--	--	(O) NJ St. Lib. (NJ-2)
1870 Industry	--	--	(O) NJ St. Lib. (NJ-2)
1880 Manufactures	--	--	(O) NJ St. Lib. (NJ-2)
1850 Agriculture	--	--	(O) NJ St. Lib. (NJ-2)
1860 Agriculture	--	--	(O) NJ St. Lib. (NJ-2)
1870 Agriculture	--	--	(O) NJ St. Lib. (NJ-2)
1880 Agriculture	--	--	(O) NJ St. Lib. (NJ-2)
1850 Mortality	M1810, 1 roll	802952	(O) NJ St. Lib. Online: www.ancestry.com/search/collections/usmortality.
1860 Mortality	M1810, 1 roll	802952	(O) NJ St. Lib. Online: www.ancestry.com/search/collections/usmortality.
1870 Mortality	M1810, 1 roll	802953	(O) NJ St. Lib. Online: www.ancestry.com/search/collections/usmortality.
1880 Mortality	M1810, 1 roll	802954	(O) NJ St. Lib. Online: www.ancestry.com/search/collections/usmortality.
1850 Slave	M432, 1 roll	--	(O) NARA See www.ancestry.com/search/collections/1850slaveschedules.
1850 Social Statistics	--	--	(O) NJ St. Lib. (NJ-2)
1860 Social Statistics	--	--	(O) NJ St. Lib. (NJ-2)
1870 Social Statistics	--	--	(O) NJ St. Lib. (NJ-2)
1880 Def/Dep/Del Classes	A3469, 5 rolls	--	(O) NJ St. Lib. Online: www.ancestry.com/search/collections/1880uscensusddd.
1935 Business-Advertising	M1797, 1 rolls	--	(O) Info: www.archives.gov/research/census/nonpopulation/new-jersey.html.
1935 Business-Banking	M2066, 6 rolls	--	(O) Info: www.archives.gov/research/census/nonpopulation/new-jersey.html.
1935 Business-Misc.Enterprises	M2067, 1 roll	--	(O) Info: www.archives.gov/research/census/nonpopulation/new-jersey.html.
1935 Business-Trucking	M2068, 1 roll	--	(O) Info: www.archives.gov/research/census/nonpopulation/new-jersey.html.
1935 Business-Warehousing	M2069, 1 roll	--	(O) Info: www.archives.gov/research/census/nonpopulation/new-jersey.html.
1935 Business-Radio Stations	M2070, 1 roll	--	(O) Info: www.archives.gov/research/census/nonpopulation/new-jersey.html.

New Jersey Notes:

NJ-1. See *Records of the 1820 Census of Manufactures* (NARA Series M279, 27 rolls). Roll 17 contains New Jersey, Delaware, and the District of Columbia. See the FHL catalog page:
www.familysearch.org/search/catalog/280127.

NJ-2. New Jersey's original Non-Population schedules are located at the New Jersey State Library, Trenton, NJ, see www.njstatelib.org.

New Mexico

Non-Population Schedules Year & Type of Schedule	NARA Series, No. of Rolls	FHL Film No.	(O) Location of Originals (See Notes) URL: online database, digital images, or info page.
1885 Manufactures	M846, 6 rolls	--	(O) NARA (NM-1)
1885 Agriculture	M846, 6 rolls	--	(O) NARA (NM-1)
1885 Mortality	M846, 6 rolls	--	(O) NARA (NM-1). Online: www.ancestry.com/search/collections/usmortality.
1935 Business-Advertising	M1797, 1 roll	--	(O) Info: www.archives.gov/research/census/nonpopulation/new-mexico.html.
1935 Business-Banking	M2066, 7 rolls	--	(O) Info: www.archives.gov/research/census/nonpopulation/new-mexico.html.
1935 Business-Misc.Enterprises	M2067, 1 roll	--	(O) Info: www.archives.gov/research/census/nonpopulation/new-mexico.html.
1935 Business-Trucking	M2068, 2 rolls	--	(O) Info: www.archives.gov/research/census/nonpopulation/new-mexico.html.
1935 Business-Warehousing	M2069, 1 roll	--	(O) Info: www.archives.gov/research/census/nonpopulation/new-mexico.html.
1935 Business-Radio Stations	M2070, 1 roll	--	(O) Info: www.archives.gov/research/census/nonpopulation/new-mexico.html.

New Mexico Notes:
NM-1. New Mexico's original Non-Population schedules are located at the National Archives, Washington, DC. See www.archives.gov/research/census/nonpopulation/new-mexico.html.

New York

Non-Population Schedules Year & Type of Schedule	NARA Series, No. of Rolls	FHL Film No.	(O) Location of Originals (See Notes) URL: online database, digital images, or info page.
1810 Manufactures	M1792, 1 roll	2155487	(O) NARA (NY-1). FHL copy digitized.
1820 Manufactures	M279, 7 rolls	1024496	(O) NARA (NY-2)
1850 Industry	--	--	(O) NY St. Lib. (NY-3)
1860 Industry	--	--	(O) NY St. Lib. (NY-3)
1870 Industry	--	1415142	(O) NY St. Lib. (NY-3)
1880 Manufactures	--	--	(O) NY St. Lib. (NY-3)
1850 Agriculture	--	--	(O) NY St. Lib. (NY-3)
1860 Agriculture	--	--	(O) NY St. Lib. (NY-3)
1870 Agriculture	--	--	(O) NY St. Lib. (NY-3)
1880 Agriculture	--	--	(O) NY St. Lib. (NY-3)
1850 Mortality	--	1415128	(O) NY St. Lib. Online: www.ancestry.com/search/collections/usmortality.
1860 Mortality	--	1415129	(O) NY St. Lib. Online: www.ancestry.com/search/collections/usmortality.
1870 Mortality	--	1415132	(O) NY St. Lib. Online: www.ancestry.com/search/collections/usmortality.
1880 Mortality	--	1415136	(O) NY St. Lib. Online: www.ancestry.com/search/collections/usmortality.
1850 Social Statistics	--	--	(O) NY St. Lib. (NY-3)
1860 Social Statistics	--	--	(O) NY St. Lib. (NY-3)
1870 Social Statistics	--	--	(O) NY St. Lib. (NY-3)
1880 Def/Dep/Del Classes	--	--	(O) NY St. Lib. Online: www.ancestry.com/search/collections/1880uscensusddd.
1935 Business-Advertising	M1797, 1 roll	--	(O) Info: www.archives.gov/research/census/nonpopulation/new-york.html.
1935 Business-Banking	M2066, 14 rolls	--	(O) Info: www.archives.gov/research/census/nonpopulation/new-york.html.
1935 Business-Misc.Enterprises	M2067, 9 rolls	--	(O) Info: www.archives.gov/research/census/nonpopulation/new-york.html.
1935 Business-Trucking	M2068, 8 rolls	--	(O) Info: www.archives.gov/research/census/nonpopulation/new-york.html.
1935 Business-Warehousing	M2069, 2 rolls	--	(O) Info: www.archives.gov/research/census/nonpopulation/new-york.html.
1935 Business-Radio Stations	M2070, 1 roll	--	(O) Info: www.archives.gov/research/census/nonpopulation/new-york.html.

New York Notes:

NY-1. See *Manufacturing Schedules Contained in the 1810 Population Census Schedules of New York State,* includes selected pages from the 1810 population census schedules for Broome, Chenango, Clinton, Cayuga, Dutchess, Essex, Genesee, Niagara, Orange, and Queens Counties. Filmed by NARA, Series 1792, 1 roll. Digitized by FamilySearch International. To access the digital images, see the FHL catalog page: **www.familysearch.org/search/catalog/720499.** ADDED NOTE: 1810 Manufactures lists were extracted from New York counties only. Population census schedules for all states, including New York, were filmed by NARA as part of Series M252, *Third Census of the United States, 1810,* (NY rolls 26-37). In all states, the 1810 Manufactures pages were added to the end of each county's heads of household name list. This 1810 Manufactures list was the first Non-Population schedule ever produced, and the only one handled this way. All subsequent Non-Population schedules were prepared on separate forms and reported separately from the Population schedules.

NY-2. See *Records of the 1820 Census of Manufactures* (NARA Series M279, 27 rolls). New York is on Rolls 5-11. See the FHL catalog page: **www.familysearch.org/search/catalog/280127.**

NY-3. New York's original Non-Population schedules, 1850-1880, are located at the New York State Library, Albany, NY, see **www.nysl.nysed.gov.** New York is included in *U.S., Selected Federal Census Non-Population Schedules, 1850-1880* [Online Database], digitized and indexed at the Ancestry.com website. See **www.ancestry.com/search/collections/nonpopcensus.**

North Carolina

Non-Population Schedules Year & Type of Schedule	NARA Series, No. of Rolls	FHL Film No.	(O) Location of Originals (See Notes) URL: online database, digital images, or info page.
1820 Manufactures	M279, 1 roll	1024510	(O) NARA (NC-1)
1850 Industry	M1805, 1 roll	--	(O) NC St. Archives (NC-2)
1860 Industry	M1805, 1 roll	--	(O) NC St. Archives (NC-2)
1870 Industry	M1805, 1 roll	--	(O) NC St. Archives (NC-2)
1880 Manufactures	M1805, 2 rolls	--	(O) NC St. Archives (NC-2)
1850 Agriculture	--	--	(O) NC St. Archives (NC-2)
1860 Agriculture	--	--	(O) NC St. Archives (NC-2)
1870 Agriculture	M1805, 1 roll	--	(O) NC St. Archives (NC-2)
1880 Agriculture	--	--	(O) NC St. Archives (NC-2)
1850 Mortality	M1805, 1 roll	--	(O) NC St. Arch. Online: www.ancestry.com/search/collections/usmortality.
1860 Mortality	M1805, 1 roll	--	(O) NC St. Arch. Online: www.ancestry.com/search/collections/usmortality.
1870 Mortality	M1805, 1 roll	--	(O) NC St. Arch. Online: www.ancestry.com/search/collections/usmortality.
1880 Mortality	M1805, 2 rolls	--	(O) NC St. Arch. Online: www.ancestry.com/search/collections/usmortality.
1850 Slave	M432, 1 roll	--	(O) NARA See www.ancestry.com/search/collections/1850slaveschedules.
1860 Slave	M653, 1 roll	--	(O) NARA See www.ancestry.com/search/collections/1860slaveschedules.
1850 Social Statistics	--	--	(O) NC St. Archives (NC-2)
1860 Social Statistics	--	--	(O) NC St. Archives (NC-2)
1870 Social Statistics	--	--	(O) NC St. Archives (NC-2)
1880 Def/Dep/Del Classes	--	--	(O) NC St. Archives (NC-2)
1935 Business-Advertising	M1797, 1 roll	--	(O) Info: www.archives.gov/research/census/nonpopulation/north-carolina.html.
1935 Business-Banking	M2066, 6 rolls	--	(O) Info: www.archives.gov/research/census/nonpopulation/north-carolina.html.
1935 Business-Misc.Enterprises	M2067, 1 roll	--	(O) Info: www.archives.gov/research/census/nonpopulation/north-carolina.html.
1935 Business-Trucking	M2068, 1 roll	--	(O) Info: www.archives.gov/research/census/nonpopulation/north-carolina.html.
1935 Business-Warehousing	M2069, 1 roll	--	(O) Info: www.archives.gov/research/census/nonpopulation/north-carolina.html.
1935 Business-Radio Stations	M2070, 1 roll	--	(O) Info: www.archives.gov/research/census/nonpopulation/north-carolina.html.

North Carolina Notes:

NC-1. See *Records of the 1820 Census of Manufactures* (NARA Series M279, 27 rolls). Roll 19 contains North Carolina, South Carolina, and Georgia. See the FHL catalog page: **www.familysearch.org/search/catalog/280127.**

NC-2. North Carolina's original Non-Population schedules are located at the North Carolina State Archives, Raleigh, NC, see **https://archives.ncdcr.gov.** North Carolina is included in *U.S., Selected Federal Census Non-Population Schedules, 1850-1880* [Online Database], digitized and indexed at the Ancestry.com website. See **www.ancestry.com/search/collections/nonpopcensus.**

North Dakota (1889-1935) – See Dakota Territory for earlier schedules.

Non-Population Schedules Year & Type of Schedule	NARA Series, No. of Rolls	FHL Film No.	(O) Location of Originals (See Notes) URL: online database, digital images, or info page.
1935 Business-Advertising	M1797, 1 rolls	--	(O) Info: www.archives.gov/research/census/nonpopulation/north-dakota.html.
1935 Business-Banking	M2066, 8 rolls	--	(O) Info: www.archives.gov/research/census/nonpopulation/north-dakota.html.
1935 Business-Misc.Enterprises	M2067, 1 roll	--	(O) Info: www.archives.gov/research/census/nonpopulation/north-dakota.html.
1935 Business-Trucking	M2068, 1 roll	--	(O) Info: www.archives.gov/research/census/nonpopulation/north-dakota.html.
1935 Business-Warehousing	M2069, 1 roll	--	(O) Info: www.archives.gov/research/census/nonpopulation/north-dakota.html.
1935 Business-Radio Stations	M2070, 1 roll	--	(O) Info: www.archives.gov/research/census/nonpopulation/north-dakota.html.

Ohio

Non-Population Schedules Year & Type of Schedule	NARA Series, No. of Rolls	FHL Film No.	(O) Location of Originals (See Notes) URL: online database, digital images, or info page.
1820 Manufactures	M279, 5 rolls	1024512	(O) NARA (OH-1)
1850 Industry	T1159, 2 rolls	1602336	(O) OH St. Lib. (OH-2)
1860 Industry	T1159, 1 roll	1602352	(O) OH St. Lib. (OH-2)
1870 Industry	T1159, 5 rolls	1602368	(O) OH St. Lib. (OH-2)
1880 Manufactures	T1159, 6 rolls	1602417	(O) OH St. Lib. (OH-2)
1850 Agriculture	T1159, 11 rolls	1602325	(O) OH St. Lib. (OH-2)
1860 Agriculture	T1159, 12 rolls	1602340	(O) OH St. Lib. (OH-2)
1870 Agriculture	T1159, 13 rolls	1602355	(O) OH St. Lib. (OH-2)
1880 Agriculture	T1159, 44 rolls	1602373	(O) OH St. Lib. (OH-2)
1850 Mortality	T1159, 2 rolls	1602426	(O) OH St. Lib. Online: www.ancestry.com/search/collections/usmortality.
1860 Mortality	T1159, 2 rolls	1602353	(O) OH St. Lib. Online: www.ancestry.com/search/collections/usmortality.
1880 Mortality	T1159, 3 rolls	1602428	(O) OH St. Lib. Online: www.ancestry.com/search/collections/usmortality.
1880 Def/Dep/Del Classes	T1159, 3 rolls	1602423	(O) OH St. Lib. Online: www.ancestry.com/search/collections/1880uscensusddd.
1935 Business-Advertising	M1797, 1 roll	--	(O) Info: www.archives.gov/research/census/nonpopulation/ohio.
1935 Business-Banking	M2066, 9 rolls	--	(O) Info: www.archives.gov/research/census/nonpopulation/ohio.
1935 Business-Misc.Enterprises	M2067, 4 rolls	--	(O) Info: www.archives.gov/research/census/nonpopulation/ohio.
1935 Business-Trucking	M2068, 7 rolls	--	(O) Info: www.archives.gov/research/census/nonpopulation/ohio.
1935 Business-Warehousing	M2069, 1 roll	--	(O) Info: www.archives.gov/research/census/nonpopulation/ohio.
1935 Business-Radio Stations	M2070, 1 roll	--	(O) Info: www.archives.gov/research/census/nonpopulation/ohio.

Ohio Notes:

OH-1. See *Records of the 1820 Census of Manufactures* (NARA Series M279, 27 rolls). Ohio is on Rolls 21-25. See the FHL catalog page: **www.familysearch.org/search/catalog/280127.**

OH-2. Ohio's original Non-Population schedules are located at the State Library of Ohio, Columbus, OH, filmed by NARA, Series T1159, 104 rolls, see **https://library.ohio.gov**. The FHL acquired the NARA film and to date has digitized just a few rolls. To see which rolls are digitized and available online search the FHL catalog for the first film number in the 104-roll series: FHL film #102325 (1850 Agriculture).

Oklahoma

Non-Population Schedules Year & Type of Schedule	NARA Series, No. of Rolls	FHL Film No.	(O) Location of Originals (See Notes) URL: online database, digital images, or info page.
1935 Business-Advertising	M1797, 1 roll	--	(O) Info: www.archives.gov/research/census/nonpopulation/oklahoma.html.
1935 Business-Banking	M2066, 7 rolls	--	(O) Info: www.archives.gov/research/census/nonpopulation/oklahoma.html.
1935 Business-Misc.Enterprises	M2067, 1 roll	--	(O) Info: www.archives.gov/research/census/nonpopulation/oklahoma.html.
1935 Business-Trucking	M2068, 2 rolls	--	(O) Info: www.archives.gov/research/census/nonpopulation/oklahoma.html.
1935 Business-Warehousing	M2069, 1 roll	--	(O) Info: www.archives.gov/research/census/nonpopulation/oklahoma.html.
1935 Business-Radio Stations	M2070, 1 roll	--	(O) Info: www.archives.gov/research/census/nonpopulation/oklahoma.html.

Oregon

Non-Population Schedules Year & Type of Schedule	NARA Series, No. of Rolls	FHL Film No.	(O) Location of Originals (See Notes) URL: online database, digital images, or info page.
1850 Industry	--	--	(O) OR St. Lib. (OR-1)
1860 Industry	--	--	(O) OR St. Lib. (OR-1)
1870 Industry	--	--	(O) OR St. Lib. (OR-1)
1880 Manufactures	--	--	(O) OR St. Lib. (OR-1)
1850 Agriculture	--	--	(O) OR St. Lib. (OR-1)
1860 Agriculture	--	--	(O) OR St. Lib. (OR-1)
1870 Agriculture	--	--	(O) OR St. Lib. (OR-1)
1880 Agriculture	--	--	(O) OR St. Lib. (OR-1)

Oregon, Cont'd

Non-Population Schedules Year & Type of Schedule	NARA Series, No. of Rolls	FHL Film No.	(O) Location of Originals (See Notes) URL: online database, digital images, or info page.
1850 Mortality	--	--	(O) OR St. Lib. Online: www.ancestry.com/search/collections/usmortality.
1860 Mortality	--	--	(O) OR St. Lib. Online: www.ancestry.com/search/collections/usmortality.
1870 Mortality	--	--	(O) OR St. Lib. Online: www.ancestry.com/search/collections/usmortality.
1880 Mortality	--	--	(O) OR St. Lib. Online: www.ancestry.com/search/collections/usmortality.
1850 Social Statistics	--	--	(O) OR St. Lib. (OR-1)
1860 Social Statistics	--	--	(O) OR St. Lib. (OR-1)
1870 Social Statistics	--	--	(O) OR St. Lib. (OR-1)
1880 Def/Dep/Del Classes	--	--	(O) OR St. Lib. Online: www.ancestry.com/search/collections/1880uscensusddd.
1935 Business-Advertising	M1797, 1 roll	--	(O) Info: www.archives.gov/research/census/nonpopulation/oregon.html.
1935 Business-Banking	M2066, 7 rolls	--	(O) Info: www.archives.gov/research/census/nonpopulation/oregon.html.
1935 Business-Misc.Enterprises	M2067, 2 rolls	--	(O) Info: www.archives.gov/research/census/nonpopulation/oregon.html.
1935 Business-Trucking	M2068, 1 roll	--	(O) Info: www.archives.gov/research/census/nonpopulation/oregon.html.
1935 Business-Warehousing	M2069, 1 roll	--	(O) Info: www.archives.gov/research/census/nonpopulation/oregon.html.
1935 Business-Radio Stations	M2070, 1 roll	--	(O) Info: www.archives.gov/research/census/nonpopulation/oregon.html.

Oregon Notes:
OR-1. Oregon's original Non-Population schedules are located at the State Library of Oregon, Salem, OR. See www.oregon.gov/library/Pages/default.aspx.

Pennsylvania

Non-Population Schedules Year & Type of Schedule	NARA Series, No. of Rolls	FHL Film No.	(O) Location of Originals (See Notes) URL: online database, digital images, or info page.
1820 Manufactures	M279, 4 rolls	1024503	(O) NARA (PA-1). See www.familysearch.org/search/catalog/280127.
1850 Industry	T1157, 5 rolls	1578849	(O) NARA (PA-1)
1860 Industry	T1157, 4 rolls	1578854	(O) NARA (PA-1)
1870 Industry	M1796, 4 rolls	899753	(O) NARA (PA-1)
1880 Manufactures	M1796, 5 rolls	899759	(O) NARA (PA-1)
1850 Agriculture	T1138, 9 rolls	1602240	(O) NARA (PA-1). Check FHL film No. for digital images on certain rolls.
1860 Agriculture	T1138, 10 rolls	1602249	(O) NARA (PA-1). Check FHL film No. for digital images on certain rolls.
1870 Agriculture	T1138, 14 rolls	1602259	(O) NARA (PA-1). Check FHL film No. for digital images on certain rolls.
1880 Agriculture	T1138, 29 rolls	1602273	(O) NARA (PA-1). Check FHL film No. for digital images on certain rolls.
1850 Mortality	M1838, 2 rolls	899736	(O) NARA Online: www.ancestry.com/search/collections/usmortality.
1860 Mortality	M1838, 2 rolls	899738	(O) NARA Online: www.ancestry.com/search/collections/usmortality.
1870 Mortality	M1838, 3 rolls	899740	(O) NARA Online: www.ancestry.com/search/collections/usmortality.
1880 Mortality	M1838, 6 rolls	899743	(O) NARA Online: www.ancestry.com/search/collections/usmortality.
1850 Social Statistics	M597, 5 rolls	1602302	(O) NARA (PA-1)
1860 Social Statistics	M597, 3 rolls	1602307	(O) NARA (PA-1)
1870 Social Statistics	M597, 1 roll	1602310	(O) NARA (PA-1)
1880 Def/Dep/Del Classes	M597, 14 rolls	1602311	(O) NARA Online: www.ancestry.com/search/collections/1880uscensusddd.
1935 Business-Advertising	M1797, 1 rolls	--	(O) Info: www.archives.gov/research/census/nonpopulation/pennsylvania.html.
1935 Business-Banking	M2066, 8 rolls	--	(O) Info: www.archives.gov/research/census/nonpopulation/pennsylvania.html.
1935 Business-Misc.Enterprises	M2067, 4 roll	--	(O) Info: www.archives.gov/research/census/nonpopulation/pennsylvania.html.
1935 Business-Trucking	M2068, 6 rolls	--	(O) Info: www.archives.gov/research/census/nonpopulation/pennsylvania.html.
1935 Business-Warehousing	M2069, 1 roll	--	(O) Info: www.archives.gov/research/census/nonpopulation/pennsylvania.html.
1935 Business-Radio Stations	M2070, 1 roll	--	(O) Info: www.archives.gov/research/census/nonpopulation/pennsylvania.html.

Pennsylvania Notes:
PA-1. Pennsylvania's original Non-Population schedules are located at the National Archives (NARA), Washington, DC. For each series of microfilm (M279, T1157, M1796, T1138, M1838, M597), 112 rolls total, a roll number and counties on each roll can be reviewed at the NARA Non-Population website for Pennsylvania, see **www.archives.gov/research/census/nonpopulation/pennsylvania.html**.

Puerto Rico

Non-Population Schedules Year & Type of Schedule	NARA Series, No. of Rolls	FHL Film No.	(O) Location of Originals (See Notes) URL: online database, digital images, or info page.
1930 Non-Population Schedules	M1896, Roll 1	--	(O) NARA (PR-1). Nonfarm Livestock, Adjuntas – Las Piedras.
1930 Non-Population Schedules	M1896, Roll 2	--	(O) NARA (PR-1). Nonfarm Livestock, Loiza – Yauca.
1935 Social & Population	M1881, 88 rolls	--	(O) NARA (PR-2).
1935 Agriculture	M1882, 136 rolls	--	(O) NARA (PR-2).

Puerto Rico Notes:

PR-1. All of the census forms were printed in Spanish. The 1930 records consist of *Forma 15-60, Tabla Para Ganado Fuera de Fincas-Puerto Rico,* with space for 28 proprietors of livestock on each side. This schedule was used to report all livestock kept in "establos, ranchos, corrales, caballerizas, patios," ("stables, ranches, corrals, horse stables, courtyards,") and other "lugares" ("places") near cities and towns.

PR-2. A full census was taken for the Territory of Puerto Rico in 1935, including Population Schedules and Non-Population Schedules (Social & Agriculture). More information is pending at the NARA website, see www.archives.gov/research/census/nonpopulation/puerto-rico.html.

Rhode Island

Non-Population Schedules Year & Type of Schedule	NARA Series, No. of Rolls	FHL Film No.	(O) Location of Originals (See Notes) URL: online database, digital images, or info page.
1820 Manufactures	M279, 1 roll	1024493	(O) NARA (RI-1). FHL film Digitized.
1870 Industry	--	--	(O) RI St. Archives (RI-2)
1875 RI Manufactures	--	--	(O) RI St. Archives (RI-2)
1885 RI Manufactures	--	--	(O) RI St. Archives (RI-2)
1870 Agriculture	--	--	(O) RI St. Archives (RI-2)
1870 Mortality	--	--	(O) RI St. Arch. Online: www.ancestry.com/search/collections/usmortality.
1870 Social Statistics	--	--	(O) RI St. Archives (RI-2)
1935 Business-Advertising	M1797, 1 roll	--	(O) Info: www.archives.gov/research/census/nonpopulation/rhode-island.html.
1935 Business-Banking	M2066, 7 rolls	--	(O) Info: www.archives.gov/research/census/nonpopulation/rhode-island.html.
1935 Business-Misc. Enterprises	M2067, 1 roll	--	(O) Info: www.archives.gov/research/census/nonpopulation/rhode-island.html.
1935 Business-Trucking	M2068, 1 roll	--	(O) Info: www.archives.gov/research/census/nonpopulation/rhode-island.html.
1935 Business-Warehousing	M2069, 1 roll	--	(O) Info: www.archives.gov/research/census/nonpopulation/rhode-island.html.
1935 Business-Radio Stations	M2070, 1 roll	--	(O) Info: www.archives.gov/research/census/nonpopulation/rhode-island.html.

Rhode Island Notes:

RI-1. See *Records of the 1820 Census of Manufactures* (NARA Series M279, 27 rolls). Roll 2 contains Massachusetts and Rhode Island. See the FHL catalog page: www.familysearch.org/search/catalog/280127.

RI-2. Rhode Island's original Non-Population schedules are located at the Rhode Island State Archives, Providence, RI. The collection includes Non-Population schedules from the 1875 and 1885 RI State Censuses. See http://sos.ri.gov/divisions/state-archives.

South Carolina

Non-Population Schedules Year & Type of Schedule	NARA Series, No. of Rolls	FHL Film No.	(O) Location of Originals (See Notes) URL: online database, digital images, or info page.
1820 Manufactures	M279, 1 roll	1024510	(O) NARA (SC-1)
1850 Industry	--	--	(O) SCDAH (SC-2)
1860 Industry	--	--	(O) SCDAH (SC-2)
1870 Industry	--	--	(O) SCDAH (SC-2)
1880 Manufactures	--	--	(O) SCDAH (SC-2)

South Carolina, Cont'd

Non-Population Schedules Year & Type of Schedule	NARA Series, No. of Rolls	FHL Film No.	(O) Location of Originals (See Notes) URL: online database, digital images, or info page.
1850 Agriculture	--	--	(O) SCDAH (SC-2)
1860 Agriculture	--	--	(O) SCDAH (SC-2)
1870 Agriculture	--	--	(O) SCDAH (SC-2)
1880 Agriculture	--	--	(O) SCDAH (SC-2)
1850 Mortality	--	--	(O) SCDAH Online: www.ancestry.com/search/collections/usmortality.
1860 Mortality	--	--	(O) SCDAH Online: www.ancestry.com/search/collections/usmortality.
1870 Mortality	--	--	(O) SCDAH Online: www.ancestry.com/search/collections/usmortality.
1880 Mortality	--	--	(O) SCDAH Online: www.ancestry.com/search/collections/usmortality.
1850 Slave	M432, 1 roll	--	(O) NARA See www.ancestry.com/search/collections/1850slaveschedules.
1860 Slave	M653, 1 roll	--	(O) NARA See www.ancestry.com/search/collections/1860slaveschedules.
1850 Social Statistics	--	--	(O) SCDAH (SC-2)
1860 Social Statistics	--	--	(O) SCDAH (SC-2)
1870 Social Statistics	--	--	(O) SCDAH (SC-2)
1880 Def/Dep/Del Classes	--	--	(O) SCDAH Online: www.ancestry.com/search/collections/1880uscensusddd.
1935 Business-Advertising	M1797, 1 roll	--	(O) Info: www.archives.gov/research/census/nonpopulation/south-carolina.html.
1935 Business-Banking	M2066, 8 rolls	--	(O) Info: www.archives.gov/research/census/nonpopulation/south-carolina.html.
1935 Business-Misc.Enterprises	M2067, 1 roll	--	(O) Info: www.archives.gov/research/census/nonpopulation/south-carolina.html.
1935 Business-Trucking	M2068, 2 rolls	--	(O) Info: www.archives.gov/research/census/nonpopulation/south-carolina.html.
1935 Business-Warehousing	M2069, 2 rolls	--	(O) Info: www.archives.gov/research/census/nonpopulation/south-carolina.html.
1935 Business-Radio Stations	M2070, 1 roll	--	(O) Info: www.archives.gov/research/census/nonpopulation/south-carolina.html.

South Carolina Notes:

SC-1. See *Records of the 1820 Census of Manufactures* (NARA Series M279, 27 rolls). Roll 19 contains North Carolina, South Carolina, and Georgia. See the FHL catalog page: **www.familysearch.org/search/catalog/280127**.

SC-2. South Carolina's original Non-Population schedules are located at the South Carolina Department of Archives & History (SCDAH), Columbia, SC. See **https://scdah.sc.gov**. South Carolina is included in *U.S., Selected Federal Census Non-Population Schedules, 1850-1880* [Online Database], digitized and indexed at the Ancestry.com website. See **www.ancestry.com/search/collections/nonpopcensus**.

South Dakota (1889-1935) – See Dakota Territory for earlier schedules.

Non-Population Schedules Year & Type of Schedule	NARA Series, No. of Rolls	FHL Film No.	(O) Location of Originals (See Notes) URL: online database, digital images, or info page.
1935 Business-Advertising	M1797, 1 roll	--	(O) Info: www.archives.gov/research/census/nonpopulation/south-dakota.html.
1935 Business-Banking	M2066, 6 rolls	--	(O) Info: www.archives.gov/research/census/nonpopulation/south-dakota.html.
1935 Business-Misc.Enterprises	M2067, 1 roll	--	(O) Info: www.archives.gov/research/census/nonpopulation/south-dakota.html.
1935 Business-Trucking	M2068, 2 rolls	--	(O) Info: www.archives.gov/research/census/nonpopulation/south-dakota.html.
1935 Business-Warehousing	M2069, 1 roll	--	(O) Info: www.archives.gov/research/census/nonpopulation/south-dakota.html.
1935 Business-Radio Stations	M2070, 1 roll	--	(O) Info: www.archives.gov/research/census/nonpopulation/south-dakota.html.

Tennessee

Non-Population Schedules Year & Type of Schedule	NARA Series, No. of Rolls	FHL Film No.	(O) Location of Originals (See Notes) URL: online database, digital images, or info page.
1820 Manufactures	M279, 1 roll	1024517	(O) NARA. (TN-1). FHL film Digitized.
1850 Industry	T1135, 3 rolls	1549473	(O) Duke Univ. (TN-2)
1860 Industry	T1135, 1 roll	1549474	(O) Duke Univ. (TN-2)
1870 Industry	T1135, 2 rolls	1549475	(O) Duke Univ. (TN-2)
1880 Manufactures	T1135, 2 rolls	1549476	(O) Duke Univ. (TN-2)
1850 Agriculture	T1135, 5 rolls	1549444	(O) Duke Univ. (TN-2)
1860 Agriculture	T1135, 5 rolls	1549449	(O) Duke Univ. (TN-2)

Tennessee, Cont'd

Non-Population Schedules Year & Type of Schedule	NARA Series, No. of Rolls	FHL Film No.	(O) Location of Originals (See Notes) URL: online database, digital images, or info page.
1870 Agriculture	T1135, 6 rolls	1549454	(O) Duke Univ. (TN-2)
1880 Agriculture	T1135, 2 rolls	1549460	(O) Duke Univ. (TN-2)
1850 Mortality	M655, 1 roll	422433	(O) NARA (TN-3). Online: www.ancestry.com/search/collections/usmortality.
1860 Mortality	M655, 1 roll	422434	(O) NARA (TN-3). Online: www.ancestry.com/search/collections/usmortality.
1870 Mortality	M655, 2 rolls	--	(O) NARA (TN-3). Online: www.ancestry.com/search/collections/usmortality.
1880 Mortality	M655, 3 rolls	422436	(O) NARA (TN-3). Online: www.ancestry.com/search/collections/usmortality.
1850 Slave	M432, 1 roll	--	(O) NARA See www.ancestry.com/search/collections/1850slaveschedules.
1860 Slave	M653, 1 roll	--	(O) NARA See www.ancestry.com/search/collections/1860slaveschedules.
1850 Social Statistics	T1135, 1 roll	1549478	(O) Duke Univ. (TN-2)
1860 Social Statistics	T1135, 1 roll	1549479	(O) Duke Univ. (TN-2)
1870 Social Statistics	T1135, 1 roll	1549480	(O) Duke Univ. (TN-2)
1880 Def/Dep/Del Classes	T1135, 2 rolls	1549481	(O) Duke Univ. Online: www.ancestry.com/search/collections/1880uscensusddd.
1935 Business-Advertising	M1797, 1 roll	--	(O) Info: www.archives.gov/research/census/nonpopulation/tennessee.html.
1935 Business-Banking	M2066, 8 rolls	--	(O) Info: www.archives.gov/research/census/nonpopulation/tennessee.html.
1935 Business-Misc.Enterprises	M2067, 1 roll	--	(O) Info: www.archives.gov/research/census/nonpopulation/tennessee.html.
1935 Business-Trucking	M2068, 2 rolls	--	(O) Info: www.archives.gov/research/census/nonpopulation/tennessee.html.
1935 Business-Warehousing	M2069, 2 rolls	--	(O) Info: www.archives.gov/research/census/nonpopulation/tennessee.html.
1935 Business-Radio Stations	M2070, 1 roll	--	(O) Info: www.archives.gov/research/census/nonpopulation/tennessee.html.

Tennessee Notes:

TN-1. See *Records of the 1820 Census of Manufactures* (NARA Series M279, 27 rolls). Roll 26 and 27 contains Tennessee. See the FHL catalog page: **www.familysearch.org/search/catalog/280127**.

TN-2. Tennessee's original Non-Population schedules are located at Rubenstein Library - Library Service Center, Manuscripts, Duke University, Durham, NC. Search for "non-population" at the search dialog box, see **https://library.duke.edu**. Filmed by NARA (Series 1135, 40 rolls), acquired by FHL, see the catalog page: **www.familysearch.org/search/catalog/589494**.

TN-3. Tennessee's original 1850, 1860, 1870 and 1880 Mortality Schedules spent some time at the DAR Library in Washington, DC, but were later returned to the National Archives. While there, the DAR undertook a full index to the names from all census years. The NARA microfilm (Series T655, 8 rolls) includes the index (as does the FHL film). The FHL has the film for 1850, 1860, and 1880 (missing 1870). To access the digital images, starting with FHL film #422433 (1850), see the FHL catalog page: **www.familysearch.org/search/catalog/783171**.

Texas

Non-Population Schedules Year & Type of Schedule	NARA Series, No. of Rolls	FHL Film No.	(O) Location of Originals (See Notes) URL: online database, digital images, or info page.
1850 Industry	T1134, 1 roll	1421044	(O) TX St. Lib. (TX-1). Digitized.
1860 Industry	T1134, 2 rolls	1421044	(O) TX St. Lib. (TX-1). Digitized.
1870 Industry	T1134, 1 roll	1421045	(O) TX St. Lib. (TX-1)
1880 Manufactures	T1134, 4 rolls	1421047	(O) TX St. Lib. (TX-1)
1850 Agriculture	T1134, 2 rolls	--	(O) TX St. Lib. (TX-1)
1860 Agriculture	T1134, 5 rolls	--	(O) TX St. Lib. (TX-1)
1870 Agriculture	T1134, 7 rolls	--	(O) TX St. Lib. (TX-1)
1880 Agriculture	T1134, 32 rolls	--	(O) TX St. Lib. (TX-1)
1850 Mortality	T1134, 2 rolls	--	(O) TX St. Lib. Online: www.ancestry.com/search/collections/usmortality.
1860 Mortality	T1134, 2 rolls	--	(O) TX St. Lib. Online: www.ancestry.com/search/collections/usmortality.
1870 Mortality	T1134, 2 rolls	--	(O) TX St. Lib. Online: www.ancestry.com/search/collections/usmortality.
1880 Mortality	T1134, 5 rolls	--	(O) TX St. Lib. Online: www.ancestry.com/search/collections/usmortality.
1850 Slave	M432, 2 rolls	--	(O) NARA See www.ancestry.com/search/collections/1850slaveschedules.
1860 Slave	M653, 4 rolls	--	(O) NARA See www.ancestry.com/search/collections/1860slaveschedules.

Texas, Cont'd

Non-Population Schedules Year & Type of Schedule	NARA Series, No. of Rolls	FHL Film No.	(O) Location of Originals (See Notes) URL: online database, digital images, or info page.
1850 Social Statistics	T1134, 1 roll	--	(O) TX St. Lib. (TX-1)
1860 Social Statistics	T1134, 2 rolls	--	(O) TX St. Lib. (TX-1)
1870 Social Statistics	T1134, 1 roll	--	(O) TX St. Lib. (TX-1)
1880 Def/Dep/Del Classes	T1134. 5 rolls	--	(O) TX St. Lib. Online: www.ancestry.com/search/collections/1880uscensusddd.
1935 Business-Advertising	M1797, 1 roll	--	(O) Info: www.archives.gov/research/census/nonpopulation/texas.html.
1935 Business-Banking	M2066, 8 rolls	--	(O) Info: www.archives.gov/research/census/nonpopulation/texas.html.
1935 Business-Misc.Enterprises	M2067, 1 roll	--	(O) Info: www.archives.gov/research/census/nonpopulation/texas.html.
1935 Business-Trucking	M2068, 2 rolls	--	(O) Info: www.archives.gov/research/census/nonpopulation/texas.html.
1935 Business-Warehousing	M2069, 2 rolls	--	(O) Info: www.archives.gov/research/census/nonpopulation/texas.html.
1935 Business-Radio Stations	M2070, 1 roll	--	(O) Info: www.archives.gov/research/census/nonpopulation/texas.html.

Texas Notes:

TX-1. All Texas original Non-Population schedules are located at the Texas State Library & Archives Commission, Austin, TX, filmed by NARA, series T1134, 59 rolls, see **www.tsl.texas.gov**. Texas is included in *U.S., Selected Federal Census Non-Population Schedules, 1850-1880* [Online Database], digitized and indexed at the Ancestry.com website. See **www.ancestry.com/search/collections/nonpopcensus**.

Utah

Non-Population Schedules Year & Type of Schedule	NARA Series, No. of Rolls	FHL Film No.	(O) Location of Originals (See Notes) URL: online database, digital images, or info page.
1860 Industrial	--	1550328	(O) UT Hist. Soc.
1870 Industrial	--	1550328	(O) UT Hist. Soc.
1850 Agriculture	--	1550328	(O) UT Hist. Soc.
1870 Agriculture	--	1550328	(O) UT Hist. Soc.
1880 Agriculture	T9, 1 roll	1255336	(O) NARA Cache Co UT only.
1880 Agriculture	--	205643	(O) LDS Church Historian. All UT counties except Cache Co
1850 Mortality	--	1550328	(O) UT Hist. Soc. Online: https://search.ancestry.com/search/db.aspx?dbid=8756.
1860 Mortality	--	1550328	(O) UT Hist. Soc. See www.ancestry.com/search/collections/usmortality.
1870 Mortality	M1807, 1 roll	1550298	(O) NARA Online: https://search.ancestry.com/search/db.aspx?dbid=8756.
1880 Mortality	--	1550325	(O) LDS Church Historian. See www.ancestry.com/search/collections/usmortality.
1850 Social Statistics	--	1550328	(O) UT Hist. Soc.
1860 Social Statistics	--	1550328	(O) UT Hist. Soc.
1870 Social Statistics	--	1550328	(O) UT Hist. Soc.
1935 Business-Advertising	M1797, 1 rolls	--	(O) Info: www.archives.gov/research/census/nonpopulation/utah.html.
1935 Business-Banking	M2066, 8 rolls	--	(O) Info: www.archives.gov/research/census/nonpopulation/utah.html
1935 Business-Misc.Enterprises	M2067, 1 roll	--	(O) Info: www.archives.gov/research/census/nonpopulation/utah.html
1935 Business-Trucking	M2068, 2 rolls	--	(O) Info: www.archives.gov/research/census/nonpopulation/utah.html
1935 Business-Warehousing	M2069, 1 roll	--	(O) Info: www.archives.gov/research/census/nonpopulation/utah.html
1935 Business-Radio Stations	M2070, 1 roll	--	(O) Info: www.archives.gov/research/census/nonpopulation/utah.html

Vermont

Non-Population Schedules Year & Type of Schedule	NARA Series, No. of Rolls	FHL Film No.	(O) Location of Originals (See Notes) URL: online database, digital images, or info page.
1820 Manufactures	M279, 1 roll	1024494	(O) NARA (VT-1)
1850 Industry	M1798, 1 roll	--	(O) VT St. Lib. (VT-2)
1860 Industry	M1798, 1 roll	--	(O) VT St. Lib. (VT-2)
1870 Industry	M1798, 1 roll	--	(O) VT St. Lib. (VT-2)
1880 Manufactures	--	--	(O) VT St. Lib. (VT-2)
1850 Agriculture	M1798, 2 rolls	--	(O) VT St. Lib. (VT-2)
1860 Agriculture	M1798, 2 rolls	--	(O) VT St. Lib. (VT-2)

Vermont, Cont'd

Non-Population Schedules Year & Type of Schedule	NARA Series, No. of Rolls	FHL Film No.	(O) Location of Originals (See Notes) URL: online database, digital images, or info page.
1870 Agriculture	M1798, 2 rolls	--	(O) VT St. Lib. (VT-2)
1880 Agriculture	--	--	(O) VT St. Lib. (VT-2)
1850 Mortality	M655, 1 roll	--	(O) NARA Online: www.ancestry.com/search/collections/usmortality.
1860 Mortality	M655, 1 roll	--	(O) NARA Online: www.ancestry.com/search/collections/usmortality.
1870 Mortality	M1807, 2 rolls	1550298	(O) NARA Online: www.ancestry.com/search/collections/usmortality.
1880 Mortality	M655, 3 rolls	1405371	(O) NARA Online: www.ancestry.com/search/collections/usmortality.
1850 Social Statistics	--	--	(O) VT St. Lib. (VT-2)
1860 Social Statistics	--	--	(O) VT St. Lib. (VT-2)
1870 Social Statistics	--	--	(O) VT St. Lib. (VT-2)
1880 Def/Dep/Del Classes	--	--	(O) VT St. Lib. (VT-2)
1935 Business-Advertising	M1797, 1 roll	--	(O) Info: www.archives.gov/research/census/nonpopulation/vermont.html.
1935 Business-Banking	M2066, 4 rolls	--	(O) Info: www.archives.gov/research/census/nonpopulation/vermont.html
1935 Business-Misc.Enterprises	M2067, 1 roll	--	(O) Info: www.archives.gov/research/census/nonpopulation/vermont.html
1935 Business-Trucking	M2068, 2 rolls	--	(O) Info: www.archives.gov/research/census/nonpopulation/vermont.html
1935 Business-Warehousing	M2069, 1 roll	--	(O) Info: www.archives.gov/research/census/nonpopulation/vermont.html
1935 Business-Radio Stations	M2070, 1 roll	--	(O) Info: www.archives.gov/research/census/nonpopulation/vermont.html

Vermont Notes:

VT-1. See *Records of the 1820 Census of Manufactures* (NARA Series M279, 27 rolls). Roll 3 contains Vermont. See the FHL catalog page: **www.familysearch.org/search/catalog/280127.**

VT-2. Vermont's original Non-Population schedules are located at the Vermont State Library, Barre, VT, see **https://libraries.vermont.gov/state_library.**

Virgin Islands of the U.S.

Non-Population Schedules Year & Type of Schedule	NARA Series, No. of Rolls	(O) Location of Originals (See Notes) URL: online database, digital images, or info page.
1917 Agriculture	M1891, 1 roll	(O) NARA. See www.archives.gov/research/census/nonpopulation/virgin-islands.html
1930 Agriculture	M1891, 1 roll	(O) NARA. See www.archives.gov/research/census/nonpopulation/virgin-islands.html

Virginia

Non-Population Schedules Year & Type of Schedule	NARA Series, No. of Rolls	FHL Film No.	(O) Location of Originals (See Notes) URL: online database, digital images, or info page.
1820 Manufactures	M279, 1 roll	1024509	(O) NARA (VA-1)
1850 Industry	T1132, 1 roll	--	(O) VA St. Lib.(VA-2)
1860 Industry	T1132, 1 roll	29745	(O) VA St. Lib.(VA-2) (VA-3)
1870 Industry	T1132, 1 roll	--	(O) VA St. Lib.(VA-2)
1880 Manufactures	T1132, 2 rolls	--	(O) VA St. Lib.(VA-2)
1850 Agriculture	T1132, 3 rolls	--	(O) VA St. Lib.(VA-2)
1860 Agriculture	T1132, 3 rolls	--	(O) VA St. Lib.(VA-2) (VA-3)
1870 Agriculture	T1132, 5 rolls	29739	(O) VA St. Lib.(VA-2)
1880 Agriculture	T1132, 8 rolls	--	(O) VA St. Lib.(VA-2)
1850 Mortality	T1132, 1 roll	1421031	(O) VA St. Lib. Online: www.ancestry.com/search/collections/usmortality.
1860 Mortality	M1808 (VA-3)	1421032	(O) VA St. Lib. Online: www.ancestry.com/search/collections/usmortality.
1870 Mortality	T1132, 1 roll	1421033	(O) VA St. Lib. Online: www.ancestry.com/search/collections/usmortality.
1880 Mortality	T1132, 2 rolls	--	(O) VA St. Lib. Online: www.ancestry.com/search/collections/usmortality.
1850 Slave	M432, 11 rolls	--	(O NARA See www.ancestry.com/search/collections/1850slaveschedules.
1860 Slave	M653, 12 rolls	--	(O) NARA See www.ancestry.com/search/collections/1860slaveschedules.
1850 Social Statistics	T1132, 1 roll	--	(O) VA St. Lib.(VA-2)
1860 Social Statistics	T1132, 1 roll	--	(O) VA St. Lib.(VA-2) (VA-3)

Virginia, Cont'd

Non-Population Schedules Year & Type of Schedule	NARA Series, No. of Rolls	FHL Film No.	(O) Location of Originals (See Notes) URL: online database, digital images, or info page.
1870 Social Statistics	T1132, 1 roll	29743	(O) VA St. Lib.(VA-2)
1935 Business-Advertising	M1797, 1 roll	--	(O) Info: www.archives.gov/research/census/nonpopulation/virginia.html.
1935 Business-Banking	M2066, 6 rolls	--	(O) Info: www.archives.gov/research/census/nonpopulation/virginia.html.
1935 Business-Misc.Enterprises	M2067, 1 roll	--	(O) Info: www.archives.gov/research/census/nonpopulation/virginia.html.
1935 Business-Trucking	M2068, 1 roll	--	(O) Info: www.archives.gov/research/census/nonpopulation/virginia.html.
1935 Business-Warehousing	M2069, 1 roll	--	(O) Info: www.archives.gov/research/census/nonpopulation/virginia.html.
1935 Business-Radio Stations	M2070, 1 roll	--	(O) Info: www.archives.gov/research/census/nonpopulation/virginia.html.

Virginia Notes:

VA-1. See *Records of the 1820 Census of Manufactures* (NARA Series M279, 27 rolls). Roll 1 contains Virginia. See the FHL catalog page: **www.familysearch.org/search/catalog/280127.**

VA-2. Virginia's original Non-Population schedules are located at the Library of Virginia, Richmond, VA, see **www.lva.virginia.gov.** Virginia is included in *U.S., Selected Federal Census Non-Population Schedules, 1850-1880* [Online Database], digitized and indexed at the Ancestry.com website. See **www.ancestry.com/search/collections/nonpopcensus.**

VA-3. See **NARA Series M1808:** *Eighth Census of the United States for the Northern District of Halifax County, Virginia, 1860: Schedules of Free Inhabitants, Slave Inhabitants, Mortality, Agriculture, Industry, and Social Statistics* (1 roll), reproduces original schedules held by the Duke University Library, which may have been a "rough draft" kept by Assistant Marshal John H. Taylor. The major difference between M1808 and T1132 in the mortality schedules: (1) M1808 indicates the slave owner's surname for each deceased slave; T1132 merely indicates the slave's first name; and (2) M1808 gives each slave's occupation as "slave" while T1132 indicates each slave's specific position (field hand, house servant, miller, etc.). See **www.archives.gov/research/census/nonpopulation/virginia.html.**

Washington

Non-Population Schedules Year & Type of Schedule	NARA Series, No. of Rolls	FHL Film No.	(O) Location of Originals (See Notes) URL: online database, digital images, or info page.
1860 Industry	A1154, 1 roll	1549530	(O) WA St. Lib. (WA-1)
1870 Industry	A1154, 1 roll	1549532	(O) WA St. Lib. (WA-1)
1880 Manufactures	A1154, 1 roll	1549534	(O) WA St. Lib. (WA-1)
1860 Agriculture	A1154, 1 roll	1549529	(O) WA St. Lib. (WA-1)
1870 Agriculture	A1154, 1 roll	1549531	(O) WA St. Lib. (WA-1)
1880 Agriculture	A1154, 1 roll	1549533	(O) WA St. Lib. (WA-1)
1860 Mortality	A1154, 1 roll	1421001	(O) WA St. Lib. Online: www.ancestry.com/search/collections/usmortality.
1870 Mortality	A1154, 1 roll	1421001	(O) WA St. Lib. Online: www.ancestry.com/search/collections/usmortality.
1880 Mortality	A1154, 1 roll	1421001	(O) WA St. Lib. Online: www.ancestry.com/search/collections/usmortality.
1860 Social Statistics	A1154, 1 roll	--	(O) WA St. Lib. (WA-1)
1870 Social Statistics	A1154, 1 roll	--	(O) WA St. Lib. (WA-1)
1880 Def/Dep/Del Classes	A1154, 1 roll	1549443	(O) WA St. Lib. Online: www.ancestry.com/search/collections/1880uscensusddd.
1935 Business-Advertising	M1797, 1 roll	--	(O) Info: www.archives.gov/research/census/nonpopulation/washington.html.
1935 Business-Banking	M2066, 7 rolls	--	(O) Info: www.archives.gov/research/census/nonpopulation/washington.html.
1935 Business-Misc.Enterprises	M2067, 2 rolls	--	(O) Info: www.archives.gov/research/census/nonpopulation/washington.html.
1935 Business-Trucking	M2068, 2 rolls	--	(O) Info: www.archives.gov/research/census/nonpopulation/washington.html.
1935 Business-Warehousing	M2069, 1 roll	--	(O) Info: www.archives.gov/research/census/nonpopulation/washington.html.
1935 Business-Radio Stations	M2070, 1 roll	--	(O) Info: www.archives.gov/research/census/nonpopulation/washington.html.

Washington Notes:

WA-1. Washington's original Non-Population schedules are located at the Washington State Library, Olympia, WA, see **www.sos.wa.gov/library**. Washington (Territory) is included in ***U.S., Selected Federal Census Non-Population Schedules, 1850-1880*** [Online Database], digitized and indexed at the Ancestry.com website. See **www.ancestry.com/search/collections/nonpopcensus**.

West Virginia

Non-Population Schedules Year & Type of Schedule	NARA Series, No. of Rolls	FHL Film No.	(O) Location of Originals (See Notes) URL: online database, digital images, or info page.
1870 Industry	--	--	(O) WV Arch. & Hist. (WV-1)
1880 Manufactures	--	--	(O) WV Arch. & Hist. (WV-1)
1850 Agriculture	--	--	(O) WV Arch. & Hist. (WV-1)
1860 Agriculture	--	--	(O) WV Arch. & Hist. (WV-1)
1870 Agriculture	--	--	(O) WV Arch. & Hist. (WV-1)
1880 Agriculture	--	--	(O) WV Arch. & Hist. (WV-1)
1850 Mortality	--	944493	(O) WV A&H. Online: www.ancestry.com/search/collections/usmortality.
1860 Mortality	--	944493	(O) WV A&H. Online: www.ancestry.com/search/collections/usmortality.
1870 Mortality	--	944493	(O) WV A&H. Online: www.ancestry.com/search/collections/usmortality.
1880 Mortality	--	944494	(O) WV A&H. Online: www.ancestry.com/search/collections/usmortality.
1880 Def/Dep/Del Classes	--	--	(O) WV Arch. & Hist. (WV-1)
1935 Business-Advertising	M1797, 1 roll	--	(O) Info: www.archives.gov/research/census/nonpopulation/west-virginia.html.
1935 Business-Banking	M2066, 8 rolls	--	(O) Info: www.archives.gov/research/census/nonpopulation/west-virginia.html.
1935 Business-Misc.Enterprises	M2067, 1 roll	--	(O) Info: www.archives.gov/research/census/nonpopulation/west-virginia.html.
1935 Business-Trucking	M2068, 3 rolls	--	(O) Info: www.archives.gov/research/census/nonpopulation/west-virginia.html.
1935 Business-Warehousing	M2069, 1 roll	--	(O) Info: www.archives.gov/research/census/nonpopulation/west-virginia.html.
1935 Business-Radio Stations	M2070, 1 roll	--	(O) Info: www.archives.gov/research/census/nonpopulation/west-virginia.html.

West Virginia Notes:

WV-1. West Virginia's original Non-Population schedules, 1860-1880, are located at the West Virginia Archives & History, Charleston, WV, see **www.wvculture.org/history/archivesindex.aspx**.

Wisconsin

Non-Population Schedules Year & Type of Schedule	NARA Series, No. of Rolls	FHL Film No.	(O) Location of Originals (See Notes) URL: online database, digital images, or info page.
1850 Industry	--	--	(O) WI St. Hist. Soc. (WI-1)
1860 Industry	--	--	(O) WI St. Hist. Soc. (WI-1)
1870 Industry	--	--	(O) WI St. Hist. Soc. (WI-1)
1880 Manufactures	--	--	(O) WI St. Hist. Soc. (WI-1)
1850 Agriculture	--	--	(O) WI St. Hist. Soc (WI-1).
1860 Agriculture	--	--	(O) WI St. Hist. Soc. (WI-1)
1870 Agriculture	--	--	(O) WI St. Hist. Soc. (WI-1)
1880 Agriculture	--	--	(O) WI St. Hist. Soc. (WI-1)
1850 Mortality	--	--	(O) WISHS Online: www.ancestry.com/search/collections/usmortality.
1860 Mortality	--	--	(O) WISHS Online: www.ancestry.com/search/collections/usmortality.
1870 Mortality	--	--	(O) WISHS Online: www.ancestry.com/search/collections/usmortality.
1880 Mortality	--	1032684	(O) WISHS Online: www.ancestry.com/search/collections/usmortality.
1850 Social Statistics	--	--	(O) WI St. Hist. Soc. (WI-1)
1860 Social Statistics	--	--	(O) WI St. Hist. Soc. (WI-1)
1870 Social Statistics	--	--	(O) WI St. Hist. Soc. (WI-1)
1880 Def/Dep/Del Classes	--	--	(O) WI St. Hist. Soc.. (WI-1)

Wisconsin, Cont'd

Non-Population Schedules Year & Type of Schedule	NARA Series, No. of Rolls	FHL Film No.	(O) Location of Originals (See Notes) URL: online database, digital images, or info page.
1935 Business-Advertising	M1797, 1 roll	--	(O) Info: www.archives.gov/research/census/nonpopulation/wisconsin.html.
1935 Business-Banking	M2066, 8 rolls	--	(O) Info: www.archives.gov/research/census/nonpopulation/wisconsin.html.
1935 Business-Misc.Enterprises	M2067, 2 rolls	--	(O) Info: www.archives.gov/research/census/nonpopulation/wisconsin.html.
1935 Business-Trucking	M2068, 5 rolls	--	(O) Info: www.archives.gov/research/census/nonpopulation/wisconsin.html.
1935 Business-Warehousing	M2069, 1 roll	--	(O) Info: www.archives.gov/research/census/nonpopulation/wisconsin.html.
1935 Business-Radio Stations	M2070, 1 roll	--	(O) Info: www.archives.gov/research/census/nonpopulation/wisconsin.html.

Wisconsin Notes:

WV-1. Wisconsin's original Non-Population schedules, 1850-1880, are located at the Wisconsin State Historical Society, Madison, WI, see **www.wisconsinhistory.org**.

Wyoming

Non-Population Schedules Year & Type of Schedule	NARA Series, No. of Rolls	FHL Film No.	(O) Location of Originals (See Notes) URL: online database, digital images, or info page.
1880 Agriculture	M1794, 1 roll	--	(O) Duke Univ. (WY-1)
1935 Business-Advertising	M1797, 1 roll	--	(O) NARA Info: www.archives.gov/research/census/nonpopulation/wyoming.html.
1935 Business-Banking	M2066, 6 rolls	--	(O) NARA Info: www.archives.gov/research/census/nonpopulation/wyoming.html.
1935 Business-Misc.Enterprises	M2067, 1 roll	--	(O) NARA Info: www.archives.gov/research/census/nonpopulation/wyoming.html.
1935 Business-Trucking	M2068, 2 rolls	--	(O) NARA Info: www.archives.gov/research/census/nonpopulation/wyoming.html.
1935 Business-Warehousing	M2069, 1 roll	--	(O) NARA Info: www.archives.gov/research/census/nonpopulation/wyoming.html.
1935 Business-Radio Stations	M2070, 1 roll	--	(O) NARA Info: www.archives.gov/research/census/nonpopulation/wyoming.html.

Wyoming Notes:

WY-1. Wyoming's original Non-Population schedule for the 1880 Agriculture is located at Rubenstein Library-Library Service Center, Manuscripts, Duke University, Durham, NC. Search for "non-population" at the search dialog box, see **https://library.duke.edu**.

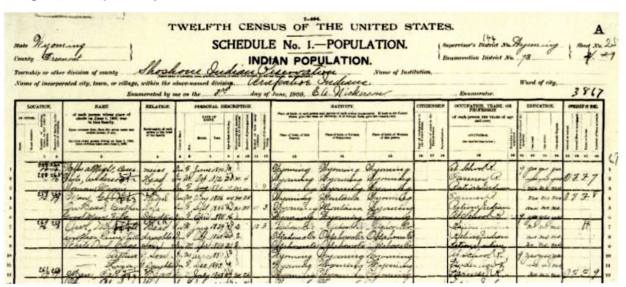

Wyoming is a fitting example to use for the *Indian Population* Schedules. In 1900, all Indians were enumerated separately from whites, generally by their tribal affiliations. This page is from the enumeration of the Indian Population of the Shoshone Indian Reservation, specifically, the Arapahoe Indians living on that reservation. The Indian Population was separated from the regular population schedules because, per the 1787 Constitution of the U.S., Indians were not part of the count for apportionment (until 1924 when the Supreme Court declared U.S. Citizenship for all American Indians).

Section 4 – Census Samples & Worksheets

Contents

Population Schedules:
- 1790 Federal Census 148
- 1800 Federal Census 150
- 1810 Federal Census 152
- 1820 Federal Census 154
- 1830 Federal Census 156
- 1840 Federal Census 158
- 1850 Federal Census 160
- 1860 Federal Census 162
- 1870 Federal Census 164
- 1880 Federal Census 166
- 1880 Short Form 168
- 1885 State Census – 5 States 170
- 1890 Short Form 172
- 1890 Union Veterans Schedule 174
- 1900 Federal Census 176
- 1910 Federal Census 178
- 1920 Federal Census 180
- 1930 Federal Census 182
- 1940 Federal Census 184
- 1950 Federal Census 186

Industry/Manufactures Schedules:
- 1820 Manufactures 188
- 1850 Products of Industry 190
- 1860 Products of Industry 192
- 1870 Products of Industry 194
- 1880 Manufactures-General 196
- 1880 Manufactures-Boots, Shoes (Sample) 198
- 1880 Manufactures-Flour Mills & Grist Mills (Sample) 199
- 1880 Manufactures-Lumber Yards & Saw Mills (Sample) 200
- 1880 Manufactures-Agricultural Implements (Sample) 201
- 1885 Manufactures-General 202

Agriculture Schedules:
- 1850 Agriculture, p. 1 (Sample) 204
- 1850 Agriculture, p. 2 (Sample) 205
- 1860 Agriculture, p. 1 (Sample) 206
- 1860 Agriculture, p. 2 (Sample) 207
- 1870 Agriculture, p. 1 (Sample) 208
- 1870 Agriculture-p. 2 (Sample) 209
- 1880 Agriculture (Sample) 210
- 1885 Agriculture (Sample) 211

Mortality Schedules:
- 1850 Mortality Schedule 212
- 1860 Mortality Schedule 214
- 1870 Mortality Schedule 216
- 1880 Mortality Schedule 218
- 1885 Mortality Schedule 220

Slave Schedules:
- 1850 Slave Schedule 222
- 1860 Slave Schedule 224

Social Statistics Schedules:
- 1850, 1860, 1870 Social Statistics (Sample) 226
- **Defective/Dependent/Delinquent Classes**
- 1880 Insane Inhabitants & Idiots (Sample) 227
- 1880 Deaf-Mutes & Blind Inhabitants (Sample) 228
- 1880 Homeless Children & Prisoners (Sample) 229
- 1880 Pauper & Indigent Inhabitants (Sample) 230

Soundex Extraction Forms:
- 1880 Soundex 232
- 1900 Soundex 234
- 1910 Soundex/Miracode 236
- 1920 Soundex 238
- 1930 Soundex 240

Census Comparison Sheets:
- 1790-1840 Census Worksheet 242
- Census Comparison Sheet 244

1790 Census Pages, prepared for Nash County, North Carolina. There were no pre-printed forms, so the Asst. Marshal prepared the format for the name lists by hand. Note that the last column was the "Amount" (total number of persons in a household), a column added by the Asst. Marshal on his own. Also, note that this Nash Co NC Asst. Marshal arranged his names by the first letter of their surnames – evidence that these pages were copied from his original door-to-door name lists.

1790 Federal Census

Researcher: Date:

Heads of household extracted from the original text of the 1790 Population Schedules

NARA Microfilm Series M637 Roll no. Page no. STATE & COUNTY	Name of HEAD OF HOUSEHOLD	FREE WHITES			Slaves	Other free persons
		Males 16 & over	Males 0-15	Females		

Names of Heads of Families	Free white males					Free white females					All other free persons except Indians not taxed
	Under 10	10 and under 16	16 and under 26 including heads of families	26 and under 45 including heads of families	45 and upward including heads of families	Under 10	10 and under 16	16 and under 26 including heads of families	26 and under 45 including heads of families	45 and upward including heads of families	
Abner Danforth	3	2	..	1	..	1	..	..	1	..	..
Gershom House	..	1	2	..	1	3	1	..	1	..	..
Isaac Clough	1	..	..	1	..	1	..	1	..	..	..
David Given	1	1	2	1	..	1	..	1	..	..	2
John Pease	..	..	..	..	..	..	..	..	..	..	..
John Mattes	1	..	..	1	..	..	..	..	1	1	..
Joseph House	1	..	..	1	..	..	..	..	1	..	..
Jacob Hacker	1	1	..	1	..	1	..	..	1	..	..
Caleb Jones	2	2	1	..	..	2	..	..	1	..	..
Lemuel Jones	2	..	..	1	..	1	..	2	1	..	..
Stephen Jones	2	..	..	1	..	4	2	..	1	..	..
Carr Verney	1	..	..	1	..	1	..	..	1	..	..
George Philbrook	2	2	..	..	1	1	2	2	..	..	..
Noel Goddard	1	..	..	1	..	1	..	..	1	..	..
Walter Davis	2	..	..	..	2	..	..	1	1	..	..
Hannah Rogers	2	..	..	..	..	..	..	..	1	..	..
David Getchell	..	..	..	1	..	..	1	..	..	..	..
Edward Jones	2	4	..	1	..	..	..	4	1	..	..
Jeremiah Hacker	..	..	..	..	1	..	..	..	1	..	..
Jeremiah Hacker, Jr	2	1	..	1	..	2	3	..	1	..	..
David Pierce	..	..	2	..	1	..	1	..	1	..	..
Joshua Gardiner	1	..	..	2	1	..	..	..	1	1	..
Robert Goddard	3	..	2	..	1	2	..	1	1	..	..
Silas Goddard	1	1	1	1	..	1	..	..	1	..	..
	16	15	10	17	10	22	12	10	15	10	2

Whole number in the town of Brunswick is 1842

1800 Census Pages, prepared for Brunswick, Cumberland County, Massachusetts (part of the **Maine** Federal District Court area). Note there are only 12 columns, as a column indicating the number of slaves was not needed. (Slavery was abolished in Massachusetts in 1789).

1800 Federal Census

Researcher: _____ Date: _____

Heads of households extracted from the original text of the 1800 Population Schedules

NARA Microfilm Series M32 Roll no.: State: County: Township:

Page	Name of HEAD OF HOUSEHOLD	FREE WHITE MALES					FREE WHITE FEMALES					Other free person	Slaves
		0 thru 9	10 thru 15	16 thru 25	26 thru 44	45 and over	0 thru 9	10 thru 15	16 thru 25	26 thru 44	45 and over		

1810 Census Page, prepared for Smyrna, Duck Creek Hundred, Kent County, Delaware.

1810 Federal Census

Researcher: Date:

Heads of households extracted from the original text of the 1810 Population Schedules

NARA Microfilm Series M252 Roll no.: State: County: Township:

Page	Name of HEAD OF HOUSEHOLD	FREE WHITE MALES					FREE WHITE FEMALES					Other free person	Slaves
		0 thru 9	10 thru 15	16 thru 25	26 thru 44	45 and over	0 thru 9	10 thru 15	16 thru 25	26 thru 44	45 and over		

154 • 1820 Federal Census

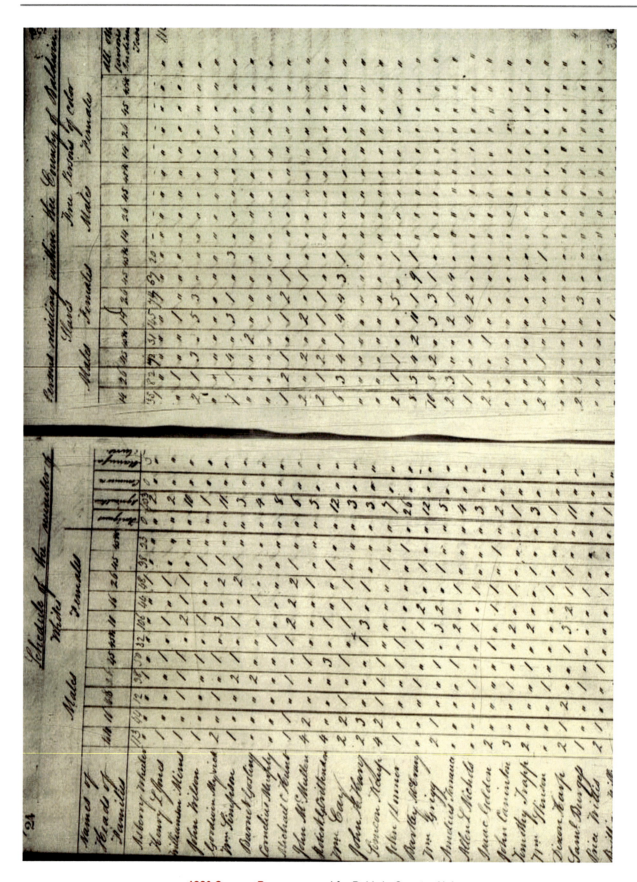

1820 Census Page, prepared for Baldwin County, Alabama.

1820 Federal Census

Heads of households extracted from the original text of the 1820 Population Schedules

NARA Microfilm Series M33   Roll no.:   State: County: Township: Researcher: Date:

Page	Name of HEAD OF HOUSEHOLD	FREE WHITES											No. of persons engaged in:			SLAVES								FREE COLORED						
		Males					Females					Foreigners not naturalized	Agriculture	Commerce	Manufacture	Males				Females				Males				Females				All other persons
		0 thru 9 years	10 thru 15 years	16 thru 18 years	16 thru 25 years	26 thru 44 years	45 years and over	0 thru 9 years	10 thru 15 years	16 thru 25 years	26 thru 44 years	45 years and over					0 thru 13 years	14 thru 25 years	26 thru 44 years	45 years and over	0 thru 13 years	14 thru 25 years	26 thru 44 years	45 years and over	0 thru 13 years	14 thru 25 years	26 thru 44 years	45 years and over	0 thru 13 years	14 thru 25 years	26 thru 44 years	45 years and over	

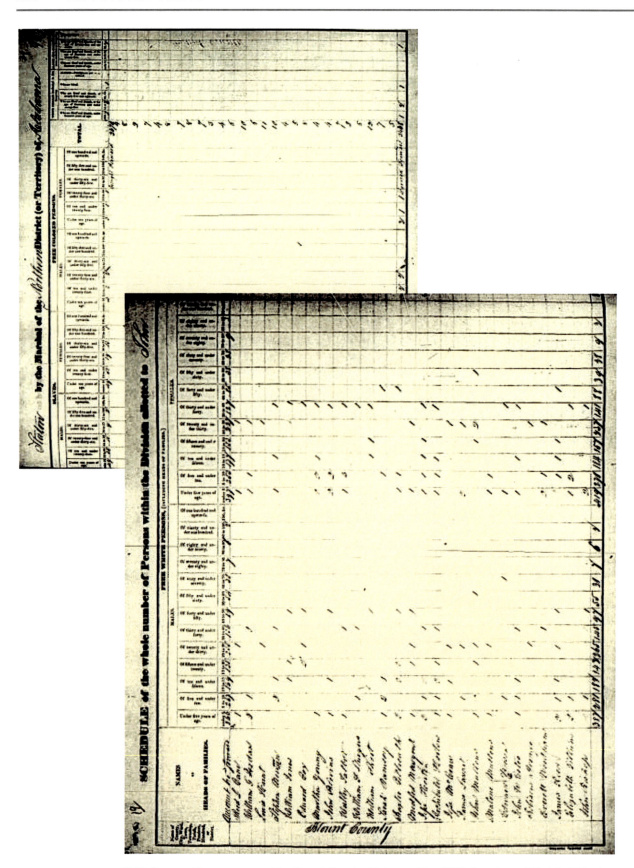

1830 Census Pages, prepared for Blount County, Alabama. The 1830 Secretary of State's Office in Washington, DC, provided printed forms to the Assistant Marshals for the first time.

1830 Federal Census

Extracted from the original text of the 1830 Census Schedules

NARA Microfilm Series M19 Roll no.:

Page: State: County: Township:

Researcher: Date:

Name of HEAD OF HOUSEHOLD	FREE WHITE PERSONS - including heads of families																							FREE COLORED													White persons who are:				SLAVES				Other information
	Males											Females											Males						Females						TOTAL PERSONS	Deaf & dumb			Blind	Aliens	Males		Females		
	0 thru 4 years	5 thru 9 years	10 thru 14 years	15 thru 19 years	20 thru 29 years	30 thru 39 years	40 thru 49 years	50 thru 59 years	60 thru 69 years	70 thru 79 years	80 thru 89 years	90 thru 99 years	100 years and over	0 thru 4 years	5 thru 9 years	10 thru 14 years	15 thru 19 years	20 thru 29 years	30 thru 39 years	40 thru 49 years	50 thru 59 years	60 thru 69 years	70 thru 79 years	80 thru 89 years	90 thru 99 years	100 years and over	0 thru 9 years	10 thru 23 years	24 thru 35 years	36 thru 54 years	55 thru 99 years	100 years and over	0 thru 9 years	10 thru 23 years	24 thru 35 years	36 thru 54 years	55 thru 99 years	100 years and over		0 - 13	14 - 24	23 & over							
1																																														
2																																														
3																																														
4																																														
5																																														
6																																														
7																																														
8																																														
9																																														

NOTES

1
2
3
4
5
6
7
8
9

158 • 1840 Federal Census

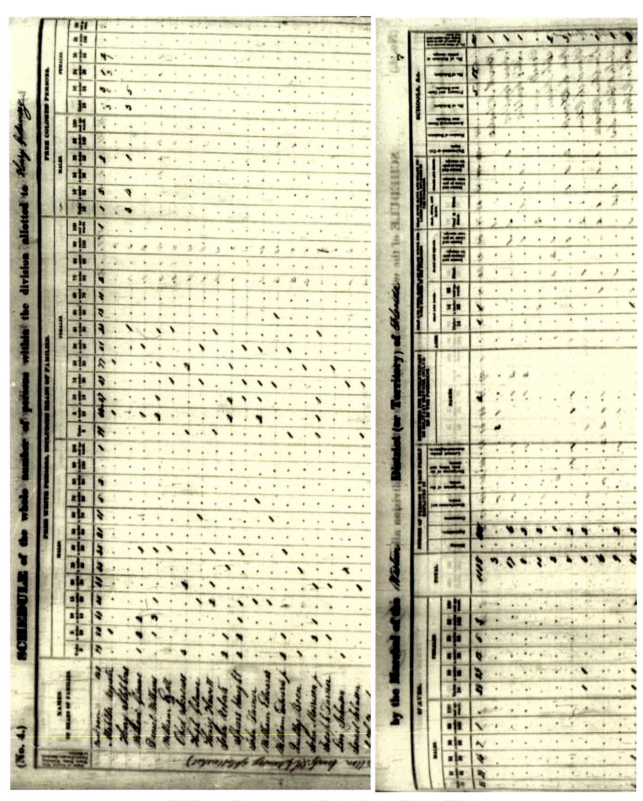

1840 Census Pages, prepared for the Western District of Florida.

1840 Federal Census

Extracted from the original text of the 1840 Census Schedules

NARA Microfilm Series M704 Roll no.: State: County: Township:

Page: Researcher: Date:

Name of HEAD OF HOUSEHOLD	FREE WHITE PERSONS - including heads of families																						FREE COLORED														TOTAL PERSONS	White persons who are:		
	Males												Females												Males						Females							Deaf & dumb	Blind	Aliens
	0 thru 4 years	5 thru 9 years	10 thru 14 years	15 thru 19 years	20 thru 29 years	30 thru 39 years	40 thru 49 years	50 thru 59 years	60 thru 69 years	70 thru 79 years	80 thru 89 years	90 thru 99 years	100 years and over	0 thru 4 years	5 thru 9 years	10 thru 14 years	15 thru 19 years	20 thru 29 years	30 thru 39 years	40 thru 49 years	50 thru 59 years	60 thru 69 years	70 thru 79 years	80 thru 89 years	90 thru 99 years	100 years and over	0 thru 9 years	10 thru 23 years	24 thru 35 years	36 thru 54 years	55 thru 99 years	100 years and over	0 thru 9 years	10 thru 23 years	24 thru 35 years	36 thru 54 years	55 thru 99 years	100 years and over		0 - 13	14 - 24	23 & over			
1																																													1
2																																													2
3																																													3
4																																													4
5																																													5
6																																													6
7																																													7
8																																													8
9																																													9

	No. of Persons in Each Family Employed in:						SLAVES				Schools Etc.
	Mining	Agriculture	Commerce	Manufactures and trades.	Navigation of the ocean	Navigation of canals, lakes, and rivers	Learned professions and engineers	Males		Females		
1												1
2												2
3												3
4												4
5												5
6												6
7												7
8												8
9												9

Revolutionary War / Military Pensioners

	Name	Age
1		
2		
3		
4		
5		
6		
7		
8		
9		

1850 Census Page, prepared for "Auburn & Vicinity," Sutter County, California.

1850 Federal Census

NARA Microfilm Series M432 Roll no.: Researcher: Date:

Page State: County: Township:

Extracted from the original text of the 1850 Census Schedules

1	2	3	4	5	6	7	8	9	10	11	12	13
Dwelling-house no.	Family no.	Name of Person	Age	Sex	Color	Occupation	Value of real estate owned	Birthplace	Married within year	Attended school	Cannot read or write	Whether deaf and dumb, blind, insane, idiotic, pauper, or convict

Description: Age | Sex | Color

1860 Census Page, prepared for the 1st Ward, Buffalo City, Erie County, New York.

1860 Federal Census

Researcher: Date:

Extracted from the original text of the 1860 Census Schedules

NARA Microfilm Series M653   Roll no.:   State: County: Township:

Page	Dwelling-house no.	Family no.	Name of Person	Age	Sex	Color	Occupation	Real estate	Personal estate	Birthplace	Married within year	Attended school	Cannot read or write	Whether deaf and dumb, blind, insane, idiotic, pauper, or convict
1	2		3	4	5	6	7	8	9	10	11	12	13	14

1870 Census Page, prepared for the town of Carlin, Elko County, Nevada.

1870 Federal Census

NARA Microfilm Series M593   Roll no.:   State: County: Township: Date:

Researcher:

Extracted from the original text of the 1870 Census Schedules

1	2	3	4	5	6	7	8	9	10	11	12	13	14	15	16	17	18	19	20
Dwelling-house no.	Family no.	Name of Person	Age	Sex	Color	Occupation	Value of real estate	Value of personal estate	Birthplace	Father of foreign birth	Mother of foreign birth	If born within year	If married within year	Attended school	Cannot read	Cannot write	Whether deaf and dumb, blind, insane, or idiots	Male over 21	Denied vote

Page

1880 Census Page, prepared for the Town of Allegany, Cattaraugus County, New York.

1880 Federal Census

Researcher: Date:

Extracted from the original text of the 1880 Census Schedules

NARA Microfilm Series T9 Roll no.: State: County: Township:

E.D.
Page

House no.	Dwelling no.	Family no.	Name of Person	Color	Sex	Age	If born within year	Relationship to Head	Single	Married	Widowed / Div.	If married within year	Profession or Trade	Months Unemployed	Sickness / disability	Blind	Deaf or dumb	Idiotic	Insane	Crippled, etc.	Attended school	Cannot read	Cannot write	Person	Father	Mother	City / Town
1	2		3	4	5	6	7	8	9	10	11	12	13	14	15	16	17	18	19	20	21	22	23	24	25	26	

Street: _____

Column groups: **In cities** (House no., Dwelling no., Family no.); **Personal** (Color, Sex, Age, If born within year, Relationship to Head); **Civil Condition** (Single, Married, Widowed/Div., If married within year); **Occupation** (Profession or Trade, Months Unemployed); **Health** (Sickness/disability, Blind, Deaf or dumb, Idiotic, Insane, Crippled etc.); **Education** (Attended school, Cannot read, Cannot write); **Birthplace of** (Person, Father, Mother); City / Town

168 • 1880 Federal Census (Short Form)

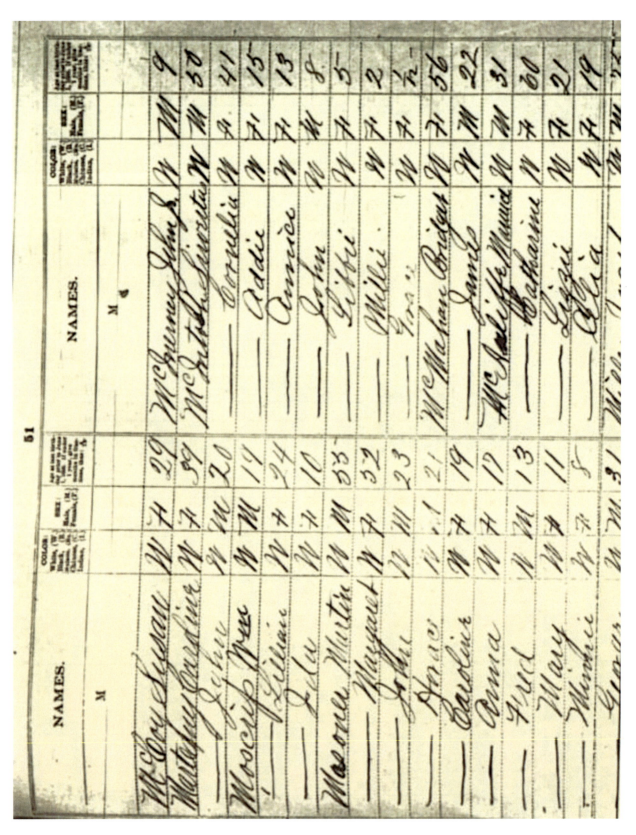

1880 Federal Census (Short Form), Town of Allegany, Cattaraugus Co NY. The Short Form was an index to the names from the full 1880 schedules. Note the family of Martin Masoner and wife Margaret. Compare the names here with the names on the full schedules. (page 166, lines 16-24).

1880 Federal Census (Short Form)

Location: _____ FHL Film No. _____ Name of Researcher: _____ Date extracted: _____

County: _____ State: _____

Page No on Original (if applicable): _____ Microfilm frame number (from beginning of E.D.): _____

NAMES First letter of surname, this page ____	COLOR White ..... (W) Black ..... (B) Mulatto ..... (M) Chinese ..... (C) Indian ..... (I)	SEX Male (M) Female (F)	AGE at last birthday if prior to June 1, 1880. If under 1 year, give number in fractions, thus: 3/12

NAMES First letter of surname, this page ____	COLOR White ..... (W) Black ..... (B) Mulatto ..... (M) Chinese ..... (C) Indian ..... (I)	SEX Male (M) Female (F)	AGE at last birthday if prior to June 1, 1880. If under 1 year, give number in fractions, thus: 3/12

1885 Colorado State Census (taken with Federal Assistance). Same form used for Colorado, Dakota Territory, Florida, Nebraska, and New Mexico Territory.

1885 Census (taken with federal assistance)
Colorado, Dakota Territory, Florida, Nebraska, or New Mexico Territory

NARA Microfilm Series: _____ Roll no.: _____ State: _____ County: _____ Township: _____ Date: _____

E.D.: _____ Researcher: _____

Page: _____

Extracted from the original text of the 1885 Census Schedules

Street	House no. (1)	In cities: Dwelling no. / Family no. (2)	Name of Person (3)	Color (4)	Sex (5)	Age (6)	Personal: If born within year (7)	Relationship to Head (8)	Single (9)	Married (10)	Civil Condition: Widowed/Div. (11)	If married within year (12)	Occupation: Profession or Trade (13)	Months Unemployed (14)	Sickness/disability (15)	Blind (16)	Deaf or dumb (17)	Idiotic (18)	Health: Insane (19)	Crippled, etc. (20)	Attended school (21)	Cannot read (22)	Education: Cannot write (23)	Birthplace of Person (24)	Father (25)	City/Town Mother (26)

172 • 1890 Federal Census (Short Form)

	NAME	COLOR	SEX	AGE	BIRTHPLACE
Davisboro					
GM 4th Dis. Li	Caroline E. Kendall	W	F	64	Ga
	Cora Kendall	W	F	31	Ga
	Leo J. Kendall	W	F	27	Ga
	Frank Kendall	W	Sn	21	Ga
	Jennie J. Johnson	W	Sn	8	Ga
	Seth S. Hodges	W	Sn	40	Ga
	Milan Hodges	W	F	35	Ga
	Bessie R. Hodges	W	F	12	Ga
	Maud Hodges	W	F	3	Ga
	Otis Hodges	W	Sn	6	Ga
	Sarah Hodges	W	F	70	Ga
	Willie Hodges	W	Sn	25	Ga
Davisboro	Thomas J. Orr	W	Sn	38	Ga
	Susie H. Orr	W	F	32	Ga
	Lillian Orr	W	F	7	Ga
	Thomas Orr	W	Sn	5	Ga
	Bessie E. Orr	W	F	8	Ga
	Nancy M. Orr	W	F	67	Ga
	Nathan A. Chance	W	Sn	38	Ga
	Laurah L. Chance	W	F	22	Ga
	Hannah P. Chance	W	F	8	Ga
	Claude Chance	W	F	9 mo.	Ga
	William E. Grubbs	W	Sn	25	Ga
	Vattie F. Grubbs	W	F	25	Ga
	James H. Grubbs	W	Sn	1	Ga

1890 Short Form. The page above is an index to the residents of Davisboro, Washington County, Georgia. Unlike the 1880 Short Form, the 1890 form listed the names of persons in the same order they appeared on the full schedules. (The full schedules were lost in a fire in 1921 that took place in the Census Bureau's basement storage area of the Commerce Building, Washington, DC).

1890 Federal Census (Short Form)

Eleventh Census of the United States

RESIDENCE.	NAME.	COLOR.	SEX.	AGE.	BIRTHPLACE.

1890 Special Schedule – Surviving Soldiers, Sailors, Marines, and Widows. The sample page above was prepared for Seattle, King County, Washington.

1890 Veterans Schedule

Extracted from the original text of the 1890 special schedules for surviving soldiers, sailors, marines, and widows

NARA Microfilm Series M123   Roll no.:   State: County: Subdistrict: Researcher: Date:

House no. 1	Family no. 2	Name of surviving soldiers, sailors, marines, or widows 3	Rank 4	Company 5	Name of Regiment or Vessel 6	Date of enlistment			Date of discharge			Length of service		
						day	month 7	year	day	month 8	year	yrs	mos 9	days
1														
2														
3														
4														
5														
6														
7														
8														
9														
10														

	Post Office address 10	Disability incurred 11	Remarks 12
1			
2			
3			
4			
5			
6			
7			
8			
9			
10			

1900 Census page, prepared for the city of Aurora, Kane County, Illinois.

1900 Federal Census

Extracted from the original text of the 1900 Census Schedules

NARA Microfilm Series T623 Roll no.: State: County: Subdistrict: Researcher: Date:

City / Town: Ward:

Page E.D.

1	2	3	4	5	6	7	8	9	10	11	12	13	14	15	16	17	18	19	20	21	22	23	24	25	26	27	28
Street	House no. / Family no.	Name of Person	Relationship to Head	Color or Race	Sex	Month (Date of Birth)	Year (Date of Birth)	Age, last birthday	Marital status	Years married	Children born	Children living / Person	Father (Birthplace of)	Mother (Birthplace of)	Year of immigration	Number years in U.S.	Naturalization	Occupation	Months not employed		Months at school	Can read	Can write	Can speak English	Own / Rent	Free / Mortgaged	Farm / House No.

Personal Description: columns 5–13
Birthplace of: columns 14–15
Citizenship: columns 16–18
Education: columns 23–25

1910 Census Page, prepared for the city of Roseburg, Douglas County, Oregon.

1910 Federal Census

Researcher: Date:

Extracted from the original text of the 1910 Census Schedules

NARA Microfilm Series T624   Roll no.:   State: County: Subdistrict:

City / Town: Ward:

Page   E.D.

Street	House no.	Family no.	Name of Person	Relationship to Head	Sex	Color or Race	Age, last birthday	Marital status	Years married	Children born	Children living	Birthplace of: Person	Birthplace of: Father	Birthplace of: Mother	Year of Immigration	Naturalization	Language spoken	Trade of profession	Type of business	Employer, employee, or works on own account	Out of work?	Weeks out	Can read	Can write	Attended school	Owned / Rented	Free / Mortgaged	Farm / House	Farm schedule no.	Veteran	Blind	Deaf
1	2		3	4	5	6	7	8	9	10	11	12	13	14	15	16	17	18	19	20	21	22	23	24	25	26	27	28	29	30	31	32

Personal Description: columns 5–12
Birthplace of: columns 13–15
Occupation: columns 18–23
Education: columns 24–26
Home Ownership: columns 27–30

1920 Census Page, prepared for the city of Roseburg, Douglas County, Oregon.

1920 Federal Census

Researcher: Date:

Extracted from the original text of the 1920 Census Schedules

NARA Microfilm Series T625   Roll no.:   State: County: Subdistrict:

City / Town: Ward:

Page   E.D.

1	2	3	4	5	6	7	8	9	10	11	12	13	14	15	16	17	18	19	20	21	22	23	24	25	26	27	28	29
Street address	House no.	Dwelling no.	Family no.	Name of Person	Relationship to Head	Home owned or rented	Free / Mortgaged	Sex	Color or race	Age, last birthday	Marital status	Year of immigration	Naturalization	Year naturalized	Attended school	Can read	Can write	Place of birth	Mother tongue	Place of birth	Mother tongue	Place of birth	Mother tongue	Speaks English?	Trade of profession	Type of business	Employer, employee, or works on own account	farm

Columns 7–8: Home owned or rented / Free / Mortgaged
Columns 9–13: Personal
Columns 14–15: Citizenship
Columns 16–18: Education
Columns 19–25: Nativity and mother tongue (Person / Father / Mother)
Columns 26–29: Occupation

1930 Census Page, prepared for Catlow Election District, Harney County, Oregon.

1930 Federal Census

Extracted from the original text of the 1930 Census Schedules

Researcher: Date:

State:	Incorporated place:	Enumeration district no.:	NARA Microfilm Series:	Roll no.:
County:	Ward of city:	Supervisor's district no.:		Sheet no.:
Township, Town, Precinct, etc.:	Unincorporated place:	Institution:	Enumeration date:	

Place of Abode			Name	Relationship to head of house	Home data				Personal description				Education		Place of birth of each person enumerated and of his or her parents.		Language spoken in home before coming to the U.S.	Year of immigration to the U.S.	Naturalization	Speaks English?	Occupation and Industry				At work yesterday?	Unemploymt Sched no.	Veteran?	Farm
Street, ave., road, etc.	House no. (in cities)	No. of dwelling house in order of enumeration	Family no.	Name of Person — Each person whose place of abode on April 1, 1930, was in this family.		Home owned or rented	Value of home or monthly payment	Radio set	Live on farm?	Sex	Color or race	Age, last birthday	Marital condition	Age, 1st marriage	Attended school?	Can read & write?	Person	Father	Mother					Trade or profession or kind of work	Industry or business	Census office code	Class of work			What war?	
1	2	3	4	5	6	7	8	9	10	11	12	13	14	15	16	17	18	19	20	21 ABC	22	23	24	25	26	D 27	28	29	30	31	32

1940 Census Page, prepared for Edgewood Precinct (near Port Angeles), Clallam County, Washington.

1940 Federal Census

1940 Census Form, Courtesy of the National Archives. The online PDF version was designed to print on 2 pages, legal size paper (8-1/2x14"). see www.archives.gov/files/research/census/1940/1940.pdf.

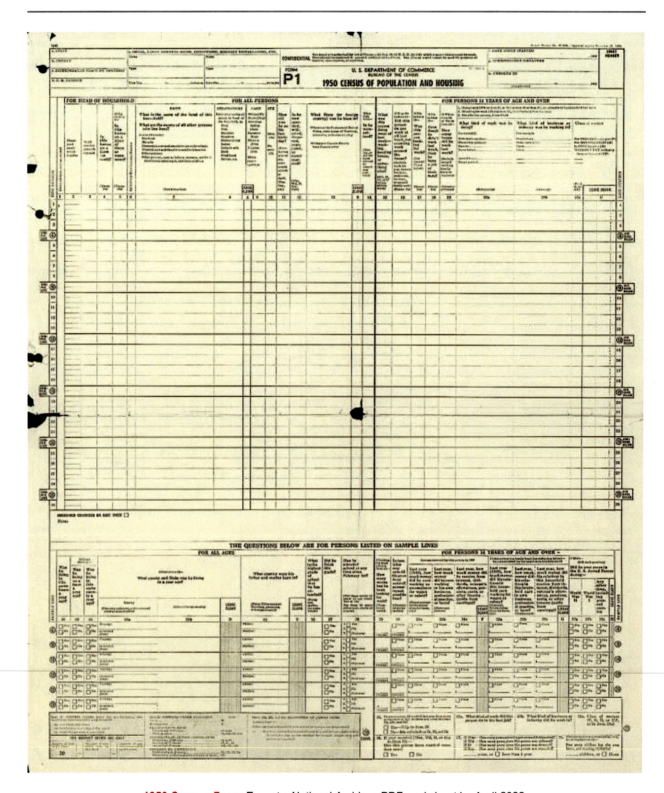

1950 Census Form. Expect a National Archives PDF worksheet by April 2022.

Content of the 1950 Population Schedules

The 1950 census questionnaire had 20 numbered columns, labeled as follows:

For Head of Household: Column 1) Name of street, avenue, or road. 2) House (and apartment) number. 3) Serial number of dwelling unit. 4) Is this house on a farm (or ranch)? (Yes or No). 5) If No in item 4 – Is this house on a place of three or more acres? (Yes or No). 6) Agriculture Questionnaire Number.

For All Persons: 7) Name: What is the name of the head of this household? What are the names of all other persons who live here? List in this order: The Head, His wife, Unmarried sons and daughters (in order of age), Married sons and daughters and their families, Other relatives, Other persons, such as lodgers, roomers, maids or hired hands who live in, and their relatives. 8) **Relationship** of person to head of household, as Head, Wife, Daughter, Grandson, Mother-in-law, Lodger, Lodger's wife, Maid, Hired Hand, Patient, etc. 9) **Race:** White (W), Negro (Neg), American Indian (Ind), Japanese (Jap), Chinese (Chi), Filipino (Fil), Other race-spell out. 10) **Sex:** Male (M), Female (F), 11) How old was he on his last birthday? (If under one year of age, enter month of birth as April, May, Dec., etc.). 12) **Marital Status:** Is he now married, widowed, divorced, separated, or never married (Mar, Wd, D, Sep, Nev). 13) **Place of Birth:** What State (or foreign country) was he born in? If born outside Continental United States, enter name of Territory, possession, or foreign country. Distinguish Canada-French from Canada-other. 14) If foreign born – Is he naturalized? (Yes, No, or AP for born abroad of American Parents).

For Persons 14 years of Age and Over: 15) What was this person doing most of last week – working, keeping house, or something else? (Wk, H, Ot, or U for unable to work). 16) If H or Ot in Item 15 – Did this person do any work at all last week, not counting work around the house? (Include work for pay, in own business, profession, or farm, or un-paid family work (Yes or No). 17) If No in Item 16 – Was this person looking for work? (Yes or No). 18) If No in Item 17 – does he have a job or business? (Yes or No).
19) If Wk in Item 15 or Yes in item 16 – How many hours did he work last week? (Number of hours).
20a (Occupation): What kind of work was he doing? 20b (Industry): What kind of business or industry was he working in? 20c) Class of Worker: Private (P), Government (G), Own business (O), Without pay (family or farm business) (NP).

Questions For Persons Listed on Sample Lines 4, 9, 14, 19, 24, and 29.

For All Ages: Columns 21-24) Residence & Housing questions. 25) Place of birth of parents. 26-28) Education questions.

For Persons 14 years of Age and Over: Columns 29-32) Employment & Wages questions. 33-35) Military Service questions.

1950 Census Publications

Digital Capture: Prior to the April 2022 opening date of the 1950 population schedules, approximately 5,000 rolls of microfilm will be digitized for the National Archives. The 1940 census was digitized for the National Archives by FamilySearch International. The images were made available to several interested websites for shared indexing. Soon after the April 2022 opening, expect the digitized images of the 1950 census to be made accessible online. It is likely one can find the images by starting with a FamilySearch.org catalog search, see **www.familysearch.org/search/catalog/search.** For the "Place" use "United States," then click on Search. At the list of categories, look for "United States – Census – 1950."

1820 Manufactures: Example of a schedule prepared by hand, following the numbered questions shown on the example on the right.

1820 Manufactures: Examples of pre-printed forms given to the enumerators. Some Ass't Marshals chose to answer the questions on the printed questionnaire, others chose to write out the answers at the space provided at the end of the form. Both examples are from Boston, Suffolk County, Massachusetts.

1820 Manufactures

Name of Corporation, Company, or individual:

Name of the County, Parish, Township, Town, or City where the Manufacture exists.		
RAW MATERIALS EMPLOYED	1. The kind?	
	2. The quantity annually consumed?	
	3. The cost of the annual consumption?	
NUMBER OF PERSONS EMPLOYED	4. Men?	
	5. Women?	
	6. Boys and Girls?	
MACHINERY	7. Whole quantity and kind of Machinery?	
	8. Quantity of Machinery in operation?	
EXPENDITURES	9. Amount of Capital invested?	
	10. Amount paid annually for wages?	
	11. Amount of Contingent Expenses?	
PRODUCTION	12. The nature and names of Articles Manufactured?	
	13. Market Value of the Articles which are annually Manufactured?	
	14. General Remarks concerning the Establishment, as to its actual and past condition, the demand for, and sale of, its Manufactures?	

Answers to the above Questions –
   No. 1.

SCHEDULE 5.—Products of Industry in the Township of Comstock in the County of Kalamazoo State of Michigan during the Year ending June 1, 1850, as enumerated by me, N. Fitts Ass't Marshal

Name of Corporation, Company, or Individual, producing Articles to the Annual Value of $500	Name of Business, Manufacture, or Product	Capital invested in Real and Personal Estate in the Business	Raw Material used, including Fuel			Kind of motive power, machinery, structure, or resource	Average number of hands employed		Wages	Annual Product		
			Quantities	Kinds	Values		Male	Female		Quantities	Kinds	Value
1	2	3	4	5	6	7	8	9	10-11	12	13	14
David Ford	Flouring Mill	11000	2000	Bushels	12500	Water	3		45	4000	Bbl Flour	13000
"	Saw Mill	300	500	Logs	845	Water	1		26	200000 ft	Lumber	1400
Enos S Kellogg	Flouring Mill	11500	2000		12500	Water	3		45	4000	Bbl Flour	16000
A. M. Burlingham	Saw Mill	800	1500	Logs	2250	Water	2		52	600000 ft	Lumber	4200
Sheldon Mather	Saw Mill	800	1000	Logs	1500	Water	2		52	100000		2000
Pascual Short	Flour Mill	4000	3000	Wheat	1000			1	30	Custom Work		1000
Jesse Earl	Saw Mill	300	500	Logs	500			1	26	150,000 ft	Lumber	1100
		20,500			31,125		13		336			42450

1850 Products of Industry

SCHEDULE 5. – Products of Industry in _____ in the County of _____ State of _____ during the year ending June 1, 1850, as enumerated by me _____ Ass't Marshal.

Name of Corporation, Company, or individual, Producing Articles to the Annual Value of $500.	Name of Business, Manufacture, or Product	Capital Invested in Real and Personal Estate in the Business	Raw Material used, including Fuel.			Kind of motive power, machinery, structure, or Resource	Average No. of Hands		Wages		Annual Product.		
			Quantities.	Kinds.	Values.		Males.	Females.	Average mo. cost of male labor	Average mo. cost of female labor	Quantities.	Kinds.	Values.
1	2	3	4	5	6	7	8	9	10	11	12	13	14

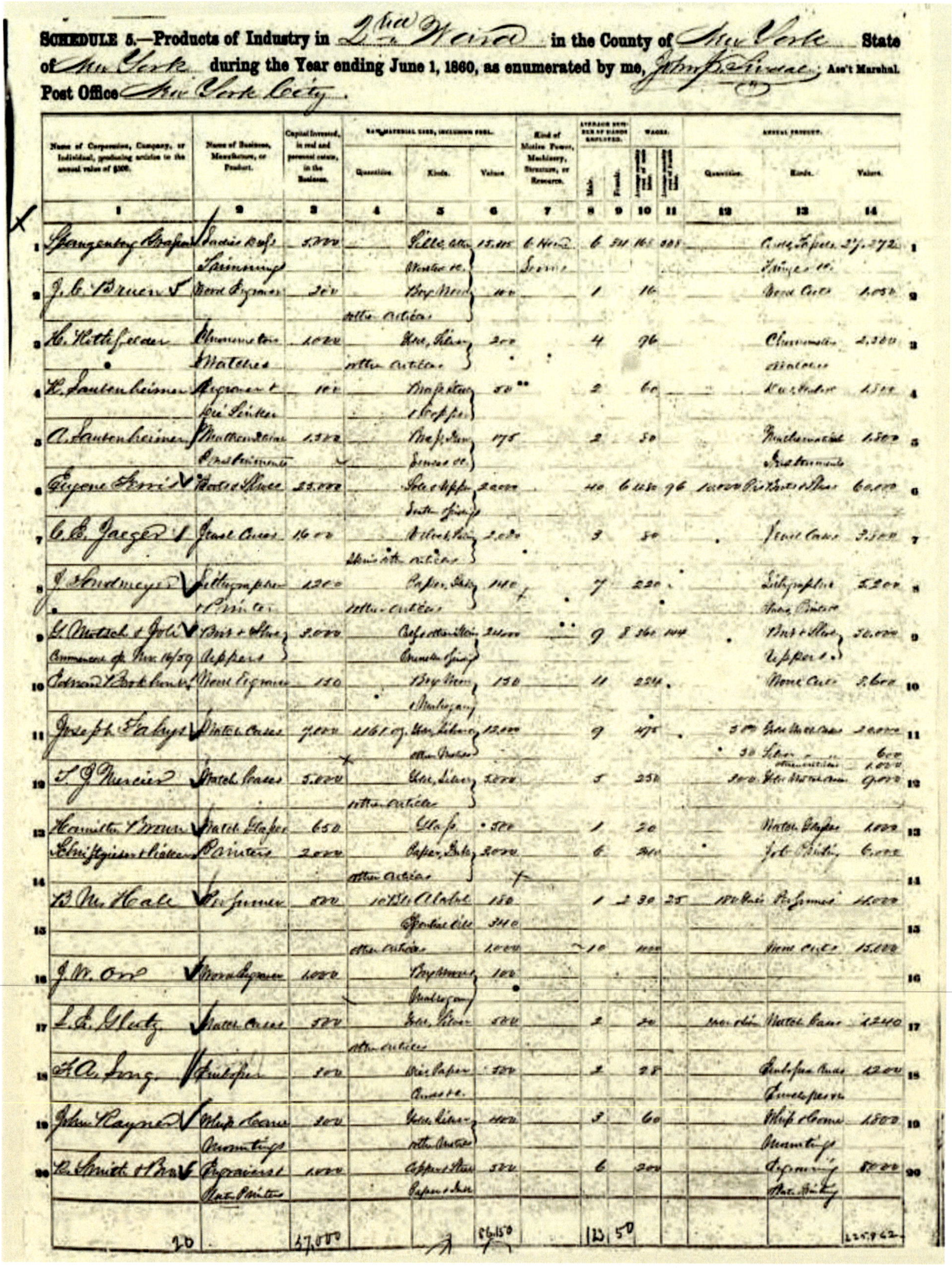

SCHEDULE 5.—Products of Industry in 2nd Ward in the County of New York State of New York during the Year ending June 1, 1860, as enumerated by me, John P. [illegible] Ass't Marshal.
Post Office New York City.

Name of Corporation, Company, or Individual, producing articles to the annual value of $500.	Name of Business, Manufacture, or Product.	Capital invested, in real and personal estate, in the Business.	Raw material used, including fuel: Quantities.	Kinds.	Values.	Kind of Motive Power, Machinery, Structure, or Resource.	Average number of hands employed: Male.	Female.	Wages: Average monthly cost of male labor.	Average monthly cost of female labor.	Annual product: Quantities.	Kinds.	Values.
1	2	3	4	5	6	7	8	9	10	11	12	13	14
1 Spangenberg & Hopper	Ladies Hose Trimmings	5,000		Silk, Cotton, Worsted &c.	15,115	6 Horse Steam	6	50	165	305		Cords, Tassels &c., Fringes &c.	27,272
2 J. C. Bruen	Wood Engraver	500	other articles	Box Wood	100		1		16			Wood Cuts	1,050
3 H. Hitchcock	Chronometers & Watches	1000	other articles	Steel, Silver	200		4		96			Chronometers, Watches	2,300
4 H. Lautenheimer	Engraver & Die Sinker	100		Brass, Steel, Copper	50		2		60			[illegible]	1,500
5 A. Lautenheimer	Mathematical Instruments	1,500		Brass, Silver &c.	175		2		50			Mathematical Instruments	1,500
6 Eugene Ferris	[illegible]	25,000		[illegible]	2,000		40	6	450	96	1,000	[illegible]	6,000
7 C. E. Jaeger	Jewel Cases	1600	Skins & other articles	Velvet, Silk	2,000		3		80			Jewel Cases	3,500
8 J. Sondmeyer	Lithographer & Printer	1200	other articles	Paper, Ink	140		7		220			Lithographs, Show Bills	5,200
9 G. Mutsch & John, Commenced Nov 16/59	Boots & Shoes, Uppers	5,000		Leather, Findings	24,000		9	8	360	144		Boots & Shoes, Uppers	50,000
10 Edward Bookhout	Wood Engraver	150		Box Wood, Mahogany	150		11		254			Wood Cuts	5,600
11 Joseph Fahys	Watch Cases	7,000	1161 oz.	Gold, Silver, other materials	12,000		9		475		350; 30	Gold Watch Cases; Silver [illegible]	20,000; 600; 1,000
12 T. G. Mercier	Watch Cases	5,000	other articles	Gold, Silver	5,000		5		250		200	Gold Watch Cases	9,000
13 Hamilton & Moore	Watch Glasses	650		Glass	500		1		20			Watch Glasses	1,000
14 [illegible] & Nickerson	Printers	2000	other articles	Paper, Ink	2,000		6		300			Job Printing	6,000
15 B. M. Hall	Perfumer	800	10 Bbl.; other articles	Alcohol; Essential Oils	150; 340; 1,000		1	2	30	25	1800 [illegible]	Perfumes	4,000
							10		400			Wood Cuts	15,000
16 J. W. Orr	Wood Engraver	1000		Box Wood, Mahogany	100								
17 L. E. Glutz	Watch Cases	500	other articles	Gold, Silver	500		2		20		[illegible]	Watch Cases	1240
18 H. A. Long	Publisher	500		Print Paper, [illegible] &c.	500		2		28			Publishing Books, [illegible]	1200
19 John Rayner	Whip & Cane Mountings	500		Gold, Silver, other metals	400		3		60			Whip & Cane Mountings	1800
20 R. Smith & Bro.	Engravers & Plate Printers	1000		Copper Plates, Paper & Ink	500		6		200			Engraving, Plate Printing	8000
20		57,000			66,150		113	50					125,962

1860 Products Of Industry, prepared for Ward 2, City of New York, New York County, New York.

1860 Products of Industry

SCHEDULE 5. – Products of Industry in _____ in the County of _____ State of _____ during the year ending June 1, 1860, as enumerated by me _____ Ass't Marshal.

Post Office _____

NAME of Corporation, Company, or individual, Producing Articles to the Annual Value of $500.	Name of Business, Manufacture, or Product	Capital Invested in Real and Personal Estate in the Business	Raw Material used, including Fuel.			Kind of motive power, machinery, structure, or Resource	Average No. of Hands		Wages		Annual Product.		
			Quantities.	Kinds.	Values.		Males.	Females.	Average mo. cost of male labor	Average mo. cost of female labor	Quantities.	Kinds.	Values.
1	2	3	4	5	6	7	8	9	10	11	12	13	14

Page No. 2

SCHEDULE 4.—Products of Industry in Murray Township, in the County of Alameda, State of California, during the year ending June 1, 1870, as enumerated by me. Stephen A Burpee, Ass't Marshal

Post Office: Pleasanton

#	Name of Corporation, Company, or Individual producing to value of $500 annually	Name of Business, Manufacture, or Product	Capital	Motive Power	Materials — Name or Description	Males above 16	Females above 15	Children & youth	Total amount paid during year	Number of months in operation	Materials — Kinds	Quantities	Values	Products — Kinds	Quantities	Values
1	Malley T.	Shoe Shop	500	Hand	Webster	1	1		300	12	Sole Leather / Upper "	25 sides / 4 doz	125 / 200 / 325	Boots / Shoes / Repairs	100 pair	800 / 200 / 1000
2	Minor Charles	Watch fty	100	Hand		1				12	Jewels	2 doz	20	Repairing Watches	300	500
3	Brian James	Harness Sp	300	Hand		1			600	12	Leather / Hardware	2500 lbs / "	650 / 250 / 850	Harness / Saddles / Bridles / Repairing	30 set / 8 / 50	900 / 160 / 150 / 500 / 1710
4	Campbell R & Co	Blacksmith & Wheel Wright Shop	4000	Hand			6		3600	12	Iron / Coal / Steel	4 ton / 15 " / 200 lbs	300 / 600 / 380 / 1280	Horse Shd / Repairing	700 shoes	300 / 3000 / 6000
5	Hartz Thomas	Shoe Shop	300	Hand		1			100	12	Sole Leather / Upper	12 sides / 100 pair	175 / 250 / 425	Boots / Repairing	50 pair	600 / 300 / 900
6	Anthony J. A.	Tin Shop	1200	Hand	Tinning 2 / Burning 2 / Turning 1 / Ironing 1 / Nailing	1			200	12	Tin / Iron	12 box / 200 lbs	156 / 200 / 356	Tinware / all kinds / Repairing / Stove Pipe	300	200 / 600 / 150 / 275
7	McKenna Mich	Shoe Shop	200	Hand		1			50	12	Sole Leather / Upper Skins 12	12 sides	100 / 100 / 200	Boots / Repairs	50 pair	600 / 100 / 700
8	Milinth William & Co	Blacksmith Shop	2000	Hand			6		3000	12	all materials		1100	all products		
9	Bastion George	Shoe Shop	200	Hand	Horses	1	1		100	12	Sole Leather / Upper Skins	12 side / 9 doz	150 / 100 / 250	Boots / Repairs	50 pair	600 / 100 / 700
10	CJ Stevens & Co	Flour Mill	1000	Steam 60	Extra mill Stone / Wheat 2 / Barley 1				400	8	Grain / Mill supplies	Iron 20 / 200	20200 / 2050 / 22250	Flour / Feed / General Produce		

Capacity per day 5 to 6 tons 2 fans

1870 Products of Industry

Page No. _____

SCHEDULE 4. – Products of Industry in _____ in the County of _____ State of _____ during the year ending June 1, 1870, as enumerated by me

Post Office _____   _____ Ass't Marshal.

NAME of Corporation, Company, or individual, Producing Articles to the Annual Value of $500.	NAME of Business, Manufacture, or Product	CAPITAL (Real & Personal) Invested in the business	MOTIVE POWER		MACHIINES		Avg. No. of Hands Employed			Total Amount paid in wages during year.	No. of months in operation part / full time	MATERIALS			PRODUCTION		
			Kind of Power (Steam, Water, etc.	No. of Horsepower	Name or Description	Number of.	Males above 16 years.	Females above 15 years.	Children and youth.			Kinds.	Quantities	Values	Kinds.	Quantities	Values
1	2	3	4	5	6	7	8	9	10	11	12	13	14	15	16	17	18

1880 Manufactures – Products of Industry, prepared for the Town of Woburn, Middlesex County, Massachusetts.

1880 Manufactures — Products of Industry in _____, in the county of _____, State of _____, during the twelve months beginning June 1, 1870, and ending May 31, 1880, as enumerated by me.

Post Office: _____   Enumerator: _____

1	2	3	4	Average No. of Hands employed			No. of Hours per day		Wages and Hours of Labor			Months in Operation					18	19	Power used in Manufacture									
																				If water power is used.					If steam power is used			
				5	6	7	8	9	10	11	12	13	14	15	16	17			20	21	Wheels.				27	28	29
Name of Corporation, Company, or Individual producing to the value of $500 annually.	Name of Business, Manufacture, or Product.	Capital (real and personal invested.	No. of Hands Employed.	Males 16 & over	Females 16 & over	Children & Youths	May to Nov.	Nov to May	Avg Day's Wages (skilled)	Avg Day's Wages (Non-skilled)	Total Amount Paid in Wages During the Year.	On Full Time.	On 3/4 Time Only.	On 2/3 Time Only.	On 1/2 Time only.	Idle.	Value of Material	Value of Product	On what River or Stream	Height in Fall, in Feet	Number.	Kind.	Breadth, in Feet	RPM	Horse Power.	No. of Boilers.	No. of Engines.	Horse Power

Supervisor's Dist. No. 60

Enumeration Dist. No. 151

74

Received July 28, 1880.

Special Schedules of Manufactures—Nos. 3 and 4.

BOOTS AND SHOES.—LEATHER (TANNED AND CURRIED).

Products of Industry in Danvers, in the County of Essex, State of Massachusetts

during the twelve months beginning June 1, 1879, and ending May 31, 1880, as enumerated by me.

Israel H. Putnam

BOOTS AND SHOES.

Mudge E. & A. Co	150,000	250	160	86	4	10	10	[illegible]	[illegible]	75,000	[illegible]	2	2	[illegible]	60		2	15,000	186,645
Tulloch James W.	2,000	8	15	[illegible]	—	10	10	[illegible]	[illegible]	1,000	11	—	1	—	3	1		600	1,500
Daugherty William	1000	4	3	—	—	10	10	[illegible]	[illegible]	1000	12	—	—	—	—	—	—	200	500
White & Putnam	15,000	45	35	10	—	10	8	200	175	8,000	9	2	1	—	9	1	—	3,200	4,545
Martin George A. & Son	38,000	143	80	60	3	10	10	235	200	38,414	[illegible]	[illegible]	2	[illegible]	42	1		7,043	38,910
Clapp Granville W.	7,000	00	50	—	—	10	10	200	150	12,000	8	2	2	—	3	2		[illegible]	[illegible]

BOOTS AND SHOES—Continued.

	5,000	200,000			300,000	300,000		300,000	1	1	1	25
3000	400	7,500			21,000	11,000		11,000	1	—	—	—
	700	3,200			6,500	4,000		4,000	1	—	—	—
15,800	5,000	[illegible]			40,000	50,000		50,000		—	—	1
20,000	23,020	113,291			179,600	178,694	400	179,094		1	1	15
50,000	[illegible]	[illegible]			40,000	48,000		48,000	592094	—	—	—

LEATHER (TANNED AND CURRIED).

[illegible]	8,000	30	30	—	—	10	10	200	125	7,000	5	—	1	6	$11,000	160,000	87,000

LEATHER (TANNED AND CURRIED)—Continued.

160,000	$14,000	[illegible]	14,000	160,000	1	1	30

1880 Manufactures – Boots & Shoes – Leather (Tanned and Curried),
prepared for the Town of Danvers, Essex County, Massachusetts.

Special Schedules of Manufactures—Nos. 7 and 8.

FLOUR AND GRIST MILLS—CHEESE, BUTTER, AND CONDENSED MILK FACTORIES.

Products of Industry in Woburn, in the County of Middlesex, State of Massachusetts, during the twelve months beginning June 1, 1879, and ending May 31, 1880, as enumerated by me.

James N. Dow, Special Agent

1880 Manufactures – Lumber/Saw Mills, Brick Yards & Tile Works

Special Schedules of Manufactures—Nos. 5 and 6.

LUMBER MILLS AND SAW-MILLS—BRICK YARDS AND TILE WORKS.

Products of Industry in *Woburn*, in the County of *Middlesex*, State of *Massachusetts* during the twelve months beginning June 1, 1879, and ending May 31, 1880, as enumerated by me.

James N. Dow, Special Agt.

LUMBER MILLS AND SAW-MILLS

Name	Capital	Avg. employees	Hours of labor	Months in operation	Saws	Materials	Sawed products
S. Richardson & Son	15,000	2 / 2	10 / 9 / 150 / 105 / 500	12 / 7	1	7.00 / 215	1875 / 175

LUMBER MILLS AND SAW-MILLS—Continued

Sawed products (cont.)	Remanufactures	Power used in manufacture
2875 / 1075 / 1075 / 100	Massachusetts / 100 / 100	Mystic 9½ 1 / Lowell 3½ 65 20

BRICK YARDS AND TILE WORKS

(no entries)

BRICK YARDS AND TILE WORKS—Continued

(no entries)

AGRICULTURAL IMPLEMENTS.

Products of Industry in Minden, in the County of Sanilac, State of Michigan during the twelve months beginning June 1, 1879, and ending May 31, 1880, as enumerated by me.

William A. Mills

Name	Capital											Power
Mudge & Shade	700	3	3		10	10	1.50	75	8	2	2	Horse Power

AGRICULTURAL IMPLEMENTS—Continued.

Materials										Products								
50 plows			$152.00								100							

AGRICULTURAL IMPLEMENTS—Continued.

																		Total value of all products
																		4000

SCHEDULE 3.—Manufactures—Products of Industry in District No. 6, in the County of Polk, State of Fla., during the twelve months beginning June 1, 1884, and ending May 31, 1885, as enumerated by me.

Post Office: Auburndale

G. L. Lightsey, Asst.
For J. L. Wheeler, Enumerator

Name	Capital	Greatest no. of hands	Avg day's wages skilled	Avg day's wages ord.	Months in operation, full time	Value of materials	Value of products	Kind of power	Horse-power	No. of boilers	No. of engines	Horse-power
L. C. Bort	Lumber	2500 10	10 .95	1.25	12	1700 2m		Steam	20	1	1	30
H. M. Vickmen	Lugar be	1000 10 10	11	1.00	7	900 2m		Cob burner	30	1	1	30
Settles	digar be	3000 10 10	20	1.25	10	1000 dato	Loris		25	1	1	25
D. McLord	Lumber	3000 18 10	10 .95 1.25 3600	1.25	12	600		Horse boat	21	1	1	21
H. L. Overchur	Lige Brill	1500 12	10	1.25	6				15	3	2	20
Bellmay el L. your	dingle Weaks	2000 50	10 .55 1.25	1.25	1/2	900 3m/m	Big Bust					
Jos D. Bye Leet		3000 10 10	10 .55 1.25			800 1m	Eli Morgan		20	1		

1885 Manufactures Schedule, Prepared for Auburndale, Polk County, Florida.

1885 Manufactures — Taken with federal assistance in Colorado, Dakota Territory, Florida, Nebraska, and New Mexico Territory.

Products of Industry in _____, **in the county of** _____, **State of** _____, during the twelve months beginning June 1, 1884, and ending May 31, 1885, as enumerated by me.

Post Office: _____ *Enumerator* _____

1	2	3	4	Average No. of Hands employed			No. of Hours per day		Wages and Hours of Labor			Months in Operation					18	19	20	If water power is used					If steam power is used		
Name of Corporation, Company, or Individual producing to the value of $500 annually.	Name of Business, Manufacture, or Product.	Capital (real and personal invested).	No. of Hands Employed.	Males 16 & over	Females 16 & over	Children & Youths	May to Nov.	Nov to May	Avg Day's Wages (skilled)	Avg Day's Wages (Non-skilled)	Total Amount Paid in Wages During the Year.	On Full Time.	On 3/4 Time Only.	On 2/3 Time Only.	On 1/2 Time only.	Idle.	Value of Material	Value of Product	On what River or Stream	Height in Fall, in Feet	Number.	Kind.	Breadth, in Feet	RPM	Horse Power.	No. of Boilers.	No. of Engines.	Horse Power
				5	6	7	8	9	10	11	12	13	14	15	16	17	18	19	20	21	22	23	24	25	26	27	28	29

1850 Agriculture Schedule – Page 1. Prepared for The Township of Reading, Hillsdale County, Michigan.

1850 Agriculture Schedule – Page 2. Prepared for The Township of Reading, Hillsdale County, Michigan.

County of Hillsdale State of Michigan during the Year ending June 1, 1850

#	20	21	22	23	24	25	26	27	28	29	30	31	32	33	34	35	36	37	38	39	40	41	42	43	44	45	46
1		32	2	10							100	3										652		10		13	47
2		70	30	100							200	20														12	23
3			1	30							200	4															10
4				30							200													13	60		30
5		15	2	100							250	4	2									1000		13		8	23
6				100							200	4															15
7		15	2	30							150	10														15	21
8				60							400	30										100			25	10	43
9		24	4	60							100	15	5									300				13	66
10		100		200							200	12	6									1100				25	30
11		63		60							200	2										300				15	40
12		30		25							200	10										400				10	2
13		30	2	300			6				200	150	30	11								1000			300	30	13
14				100							100	7										100		20			30
15		20		40		5					300	13										600				25	30
16		60		100			20				200	10										600				30	16
17		10	2	22		5					300	5										300		6		8	12
18		15	2	50							200	100	9	4								400				16	32
19		9		30							200	100	6									100				20	42
20		30		100							400	200	30									600				30	100
21		25		40			20				200	6										232		100	26	44
22		13		25							200	6										140		5		15	17
23		27		60							200	100	10									600		6	30	16	30
24		26		50							100											200				2	12
25			2	30	10						300	1													54		45
26		120		70							200	5										432					64
27		9	1	40		60					100											326		132	10	18	
28				100							300											400				18	25
29		40		45							300											300			100	11	30
30		20		70		35					300	4										100				25	11
31		9		40			15				100	10										300			30	9	10
32				20		20					50											100					10
33			10	30							200	7										400					13
34		25		100		5					300	12										400			100		43
35		30	3	100		45	20				300	10	7													12	22
36			5	100							300	10										200		60			29
37		50		50		5					300	18	4									300				20	40
38		6	2	100							200											100					12
39		30	2	100							200	8	1									50		2			13
40		30		100		100					100	8														20	10
41		30		120		5					200	10	2									200			100	45	30

1860 Productions of Agriculture – Page 1

Page No. _____
SCHEDULE 4.—Productions of Agriculture in Hardwick in the County of Worcester in the Post Office Hardwick.

#	Name of Owner, Agent, or Manager of the Farm	Acres Improved	Acres Unimproved	Cash Value of Farm	Value of Farming Implements	Horses	Asses/Mules	Milch Cows	Working Oxen	Other Cattle	Sheep	Swine	Value of Livestock	Wheat	Rye	Indian Corn	Oats	Rice	Tobacco	Ginned Cotton	Wool
1	David Aiken	75	70	1,500	150	1		8	2			6	500			50	50				
2	John Wheeler	120	30	5,000	75	1		15	2	8		8	819	16		100	50				
3	Timothy Rich	60	30	800	20	1		5	2			2	200			10	4				
4	James B. Patrell	50	100	1,000	50	1		3	2	2	1		250			15	60				
5	Lewis Aiken	1		3,000	15	1		1				1	150								
6	E. Darius Robinson	8	17	3,000	40	2		1					400								
7	Sally S. Morley	86	26	9,800	75	2		7	2	5		2	580	5	11	60	30				
8	Michael Brady	50	5	1,000	40	1		3	2	2		1	300			5	25				
9	George C. Howard	11		1,000	15	1		2				1	150	30		15					
10	Nathan M. Robinson	12	8	800	10			2				1	70			15	15				
11	Patrick Alley	60	10	1,000	10	1		6		1		1	175			10					
12	Thomas Higgins	25	18	450	5			1		4		2	125			20	10				
13	Anson Ramsdell	60	200	3,200	75	4		5	2			1	300			20	45				
14	Edmund Moore	100	50	2,000	25	1		6	2	5		2	300			10	40				
15	Cahista Cummings	25	5	450				3		1		1	110			20	15				
16	Calvin Paget	25	5	100	15	1		2				2	100			30	25				
17	George T. Alley	20	20	700	10	1		2				1	150			20					
18	Patrick Sullivan	40	60	1,400	25	1		10	2			4	450			20	30				
19	Lucia Morten	30	26	1,600	15			1			4		50			12					
20	Samuel Kendall	100	50	4,500	40	1		9	2	11	18	2	520		6	35	6				60
21	Benj. W. Sherman	69	16	4,000	100	1		5	2	15		2	600			60	60				
22	Wells Berry	30	16	3,000	75	1		3	2	5		2	330		10	30	15				
23	John B. Mitchell	50	15	3,000	25	1		6	2	5		4	440		25	50	135				
24	Amos Barnes	65	107	1,800	20	1		4	2	5		1	416			40	46				
25	Peter Carr	20	6	350	25	2		1				1	200			25	20				
26	John King	50	30	1,100	50	1		2	2	2		2	200			15	20				
27	Hiram S. Douglas	45	20	1,100	50	1		2		2		1	180	14		35	25				
28	Bizarah Johnson	75	25	1,800	30	1		4	2	6		2	340			25	66				
29	Alvin Cleveland	70	60	2,000	30	1		5	2	2		2	340			25	50				
30	William E. Dart	35	3	1,600	17	2		3		1		1	200			30	20				
31	Arvey D. Morland	80	45	2,000	200	2		4	2	2		1	438			75	50				
32	E. Willis Robinson	70	25	1,000	25	1		5	2	2			275	8		40	30				
33	James Sturtevant	40	75	800	25	1		1	2	1	2		125			40	30				10
34	Leander Sibley	70	10	1,700	40	1		5	2	4		8	340			5	40				
35	Lucius Barnes	50	7	1,000	25	1		3	2	2	2	1	350			5	40				12
36	Joseph P. Snow	30	30	800	15	1		3		5	2	1	160			50	30				6
37	John James	50	30	1,100	20	1		3		3		3	125			20	30				
38	Asa Sturtevant	75	80	2,000	40	1		3	2	7		1	360			40	80				
39	Augustus D. Blackm.	45	30	1,800	25	1		4	2	2		2	200			100	50				5
40	Isaac Burt	40	20	1,000	20	1		6		1		2	175			20					

1860 Agriculture Schedule – Page 1. Prepared for the Town of Hardwick, Worcester County, Massachusetts.

State of Mass. enumerated by me, on the 9th day of July, 1860.
Joseph W. [?], Ass't Marshal.

YEAR ENDING JUNE 1, 1860.

#	28	29	30	31	32	33	34	35	36	37	38	39	40	41	42	43	44	45	46	47	48
1	3	50					300	600	5											90	86
2		200	15		25		800	1000	60								6			50	250
3		50	10	4	10		900	500	8											50	50
4	1	50		3	25		100	1400	22	1										40	100
5	2	175			40		100	900	25											25	100
6		200	1	11	15		20	750	35											50	150
7	4	150			50	100	200	750	40											40	400
8	12	125		16	20	20	15	300	2000	40										90	195
9		50	10			4	100	1500	15											15	200
10		60			8		75	300	8											20	91
11	1	150			20		50	1000	20											25	100
12	2	100					100	400	10								10			40	60
13		150	2	12	18		200	400	30											25	34
14	4	150	15	15	10		150	300	50										5	30	15
15		40					200	300	10											20	68
16	10	200	30		25		150	500	50											25	86
17		100			25		200	600	60											20	150
18		100			25		300	2300	15											15	95
19	2	125			20		350	4500	55								9			50	475
20		200			30		400	4000	40											30	575
21		150					100	4000	25											50	250
22		200	8		15		100	2000	40								100			25	465
23	3	150			30		150	6000	60										20	20	350
24		150			15		200	3000	40											30	150
25		150			12		225	4000	40										15	50	300
26	6	125			10		100	300	35											15	350
27		75					100	300	40											20	110
28		100	8		10		300	350	40											15	100
29		100	25		15		250	400	40											25	108
30		100			5		200	1000	20											30	100
31		30			12		300	400	15											20	90
32		10					100	1180	10											25	75
33	1	75			50		250	8500	40											25	300
34		50					400	3500	20											15	210
35	1	100			20	3	100	4000	50											30	25
36	1	175	5		5		100	330	40											20	150
37		25			10		100	400	40											30	350
38	2	25		3	50		250	1000	40											40	325
39	6	100			20		100		25											10	75
40		65			25		100	400	10											20	30

1860 Agriculture Schedule – Page 2. Prepared for the Town of Hardwick, Worcester County, Massachusetts.

SCHEDULE 3.—Productions of Agriculture in Etna, in the County of Penobscot, in the
Post Office: Etna.

Name	2	3	4	5	6	7	8	9	10	11	12	13	14	15	16	17	18	19	20	21	22	23	24
Borden Arthur	67		2	100	50			1		1	4	10		350				10	10				
Borden Levi	95	10		800	25			1		2	2	8	1	285				25	50				
Brown Levi	50	25		1200	100			1		1	2	5	9	1	300			11	10	17			
Stevens Wheelwright	100	45		2500	70			1		2	2	4	17	1	520	15		85	10	15	15		
Brown Charles C	75	10		1500	100		2	2		2	3	16		614	20				80		10		
Corpel or Stephen	20	20		500	20			1		1				325				15					
Leonard Henry P	100	60		1000	100			1		2	2	11	1	583	70			50	30				
Friend Benjamin	60	100		1200	150	50	4	2		3	20		140				25	50					
Friend James C	35	25		100	75			1		1	4	8		471				5	5				
Edwards Edward	14	11		500				1		1		6		189				18	42				
Ingalls Abraham	30	10		400	30			1		2		4		196	10			10					
Friend Amos J	75			500	10			1		2	1	11		359									
Crabtree Aaron C	80	30		700	50			1		2	4	15		522				12	25				
Harding Absalom	75	40		2500	100	100	1		4	2	7	24	2	735				100	35				
Hardy Henry P	75	25		2000	250	100	2		2	3	6		750	35			20						
Hardy Charles	52	25		600	90		3							300				50	5				
Whitten Nathan	150	60		3000	100	225	2	2	2	6	20	1	500	15			10	80		60			
White Jefferson	35	20		2000	200		1		3	2	4	21	1	500	20			30	15				
Whitter Elisha W	70	20		1500	100		2		3	2	18	1	335	15			45	40		27			
Abbott Samuel	75	35	40	3000	100	225	1	2	4	11	1	574	20			100	15						
Weaver Lindley	40	10		650				1		1				165									
Friend Henry L	25			200	100	75	2		2				380				20						
Stevens William	100	60		1500	100		2		2	3	17	2	418				40	21					
Borden Albion	40	25		1000	50		1		2	1	7	1	500	25			10	40					
Friend Bradbury L	30	40		1200	50		1		1	3	5		315	30			6	15					
Moseley Hannah	65			1800	90			1		4	3	20	1	570									
Abbott Moses	50	90		3580	100		2		4	2	5	18	1	853	35			12	50	12			

1870 Agriculture Schedule – Page 2. Prepared for the Town of Etna, Penobscot County, Maine.

#	25	26	27	28	29	30	31	32	33	34	35	36	37	38	39	40	41	42	43	44	45	46	47	48	49	50	51	52
1	30	3	75						150			12														18	72	361
2	30	6	150						300			15														20	77	494
3	35	4	300		10				150			20												20		10	65	515
4	50	15			50				300			20														60	75	745
5	100	10	100		25				300			18										16m		75		16	125	784
6		4	40		10				150			5																166
7	70	9	160		25				300			15												120		20	45	543
8	116	8	300						300			20														12	100	700
9	67	3	60						200			10												134		134	20	445
10	40	8	180		10				150			10															32	370
11	25	6	80						300			11														20	60	396
12	30	2	35		20				300			10														40	40	328
13	40	7	75						300			8														80	100	581
14	70	5	500		20				400			20												75		40	276	1193
15	100	7	400		10				300			40												20	25	25	369	1461
16			150									5											250					490
17	100	7	300		10				300			40												45		40	72	1032
18	90	8	150		15				400			20														20	60	775
19	45	7	280		20				150			25														30	97	810
20	75	5	500		50				300			30												200		80	75	800
21			10									12																160
22		10	300						150			4															145	785
23	50	13	400						300			10															105	680
24	30	7	200						300			25														36	80	500
25	12	7	150		12				300			5														24	100	437
26	80		35						400			20														32	132	568
27	100	8	400		12				500			40														100	225	1350

1880 Agriculture Schedule. Prepared for the town of Franklin, Franklin County, Nebraska.

1885 Agriculture Schedule. Prepared for Polk County, Florida.

1850 Mortality Schedule

SCHEDULE 3.—Persons who Died during the Year ending 1st June, 1850, in the City of Washington in the County of Washington, ~~State of~~ Dis. of Columbia, enumerated by me, E. F. Queen Ass't Marshal

#	NAME OF EVERY PERSON WHO DIED during the Year ending 1st June, 1850, whose usual Place of Abode at the Time of his Death was in his Family.	Age	Sex	Colour, White, Black, or Mulatto	Free or Slave	Married or widowed	PLACE OF BIRTH. Naming the State, Territory, or Country.	The Month in which the Person died.	PROFESSION, OCCUPATION, OR TRADE.	DISEASE, OR CAUSE OF DEATH.	Number of DAYS ILL
1	Francis Grimes	1	M	M	S		D.C.	Augr		Brain fever	2 d
2	Margaret Grimes	1	F	M			ditto	June		Diarrhea	3 wo
3	J. Steel	½	M				ditto	July		Diarrhea	1 mo
4	J. Wesley	5	M				Va	Feby		Hoop Cough	2 mo
5	M. A. Murton	½	F				D.C.	May		Fever	3 day
6	Elizabeth Walter	6	F				ditto	ditto		Bilious fever	5 da
7	B. E. Gates	1	F				ditto	July		Diarrhea	4 da
8	S. Brown	3	F	M	F		ditto	Jany		Lung fever	1 mo
9	L. Johnson	6	F				ditto	Mch		Brain fever	12 da
10	J. E. Sails	2	M				ditto	Jany		Chronic	26 da
11	Chr. Columbus	3	M				ditto	June		Brain fever	4 day
12	M. J. Jackson	1	F				ditto	July		Chol. Infantum	4 d
13	E. M. Morgan	20	F				Va	Novr		Consump.	1 mo
14	Jane Storm	6	F				M.d.	March		Dysentery	1 wo
15	Chas. Harris	7	M				D.C.	Feby		Dysentery	4 wo
16	F. Harris	5	M				ditto	March		Dysentery	4 da
17	S. Harris	3	F				ditto	March		Dysentery	4 da
18	W. Fitzgerald	1	M				ditto	March		Dysentery	2 da
19	W. Stoops	31	M				Va	June	None	Consump.	1 mo
20	Henry Piper	57	M				ditto	Novr		Old age	3 mo
21	A. Hunt	6	F				D.C.	Mar		Br. fever	1 do
22	W. Shreves	½	M				ditto	Mar		Dysentery	4 da
23	D. Nelson	1	M				ditto	Sept		Summer Comp.	2 mo
24	N. Collins	58	M				M.d.	Sept	Farmer	Old age	6 mo
25	W. Johnson	39	F				ditto	Jany		Consump.	1 yr
26	J. Johnson	52	M		M		ditto	April	Laborer	Consump.	1 wo
27	W. Mitchell	4	M				D.C.	Augr		Diarrhea	2 wo
28	N. Donalson	½	F				ditto	Augr		Sudden	
29	W. Umpress	82	M	B	F		M.d.	Sept	ditto	Dis. from old age	10 da
30	M. Flaherty	74	F				Ireland	May		Old age	2 yr
31	W. Hoover	6	M				D.C.	Oct		Dropsy	3 wo
32	H. Stuart	1	M				ditto	Augt		Dysentery	3 wo
33	E. C. Carpenter	17	F				M.d.	Sept		Bilious fever	1 do
34	J. Prather	37	M				ditto	Nov	Carpenter	Dysentery	1 mo
35	E. Prather	30	F				ditto	Nov		Consump.	5 wo

1850 Mortality Schedule. Prepared for the City of Washington, Washington County, District of Columbia.

1850 Mortality Schedule

Researcher: _____ Date: _____

Extracted from the original text of the 1850 census (Mortality) schedules

NARA Microfilm Pub. No.: _____ Roll no.: _____ State: _____ County: _____ Subdistrict: _____

Page _____

1	2	3	4	5	6	7	8	9	10	11
NAME OF DECEASED — Name of each person who died during the year ending June 1, 1850	Age	Sex	Color	Free or Slave	Married or Widowed	Birthplace	Month of Death	Occupation	Disease or Cause of Death	No. of days ill

1860 Mortality Schedule

Page No. 1

SCHEDULE 3.—Persons who Died during the Year ending 1st June, 1860, in Battersville Dist in the County of Allen State of Kentucky, enumerated by me, J N Pry Ass't Marshal.

Name of Every Person Who Died	Age	Sex	Color	Free or Slave	Married or Widowed	Place of Birth	The Month in which the person died	Profession, Occupation, or Trade	Disease or Cause of Death	Number of Days Ill
Richard	8	M	B	S		Ky	Sept	Farm hand	African Consump	175
John Lightfoot	62	M			M	Va	Apr	Farmer	Consumption	276
S E Lightfoot	1	F				Ky	Sept		Fever	91
C E Hancock	½	M				" "	April		Unknown	6
C J Ingram	2	M				" "	July		Scarlet Fever	15
Williamson McB	59	M			M	Va	Apr		Typhoid Fever	9
P J Evans	1	F				Ky	July		Whooping Cough	50
Isabella Dixon	22	F				Ky	May	Seamstress	Lung Disease	60
A J Thacker	½	F				" "	Dec		Unknown	Sudden
Thomas	35	M	B	S		" "	Jan	Farm hand	Consumption	200
S E J Nelson	½	F				" "	Dec		Unknown	1
C J Dyer	½	F				" "	Apr		" "	60
infant Jackson	½	M				" "	Nov		" "	Sudden
infant Hunt	½	M				" "	Jan		" "	" "
J J Logan	10/12	M				" "	June		Whooping Cough	17
M H Moore	½	F				" "	Nov		Croup	3
Ann Anderson	67	F			W	Tenn	March	none	Cold	49
infant Rather	½	M				Ky	Aug		Unknown	5
Cynthia Jeske	54	F			M	" "	Oct	Housekpg	Consumption	9
J W Drisdelle	18	M				" "	Sept		Croup	5
M E Clyde	12	F				" "	May		Consumption	6
Daniel	42	M	B	S		Tenn	Apr	Farm hand	African Consump	240
Dan Tucker	14	M	B	S		Ky	Apr	" "	" "	120
Mary	28	F	B	S		" "	July	House Serv't	Dropsy	1 m
E McCarter	12	F			M	Tenn	Aug	Housekpg	Consumption	2 m
Sanllican	½	F				Ky	July		Cholera Infantum	2
Lucy	27	F	M	S		Tenn		House Serv't	Fever	4 m
Harriet	18	F	B	S		" "	Apr		Scrofula	14 m
Alice	2	F	B	S		" "	March			18
Hannah	21	F	B	S		July			Poison	90
Infant	½	F	B	S		Ky	" "			Sudden
A Nelson	21	F			M	" "	Aug	Housekpg	Chronic	180
Nancy Shea	45	F	W	F		" "	May		Consumption	12 m
Arthena Castile	½	F				" "	June		Whooping Cough	21
C A Jones	18	M				" "	Oct	Farmer	Consumption	11 m

1860 Mortality Schedule. Prepared for Allen County, Kentucky.

1860 Mortality Schedule

Researcher: Date:

Extracted from the original text of the 1860 census (Mortality) schedules

NARA Microfilm Pub. No.:   Roll no.:   State: County: Subdistrict:

Page

NAME OF DECEASED — Name of each person who died during the year ending June 1, 1860 (1)	Age (2)	Sex (3)	Color (4)	Free or Slave (5)	Married or Widowed (6)	Birthplace (7)	Month of Death (8)	Occupation (9)	Disease or Cause of Death (10)	No. of days ill (11)

1870 Mortality Schedule

SCHEDULE 2.—Persons who Died during the Year ending 1st June, 1870, in 1st Ward, in the County of Assumption, State of Louisiana, enumerated by me, Willard N. Dyer, Ass't Marshal.

#	Family #	Name	Age	Sex	Color	M/W	Place of Birth	F	M	Month of Death	Profession	Cause of Death
1	23	Benjamin Julianne	50	F	B	m	Va.			June		Childbirth
2	"	Antoine	½	M	B		La.			Nov.		Pernicious fever
3	59	Martinez Valerie	½	M	W		"			Oct.		Hooping cough
4	41	Caroline Joseph	12	M	W		"			April		Eating Dirt
5	43	Martiny Charles	½	M	W		"			July		Pernicious fever
6	56	Boudreau Brique	1	M	W		"			March		Small pox
7	57	Charlet Emile	½	M	W		"			July		Catarrh
8	66	Roberts Josephine	5	F	B		"			Aug.		Inf. Convulsions
9	81	Barbin Delphin	1	M	W		"			Aug.		Hooping Cough
10	81	Caroline Joseph	15	M	W		"			May	farm laborer	Small pox
11	88	Thibodaux Margaret	76	F	W	W	La.			Jan.		Chronic Dysentery
12	"	Bomilliard Virgile	35	M	W	M	La.			Jan.		Childbirth
13	92	Turville Louis	½	M	W		"			Aug.		Pernicious fever
14	141	Smith Henry	30	M	B	M	"			Aug.		Chronic Dysentery
15	"	Mary	2	F	B		"			May		Pernicious fever
16	146	Matt William	3	M	B		"			Sept.		Hooping cough
17	153	Golden Matilda	16	F	B		Ken.			Nov.		Burned
18	161	Butler Adele	1	F	M		La.			Dec.		Burned
19	177	Quine William	46	M	W		England	1	1	Aug.	Blacksmith	Intemperance
20	170	Goldson Matilda	18	F	B		La.			Jan.		Consumption
21	196	Young Mary	1	F	B		"			Sept.		Pernicious fever
22	217	Long Reuben	58	M	B	M	Va.			Sept.	farm laborer	Cholera Morbus
23	"	Jacob	2	M	B		La.			Sept.		Pernicious fever
24	22	Banos Antoine	½	M	W		"			Sept.		Inf. Convulsions
25	47	Sirry Narcisse	55	M	W	M	La.			May	farm laborer	Cholera Morbus
26	68	Melancon Telesfor	23	M	W		"			Feby.	Laborer	Small pox
27	95	Rouis Laurence	1	M	W		"			Oct.		Inf. Convulsions
28	130	Dalfer or Antoine	12	M	W		"			Sept.		Pernicious fever

I certify that the foregoing is a correct copy of the enumeration of my subdivision, and that the same was done according to law and instructions.

Willard N. Dyer

1870 Mortality Schedule. Prepared for Assumption Parish, Louisiana.

1870 Mortality Schedule

Researcher: Date:

Extracted from the original text of the 1870 census (Mortality) schedules

NARA Microfilm Pub. No.:   Roll no.:   State: County: Subdistrict:

Page:

1	2	3	4	5	6	7	8	9	10	11	12
Family no. (from 1870 population schedule)	NAME OF DECEASED — Name of each person who died during the year ending June 1, 1870	Age, last birthday	Sex	Color	Married or widowed	Birthplace	Father foreign born	Mother foreign born	Month of Death	Occupation	Disease or Cause of Death

218 • 1880 Mortality Schedule

1880 Mortality Schedule. Prepared for Allen County, Kentucky.

1880 Mortality Schedule

Researcher: _____ Date: _____

Extracted from the original text of the 1880 census (Mortality) schedules

NARA Microfilm Pub. No.: _____ Roll no.: _____ State: _____ County: _____ Subdistrict: _____

Page: _____ E.D.: _____

1	2	3	4	5	6	7	8	9	10	11	12	13	14	15	16	17
Family no. (from 1880 population schedules)	NAME OF DECEASED — Name of each person who died during the year ending May 31, 1880	Age	Sex	Color	Single	Married	Widowed / divorced	Person	Father	Mother	Occupation	Month of death	Disease or cause of death	Months in county	Place disease contracted	Name of attending physician

Columns 3–5: Personal Description
Columns 6–8: Marital Status
Columns 9–11: Birthplace of:

1885 Mortality Schedule, prepared for Bartow, Polk County, Florida.

1885 Mortality Schedule — Taken with federal assistance in Colorado, Dakota Territory, Florida, Nebraska, and New Mexico Territory.

SCHEDULE 5 – Persons who died during the year ending May 31, 1885, enumerated by me in _____, in the county of _____, State of _____, _____, Enumerator

Family No.–From Pop. Sched 1.	NAME of the deceased	Personal Description			Marital Status of Deceased			Nativity			Profession, Occupation or Trade.	Month of Death	Disease or Cause of Death.	How long a resident of this county. If less than 1 year, use fractions: 2/12.	If the disease was not contracted at the place of death, state that place.	Name of Attending Physician.
		Age, last birthday. Under 1 year, use fractions, 1/12, 2/12	Sex, (M or F)	Color, (W, B, M, etc.)	Single.	Married.	Widowed. Divorced D.	Birthplace of person (State, Territory, or Country)	Birthplace of Father	Birthplace of Mother						
1	2	3	4	5	6	7	8	9	10	11	12	13	14	15	16	17

1850 Slave Schedule, prepared for Kaw Township, Jackson County, Missouri.

1850 Slave Schedule

Researcher: Date:

Extracted from the original text of the 1850 census slave schedules

NARA Microfilm Pub. No. M432   Roll no.:   State: County:

Page / City, Town, or Subdistrict	Names of Slave Owners	No. of Slaves	Age	Sex	Color	Fugitives from state	No. Manumitted	Deaf & dumb, blind, insane, or idiotic
	1	2	3	4	5	6	7	8

Page No. 15

SCHEDULE 2.—Slave Inhabitants in Independance in the County of Autauga State of Alabama, enumerated by me, on the 15 day of August, 1860. W. H. Mazingale Ass't Marshal.

	NAMES OF SLAVE OWNERS	Number of Slaves	Age	Sex	Color	Fugitives from the State	Number manumitted	Deaf & dumb, blind, insane, or idiotic	No. of Slave houses	NAMES OF SLAVE OWNERS	Number of Slaves	Age	Sex	Color	Fugitives from the State	Number manumitted	Deaf & dumb, blind, insane, or idiotic	No. of Slave houses	
1		1	5	m	B						1	14	f	B					1
2		1	1	m	M				2		1	10	m	B					2
3	G. W. Ziegler	1	60	f	B						1	10	m	B					3
4		1	60	f	B						1	8	f	B					4
5		1	45	m	B						1	6	m	B					5
6		1	45	f	B						1	4	m	B					6
7		1	27	m	B						1	4	f	B					7
8		1	27	m	B						1	4	f	B					8
9		1	25	m	B						1	3	f	B					9
10		1	35	m	B						1	3	m	B					10
11		1	22	f	B						1	2	m	B					11
12		1	24	f	B						1	1	f	B					12
13		1	27	m	B						1	1	m	B					13
14		1	18	f	B						1	4/12	f	B					14
15		1	15	f	B						1	4/12	f	B				5	15
16		1	15	m	B					A. M. Rountree	1	84	m	B					16
17		1	15	m	B						1	54	f	M					17
18		1	12	m	B						1	56	f	B					18
19		1	12	m	B						1	25	m	B					19
20		1	5	m	B						1	25	m	B					20
21		1	5	f	B						1	22	f	B					21
22		1	3	m	B						1	18	f	B					22
23		1	3	m	B						1	13	m	B					23
24		1	2	f	M						1	11	m	M					24
25		1	1/2	f	M			4			1	6	f	B					25
26	J. G. Henman	1	70	m	B						1	12	m	B					26
27		1	60	m	B						1	18	f	B					27
28		1	40	f	B						1	11	m	B					28
29		1	40	f	B						1	8	m	B					29
30		1	40	f	B						1	6	m	M					30
31		1	25	f	B						1	7	m	B					31
32		1	26	m	B						1	1	m	B				5	32
33		1	18	f	B					John Ray	1	50	f	B					33
34		1	19	m	B						1	35	f	B					34
35		1	12	f	B						1	28	m	B					35
36		1	19	f	B						1	24	m	B					36
37		1	17	f	B						1	13	m	B					37

1860 Slave Schedule, prepared for Independence, Autauga County, Alabama.

1860 Slave Schedule

Researcher: Date:

Extracted from the original text of the 1860 census slave schedules

NARA Microfilm Pub. No. M653 Roll no.: State: County:

Page

City, Town, or Subdistrict	Names of Slave Owners	No. of Slaves	Description			Fugitives from state	No. Manumitted	Deaf & dumb, blind, insane, or idiotic	No. of slave houses
			Age	Sex	Color				
	1	2	3	4	5	6	7	8	9

Sample: **1850 Social Statistics Schedule,** prepared for Gun Plain (Charter Township), Allegan County, Michigan. The Census Act of 1850 authorized the 1850, 1860, and 1870 censuses, and included a description of Population Schedules and all other special schedules. Amended Census Acts of 1860 and 1870 made some changes to the subsequent schedules, but in the case of the Social Statistics Schedules, they remained the same for all three census years, 1850, 1860, and 1870.

1880 Insane Inhabitants & Idiots, prepared for the 19th Election Distr., NYC, New York County, New York.

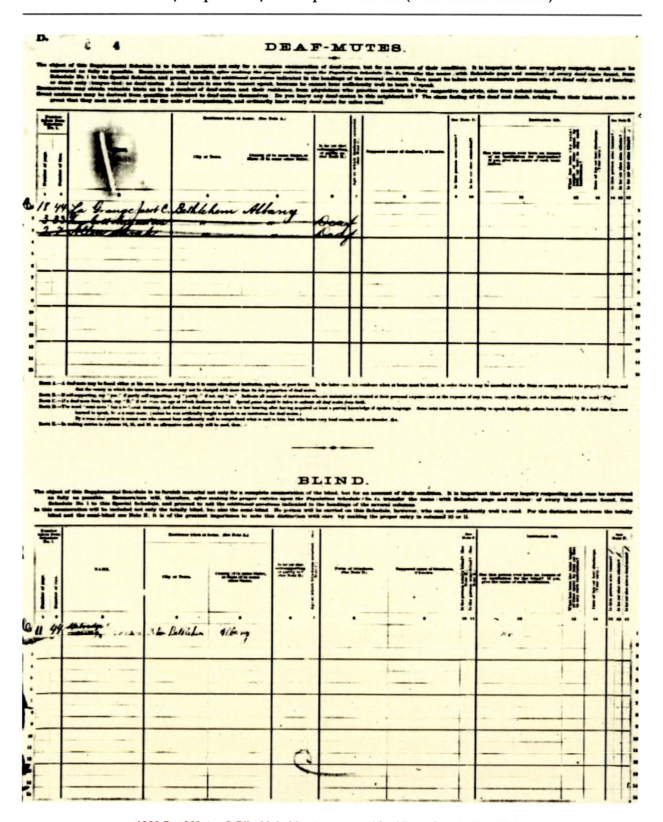

1880 Deaf-Mutes & Blind Inhabitants, prepared for Albany County, New York.

1880 Defective / Dependent / Delinquent Classes (Homeless Children & Prisoners)

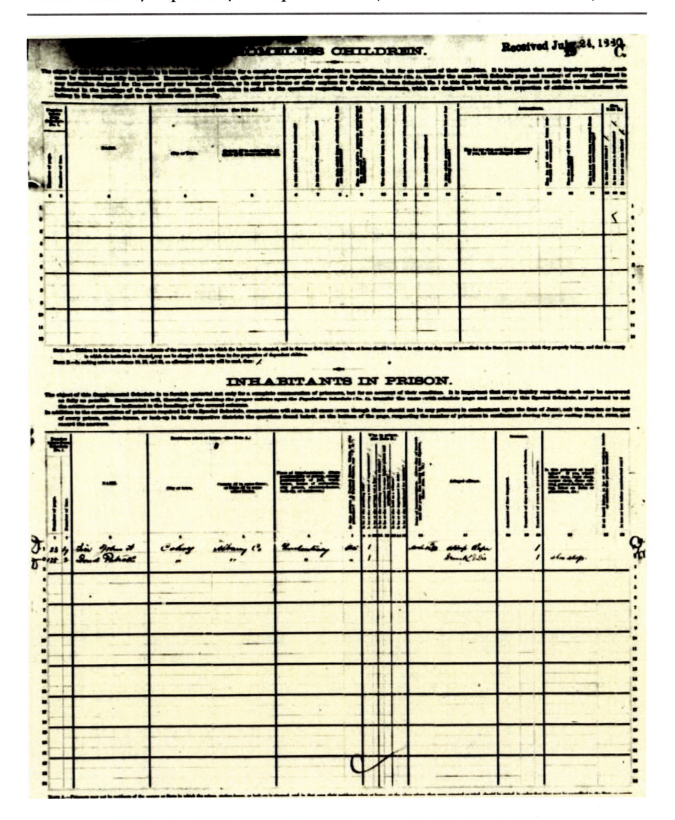

1880 Homeless Children & Inhabitants in Prison, prepared for Albany County, New York.

1880 Defective / Dependent / Delinquent Classes (Pauper & Indigents)

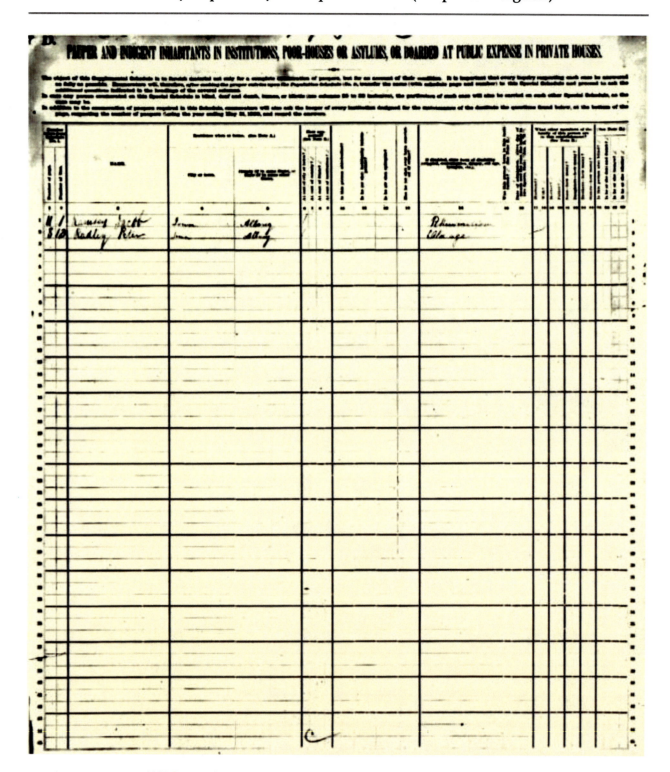

1880 Pauper & Indigent Inhabitants, prepared for Albany County, New York.

Soundex Indexes, 1880-1930

When Social Security began in 1935, the first old-age pension system was established for every citizen of the United States of the age of 65 or over. An immediate concern was how to prove an age for a person applying for social security, since not very many people could produce a birth certificate in 1935. Many people who were qualified could not prove their age.

To counter this problem, a special branch of the Census Bureau was created, called the Age Search Group. This group would take a person's application for social security and attempt to find that same person in a census record where a name and age would be given. It was soon determined that indexes would be needed to speed up the work of finding a particular person's name and age listing.

The Census Bureau hired the Rand Corporation to design an indexing system based on phonetic sounds for a name, which become known as "Soundex." Under the supervision of the Age Search Group, the Works Progress Administration (WPA) employed clerical workers to create the indexes to the 1880, 1900, 1920 and 1930 censuses. The WPA workers prepared index cards for heads of household from the 1880 census with children 10 years or younger, as well as the index cards for all heads of household from the 1900 and 1920. The 1930 Soundex was complete for 10 states only, with partial indexes for two more states.

In 1962, the Age Search Group, on their own, undertook a census index of the 1910 census but limited the index to twenty-one states. The 1910 index was the first to employ a use of computers.

Two systems for coding the names in the 1910 index were used. The coding used was either the Soundex or Miracode system, but both systems were exactly the same for coding a surname. The index cards for Miracode or Soundex differ only in the citation to a visitation (house) or page number on the full schedules.

Soundex Code

In all cases, a Soundex Code was given at the top of the index card, followed by the name of the head of the household, the names and ages of each member of the family, and a citation to the census schedules on which they appeared. The cards were then arranged by the Soundex codes for each census index, A000-Z600, and after that by the first name of the head of the household.

The code consisted of an alpha character for the surname, removing all vowels and any doubled letters, and coding up to three consonants with similar sounds:

1 = b, p, f, v
2 = c, s, k, g, j, q, x, z
3 = d, t
4 = l
5 = m, n
6 = r

For example, to code the surname MARBUTT, start with the letter M, eliminate vowels and doubled letters, thus, M-R-B-T codes as M613. If less than 3 coded letters use 0's; e.g., LEE would code as L000.

Contents – 1880-1930 Soundex Samples & Forms:

1880 Soundex………..……...232
1900 Soundex…………….…234
1910 Soundex/Miracode… 236
1920 Soundex……………….238
1930 Soundex……………….240

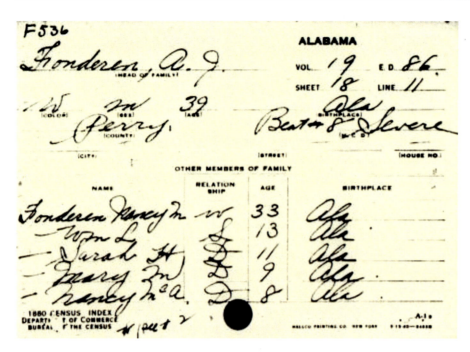

1880 Soundex Index Card (1 of 2), prepared for the family of A.J. Fonderen, Perry County, Alabama. **NOTE:** 1880 Soundex cards were prepared only for families with a child 10 years or younger.

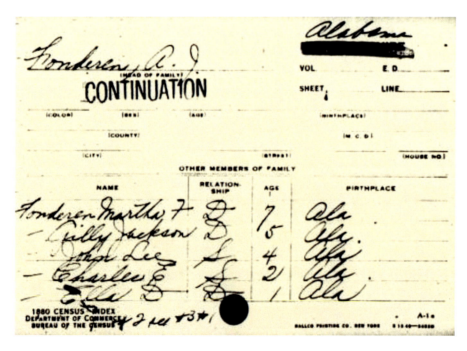

1880 Soundex Index Card (2 of 2), Continuation Card, Family of A. J. Fonderen.

1880 Soundex

Researcher: Date:

Soundex Code
- 1 = b, p, f, v
- 2 = c, s, k, g, j, q, x, z
- 3 = d, t
- 4 = l
- 5 = m, n
- 6 = r

Microfilm pub. no. (T734 - T780)

Extracted from the original text of the 1880 Soundex cards

PLACE OF RESIDENCE — Indicate house number, street, city, precinct, and township for Head of Family				MEMBERS OF HOUSEHOLD — List name of Head of Family followed by each person included in the family				Reference to 1880 population schedule			
Roll no.	State	Subdistrict	County	Name	Relationship to Head	Age	Birthplace	Vol. no.	E.D. no.	Sheet	Line

1900 Soundex Index Card (1 of 2), prepared for the family of Charles D'Fosee

1900 Soundex Index Card (2 of 2), Continuation Card, Family of Charles D'Fosee.

1900 Soundex

Researcher: _____ Date: _____

Extracted from the original text of the 1900 Soundex cards

Soundex Code
- 1 = b, p, f, v
- 2 = c, s, k, g, j, q, x, z
- 3 = d, t
- 4 = l
- 5 = m, n
- 6 = r

Microfilm Pub. no. (T1030 - T1083)	Roll no.	PLACE OF RESIDENCE — Indicate house number, street, city, precinct, and township for Head of Family			MEMBERS OF HOUSEHOLD — List name of Head of Family followed by each person included in the family		Birth						Reference to 1900 population schedules			
		State	Subdistrict	County	Name	Relationship to Head	Month	Year	Age	Birthplace	Citizenship	Vol. no.	E.D. no.	Sheet	Line

1910 Soundex Index Card – Family Card, prepared for the family of Hardie Coleman (local/county jurisdiction omitted), Alabama.

1910 Miracode Print-out, Allen County, Kansas.

1910 Soundex States: Alabama, Georgia, Louisiana (except Shreveport and New Orleans), Mississippi, South Carolina, Tennessee, and Texas.

1910 Miracode States: Arkansas, California, Florida, Illinois, Kansas, Kentucky, Louisiana (Shreveport and New Orleans only), Michigan, Missouri, North Carolina, Ohio, Oklahoma, Pennsylvania, Virginia, and West Virginia.

1910 Soundex-Miracode

Researcher: Date:

Extracted from the original text of the 1910 Soundex or Miracode records

Soundex Code	Microfilm pub. no. (T1259 - T1279)	Roll no.	PLACE OF RESIDENCE — Indicate house number, street, city, precinct, and township for Head of Family			MEMBERS OF HOUSEHOLD — List name of Head of family followed by each person included in the family				Vol. no.	Miracode only		Reference to 1910 population schedules		Soundex only
1 = b, p, f, v 2 = c, s, k, g, j, q, x, z 3 = d, t 4 = l 5 = m, n 6 = r			State	Subdistrict	County	Name	Relationship to Head	Age	Birthplace		E.D. no.	Visitation (house) no.	E.D. no.	Sheet no.	

1920 Soundex Index Card, prepared for the family of A. D. Hess, Council Bluffs, Pottawattamie County, Iowa.

1920 Soundex Index Card, prepared for Addie Hess, enumerated with her son, Ralph Hess, Dubuque, Dubuque County, Iowa. **NOTE.** Usually, another card was only prepared for persons in a household with a different surname than the head of house. This example shows that some WPA clerical workers made separate cards for any extra adult in a household grouping.

1920 Soundex

Researcher: Date:

Extracted from the original text of the 1920 Soundex cards

Soundex Code	Microfilm Pub. no. (M1548 - M1605)	Roll no.	PLACE OF RESIDENCE — Indicate house number, street, city, precinct, and township for head of household			MEMBERS OF HOUSEHOLD — List name of Head of Family followed by each person included in the family					Reference to 1920 population schedules		
1 = b, p, f, v			State	Subdistrict	County	Name	Relationship to Head	Age	Birthplace	Citizenship	Vol. no.	E.D. no.	Sheet	Line
2 = c, s, k, g, j, q, x, z														
3 = d, t														
4 = l														
5 = m, n														
6 = r														

1930 Soundex Index Card, prepared for J.C. Marbutt, Marion County, Alabama.

1930 Soundex Index Card – Continuation Card. The only way one knows that this is a continuation of the J. C. Marbutt family is that this card is next in the microfilm image sequence.

1930 Soundex

Researcher: Date:

Extracted from the original text of the 1930 Soundex cards

Soundex Code

1 = b, p, f, v
2 = c, s, k, g, j, q, x, z
3 = d, t
4 = l
5 = m, n
6 = r

Microfilm pub. no.	Roll no.	PLACE OF RESIDENCE — Indicate house number, street, city, precinct, and township for head of household			MEMBERS OF HOUSEHOLD — List name of Head of Family followed by each person included in the family					Reference to 1930 population schedules			
		State	Subdistrict	County	Name	Relationship to Head	Age	Birthplace	Citizenship	Vol. no.	E.D. no.	Sheet	Line

242 • 1790-1840 Census Worksheet

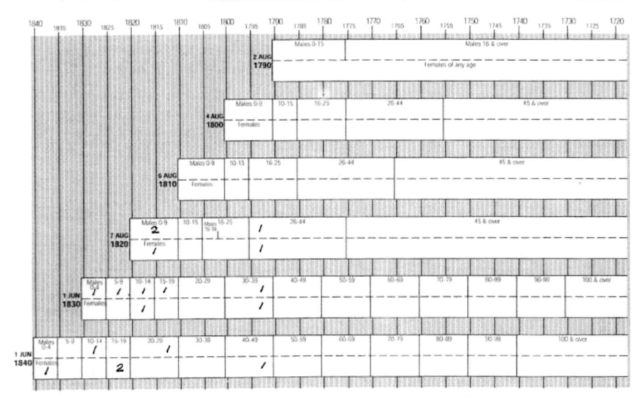

Notes:

To identify each person shown in the various age categories, information was needed from other sources. For example, It is known that Jesse, Sr. was born in about 1795, that he married Nancy Pierson in 1814, and they had two daughters (Elizabeth, b 1818; and Mary, b 1824; and four sons (John, b 1815; Jesse (Jr.), b 1816; William, b 1820; and Joel, b 1827). In the 1820 census, Jesse and Nancy both appear in the 26-44 category; with 2 sons under 5; and 1 daughter under 5. In the 1830 census, their four male children are indicated, as well as one female child.

Note that Jesse and Nancy's births can be narrowed down to a five-year period (1790-1795). This narrowing of birth years is the main purpose of the chart – comparing the numbers of males and females in each census usually gives a researcher a more precise range/year of birth for a person.

In the 1840 census, note that an older female is living with the family of Jesse Jr. Since Jesse Sr. died in early 1840, It appears that his widow moved in with their son, Jesse Jr. and family. This information does not prove anything, but gives a good clue to the whereabouts of Nancy (Pierson) Dollarhide in 1840. Note that Jesse's wife (Nancy Murphey Dollarhide) is a bit younger than him, as he is in the 20-29 category; and she is one of two females in the 15-19 category. The other female could be Jesse's younger sister (Mary, b 1824).

Without background information about these families, educated guesses about the identity of each person would be difficult. Again, the main purpose of the 1790-1840 Worksheet is to visually compare the age categories for a person in more than one census.

1790-1840 Census Worksheet

For each of the indicated years, show the number of males and females in the appropriate age brackets below. By comparing censuses, a more accurate span of years may be determined.

YEAR	HEAD OF HOUSEHOLD	STATE	COUNTY	REMARKS

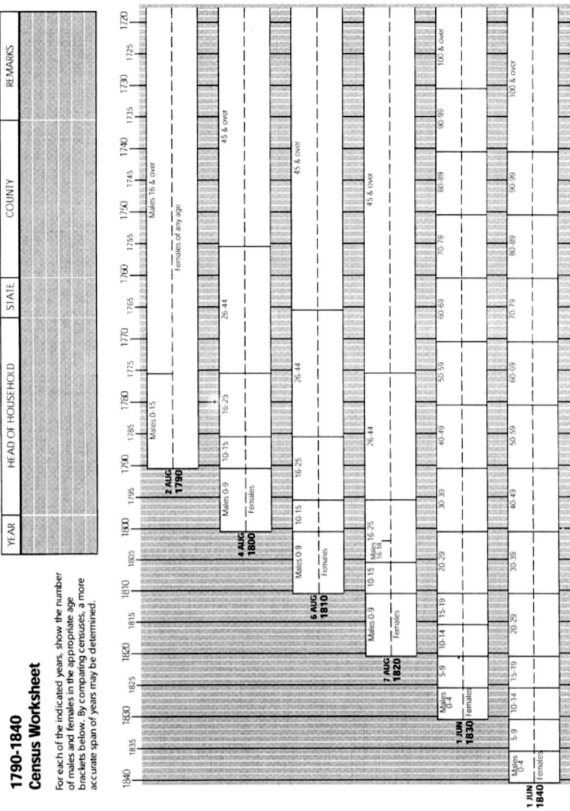

Census Comparison Sheet

Researcher:

Year 1850	State Indiana	County Jasper Co		Town or District Beaver Township	
Series	Roll No.	Page 218		Dwelling No. 36	Family No. 36
Name	Age	Sex	Occupation	Birthplace	Other Information
Jesse DOLLARHIDE	33	M	Farmer	Indiana	b 1816 (per death cert.)
Nancy M. DOLLARHIDE	25	F		"	
Amanda DOLLARHIDE	10	F		"	
Lavina DOLLLARHIDE	8	F		"	
Henry C. DOLLARHIDE	5	M		"	
John W. DOLLARHIDE	3	M		"	
Nancy M. DOLLARHIDE	1	F		"	

Year 1860	State Iowa	County Fayette Co		Town or District West Union	
Series	Roll No.	Page 156		Dwelling No. 1292	Family No. 1000
Name	Age	Sex	Occupation	Birthplace	Other Information
Jesse DOLLARHIDE	44	M	Farmer	Indiana	
Maria DOLLARHIDE	35	F		"	
Louisa DOLLARHIDE	18	F		"	Copying error, should be "Lavina"
Henry C. DOLLARHIDE	16	M	Farm Laborer	"	
John W. DOLLARHIDE	13	M		"	
Mary DOLLARHIDE	11	F		"	
Lucy DOLLARHIDE	9	F		"	
Jemima DOLLARHIDE	6	F		"	
Priscilla DOLLARHIDE	4	F		"	
Matilda DOLLARHIDE	2	F		"	

Year 1870	State Oregon	County Jackson Co		Town or District Not Stated	
Series	Roll No.	Page 59-60		Dwelling No.	Family No.
Name	Age	Sex	Occupation	Birthplace	Other Information
Henry C. DOLLARHIDE	24	M	Farmer	Indiana	Fam. No. 529
Julia A. DOLLARHIDE	23	F	Keeping House	Missouri	"
Jesse DOLLARHIDE	54	M	Farmer	Indiana	Fam. No. 530
Nancy DOLLARHIDE	48	F	Keeping House	"	"
Jemima DOLLARHIDE	17	F		"	"
Priscilla DOLLARHIDE	15	F		"	"
Matilda DOLLARHIDE	12	F		Iowa	"
Leander D. DOLLARHIDE	9	M		"	"
John W. DOLLARHIDE	20	M	Farmer	Indiana	Fam. No. 531
Sarah J. DOLLARHIDE	18	F	Keeping House	Illinois	"
Wesley DOLLARHIDE	1	M		California	"

Census Comparison Sheet

Researcher:

Year	State	County			Town or District		
	Series	Roll No.		Page No.	Dwelling No.		Family No.
Name		**Age**	**Sex**	**Occupation**	**Birthplace**		**Other Information**

Year	State	County			Town or District		
	Series	Roll No.		Page No.	Dwelling No.		Family No.
Name		**Age**	**Sex**	**Occupation**	**Birthplace**		**Other Information**

Year	State	County			Town or District		
	Series	Roll No.		Page No.	Dwelling No.		Family No.
Name		**Age**	**Sex**	**Occupation**	**Birthplace**		**Other Information**